Conference on Empirical Methods in Natural Language Processing (EMNLP 2018)

System Demonstrations

Brussels, Belgium
31 October - 4 November 2018

ISBN: 978-1-5108-7417-6

EMNLP 2018

**The Conference on
Empirical Methods in
Natural Language Processing**

Proceedings of System Demonstrations

October 31 – November 4, 2018
Brussels, Belgium

Order copies of this and other ACL proceedings from:

Association for Computational Linguistics (ACL)
209 N. Eighth Street
Stroudsburg, PA 18360
USA
Tel: +1-570-476-8006
Fax: +1-570-476-0860
acl@aclweb.org

Introduction

Welcome to the proceedings of the system demonstrations session. This volume contains the papers of the system demonstrations presented at the 2018 Conference on Empirical Methods in Natural Language Processing (EMNLP), which was held in Brussels, Belgium on October 31 - November 4, 2018.

The system demonstrations session includes papers describing systems ranging from early research prototypes to mature production-ready software. We received 77 submissions, 4 of which were either invalid or withdrawn by the authors. Of the 73 valid submissions, 29 (40%) were selected for inclusion in the proceedings after review of three members of the program committee. We thank all authors for their submissions, and the 162 members of the program committee for their timely and thoughtful reviews.

Best regards,
Eduardo Blanco and Wei Lu
EMNLP 2018 System Demonstration Co-Chairs

Organizers:

Eduardo Blanco, University of North Texas
Wei Lu, Singapore University of Technology and Design

Program Committee:

Table of Contents

SyntaViz: Visualizing Voice Queries through a Syntax-Driven Hierarchical Ontology
Md Iftekhar Tanveer and Ferhan Ture 1

TRANX: A Transition-based Neural Abstract Syntax Parser for Semantic Parsing and Code Generation
Pengcheng Yin and Graham Neubig 7

Data2Text Studio: Automated Text Generation from Structured Data
Longxu Dou, Guanghui Qin, Jinpeng Wang, Jin-Ge Yao and Chin-Yew Lin 13

Term Set Expansion based NLP Architect by Intel AI Lab
Jonathan Mamou, Oren Pereg, Moshe Wasserblat, Alon Eirew, Yael Green, Shira Guskin, Peter
Izsak and Daniel Korat 19

MorAz: an Open-source Morphological Analyzer for Azerbaijani Turkish
Berke Özenç, Razieh Ehsani and Ercan Solak 25

An Interactive Web-Interface for Visualizing the Inner Workings of the Question Answering LSTM
Ekaterina Loginova and Günter Neumann 30

Visual Interrogation of Attention-Based Models for Natural Language Inference and Machine Comprehension
Shusen Liu, Tao Li, Zhimin Li, Vivek Srikumar, Valerio Pascucci and Peer-Timo Bremer 36

DERE: A Task and Domain-Independent Slot Filling Framework for Declarative Relation Extraction
Heike Adel, Laura Ana Maria Bostan, Sean Papay, Sebastian Padó and Roman Klinger 42

Demonstrating Par4Sem - A Semantic Writing Aid with Adaptive Paraphrasing
Seid Muhie Yimam and Chris Biemann 48

Juman++: A Morphological Analysis Toolkit for Scriptio Continua
Arseny Tolmachev, Daisuke Kawahara and Sadao Kurohashi 54

Visualization of the Topic Space of Argument Search Results in args.me
Yamen Ajjour, Henning Wachsmuth, Dora Kiesel, Patrick Riehmann, Fan Fan, Giuliano Castiglia,
Rosemary Adejoh, Bernd Fröhlich and Benno Stein 60

SentencePiece: A simple and language independent subword tokenizer and detokenizer for Neural Text Processing.
Taku Kudo and John Richardson 66

CogCompTime: A Tool for Understanding Time in Natural Language
Qiang Ning, Ben Zhou, Zhili Feng, Haoruo Peng and Dan Roth 72

A Multilingual Information Extraction Pipeline for Investigative Journalism
Gregor Wiedemann, Seid Muhie Yimam and Chris Biemann 78

Sisyphus, a Workflow Manager Designed for Machine Translation and Automatic Speech Recognition
Jan-Thorsten Peter, Eugen Beck and Hermann Ney 84

KT-Speech-Crawler: Automatic Dataset Construction for Speech Recognition from YouTube Videos
Egor Lakomkin, Sven Magg, Cornelius Weber and Stefan Wermter 90

Visualizing Group Dynamics based on Multiparty Meeting Understanding
Ni Zhang, Tongtao Zhang, Indrani Bhattacharya, Heng Ji and Rich Radke 96

An Interface for Annotating Science Questions
Michael Boratko, Harshit Padigela, Divyendra Mikkilineni, Pritish Yuvraj, Rajarshi Das, Andrew McCallum, Maria Chang, Achille Fokoue, Pavan Kapanipathi, Nicholas Mattei, Ryan Musa, Kartik Talamadupula and Michael Witbrock 102

APLenty: annotation tool for creating high-quality datasets using active and proactive learning
Minh-Quoc Nghiem and Sophia Ananiadou 108

Interactive Instance-based Evaluation of Knowledge Base Question Answering
Daniil Sorokin and Iryna Gurevych 114

Magnitude: A Fast, Efficient Universal Vector Embedding Utility Package
Ajay Patel, Alexander Sands, Chris Callison-Burch and Marianna Apidianaki 120

Integrating Knowledge-Supported Search into the INCEpTION Annotation Platform
Beto Boullosa, Richard Eckart de Castilho, Naveen Kumar, Jan-Christoph Klie and Iryna Gurevych 127

CytonMT: an Efficient Neural Machine Translation Open-source Toolkit Implemented in C++
Xiaolin Wang, Masao Utiyama and Eiichiro Sumita 133

OpenKE: An Open Toolkit for Knowledge Embedding
Xu Han, Shulin Cao, Xin Lv, Yankai Lin, Zhiyuan Liu, Maosong Sun and Juanzi Li 139

LIA: A Natural Language Programmable Personal Assistant
Igor Labutov, Shashank Srivastava and Tom Mitchell 145

PizzaPal: Conversational Pizza Ordering using a High-Density Conversational AI Platform
Antoine Raux, Yi Ma, Paul Yang and Felicia Wong 151

Developing Production-Level Conversational Interfaces with Shallow Semantic Parsing
Arushi Raghuvanshi, Lucien Carroll and Karthik Raghunathan 157

When science journalism meets artificial intelligence : An interactive demonstration
Raghuram Vadapalli, Bakhtiyar Syed, Nishant Prabhu, Balaji Vasan Srinivasan and Vasudeva Varma 163

Universal Sentence Encoder for English
Daniel Cer, Yinfei Yang, Sheng-yi Kong, Nan Hua, Nicole Limtiaco, Rhomni St. John, Noah Constant, Mario Guajardo-Cespedes, Steve Yuan, Chris Tar, Brian Strope and Ray Kurzweil 169

Conference Program

SyntaViz: Visualizing Voice Queries through a Syntax-Driven Hierarchical Ontology
Md Iftekhar Tanveer and Ferhan Ture

TRANX: A Transition-based Neural Abstract Syntax Parser for Semantic Parsing and Code Generation
Pengcheng Yin and Graham Neubig

Data2Text Studio: Automated Text Generation from Structured Data
Longxu Dou, Guanghui Qin, Jinpeng Wang, Jin-Ge Yao and Chin-Yew Lin

Term Set Expansion based NLP Architect by Intel AI Lab
Jonathan Mamou, Oren Pereg, Moshe Wasserblat, Alon Eirew, Yael Green, Shira Guskin, Peter Izsak and Daniel Korat

MorAz: an Open-source Morphological Analyzer for Azerbaijani Turkish
Berke Özenç, Razieh Ehsani and Ercan Solak

An Interactive Web-Interface for Visualizing the Inner Workings of the Question Answering LSTM
Ekaterina Loginova and Günter Neumann

Visual Interrogation of Attention-Based Models for Natural Language Inference and Machine Comprehension
Shusen Liu, Tao Li, Zhimin Li, Vivek Srikumar, Valerio Pascucci and Peer-Timo Bremer

DERE: A Task and Domain-Independent Slot Filling Framework for Declarative Relation Extraction
Heike Adel, Laura Ana Maria Bostan, Sean Papay, Sebastian Padó and Roman Klinger

Demonstrating Par4Sem - A Semantic Writing Aid with Adaptive Paraphrasing
Seid Muhie Yimam and Chris Biemann

Juman++: A Morphological Analysis Toolkit for Scriptio Continua
Arseny Tolmachev, Daisuke Kawahara and Sadao Kurohashi

Visualization of the Topic Space of Argument Search Results in args.me
Yamen Ajjour, Henning Wachsmuth, Dora Kiesel, Patrick Riehmann, Fan Fan, Giuliano Castiglia, Rosemary Adejoh, Bernd Fröhlich and Benno Stein

SentencePiece: A simple and language independent subword tokenizer and detokenizer for Neural Text Processing.
Taku Kudo and John Richardson

No Day Set (continued)

CogCompTime: A Tool for Understanding Time in Natural Language
Qiang Ning, Ben Zhou, Zhili Feng, Haoruo Peng and Dan Roth

A Multilingual Information Extraction Pipeline for Investigative Journalism
Gregor Wiedemann, Seid Muhie Yimam and Chris Biemann

Sisyphus, a Workflow Manager Designed for Machine Translation and Automatic Speech Recognition
Jan-Thorsten Peter, Eugen Beck and Hermann Ney

KT-Speech-Crawler: Automatic Dataset Construction for Speech Recognition from YouTube Videos
Egor Lakomkin, Sven Magg, Cornelius Weber and Stefan Wermter

Visualizing Group Dynamics based on Multiparty Meeting Understanding
Ni Zhang, Tongtao Zhang, Indrani Bhattacharya, Heng Ji and Rich Radke

An Interface for Annotating Science Questions
Michael Boratko, Harshit Padigela, Divyendra Mikkilineni, Pritish Yuvraj, Rajarshi Das, Andrew McCallum, Maria Chang, Achille Fokoue, Pavan Kapanipathi, Nicholas Mattei, Ryan Musa, Kartik Talamadupula and Michael Witbrock

APLenty: annotation tool for creating high-quality datasets using active and proactive learning
Minh-Quoc Nghiem and Sophia Ananiadou

Interactive Instance-based Evaluation of Knowledge Base Question Answering
Daniil Sorokin and Iryna Gurevych

Magnitude: A Fast, Efficient Universal Vector Embedding Utility Package
Ajay Patel, Alexander Sands, Chris Callison-Burch and Marianna Apidianaki

Integrating Knowledge-Supported Search into the INCEpTION Annotation Platform
Beto Boullosa, Richard Eckart de Castilho, Naveen Kumar, Jan-Christoph Klie and Iryna Gurevych

CytonMT: an Efficient Neural Machine Translation Open-source Toolkit Implemented in C++
Xiaolin Wang, Masao Utiyama and Eiichiro Sumita

OpenKE: An Open Toolkit for Knowledge Embedding
Xu Han, Shulin Cao, Xin Lv, Yankai Lin, Zhiyuan Liu, Maosong Sun and Juanzi Li

No Day Set (continued)

LIA: A Natural Language Programmable Personal Assistant
Igor Labutov, Shashank Srivastava and Tom Mitchell

PizzaPal: Conversational Pizza Ordering using a High-Density Conversational AI Platform
Antoine Raux, Yi Ma, Paul Yang and Felicia Wong

Developing Production-Level Conversational Interfaces with Shallow Semantic Parsing
Arushi Raghuvanshi, Lucien Carroll and Karthik Raghunathan

When science journalism meets artificial intelligence : An interactive demonstration
Raghuram Vadapalli, Bakhtiyar Syed, Nishant Prabhu, Balaji Vasan Srinivasan and Vasudeva Varma

Universal Sentence Encoder for English
Daniel Cer, Yinfei Yang, Sheng-yi Kong, Nan Hua, Nicole Limtiaco, Rhomni St. John, Noah Constant, Mario Guajardo-Cespedes, Steve Yuan, Chris Tar, Brian Strope and Ray Kurzweil

SyntaViz: Visualizing Voice Queries through a Syntax-Driven Hierarchical Ontology

Md Iftekhar Tanveer
University of Rochester
Rochester, NY, USA
itanveer@cs.rochester.edu

Ferhan Ture
Comcast Applied AI Research
Washington DC, USA
ferhan_ture@comcast.com

Abstract

This paper describes SYNTAVIZ, a visualization interface specifically designed for analyzing natural-language queries that were created by users of a voice-enabled product. SYNTAVIZ provides a platform for browsing the ontology of user queries from a syntax-driven perspective, providing quick access to high-impact failure points of the existing intent understanding system and evidence for data-driven decisions in the development cycle. A case study on Xfinity X1 (a voice-enabled entertainment platform from Comcast) reveals that SYNTAVIZ helps developers identify multiple action items in a short amount of time without any special training. SYNTAVIZ has been open-sourced for the benefit of the community.

1 Introduction

Voice-driven interactions with computing devices are becoming increasingly prevalent. Amazon's Alexa, Apple's Siri, Microsoft's Cortana, and the Google Assistant are prominent examples. Google observed that mobile devices surpassed traditional computers in terms of search traffic (Sterling, 2015), and that 20% of mobile searches are voice queries (Pichai, 2016). As opposed to the keyword-based shorter queries received by web-based search engines, voice-enabled natural language processing (NLP) systems deal with longer, natural-language queries. This raises the question of how such data should be utilized for continuous improvements of the underlying methods.

In this paper, we introduce SYNTAVIZ, a web interface for visualizing natural-language queries based on a syntax-driven ontology, thereby enabling its user to quickly gain insights on the statistical and structural properties of large-scale customer-generated data. We provide use cases of SYNTAVIZ on a dataset of 1 million unique voice queries issued by users of the Xfinity X1 entertainment platform of Comcast—one of the largest cable companies in the United States with approximately 22 million subscribers. We are planning to make the source code of SYNTAVIZ freely available as a contribution to the community.

2 Related Work

There is a growing body of literature that deals with various text visualization techniques: Paulheim and Probst (2012) provided a survey of various ontology-enhanced user interfaces. Most prior work utilizes topic modeling to group and/or partition the collection in a way that lexically different yet semantically similar queries are clustered together. Wei et al. (2010) proposed using Latent Dirichlet Allocation (LDA) to induce topic models for an exploratory text analytics system. Hoque and Carenini (2016) utilized topic modeling and sentiment analysis to visualize blog texts and associated comments. A combination of latent topic analysis, discriminative feature selection and various ranking methods was developed by Singh et al. (2017) as part of a visualization interface for large text corpora. Dasiopoulou et al. (2015) developed a predicate-argument based ontology for exploring text elements and their relations. Their framework was demonstrated on excerpts from patent documents. Despite the similarities with our proposed approach, none of the techniques directly suits the use case described in the next section.

3 Methods

SYNTAVIZ is a web interface that visualizes a collection of queries by grouping them in human-understandable clusters. The clusters are formed in a hierarchy based on the dependency parse of the tree of the natural language queries. The design rationale and an elaborate description of so-

1

Proceedings of the 2018 Conference on Empirical Methods in Natural Language Processing (System Demonstrations), pages 1–6
Brussels, Belgium, October 31–November 4, 2018. ©2018 Association for Computational Linguistics

lution are given in the following subsections.

3.1 Need Finding

The project stemmed from a need to optimize the engineering process of the existing intent understanding system. We arranged an informal discussion with the engineering team to understand the current workflow for developing the software that understands the intent of the users from their voice queries. The discussion provided clues that the current design is based on an "open-loop" design process, where the team starts by coming up with many variations of voice queries that would describe a certain intent. For example, for the CHANNELTUNE intent, the first step would be to imagine query patterns such as "tune to ...", "switch over to ...", or simply "channel ...". The next step is to implement an algorithm to convert every such query to its corresponding intent (e.g., "tune to HBO" ⇒ CHANNELTUNE).

The design process does not involve any analysis of historical query logs. This creates the risk of potential gaps between the capabilities of the developed software and the users' expectations. Even though the engineers agreed that such data analyses would help design a better product, the lack of suitable techniques and/or a visualization/analysis tool resulted in this suboptimal process. Our conclusion from these discussions was that the development team was not able to gain useful insights about the incoming voice queries. For example, assigning the word "show" to carry an intent of watching *TV shows* (noun) might negatively impact the queries where the users say "show me ..." (verb). It is difficult to identify these adverse effects without a way to group and visualize similar queries.

Therefore, the need finding exercise revealed the importance of grouping or clustering the queries into semantic structures that reduces the informational overburden (Jones et al., 2004) and ranks the failure points of the system in proportion to real query traffic. There are at least three benefits we have identified:

1. Software developers can access the information needed to design the most effective NLP algorithms.

2. Editors can identify bugs and patterns of logical errors in the deployed system.

3. Product managers can prioritize development

efforts in a data-driven fashion, by easily identifying real cases that degrade user experience.

Ideally, all the data should be summarized and presented through a visual interface with minimum cognitive burden. We sought to find an ontology suitable for these needs. Although "topic modeling" is used as the *de facto* ontology for many text visualization projects (Wei et al., 2010; Hoque and Carenini, 2016; Singh et al., 2017), it is not suitable for this case because the voice queries are much shorter in length compared to the typical text documents used in topic modeling. In addition, one of the reasons to form clusters of sentences is to visualize the systemic mistakes made by the intent understanding system. From this point of view, it appeared natural to cluster the syntactically similar queries together.

3.2 Ontology

Based on the need finding analysis, we realized that syntactic structures would be a great basis for summarizing the voice queries for the current scenario. Dependency parse trees (Jurafsky and Martin, 2014) capture the syntactic relationships by representing the dependencies among the words with directed arrows. Figure 1 shows the dependency trees for two example sentences. Noticeably, the dependent words (represented by arrow heads) modify or complement their parents (e.g. *watch* complements *want* because it answers "want what?"). It is possible to summarize a number of voice queries into hierarchical clusters using these structures, by putting the queries containing the same *tree fragments* into the same cluster. Each cluster then could be divided into subclusters based on the structures of the subtrees within. This ontology allows the users to (1) identify common patterns of error by the NLP system because syntactically similar queries are likely to all be victims of the same weaknesses, and (2) observe the statistical distributions of the queries to the level of granularity they wish to see.

3.3 Dataset

We collected real voice queries issued by the users of Xfinity X1 TV control system within a period of seven days—totaling 32 million queries with an average length of 2.1 words. As we are interested in more "natural" queries, we filtered out the sentences with fewer than five words. In ad-

---

Algorithm 1 Building the hierarchical clusters.

Input: Query q, Dependency tree $tree$, Cluster $clust$

Output: Updated cluster c'

    procedure BUILD_CLUST(q, tree, clust)
        for node in tree **do**
            Get (word, POS, dependency) triplet from node
            Put q in clust[word, POS, dependency]
            if node has subtree **then**
        BUILD_CLUST(q, subtree, clust[word, POS, dependency])

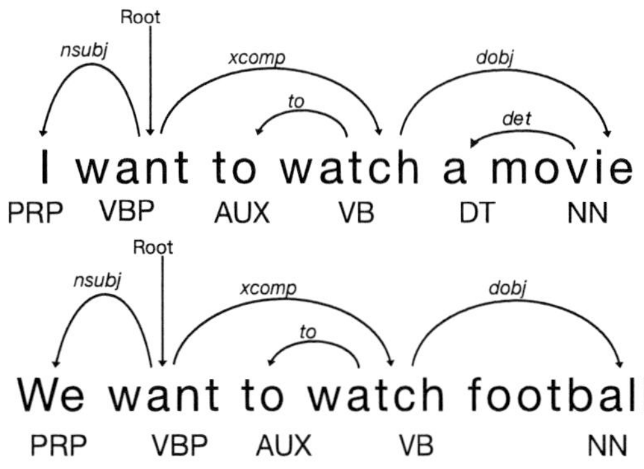

Figure 1: Examples of dependency trees.

dition, we used trigram language model (Kneser and Ney, 1995) probability to obtain queries with higher natural language probabilities. The final dataset contains 1.02 million unique queries.

3.4 Clustering

The algorithm for formulating the clusters is shown in Algorithm 1. For the convenience of discussion, let us consider the following two sentences: "I want to watch a movie" and "We want to watch football games". We extract the corresponding dependency tree using Google's "SyntaxNet" (Andor et al., 2016) parser as shown in Figure 1. Representing the tree as a directed acyclic graph, each token becomes a node and each dependency relation is a directed edge between two nodes.

Our clustering algorithm (Algorithm 1) is designed to group queries together if they have the same subpath (including the part-of-speech) in their dependency tree. Clusters are formed in a recursive manner, starting from the root. At every step, new sub-clusters are constructed based on the neighboring nodes (i.e. nodes receiving an edge from the current node). The landing node and the outgoing edge becomes the label of the sub-cluster: a triplet of the word, the part-of-speech, and the dependency relation (e.g., `a/DT/det`), which contains all queries with the same path starting from the root. For example, notice that both sentences in Figure 1 fall in the same cluster named `want/VBP/ROOT`. Under this cluster, there are three sub-clusters: `watch/VB/xcomp`, `I/PRP/nsubj`, and `we/PRP/nsubj` where the first sub-cluster contains both sentences but the other two contains only one sentence each. The sub-cluster `watch/VB/xcomp` is again divided into smaller sub-clusters. SYNTAVIZ allows the user to jump back-and-forth between the different levels of granularity through its novel interface.

3.5 Interface

The SYNTAVIZ interface is shown in Figure 2. It consists of two panes: the left pane lists labels of all the sub-clusters for the current cluster; the right pane lists all queries within the current cluster associated with other relevant information. We sort the list of sub-clusters on the left side by number of unique queries (descending)—this helps to prioritize clusters with highest impact. Clicking on the label of a sub-cluster allows the user to navigate deep into the clusters containing increasingly (syntactically) similar queries. A breadcrumb shows the current position in the hierarchical cluster and also allows the users to navigate back to the upper level clusters. In the right pane, each query contains the action taken by the existing intent understanding system. This allows the users to quickly explore the failure points of the system. The queries are also accompanied by the frequencies of their occurrences in the dataset, and a list of sub-clusters that each query belongs to.

Given the syntax-driven query ontology, we needed to decide the ranking of the sub-clusters (left pane) and queries (right pane) as well. In order to prioritize high-impact queries, we sort the list on the right side by a descending frequency of occurrences in the dataset. This arrangement provides an idea of the distribution of the queries to the user because the most prevalent ones are ranked higher in the order. In addition, a histogram of all the actions taken by the intent understanding system is shown on the upper right, which makes it possible to quickly notice any red flags in terms of system correctness.

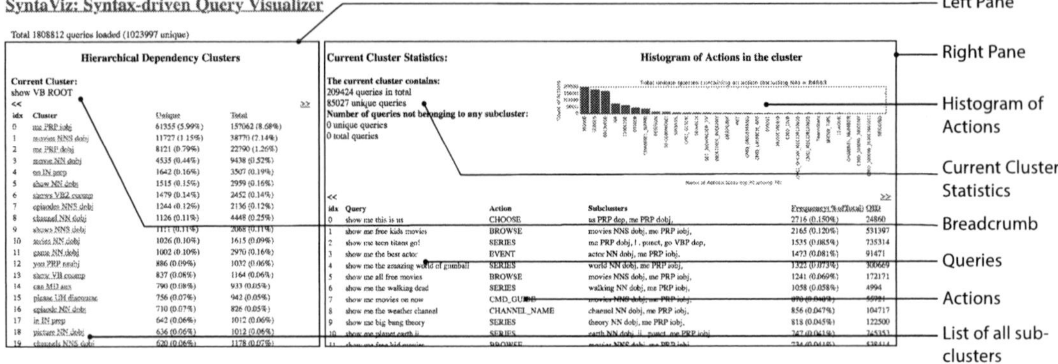

Figure 2: The complete SYNTAVIZ interface.

4 User Study

We conducted quantitative, qualitative and heuristic experiments with the users of the SYNTAVIZ interface. There were 8 participants in the study among which four were editors/annotators from the voice NLP and the customer service project, three were developers of the voice NLP project, and one was the project manager of the customer service project. All of the participants were familiar with the voice queries and the existing intent understanding methods.

4.1 Quantitative Evaluation

Several metrics were computed based on responses to statements shown in Table 1 where the participants rated whether they agree, disagree, or remain neutral with respect to each statement. We use Q1 for measuring the usefulness, Q2, Q3 for usability, Q4, Q5 for efficiency, and Q6 for the practical value of the system.

The results of the evaluation are shown in Figure 3. Six out of eight participants agreed that SYNTAVIZ helped them to quickly find the major patterns of mistakes. This shows that SYNTAVIZ provides useful information to achieve its intended use—finding patterns of mistakes in the existing system. Seven participants disagreed with the statement that the interface is complex (Q2) and six agreed that no help is needed to use the interface (Q3). The evidence that SYNTAVIZ does not cause cognitive overload or require outside help implies that it is intuitively usable. In terms of efficiency, six participants agreed that it does not take much time to learn (Q4), half of the total participants seem to be confused at some point while using the interface. We analyzed this issue in the subjective evaluation which is described in the following subsection. Finally, the majority of the participants (5 out of 8) mentioned that they will use SYNTAVIZ in their regular workflow.

4.2 Qualitative Evaluation

We asked for subjective opinions from the participants for a qualitative evaluation of SYNTAVIZ. Each participant was asked to write about the positive features, negative features, important future additions, and the impact of the interface in their current workflow. These comments provided us a spectrum of information regarding the SYNTAVIZ interface which are discussed below.

Positive Aspects. A number of positive aspects of the SYNTAVIZ interface were mentioned. Almost all the participants appreciated that the combination of syntactic ontology and the action histogram makes it easier to understand where the existing system is failing.

> "The interface makes it clear that syntactic information is very useful for drilling down the long tail of VREX commands. Once I have drilled down a few levels deep, I start to see utterances where the system failed."

They also appreciated the frequency-based ranking scheme which helped them to "know the weight of the queries and decide priorities". In addition, every participant commented positively about the simple interaction experience.

> "Simple, easy-to-learn design. Did not take long to get used to the layout and multiple sorting and drill-down features. Almost no load time. Useful and specific information."

Measures for Quantitative Evaluation
Q1: SYNTAVIZ allowed me to quickly find major patterns of mistakes in the deployed system
Q2: The interaction was unnecessarily complex.
Q3: I did not need assistance to use SYNTAVIZ.
Q4: SYNTAVIZ does not take much time to learn.
Q5: I never felt confused/lost while using the interface.
Q6: If available, I'll use SYNTAVIZ in my regular workflow.

Measures for Qualitative Evaluation
Please write some useful aspects of SYNTAVIZ
Please write some aspects of the interface that could be improved upon. Please also suggest why the proposed approach would be an improvement over the existing solution.
Please enlist some possible features that should be added in the future iterations of the interface. Please also explain why.
What immediate changes/benefits can this tool bring in your current workflow?

Table 1: All the measures for quantitative and qualitative evaluation of SYNTAVIZ.

Negative Aspects. The quantitative analysis revealed that some of the users felt confused or lost while using the interface. The underlying reason for such rating became clear in the qualitative evaluation. Many participants mentioned that the labels of the clusters are not immediately understandable. The cluster names included parts-of-speech tags from Penn Treeback Project (Santorini, 1990) (e.g. NN for Noun, JJ for Adjective), and dependency type information from Universal Dependency Project (Nivre et al., 2016). The participants commented that these codes might confuse the users. They suggested a pop-up legend or glossary would be helpful in this situation.

> "I believe that the naming can be hard to understand for many people. QID is not necessarily intuitive and for anyone who operates on a higher level, they may not be aware of what a subcluster is or what the "nn root" means after the groups on the first page."

A few participants mentioned that it is problematic to navigate back to the parent clusters by clicking the *back* button multiple times, suggesting a *Back to Home* button. In addition, these comments suggest that the existence or use of the breadcrumb is not obvious in the interface.

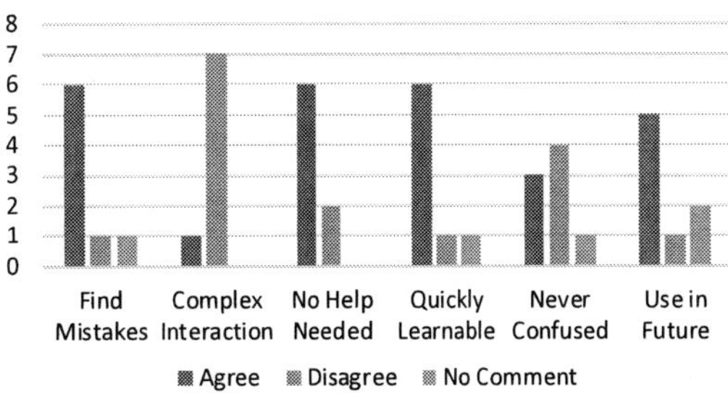

Figure 3: Results of quantitative evaluation of the SYNTAVIZ interface.

Possible Future Additions. We asked the users to suggest future additions to the interface and received a number of ideas that can improve the interface and user experience. For example, several users asked for a search capability within the interface. Interaction on SYNTAVIZ is currently exploratory and thus the experience is similar to browsing through a tree. However, the users might need to search for a specific keyword and navigate quickly to the corresponding clusters.

> "Allow the user to search for a word (or words) eg the word 'card': `card NN ROOT|credit NN nn|` and `change VB ROOT|card NN dobj|` — I wanted to find instances of 'credit card' as some of those queries may have different labels. Allow the user to filter on Action so that the user can view only queries for that action; Allow users to export queries that may need to be fixed"

Participants also mentioned some other useful features; for instance, adjusting the time span for the dataset, searching and filtering for a specific action, and comparing multiple clusters. All these ideas are implementable in a future iteration while staying within the design of the proposed visual framework.

Impact. Many participants mentioned that SYNTAVIZ will allow them to identify outliers in the data or systemic errors in the deployed system, and that it will help them to identify unsupported patterns. This was considered useful for feature prioritization from a product point of view:

> "Feature prioritization will be a big problem to solve from a product point of view. From research point of view this give great understanding of how the data

is getting clustered among queries and find potential bugs and loop holes in our NLP system."

4.3 Heuristic Evaluation

In this section, we describe a usage scenario based on the informal discussions with the developers of the X1 platform: Upon studying the ranked lists, one developer noticed a cluster labeled `record/VB/ROOT`, which refers to the group of 4587 unique queries that share the root verb "record". One of the largest sub-clusters is `oscars/NNS/dobj`, referring to the group of queries where the customers were interested in recording the Oscars event.[1] Clicking on this sub-cluster provides great insight into how customers use voice, as well as queries mishandled by the deployed system. The histogram on the upper right immediately revealed that around 60% of queries were categorized by the system as a `SEARCH` intent, whereas only 20% were linked to the correct (`RECORD`) intent. Discussions among engineers resulted in several action items to fix such issues and provide a more consistent user experience.

These errors might have seemed obvious after a short session with SYNTAVIZ, but such information is usually buried deep under the large pile of popular queries. We observed first-hand that a syntax-driven ontology is very useful at highlighting many other patterns in how customers use natural language to query the platform.

5 Conclusions

In conclusion, SYNTAVIZ is a novel visualization interface for datasets with a large number of unique natural-language queries. It is based on a hierarchical clustering of all queries, designed from a syntax-driven ontology of the dataset.

Evaluation of SYNTAVIZ shows strong evidence that the system provides useful information for finding the errors in the existing system. Based on real needs of a major voice-enabled entertainment platform, our preliminary implementation has shown great promise to improve software development cycles by providing useful analytics that help fix bugs, as well as prioritize future efforts in a data-driven fashion.

By releasing the source code of SYNTAVIZ, we are hoping to share these benefits with many other teams across the industry. The complete source code of SyntaViz is available in

`https://github.com/Comcast/SyntaViz`

References

Daniel Andor et al. 2016. Globally normalized transition-based neural networks. In *ACL'16*, volume 1, pages 2442–2452.

Stamatia Dasiopoulou et al. 2015. Representing and visualizing text as ontologies: A case from the patent domain. In *VOILA@ ISWC*, page 83.

Enamul Hoque and Giuseppe Carenini. 2016. Multiconvis: A visual text analytics system for exploring a collection of online conversations. In *IUI'16*, pages 96–107. ACM.

Quentin Jones et al. 2004. Information overload and the message dynamics of online interaction spaces: A theoretical model and empirical exploration. *Information systems research*, 15(2):194–210.

Dan Jurafsky and James H Martin. 2014. *Speech and language processing*, volume 3 (In Prep.) Chap. 14. Pearson London.

Reinhard Kneser and Hermann Ney. 1995. Improved backing-off for m-gram language modeling. In *Acoustics, Speech, and Signal Processing, 1995. ICASSP-95., 1995 International Conference on*, volume 1, pages 181–184. IEEE.

Joakim Nivre et al. 2016. Universal dependencies v1: A multilingual treebank collection. In *LREC*.

Heiko Paulheim and Florian Probst. 2012. Ontology-enhanced user interfaces: A survey. *Semantic-Enabled Advancements on the Web: Applications Across Industries*, 214.

Sundar Pichai. 2016. Google i/o keynote. Presentation.

Beatrice Santorini. 1990. Part-of-speech tagging guidelines for the penn treebank project (3rd revision). *Technical Reports (CIS)*, page 570.

Jaspreet Singh et al. 2017. Structure-aware visualization of text corpora. In *Proceedings of the 2017 Conference on Conference Human Information Interaction and Retrieval*, pages 107–116. ACM.

Greg Sterling. 2015. It's official: Google says more searches now on mobile than on desktop. `http://searchengineland.com/its-official-google-says-more-searches-now-on-mobile-than-on-desktop-220369`. Accessed: 2017-08-16.

Furu Wei et al. 2010. Tiara: a visual exploratory text analytic system. In *Proceedings of the 16th ACM SIGKDD international conference on Knowledge discovery and data mining*, pages 153–162. ACM.

---

[1] 2017 Oscars occurred during the week of our collected dataset.

TRANX: A Transition-based Neural Abstract Syntax Parser for Semantic Parsing and Code Generation

Pengcheng Yin, Graham Neubig
Language Technologies Institute
Carnegie Mellon University
{pcyin,gneubig}@cs.cmu.edu

Abstract

We present TRANX, a transition-based neural semantic parser that maps natural language (NL) utterances into formal meaning representations (MRs). TRANX uses a transition system based on the *abstract syntax description language* for the target MR, which gives it two major advantages: (1) it is highly accurate, using information from the syntax of the target MR to constrain the output space and model the information flow, and (2) it is highly generalizable, and can easily be applied to new types of MR by just writing a new abstract syntax description corresponding to the allowable structures in the MR. Experiments on four different semantic parsing and code generation tasks show that our system is generalizable, extensible, and effective, registering strong results compared to existing neural semantic parsers.[1]

1 Introduction

Semantic parsing is the task of transducing natural language (NL) utterances into formal meaning representations (MRs). The target MRs can be defined according to a wide variety of formalisms. This include linguistically-motivated semantic representations that are designed to capture the meaning of any sentence such as λ-calculus (Zettlemoyer and Collins, 2005) or the abstract meaning representations (Banarescu et al., 2013). Alternatively, for more task-driven approaches to semantic parsing, it is common for meaning representations to represent executable programs such as SQL queries (Zhong et al., 2017), robotic commands (Artzi and Zettlemoyer, 2013), smart phone instructions (Quirk et al., 2015), and even general-purpose programming languages like Python (Yin and Neubig, 2017; Rabinovich et al., 2017) and Java (Ling et al., 2016).

Because of these varying formalisms for MRs, the design of semantic parsers, particularly neural network-based ones has generally focused on a small subset of tasks — in order to ensure the syntactic well-formedness of generated MRs, a parser is usually specifically designed to reflect the domain-dependent grammar of MRs in the structure of the model (Zhong et al., 2017; Xu et al., 2017). To alleviate this issue, there have been recent efforts in neural semantic parsing with general-purpose grammar models (Xiao et al., 2016; Dong and Lapata, 2018). Yin and Neubig (2017) put forward a neural sequence-to-sequence model that generates tree-structured MRs using a series of tree-construction actions, guided by the task-specific context free grammar provided to the model *a priori*. Rabinovich et al. (2017) propose the abstract syntax networks (ASNs), where domain-specific MRs are represented by abstract syntax trees (ASTs, Fig. 2 *Left*) specified under the abstract syntax description language (ASDL) framework (Wang et al., 1997). An ASN employs a modular architecture, generating an AST using specifically designed neural networks for each construct in the ASDL grammar.

Inspired by this existing research, we have developed TRANX, a **TRAN**sition-based abstract synta**X** parser for semantic parsing and code generation. TRANX is designed with the following principles in mind:

- **Generalization ability** TRANX employs ASTs as a general-purpose intermediate meaning representation, and the task-dependent grammar is provided to the system as external knowledge to guide the parsing process, therefore decoupling the semantic parsing procedure with specificities of grammars.

- **Extensibility** TRANX uses a simple transition system to parse NL utterances into tree-

---

[1]Available at https://github.com/pcyin/tranX. An earilier version is used in Yin et al. (2018).

Proceedings of the 2018 Conference on Empirical Methods in Natural Language Processing (System Demonstrations), pages 7–12
Brussels, Belgium, October 31–November 4, 2018. ©2018 Association for Computational Linguistics

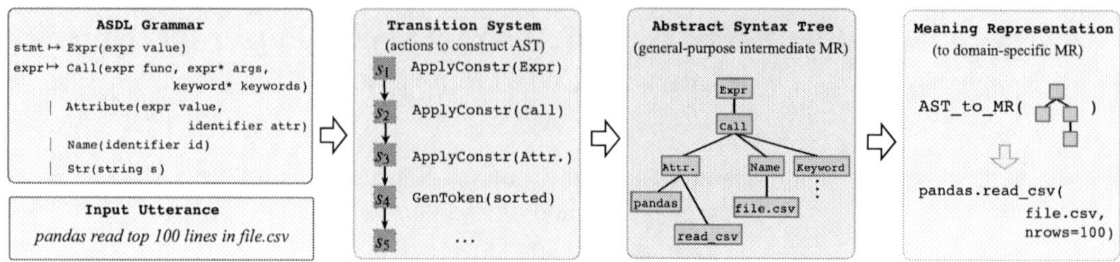

Figure 1: Workflow of TRANX

2 Methodology

structured ASTs. The transition system is designed to be easy to extend, requiring minimal engineering to adapt to tasks that need to handle extra domain-specific information.

- **Effectiveness** We test TRANX on four semantic parsing (ATIS, GEO) and code generation (DJANGO, WIKISQL) tasks, and demonstrate that TRANX is capable of generalizing to different domains while registering strong performance, out-performing existing neural network-based approaches on three of the four datasets (GEO, ATIS, DJANGO).

2 Methodology

Given an NL utterance, TRANX parses the utterance into a formal meaning representation, typically represented as λ-calculus logical forms, domain-specific, or general-purpose programming languages (e.g., Python). In the following description we use Python code generation as a running example, where a programmer's natural language intents are mapped to Python source code. Fig. 1 depicts the workflow of TRANX. We will present more use cases of TRANX in § 3.

The core of TRANX is a transition system. Given an input NL utterance x, TRANX employs the transition system to map the utterance x into an AST z using a series of tree-construction actions (§ 2.2). TRANX employs ASTs as the intermediate meaning representation to abstract over domain-specific structure of MRs. This parsing process is guided by the user-defined, domain-specific grammar specified under the ASDL formalism (§ 2.1). Given the generated AST z, the parser calls the user-defined function, AST_to_MR(·), to convert the intermediate AST into a domain-specific meaning representation y, completing the parsing process. TRANX uses a probabilistic model $p(z|x)$, parameterized by a neural network, to score each hypothesis AST (§ 2.3).

2.1 Modeling ASTs using ASDL Grammar

TRANX uses ASTs as the general-purpose, intermediate semantic representation for MRs. ASTs are commonly used to represent programming languages, and can also be used to represent other tree-structured MRs (e.g., λ-calculus). The ASDL framework is a grammatical formalism to define ASTs. See Fig. 1 for an excerpt of the Python ASDL grammar. TRANX provides APIs to read such a grammar from human-readable text files.

An ASDL grammar has two basic constructs: *types* and *constructors*. A *composite* type is defined by the set of constructors under that type. For example, the stmt and expr composite types in Fig. 1 refer to Python statements and expressions, repectively, each defined by a series of constructors. A constructor specifies a language construct of a particular type using its *fields*. For instance, the Call constructor under the composite type expr denotes function call expressions, and has three fields: func, args and keywords. Each field in a constructor is also strongly typed, which specifies the type of value the field can hold. A field with a composite type can be instantiated by constructors of the same type. For example, the func field above can hold a constructor of type expr. There are also fields with *primitive* types, which store values. For example, the id field of Name constructor has a primitive type identifier, and is used to store identifier names. And the field s in the Str (string) constructor hold string literals. Finally, each field has a cardinality (single, optional ? and sequential ∗), denoting the number of values the field holds.

An AST is then composed of multiple constructors, where each node on the tree corresponds to a typed field in a constructor (except for the root node, which denotes the root constructor). Depending on the cardinality of the field, a node can hold one or multiple constructors as its values. For instance, the func field with single car-

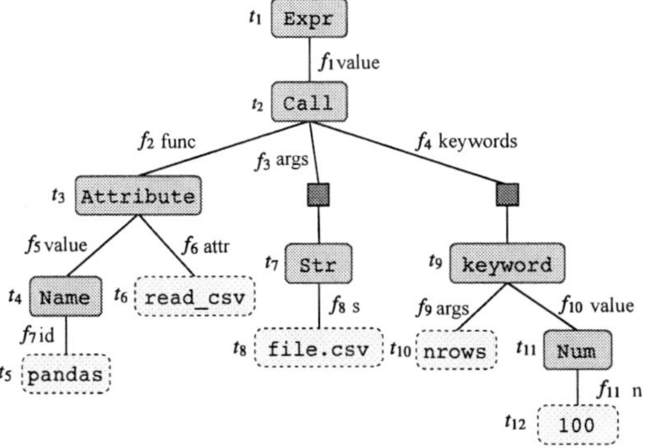

t	n_{f_t}	Action
t_1	root	Expr(expr value)
t_2	f_1	Call(expr func, expr* args, keyword* keywords)
t_3	f_2	Attribute(expr value, identifier attr)
t_4	f_5	Name(identifier id)
t_5	f_7	GENTOKEN[pandas]
t_6	f_6	GENTOKEN[read_csv]
t_7	f_3	Str(string s)
t_8	f_8	GENTOKEN[file.csv]
t_9	f_8	GENTOKEN[</f>]
t_{10}	f_3	REDUCE (close the frontier field f_3)
t_{11}	f_4	keyword(identifier arg, expr value)
t_{12}	f_9	GENTOKEN[nrows]
t_{13}	f_{10}	Num(object n)
t_{14}	f_{11}	GENTOKEN[1000]
t_{15}	f_4	REDUCE (close the frontier field f_4)

Figure 2: *Left* The ASDL AST for the target Python code in Fig. 1. Field names are labeled on upper arcs, and indexed as f_i. Purple squares denote fields with *sequential* cardinality. Grey nodes denote primitive identifier fields. Fields are labeled with time steps at which they are generated. *Right* The action sequence used to construct the AST. Each action is labeled with its frontier field n_{f_t}. APPLYCONSTR actions are represented by their constructors.

dinality in the ASDL grammar in Fig. 1 is instantiated with one `Name` constructor, while the `args` field with sequential cardinality have multiple child constructors.

2.2 Transition System

Inspired by Yin and Neubig (2017) (hereafter YN17), we develop a transition system that decomposes the generation procedure of an AST into a sequence of tree-constructing *actions*. We now explain the transition system using our running example. Fig. 2 *Right* lists the sequence of actions used to construct the example AST. In high level, the generation process starts from an initial derivation AST with a single root node, and proceeds according to a top-down, left-to-right order traversal of the AST. At each time step, one of the following three types of actions is evoked to expand the opening *frontier field* n_{f_t} of the derivation:

APPLYCONSTR[c] actions apply a constructor c to the opening composite frontier field which has the same type as c, populating the opening node using the fields in c. If the frontier field has sequential cardinality, the action appends the constructor to the list of constructors held by the field.

REDUCE actions mark the completion of the generation of child values for a field with optional (?) or multiple (*) cardinalities.

GENTOKEN[v] actions populate a (empty) primitive frontier field with a token v. For example, the field f_7 on Fig. 2 has type `identifier`, and is instantiated using a single GENTOKEN action. For fields of `string` type, like f_8, whose value could consists of multiple tokens (only one shown here), it can be filled using a sequence of GENTOKEN actions, with a special

GENTOKEN[</f>] action to terminate the generation of token values.

The generation completes once there is no frontier field on the derivation. TRANX then calls the user specified function AST_to_MR($\cdot$) to convert the generated intermediate AST z into the target domain-specific MR y. TRANX provides various helper functions to ease the process of writing conversion functions. For example, our example conversion function to transform ASTs into Python source code contains only 32 lines of code. TRANX also ships with several built-in conversion functions to handle MRs commonly used in semantic parsing and code generation, like λ-calculus logical forms and SQL queries.

2.3 Computing Action Probabilities $p(z|x)$

Given the transition system, the probability of an z is decomposed into the probabilities of the sequence of actions used to generate z

$$p(z|x) = \prod_t p(a_t|a_{<t}, x),$$

Following YN17, we parameterize the transition-based parser $p(z|x)$ using a neural encoder-decoder network with augmented recurrent connections to reflect the topology of ASTs.

Encoder The encoder is a standard bidirectional Long Short-term Memory (LSTM) network, which encodes the input utterance x of n tokens, $\{x_i\}_{i=1}^n$ into vectorial representations $\{\mathbf{h}\}_{i=1}^n$.

Decoder The decoder is also an LSTM network, with its hidden state $\mathbf{s}_t$ at each time temp given by

$$\mathbf{s}_t = f_{\text{LSTM}}([\mathbf{a}_{t-1} : \tilde{\mathbf{s}}_{t-1} : \mathbf{p}_t], \mathbf{s}_{t-1}),$$

where f_{LSTM} is the LSTM transition function, and $[:]$ denotes vector concatenation. $\mathbf{a}_{t-1}$ is the em-

9

```
expr
 = Variable(var variable)
 | Entity(ent entity)
 | Number(num number)
 | Apply(pred predicate, expr* arguments)
 | Argmax(var variable, expr domain, expr body)
 | Argmin(var variable, expr domain, expr body)
 | Count(var variable, expr body)
 | Exists(var variable, expr body)
 | Lambda(var variable, var_type type, expr body)
 | Max(var variable, expr body)
 | Min(var variable, expr body)
 | Sum(var variable, expr domain, expr body)
 | The(var variable, expr body)
 | Not(expr argument)
 | And(expr* arguments)
 | Or(expr* arguments)
 | Compare(cmp_op op, expr left, expr right)

cmp_op = Equal | LessThan | GreaterThan
```

Figure 3: The λ-calculus ASDL grammar for GEO and ATIS, defined in Rabinovich et al. (2017)

bedding of the previous action. We maintain an embedding vector for each action. $\tilde{\mathbf{s}}_t$ is the attentional vector defined as in Luong et al. (2015)

$$\tilde{\mathbf{s}}_t = \tanh(\mathbf{W}_c[\mathbf{c}_t : \mathbf{s}_t]).$$

where $\mathbf{c}_t$ is the context vector retrieved from input encodings $\{\mathbf{h}_i\}_{i=1}^n$ using attention.

Parent Feeding $\mathbf{p}_t$ is a vector that encodes the information of the parent frontier field n_{f_t} on the derivation, which is a concatenation of two vectors: the embedding of the frontier field $\mathbf{n}_{f_t}$, and $\mathbf{s}_{p_t}$, the decoder's state at which the constructor of n_{f_t} is generated by the APPLYCONSTR action. Parent feeding reflects the topology of tree-structured ASTs, and gives better performance on generating complex MRs like Python code (§ 3).

Action Probabilities   The probability of an AP-PLYCONSTR[c] action with embedding $\mathbf{a}_c$ is[2]

$$p(a_t = \text{APPLYCONSTR}[c]|a_{<t}, \boldsymbol{x})$$
$$= \text{softmax}(\mathbf{a}_c^\mathsf{T}\mathbf{W}\tilde{\mathbf{s}}_t) \quad (1)$$

For GENTOKEN actions, we employ a hybrid approach of generation and copying, allowing for out-of-vocabulary variable names and literals (e.g., *"file.csv"* in Fig. 1) in $\boldsymbol{x}$ to be directly copied to the derivation. Specifically, the action probability is defined to be the marginal probability

$$p(a_t = \text{GENTOKEN}[v]|a_{<t}, \boldsymbol{x})$$
$$= p(\text{gen}|a_t, \boldsymbol{x})p(v|\text{gen}, a_t, \boldsymbol{x}) +$$
$$p(\text{copy}|a_t, \boldsymbol{x})p(v|\text{copy}, a_t, \boldsymbol{x})$$

---

[2] REDUCE is treated as a special APPLYCONSTR action.

```
stmt = Select(agg_op? agg, idx column_idx,
                        cond_expr* conditions)
cond_expr = Condition(cmp_op op, idx column_idx,
                        string value)
agg_op = Max | Min | Count | Sum | Avg
cmp_op = Equal | GreaterThan | LessThan | Other
```

Figure 4: The ASDL grammar for WIKISQL

The binary probability $p(\text{gen}|\cdot)$ and $p(\text{copy}|\cdot)$ is given by softmax$(\mathbf{W}\tilde{\mathbf{s}}_t)$. The probability of generating v from a closed-set vocabulary, $p(v|\text{gen}, \cdot)$ is defined similarly as Eq. (1). The copy probability of copying the i-th word in $\boldsymbol{x}$ is defined using a pointer network (Vinyals et al., 2015)

$$p(x_i|\text{copy}, a_{<t}, \boldsymbol{x}) = \text{softmax}(\mathbf{h}_i^\mathsf{T}\mathbf{W}\tilde{\mathbf{s}}_t).$$

3 Experiments

3.1 Datasets

To demonstrate the generalization and extensibility of TRANX, we deploy our parser on four semantic parsing and code generation tasks.

3.1.1 Semantic Parsing

We evaluate on GEO and ATIS datasets. GEO is a collection of 880 U.S. geographical questions (*e.g.*, *"Which states border Texas?"*), and ATIS is a set of 5,410 inquiries of flight information (*e.g.*, *"Show me flights from Dallas to Baltimore"*). The MRs in the two datasets are defined in λ-calculus logical forms (*e.g.*, "lambda x (and (state x) (next_to x texas))" and "lambda x (and (flight x dallas) (to x baltimore))"). We use the pre-processed datasets released by Dong and Lapata (2016). We use the ASDL grammar defined in Rabinovich et al. (2017), as listed in Fig. 3.

3.1.2 Code Generation

We evaluate TRANX on both general-purpose (Python, DJANGO) and domain-specific (SQL, WIKISQL) code generation tasks. The DJANGO dataset (Oda et al., 2015) consists of 18,805 lines of Python source code extracted from the Django Web framework, with each line paired with an NL description. Code in this dataset covers various real-world use cases of Python, like string manipulation, I/O operation, exception handling, *etc.*

WIKISQL (Zhong et al., 2017) is a code generation task for *domain-specific* languages (*i.e.*, SQL). It consists of 80,654 examples of NL questions (*e.g.*, *"What position did Calvin Mccarty play?"*) and annotated SQL queries (*e.g.*, "SELECT Position FROM Table WHERE

Methods	GEO	ATIS
ZH15 (Zhao and Huang, 2015)	88.9	84.2
ZC07 (Zettlemoyer and Collins, 2007)	89.0	84.6
WKZ14 (Wang et al., 2014)	**90.4**	**91.3**
Neural Network-based Models		
SEQ2TREE (Dong and Lapata, 2016)	87.1	84.6
ASN (Rabinovich et al., 2017)	85.7	85.3
+ supervised attention	87.1	85.9
TRANX (w/o parent feeding)	88.2	86.2
TRANX (w/ parent feeding)	87.7	86.2

Table 1: Semantic parsing accuracies on GEO and ATIS

Methods	ACC.
Phrasal Statistical MT (Ling et al., 2016)	31.5
SEQ2TREE (Dong and Lapata, 2016)	39.4
NMT (Neubig, 2015)	45.1
LPN (Ling et al., 2016)	62.3
YN17 (Yin and Neubig, 2017)	71.6
TRANX (w/o parent feeding)	72.7
TRANX (w parent feeding)	**73.7**

Table 2: Code generation accuracies on DJANGO

Methods	ACC_{EM}	ACC_{EX}
Seq2Seq (Zhong et al., 2017)	23.4	35.9
SEQ2TREE (Dong and Lapata, 2016)	23.4	35.9
Seq2SQL (Zhong et al., 2017)	48.3	59.4
SQLNet (Xu et al., 2017)	–	68.0
PT-MAML (Huang et al., 2018)	62.8	68.0
TypeSQL (Yu et al., 2018)	–	**73.5**
TRANX		
w/ parent feeding	62.6	71.6
w/o parent feeding	**62.9**	71.7
PointSQL (Wang et al., 2017)[†]	61.5	66.8
TypeSQL+TC (Yu et al., 2018)[†]	–	**82.6**
STAMP (Sun et al., 2018)[†]	60.7	74.4
STAMP+RL (Sun et al., 2018)[†]	61.0	74.6
TRANX		
w par. feed. + answer pruning[†]	68.4	78.6
w/o par. feed. + answer pruning[†]	**68.6**	78.6

Table 3: Exact match (EM) and execution (EX) accuracies on WIKISQL. [†]Methods that use the contents of input tables.

Player = Calvin Mccarty"). Different from other datasets, each example also has a table extracted from Wikipedia, and the SQL query is executed against the table to get an answer.

Extending TRANX for WIKISQL In order to achieve strong results, existing parsers, like most models in Tab. 3, use specifically designed architectures to reflect the syntactic structure of SQL queries. We show that the transition system used by TRANX can be easily extended for WIKISQL with minimal engineering, while registering strong performance. First, we use define a simple ASDL grammar following the syntax of SQL (Fig. 4). We then augment the transition system with a special GENTOKEN action, SELCOLUMN$[k]$. A SELCOLUMN$[k]$ action is used to populate a primitive `column_idx` field in `Select` and `Condition` constructors in the grammar by selecting the k-th column in the table. To compute the probability of SELCOLUMN$[k]$ actions, we use a pointer network over column encodings, where the column encodings are given by a bidirectional LSTM network over column names in an input table. This can be simply implemented by overriding the base `Parser` class in TRANX and modifying the functions that compute action probabilities.

3.2 Results

In this section we discuss our experimental results. All results are averaged over three runs with different random seeds.

Semantic Parsing Tab. 1 lists the results for semantic parsing tasks. We test TRANX with two configurations, with or without parent feeding (§ 2.3). Our system outperforms existing neural network-based approaches. This demonstrates the effectiveness of TRANX in closed-domain semantic parsing. Interestingly, we found the model without parent feeding achieves slightly better accuracy on GEO, probably because that its relative simple grammar does not require extra handling of parent information.

Code Generation Tab. 2 lists the results on DJANGO. TRANX achieves state-of-the-art results on DJANGO. We also find parent feeding yields +1 point gain in accuracy, suggesting the importance of modeling parental connections in ASTs with complex domain grammars (*e.g.*, Python).

Tab. 3 shows the results on WIKISQL. We first discuss our standard model which only uses information of column names and do not use the contents of input tables during inference, as listed in the top two blocks in Tab. 3. We find TRANX, although just with simple extensions to adapt to this dataset, achieves impressive results and outperforms many *task-specific* methods. This demonstrates that TRANX is easy to extend to incorporate task-specific information, while maintaining its effectiveness. We also extend TRANX with a very simple *answer pruning* strategy, where we execute the candidate SQL queries in the beam against the input table, and prune those that yield empty execution results. Results are listed in the bottom two-blocks in Tab. 3, where we compare with systems that also use the contents of tables. Surprisingly, this (frustratingly) simple extension yields significant improvements, outperforming many task-specific models that use specifically designed, heavily-engineered neural networks to incorporate information of table contents.

4 Conclusion

We present TRANX, a transition-based abstract syntax parser. TRANX is generalizable, extensible and effective, achieving strong results on semantic parsing and code generation tasks.

Acknowledgements

This material is based upon work supported by the National Science Foundation under Grant No. 1815287.

References

Yoav Artzi and Luke Zettlemoyer. 2013. Weakly supervised learning of semantic parsers for mapping instructions to actions. *Transaction of ACL*.

Laura Banarescu, Claire Bonial, Shu Cai, Madalina Georgescu, Kira Griffitt, Ulf Hermjakob, Kevin Knight, Philipp Koehn, Martha Palmer, and Nathan Schneider. 2013. Abstract meaning representation for sembanking. In *Proceedings of LAW-ID@ACL*.

Li Dong and Mirella Lapata. 2016. Language to logical form with neural attention. In *Proceedings of ACL*.

Li Dong and Mirella Lapata. 2018. Coarse-to-fine decoding for neural semantic parsing. In *Proceedings of ACL*.

Po-Sen Huang, Chenglong Wang, Rishabh Singh, Wen tau Yih, and Xiaodong He. 2018. Natural language to structured query generation via meta-learning. In *Proceedings of NAACL-HLT*.

Wang Ling, Phil Blunsom, Edward Grefenstette, Karl Moritz Hermann, Tomás Kociský, Fumin Wang, and Andrew Senior. 2016. Latent predictor networks for code generation. In *Proceedings of ACL*.

Thang Luong, Hieu Pham, and Christopher D. Manning. 2015. Effective approaches to attention-based neural machine translation. In *Proceedings of EMNLP*.

Graham Neubig. 2015. lamtram: A toolkit for language and translation modeling using neural networks. http://www.github.com/neubig/lamtram.

Yusuke Oda, Hiroyuki Fudaba, Graham Neubig, Hideaki Hata, Sakriani Sakti, Tomoki Toda, and Satoshi Nakamura. 2015. Learning to generate pseudo-code from source code using statistical machine translation (T). In *Proceedings of ASE*.

Chris Quirk, Raymond J. Mooney, and Michel Galley. 2015. Language to code: Learning semantic parsers for if-this-then-that recipes. In *Proceedings of ACL*.

Maxim Rabinovich, Mitchell Stern, and Dan Klein. 2017. Abstract syntax networks for code generation and semantic parsing. In *Proceedings of ACL*.

Yibo Sun, Duyu Tang, Nan Duan, Jianshu Ji, Guihong Cao, Xiaocheng Feng, Bing Qin, Ting Liu, and Ming Zhou. 2018. Semantic parsing with syntax- and table-aware SQL generation. *CoRR*, abs/1804.08338.

Oriol Vinyals, Meire Fortunato, and Navdeep Jaitly. 2015. Pointer networks. In *Proceedings of NIPS*.

Adrienne Wang, Tom Kwiatkowski, and Luke Zettlemoyer. 2014. Morpho-syntactic lexical generalization for CCG semantic parsing. In *Proceedings of EMNLP*.

Chenglong Wang, Marc Brockschmidt, and Rishabh Singh. 2017. Pointing out SQL queries from text. Technical report.

Daniel C. Wang, Andrew W. Appel, Jeffrey L. Korn, and Christopher S. Serra. 1997. The Zephyr abstract syntax description language. In *Proceedings of DSL*.

Chunyang Xiao, Marc Dymetman, and Claire Gardent. 2016. Sequence-based structured prediction for semantic parsing. In *Proceedings of ACL*.

Xiaojun Xu, Chang Liu, and Dawn Song. 2017. SQLNet: Generating structured queries from natural language without reinforcement learning. *arXiv preprint arXiv:1711.04436*.

Pengcheng Yin and Graham Neubig. 2017. A syntactic neural model for general-purpose code generation. In *Proceedings of ACL*.

Pengcheng Yin, Chunting Zhou, Junxian He, and Graham Neubig. 2018. StructVAE: Tree-structured latent variable models for semi-supervised semantic parsing. In *Proceedings of ACL*.

Tao Yu, Zifan Li, Zilin Zhang, Rui Zhang, and Dragomir R. Radev. 2018. TypeSQL: Knowledge-based type-aware neural text-to-sql generation.

Luke Zettlemoyer and Michael Collins. 2005. Learning to map sentences to logical form structured classification with probabilistic categorial grammars. In *Proceedings of UAI*.

Luke S. Zettlemoyer and Michael Collins. 2007. Online learning of relaxed CCG grammars for parsing to logical form. In *Proceedings of EMNLP-CoNLL*.

Kai Zhao and Liang Huang. 2015. Type-driven incremental semantic parsing with polymorphism. In *Proceedings of NAACL-HLT*.

Victor Zhong, Caiming Xiong, and Richard Socher. 2017. Seq2SQL: Generating structured queries from natural language using reinforcement learning. *arXiv preprint arXiv:1709.00103*.

Data2Text Studio: Automated Text Generation from Structured Data

Longxu Dou[1][*] **Guanghui Qin**[2][*] **Jinpeng Wang**[3] **Jin-Ge Yao**[3] **and Chin-Yew Lin**[3]
[1] Harbin Institute of Technology, `dreamerdeo@hit.edu.cn`
[2] Peking University, `ghq@pku.edu.cn`
[3] Microsoft Research Asia, `{jinpwa, jinge.yao, cyl}@microsoft.com`

Abstract

Data2Text Studio is a platform for automated text generation from structured data. It is equipped with a Semi-HMMs model to extract high-quality templates and corresponding trigger conditions from parallel data automatically, which improves the interactivity and interpretability of the generated text. In addition, several easy-to-use tools are provided for developers to edit templates of pre-trained models, and APIs are released for developers to call the pre-trained model to generate texts in third-party applications. We conduct experiments on ROTOWIRE datasets for template extraction and text generation. The results show that our model achieves improvements on both tasks.

1 Introduction

Data-to-text generation, i.e., a technology which takes structured data as input and produces text that adequately and fluently describes this data as output, has various applications on the generation of sports news (Chen and Mooney, 2008; Kim and Mooney, 2010; Mei et al., 2016; Wiseman et al., 2017), product descriptions (Wang et al., 2017), weather reports (Liang et al., 2009; Angeli et al., 2010; Mei et al., 2016) and short biographies (Lebret et al., 2016; Chisholm et al., 2017). In another scenario, it is possible albeit a little awkward for a virtual assistant like Microsoft Cortana to read out structured data when responding to users' queries. it is more user friendly for a virtual assistant to identify and read out the essential part of the structured data in natural language to make it easier to understand. In these cases, it is inefficient and expensive to generate texts using human writers, while an automatic text generation system would be helpful.

There are two main challenges for data-to-text generation systems: 1) Interactivity: For a developer, it should be able to customize the text generation model and control the generated texts. 2) Interpretability: the generated texts should be consistent with the structured data. For example, we can say "with a massive 8 GB of memory" for a laptop computer while "a massive 2 GB" is inappropriate. Rule-based approaches (Moore and Paris, 1993; Hovy, 1993; Reiter and Dale, 2000; Belz, 2007; Bouayad-Agha et al., 2011) encode domain knowledge into the generation system and then produce high-quality texts, while the construction of the system is expensive and heavily depends on domain experts. Statistical approaches are employed to reduce extensive development time by learning rules from historical data (Langkilde and Knight, 1998; Liang et al., 2009; Duboue and McKeown, 2003; Howald et al., 2013). However, statistical approaches are prone to generating texts with mistakes, because they don't know how to use specific phrases under various application conditions.

To address the second challenge, we propose a Semi-HMMs model to automatically extract templates and corresponding trigger conditions from parallel training data. Trigger conditions are explicit latent semantic annotations between paired structured data and texts, which support learning how to use specific phrases under the particular condition and then improve the interactivity and interpretability of the generated text compared to traditional template-based methods. More importantly, obtaining text generation trigger conditions automatically from alignment distribution could significantly reduce human editing workload compared with other commercial systems, e.g., Word-

---

[*] Contribution during the internship at Microsoft Research Asia.

Proceedings of the 2018 Conference on Empirical Methods in Natural Language Processing (System Demonstrations), pages 13–18
Brussels, Belgium, October 31–November 4, 2018. ©2018 Association for Computational Linguistics

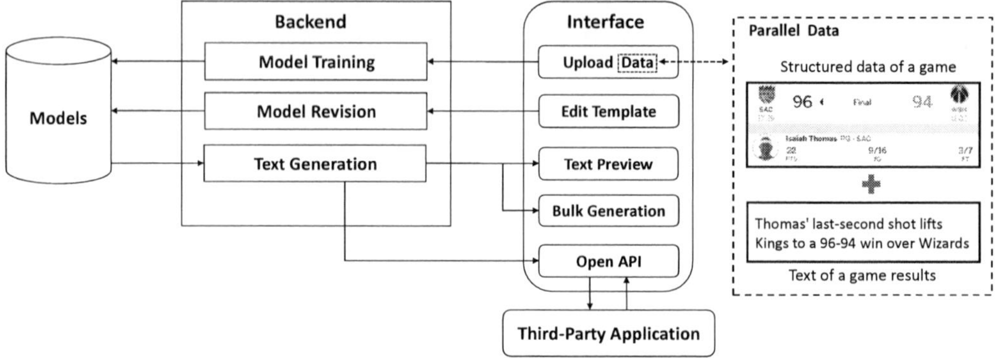

Figure 1: The simplified architecture of the Data2Text Studio.

Smith, Arria and Quill[1]. For example, although WordSmith provides functional tools to help developers create templates and generation rules, it still needs to create rules from scratch manually.

For the first challenge, we demonstrate the Data2Text Studio, a powerful platform equipped with the proposed Semi-HMMs model, to assist developers to generate texts from structured data in their own applications. Currently, this system provides several pre-trained models covering different domains: sports headline generation, resume generation, product description generation, etc. Developers can also train their own models by uploading parallel data. After model training, developers can revise the model, preview the generated texts or call the APIs to generate texts in third-party applications. All the processes are simple and friendly.

We conduct experiments on the ROTOWIRE dataset (Wiseman et al., 2017) to evaluate the performance of template extraction and overall text generation. The results show that our model achieves improvements on both tasks. The rest of this paper is organized as follows: Section 2 describes the architecture of Data2Text Studio. Section 3 proposes the main algorithm. Section 4 shows the experiment results.

2 Architecture

Fig. 1 shows the simplified architecture of the Data2Text Studio. It mainly consists of three components: 1) model training, 2) model revision and 3) text generation. For typical usages, developers can directly choose the pre-trained model to generate high-quality texts. To develop a customized text generation model: First, develop-

Figure 2: Extracted templates of NBA headlines. Bracket indicates the slot, and words in it indicates the corresponding attribute of structured data.

ers need to upload parallel data which consists of texts and corresponding structured data to train the model, and then training components will extract the templates and corresponding trigger conditions from training data automatically; secondly, developers could leverage the built-in tools to further revise the extracted templates and trigger conditions manually; finally, developers could preview the generated texts of the customized model, and the APIs are provided to generate texts in bulk or generate texts in third-party applications. In the following, we will introduce these modules in detail.

2.1 Model Training

We adopt the template-based solution for the Data2Text Studio. It can generate texts with high accuracy and fluency, which can be used in business applications directly. Several previous studies (Liang et al., 2009; Wang et al., 2017; Kondadadi et al., 2013) can be applied to extract templates from parallel data. To address the challenges introduced in Section 1, we propose a

---

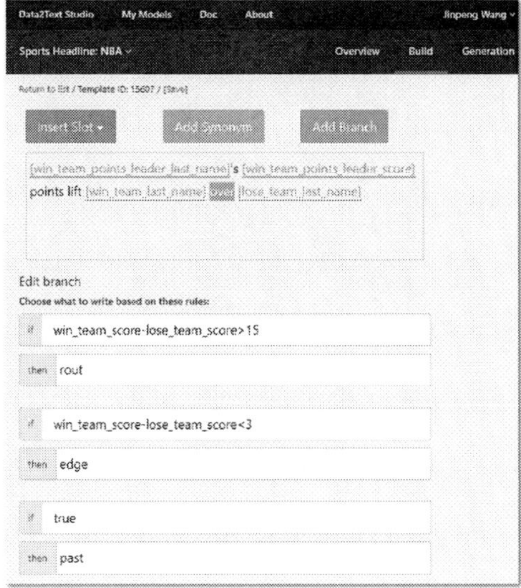
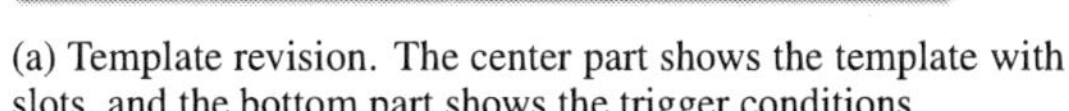
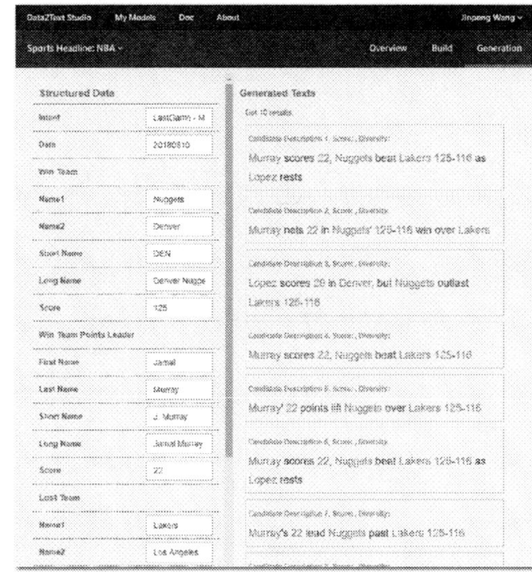

(a) Template revision. The center part shows the template with slots, and the bottom part shows the trigger conditions.

(b) Generated texts preview. Multiple headlines are generated for the same game to ensure variety.

Figure 3: Data2Text Studio Interface

Semi-HMMs model to extract templates and corresponding trigger conditions from parallel data (see Section 3.1 for the algorithm). Fig. 2 presents an example of the extracted templates from NBA Headline parallel data, which consists of the scoreboard and the corresponding news.

2.2 Model Revision

The trained model provides a better starting point for developers to avoid creating a model from scratch. If necessary, developers can revise the trained model by editing the extracted templates and their corresponding trigger conditions. Fig. 3a shows the interface of template editing. Three mechanisms are designed to manage templates and corresponding trigger conditions: 1) Data slot: the input structured data will be filled into the slot to generate texts. 2) Synonyms: it is constructed by a list of phrases, and one of them will be chosen randomly during the generation process. 3) Branch: the trigger condition to define usage scenario for the specific phrase. Our Semi-HMMs model in Section 3.1 can learn such data slots and trigger conditions automatically. Meanwhile, developers can also revise them if necessary.

2.3 Text Generation

Given the structured data, the system will generate corresponding texts with the trained model. Fig. 3b shows an example for NBA headline generation. The left-hand side shows the input struc-

tured data which contains the attributes of the game. The right-hand side shows multiple generated texts for this game to help developers check the quality of the generated texts.

2.4 API for Third-Party Applications

To use the text generation service in third-party applications, an API is created for each trained model. Once the structured data is posted through the API, the system will deliver the generated text back to third-party applications automatically. In this way, developers can leave the development work for a text generation model in the Data2Text Studio. Fig. 4 shows three application scenarios: sports headline generation, user profile generation based on LinkedIn data and car insight generation.

3 The Proposed Algorithm

In this section, we introduce the proposed algorithm for templates extraction and corresponding trigger conditions mining.

3.1 Template Extraction

A main challenge of templates extraction is the alignment between text and structured data. We adopt the model given by Liang et al. (2009), which presents a 3-tier HMMs to automatically align words to the fields of structured data. These aligned words could be strings, like brand names, or numbers copied from the data.

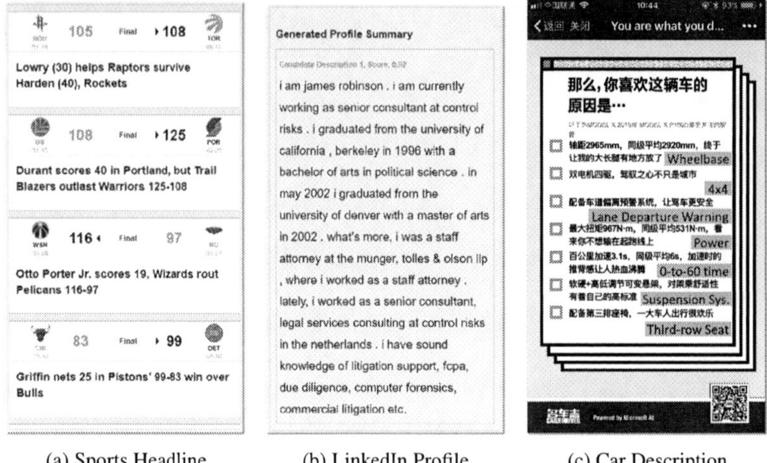

(a) Sports Headline	(b) LinkedIn Profile	(c) Car Description

Figure 4: Example applications by using the Data2Text API.

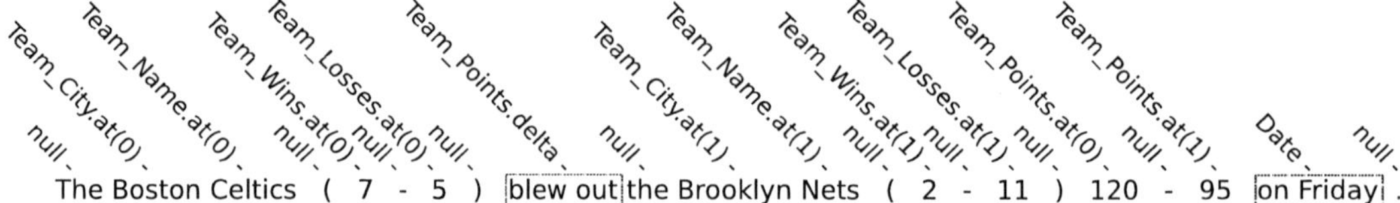

Figure 5: Example of Trigger Mechanism. Words in blue dashed boxes are particular phrases generated by our model under the specific rules. For example, *"blew out"* will be generated when *"Team_Points.delta"* overs 17 under the automatically extracted rules.

Another challenge is the lexical choice, which refers to choosing contextually-appropriate words to express non-linguistic data. For example, in a basketball game report, the author tends to use *blow out* only when the score difference is very large. Lexical choice is very subtle and differs from author to author, thus we enrich the alignment model with a Gaussian emission probability from words to numbers in the data.

The garbage collection problem is severe in the original model of Liang et al. (2009), which means that most of the words are wrongly aligned to infrequent fields that should remain unaligned (i.e, aligned to *null*). Here we incorporate the Posterior Regularization proposed by Graça et al. (2010), which could add constraints into models with latent variables while keeping the model tractable at the same time. In practice, we set a lower bound on the number of unaligned words, which could significantly alleviate the garbage collection problem.

In a nutshell, we propose a generative model, $P_s(\mathbf{w}, \pi | \mathbf{l})$, where s is the world state, namely, the structured data, $\mathbf{w}$ is the observed words, π is the segmentation of words, and $\mathbf{l}$ represents tags, which could be the fields of the structured data (e.g. `Team_Name`) or simple operations on specific fields (e.g. score difference). Let $\mathbf{c}$ be the segments of sentence $\mathbf{w}$ segmented by π. We further make a Markov assumption and factorize it into:

$$P(\mathbf{c}|\mathbf{l}) = \prod_t P(l^t|l^{t-1}) \cdot P_s(c^t|l^t), \quad (1)$$

where c^t represents the segment at time stamp t, which is annotated with tag l^t. For different types of fields, we use different methods to model $P_s(c^t|l^t)$.

During the training process, our goal is to maximize the complete data likelihood:

$$\mathcal{L}(\theta) = \prod_{(s,\mathbf{w}) \in \mathcal{D}} \sum_{\mathbf{l},\pi} P_s(\mathbf{l}, \pi, \mathbf{w}; \theta),$$

where $\mathcal{D}$ represents the whole training data. Once the model has been trained, we use Viterbi-like dynamic programming to perform the MAP inference to segment the texts and to assign the most likely tags for each span.

We derive an expectation-maximization (EM) algorithm to perform maximum likelihood estimation, and introduce a soft statistical regularization to guide the model towards a better solution. Specifically, we design a special NULL tag for unaligned words, and we "encourage" it to annotate at least half of the words. For more details, please refer to Qin et al. (2018).

3.2 Trigger Mechanism

As proposed in 3.1, we use Gaussian distribution to model the probability of alignment between numerical values and phrases. Hence our model can tell us not only where the word comes from, but also the distribution of numbers it is aligned to. For example, after training, our model successfully aligns "blow out" to the score difference, and shows that the mean value of score difference is 17 when this phrase is used. With this information, we could set a "trigger" on the aligned words. Trigger is a scheme which determines under what conditions a template could be used. For example, templates with "blow out" aligned to score difference can only be used when the score difference is around 17, where *blew out* would have a higher probability than *defeated*. So we could obtain a rule like this:

```
if team_points_delta > 17:
    use(blew out)
else:
    use(defeated)
```

With such rules, our model will be able to use different words under various conditions.

Now that the templates and triggers are ready for use, for text generation, we fill the templates with structured data under corresponding applicable trigger conditions.

4 Experiments

In this section, we will report the performance of the proposed model on template extraction and on overall text generation, both evaluated on the ROTOWIRE subset of the Wiseman et al. (2017) dataset.

	Precision	Recall	F1
Liang09	0.319	0.643	0.426
Liang09+PR	0.397	0.640	0.490
Semi-HMMs	0.254	0.765	0.381
Semi-HMMs+PR	**0.504**	**0.786**	**0.614**

Table 1: Word-level tag assignment results.

4.1 Template Extraction Evaluation

We conduct an experiment and compare with Liang et al. (2009)'s system as the baseline. It is difficult to evaluate the accuracy of tag assignment for the whole dataset, since the executable tags are not annotated in the original data. We recruit three human annotators which are familiar with basketball games to label a random sample consisting of 300 sentences from the test set. The annotators were told to judge whether each word span is related to the table, and which label they are related to. Finally, we calculate the precision and recall for non-NULL tag assignments at word-level.

The results are shown at Table 1. We can observe that our initial model indeed outperforms the baseline system in recall, while posterior regularization helps a lot to avoid distraction from irrelevant information that should be tagged as NULL without sacrificing the recall performance.

4.2 Overall Text Generation Evaluation

We also test the performance of extracted templates in overall text generation, by comparing with the baseline using the same heuristics described in Section 3.2. To generate document-level texts, we first generate a sentence describing the scoreline result for every game, followed by three sentences describing other information about team performance. While maintaining that no template is repeatedly used, we then choose the template with the highest score for the top ten players sorted by their game points. We report automatic metrics including BLEU scores and those based on relation extraction as proposed by Wiseman et al. (2017): precision & number of unique relations in generation (RG), precision & recall for content selection (CS), and content ordering (CO) score. Besides these automatic metrics for various aspects in NLG, we also conduct human evaluation on information correctness (1-5 scale ratings, the higher the better). We ask four human raters who are fluent in English and familiar with basketball to rate outputs for 30 random games. Results are shown in Table 2 with Kendall's W measuring the inter annotator agreement. We can observe that templates derived from our model indeed outperform those from the baseline system.

5 Conclusion and Future Work

To summarize, Data2Text Studio is a platform for automated text generation from structured data.

Model	RG(P%)	RG(#)	CS(P%)	CS(R%)	CO	BLEU	Correctness
Liang09+PR	85.83	33.29	14.33	31.09	6.25	8.34	2.60
SemiHMM+PR	90.47	41.79	21.63	50.17	9.63	9.45	3.58
Gold-standard	91.77	12.84	100	100	100	100	4.88

Table 2: Results for text generation. (Kendall's W=0.83 from correctness raters.)

It not only provides several pre-trained models which could generate high-quality texts from data but also is very easy to train new models by uploading parallel data. In addition, this system is equipped with the proposed Semi-HMMs model which could extract templates and corresponding trigger conditions from parallel data automatically and supports learning how to use specific phrases under the particular condition. Experiment results on the ROTOWIRE dataset show that the proposed model outperforms the baseline for template extraction and text generation.

In the future, we will integrate more powerful pre-trained models into this system in terms of data domain and text fidelity. For the template extraction model, we will learn more complex grounding rules to enhance the model power.

References

Gabor Angeli, Percy Liang, and Dan Klein. 2010. A simple domain-independent probabilistic approach to generation. In *EMNLP*, pages 502–512.

Anja Belz. 2007. Probabilistic generation of weather forecast texts. In *HLT-NAACL*, pages 164–171.

Nadjet Bouayad-Agha, Gerard Casamayor, and Leo Wanner. 2011. Content selection from an ontology-based knowledge base for the generation of football summaries. In *ENLG*, pages 72–81.

David L. Chen and Raymond J. Mooney. 2008. Learning to sportscast: a test of grounded language acquisition. In *ICML*, pages 128–135.

Andrew Chisholm, Will Radford, and Ben Hachey. 2017. Learning to generate one-sentence biographies from wikidata. *CoRR*, abs/1702.06235.

Pablo A. Duboue and Kathleen R. McKeown. 2003. Statistical acquisition of content selection rules for natural language generation. In *EMNLP*, pages 121–128.

J. V. Graça, K. Ganchev, and B. Taskar. 2010. Learning tractable word alignment models with complex constraints. *Computational Linguistics*, 36(3):481–504.

Eduard H. Hovy. 1993. Automated discourse generation using discourse structure relations. *Artificial Intelligence*, 63(1-2):341–385.

Blake Howald, Ravikumar Kondadadi, and Frank Schilder. 2013. Domain adaptable semantic clustering in statistical NLG. In *Proceedings IWCS*, pages 143–154.

Joohyun Kim and Raymond J. Mooney. 2010. Generative alignment and semantic parsing for learning from ambiguous supervision. In *COLING*, pages 543–551.

Ravi Kondadadi, Blake Howald, and Frank Schilder. 2013. A statistical NLG framework for aggregated planning and realization. In *ACL*, pages 1406–1415.

Irene Langkilde and Kevin Knight. 1998. Generation that exploits corpus-based statistical knowledge. In *ACL*, pages 704–710.

Rmi Lebret, David Grangier, and Michael Auli. 2016. Neural text generation from structured data with application to the biography domain. In *EMNLP*, pages 1203–1213.

P. Liang, M. I. Jordan, and D. Klein. 2009. Learning semantic correspondences with less supervision. In *IJCNLP*, pages 91–99.

Hongyuan Mei, Mohit Bansal, and Matthew R. Walter. 2016. What to talk about and how? selective generation using lstms with coarse-to-fine alignment. In *HLT-NAACL*, pages 720–730.

Johanna D. Moore and Cécile L. Paris. 1993. Planning text for advisory dialogues: Capturing intentional and rhetorical information. *Computational Linguistics*, 19(4):651–694.

Guanghui Qin, Jin-Ge Yao, Xuening Wang, Jinpeng Wang, and Chin-Yew Lin. 2018. Learning Latent Semantic Annotations for Grounding Natural Language to Structured Data. In *Empirical Methods in Natural Language Processing (EMNLP)*.

Ehud Reiter and Robert Dale. 2000. *Building Natural Language Generation Systems*. Cambridge University Press.

Jinpeng Wang, Yutai Hou, Jing Liu, Yunbo Cao, and Chin-Yew Lin. 2017. A statistical framework for product description generation. In *IJCNLP*, pages 187–192.

S. Wiseman, S. M. Shieber, and A. M. Rush. 2017. Challenges in data-to-document generation. In *EMNLP*, pages 2253–2263.

Term Set Expansion based NLP Architect by Intel AI Lab

Jonathan Mamou, Oren Pereg, Moshe Wasserblat,
Alon Eirew, Yael Green, Shira Guskin, Peter Izsak, Daniel Korat
Intel AI Lab, Israel
`firstname.lastname@intel.com`

Abstract

We present SetExpander, the term set expansion system based NLP Architect by Intel AI Lab. SetExpander is a corpus-based system for expanding a seed set of terms into a more complete set of terms that belong to the same semantic class. It implements an iterative end-to-end workflow and enables users to easily select a seed set of terms, expand it, view the expanded set, validate it, re-expand the validated set and store it, thus simplifying the extraction of domain-specific fine-grained semantic classes. SetExpander has been used successfully in real-life use cases including integration into an automated recruitment system and an issues and defects resolution system.[1]

1 Introduction

Term set expansion is the task of expanding a given partial set of terms into a more complete set of terms that belong to the same semantic class. For example, given a seed of personal assistant application terms like 'Siri' and 'Cortana', the expanded set is expected to include additional terms such as 'Amazon Echo' and 'Google Now'. Many NLP-based information extraction applications, such as relation extraction or document matching, require the extraction of terms belonging to fine-grained semantic classes as a basic building block. A practical approach to extracting such terms is to apply a term set expansion system. The input seed set for such systems may contain as few as 2 to 10 terms, which is practical to obtain. SetExpander uses a corpus-based approach based on the *distributional similarity hypothesis* (Harris, 1954), stating that semantically similar words appear in similar contexts. Linear bag-of-words con-

text is widely used to compute semantic similarity. However, it typically captures more *topical* and less *functional* similarity, while for the purpose of set expansion, we need to capture more functional and less topical similarity.[2] For example, given a seed term like the programming language 'Python', we would like the expanded set to include other programming languages with similar characteristics, but we would not like it to include terms like 'bytecode' or 'high-level programming language' despite these terms being semantically related to 'Python' in linear bag-of-words contexts. Moreover, for the purpose of set expansion, a seed set contains more than one term and the terms of the expanded set are expected to be as functionally similar to *all* the terms of the seed set as possible. For example, 'orange' is functionally similar to 'red' (color) and to 'apple' (fruit), but if the seed set contains both 'orange' and 'yellow' then only 'red' should be part of the expanded set. However, we do not want to capture only the term sense; we also wish to capture the granularity within a category. For example, 'orange' is functionally similar to both 'apple' and 'lemon'; however, if the seed set contains 'orange' and 'banana' (fruits), the expanded set is expected to contain both 'apple' and 'lemon'; but if the seed set is 'orange' and 'grapefruit' (citrus fruits), then the expanded set is expected to contain 'lemon' but not 'apple'.

While term set expansion has received attention from both industry and academia, there are only a handful of available implementations. Relative to prior work, the contribution of this paper is twofold. First, it presents an iterative end-to-end

---

[1]A video demo of SetExpander is available at `https://drive.google.com/open?id=1e545bB87Autsch36DjnJHmq3HWfSd1Rv` (some images were blurred for privacy reasons).

[2]We use the terminology introduced by (Turney, 2012): the *topic* of a term is characterized by the nouns that occur in its neighborhood while the *function* of a term is characterized by the syntactic context that relates it to the verbs that occur in its neighborhood.

Proceedings of the 2018 Conference on Empirical Methods in Natural Language Processing (System Demonstrations), pages 19–24
Brussels, Belgium, October 31–November 4, 2018. ©2018 Association for Computational Linguistics

workflow that enables users to select an input corpus, train multiple embedding models and combine them; after which the user can easily select a seed set of terms, expand it, view the expanded set, validate it, iteratively re-expand the validated set and store it. Second, it describes the SetExpander application that provides these abilities. SetExpander is based on a novel corpus-based set expansion algorithm. This algorithm combines multi-context term embeddings using a neural classifier in order to capture different aspects of semantic similarity and to make the system more robust across different semantic classes and different domains. The algorithm is briefly described in Section 3. Our system has been used successfully in several real-life use cases. One of them is an automated recruitment system that matches job descriptions with job-applicant resumes. Another use case involves enhancing a software development process by detecting and reducing the amount of duplicate defects in a validation system. Section 5 includes a detailed description of both use cases. The system is distributed as open source software under the Apache license as part of NLP Architect by Intel AI Lab.[3]

2 Related Work

State-of-the-art set expansion techniques return the k nearest neighbors around the seed terms as the expanded set, where terms are represented by their co-occurrence or embedding vectors in a training corpus. Vectors are constructed according to different context types, such as linear bag-of-words context (Pantel et al., 2009; Shi et al., 2010; Rong et al., 2016; Zaheer et al., 2017; Gyllensten and Sahlgren, 2018), explicit lists (Roark and Charniak, 1998; Sarmento et al., 2007; He and Xin, 2011), coordinational patterns (Sarmento et al., 2007) and unary patterns (Rong et al., 2016; Shen et al., 2017). SetExpander looks at additional context types that can capture functional semantic similarities and combines context type embeddings using a neural classifier.

Google Sets, now discontinued, was one of the earliest web applications for term set expansion. It used methods like latent semantic indexing to pre-compute lists of similar words from the web. Word Grab Bag[4] is another web application based on a method that builds lists dynamically using word2vec embeddings based on linear bag-of-word contexts, but their algorithm is not publicly described. Later, Wang and Cohen (2007) proposed the SEAL (Set Expander for Any Language) system which automatically finds semi-structured web pages that contain 'lists of' items, and then aggregates these lists so that the most promising items are ranked higher. In our paper, we describe an iterative end-to-end system, including model training and using additional context types.

Pantel et al. (2009) propose a highly scalable algorithm, implemented in the MapReduce framework, for computing semantic similarity, where terms are represented by large and sparse co-occurrence vectors. SetExpander ensures scalability by representing terms with small and dense embeddings vectors.

The current paper extends (Mamou et al., 2018) paper.

3 Algorithm Overview

3.1 Term Extraction and Representation

Our approach is based on representing any term of an (unlabeled) training corpus by its word embeddings in order to estimate the similarity between seed terms and candidate expansion terms.

Noun phrases provide good approximation for candidate terms and are extracted in our system using a noun phrase chunker.[5] Term variations, such as aliases, acronyms and synonyms, which refer to the same entity, are grouped together.[6] Next, we use term groups as input units for embedding training; this enables obtaining more contextual information compared to using individual terms, thus enhancing embedding model robustness. In the remainder of this paper, by language abuse, *term* will be used instead of term group.

While word2vec originally uses a linear bag-of-words context around the *focus term* to learn the term embeddings, the literature describes other possible context types. For each focus term, we extract *context units* of different types, as follows (see examples in Table 1).

---

[3]http://nlp_architect.nervanasys.com/
term_set_expansion.html
[4]www.wordgrabbag.com

[5]http://nlp_architect.nervanasys.com/
chunker.html

[6]For that, we use a heuristic algorithm based on text normalization, abbreviation web resources, edit distance and word2vec similarity. For example, *New York, New-York, NY, NYC* and *New York City* are grouped.

Context type	Example sentence	Focus term	Context units
Linear $win = 5$	*Siri uses voice queries and a natural language user interface.*	*Siri*	*uses, voice queries, natural language user interface*
List	*Experience in Image processing, Signal processing, Computer Vision.*	*Image processing*	*Signal processing, Computer Vision*
Dep	*Turing studied as an undergraduate ... at King's College, Cambridge.*	*studied*	*(Turing/nsubj), (undergraduate/prep_as), (King's College/prep_at)*
SP	*Apple and Orange juice drink ...*	*Apple*	*Orange*
UP	*In the U.S. state of Alaska ...*	*Alaska*	*U.S. state of __*

Table 1: Examples of extracted contexts per context type.

Linear Bag-of-Words Context. This context type is defined by neighboring context units within a fixed length window of context units, denoted by win, around the focus term. Both terms and other words can be context units. One of its implementations is word2vec (Mikolov et al., 2013), widely used for NLP tasks including set expansion.

Explicit Lists. Context units consist of terms co-occurring with the focus term in textual lists such as comma separated lists and bullet lists (Roark and Charniak, 1998).

Syntactic Dependency Context (Dep). This context type is defined by the syntactic dependency relations in which the focus term participates (Levy and Goldberg, 2014). Context units consist of terms or other words, along with the type and the direction of the dependency relation. This context type has not been used for set expansion in prior work. However, Levy and Goldberg (2014) showed that this context yields more functional similarities of a co-hyponym nature than is yielded by linear bag-of-words context, which suggests its relevance for set expansion.

Symmetric Patterns (SP). Context units consist of terms co-occurring with the focus term in symmetric patterns (Davidov and Rappoport, 2006). For example, the symmetric pattern 'X rather than Y' captures a certain semantic relatedness between the terms X and Y. This context type generalizes coordinational patterns ('X and Y', 'X or Y'), which have been used for set expansion.

Unary Patterns (UP). This context type is defined by the unary patterns in which the focus term occurs (Rong et al., 2016). Context units consist of n-grams of terms and other words, in which the focus term occurs; '__' denotes the placeholder of the focus term in Table 1.[7]

We found that indeed in different domains and for different semantic classes, better similarities are found using different context types. The different contexts thus complement each other by capturing different types of semantic relations. For example, explicit list contexts worked well for the automated recruitment system use case, while unary patterns contexts worked well for the issues and defects resolution use case (discussed in Section 5). Moreover, explicit lists, syntactic dependency, symmetric patterns and unary patterns context types tend to capture functional rather than topical semantic similarities. We train a separate term embedding model for each of the five context types and thus, for each term, we obtain five different representations.

Terms are represented by their linear bag-of-words window context embeddings using the word2vec toolkit [8] and by arbitrary context embeddings using the generic word2vecf toolkit.[9]. For each focus term in the corpus, <focus term, context unit> pairs are extracted from the corpus and are then fed to the embeddings training algorithm. Concerning linear bag-of-words context type, some hyperparameters of the term embeddings training can be tuned to optimize the set expansion task; in particular, a smaller window size

---

[7] Following Rong et al. (2016), we extract six n-grams per focus term. Given a sentence fragment $c_{-3}\ c_{-2}\ c_{-1}\ t\ c_1\ c_2\ c_3$ where t is the focus term and c_i are the context units, the following n-grams are extracted: $(c_{-3}\ c_{-2}\ c_{-1}\ t\ c_1)$, $(c_{-2}\ c_{-1}\ t\ c_1\ c_2)$, $(c_{-1}\ t\ c_1\ c_2)$, $(c_{-1}\ t\ c_1\ c_2\ c_3)$, $(c_{-1}\ t\ c_1\ c_2)$, $(c_{-1}\ t\ c_1)$.

[8] http://code.google.com/archive/p/word2vec

[9] http://bitbucket.org/yoavgo/word2vecf

seems to capture functional rather than topical semantic similarities (Levy and Goldberg, 2014).

3.2 Multi-Context Term Similarity

To make set expansion more robust, we aim to combine multi-context embeddings. Following (Berant et al., 2012), who train a Support Vector Machine (SVM) to combine different similarity score features, we train a Multilayer Perceptron (MLP) classifier that predicts whether a candidate term should be part of the expanded set based on ten similarity scores (considered as input features) obtained by the five different context types and two different similarity-scoring methods. The two similarity scores are estimated by the cosine similarity between the centroid of the seed terms and each candidate term, and by the average pairwise cosine similarity between each seed term and each candidate term; both methods ensure that the candidate term is similar to all the seed terms. MLP is trained on a labeled training set of seed terms and candidate terms.

3.3 Implementation and Evaluation

NLP Architect by Intel AI Lab [10] has been used for noun phrase chunking, dependency parsing and term embeddings model training. The performance of the algorithm was first evaluated by the Mean Average Precision at different top n values (MAP@n). MAP@10, MAP@20 and MAP@50 on an English Wikipedia based dataset [11] are respectively 0.83, 0.74 and 0.63. These figures indicate the quite useful performance of the algorithm, which was further assessed by the use cases described in Section 5.

4 System Workflow and Application

This section describes the iterative end-to-end workflow of SetExpander, as depicted in Figure 1.

Steps 1 & 2: Selecting an Input Corpus and Training Models. The first step of the flow is to **select an input corpus**, performed by selecting *Open* (not shown) from the *File* menu (see the red rectangle in Figure 2). The second step of the flow is to **train the models** based on the selected corpus, performed by selecting *Train Models* (not

shown) from the *Tools* menu (see the yellow rectangle in Figure 2). The "train models" step extracts term groups from the corpus, trains the combined term groups embedding models (Section 3.1) and the MLP classifier that predicts whether a candidate term should be part of the expanded set (Section 3.2).

Steps 3 & 4: Selecting and Expanding a Seed Set. Figure 2 also shows the seed set selection and expansion user interface. Each row in the displayed table corresponds to a different term group. The top 5000 term group names are displayed under the *Expression* column, sorted by their TF-IDF based importance score. Term groups that include more than one term are highlighted in bold, and are represented in the display, by the term with the highest importance score among the terms of the group. Hovering over such a group opens a drop-down list that displays all the terms within the group. The user can choose to exclude specific terms from the group if their semantic meaning does not align with that of the group. The *Filter* text box is used for searching for specific term groups. Upon selecting (clicking) a term group, the context view on the right hand side of Figure 2 (blurred) displays text snippets from the input corpus that include terms that are part of the selected term group (highlighted in green). The context view enables the user to verify the semantic meaning of terms in various contexts in the topical domain.

The user can **create a seed set** assembled from specific term groups by checking their *Expand* checkbox (see the red circle in Figure 2). The user can set a name for the semantic category of the seed set. This name will be used for displaying and storing the seed set and the resulting expanded set of terms. The category name can be selected from a predefined list of category names or added as a new custom category name (see the drop down list in Figure 2). Once the seed set is assembled, the user can **expand the seed set** by selecting the *Expand* option (not shown) in the *Tools* menu.

Steps 5 & 6: Edit, Validate and Re-expand. Figure 3 shows the output of the expansion process. The *Certainty* score represents the relatedness of each expanded term group to the seed set, as determined by the MLP classifier (Section 3.2). The Certainty scores of term groups that were manually selected as part of the seed set are

---

[10]https://github.com/NervanaSystems/nlp-architect

[11]Dataset is described at http://nlp_architect.nervanasys.com/term_set_expansion.html.

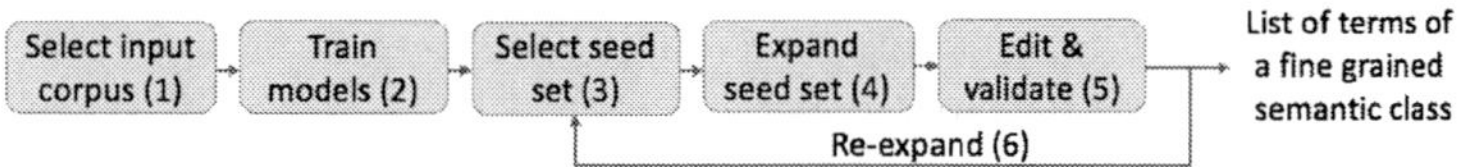

Figure 1: SetExpander end-to-end workflow.

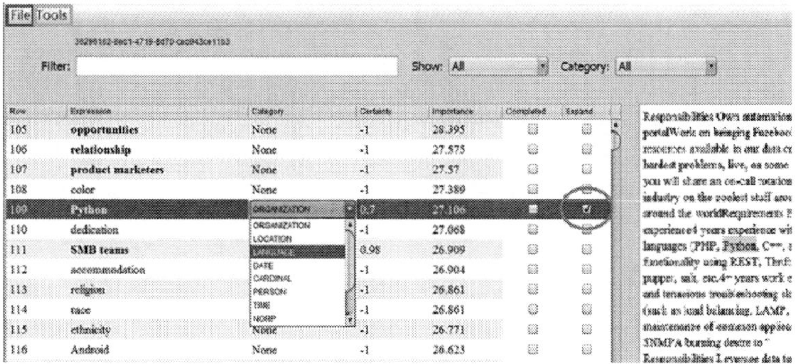

Figure 2: SetExpander user interface for seed selection and expansion.

Row	Expression	Category	Certainty
0	java	LANGUAGE	1
1	**Python**	LANGUAGE	1
2	**JavaScript**	LANGUAGE	0.92
3	SQL	LANGUAGE	0.88
4	perl	LANGUAGE	0.84
5	PHP	LANGUAGE	0.82
6	C++	LANGUAGE	0.82
7	TCL	LANGUAGE	0.81
8	ruby	LANGUAGE	0.79
9	**visual basic**	LANGUAGE	0.77

Figure 3: SetExpander user interface for expansion results output. Seed terms are 'java' and 'python'.

set to 1. The user can **validate** each expanded item by checking the *Completed* checkbox. The validated list can then be saved and later used as a fine-grained semantic class input to external applications. Following validation, the user can perform **re-expansion** by creating a new seed set based on the validated expanded terms and the original seed set terms.

5 Field Use Cases

This section describes two use cases in which SetExpander has been successfully used.

Automated Recruitment System. Human matching of applicant resumes to open positions in organizations is time-consuming and costly. Automated recruitment systems enable recruiters to speed up and refine this process. The recruiter provides an open position description and then the system scans the organizations resume repository searching for the best matches. One of the main features that affect the matching is the skills list, for example, a good match between an applicant and an open position regarding specific programming skills or experience using specific tools is significant for the overall matching. However, manual generation and maintenance of comprehensive and updated skills lists is tedious and difficult to scale. SetExpander was integrated into such a recruitment system. Recruiters used the system's user interface (Figures 2 & 3) to generate fine-grained skills lists based on small seed sets for eighteen engineering job position categories. We evaluated the recruitment system use case for different skill classes. The system achieved a precision of 94.5%, 98.0% and 70.5% at the top 100 applicants, for the job position categories of Software Machine Learning Engineer, Firmware Engineer and ADAS Senior Software Engineer, respectively.

Issues and Defects Resolution. Quick identification of duplicate defects is critical for efficient software development. The aim of automated issues and defects resolution systems is to find duplicates in large repositories of millions of software defects used by dozens of development teams. This task is challenging because the same defect may have different title names and different textual descriptions. The legacy solution relied on manually constructed lists of tens of thousands of terms, which were built over several weeks. Our term set expansion application was integrated into such a system and was used for generating domain specific semantic categories such as product names, process names, technical terms, etc. The integrated system enhanced the duplicate defects detection precision by more than 10% and sped-up the term list generation process from several weeks to hours.

6 Conclusion

We presented SetExpander, a corpus-based system for set expansion which enables users to select a seed set of terms, expand it, validate it, re-expand the validated set and store it. The expanded sets can then be used as a domain specific semantic classes for downstream applications. Our system was used in several real-world use cases, among them, an automated recruitment system and an issues and defects resolution system.

References

J. Berant, I. Dagan, and J. Goldberger. 2012. Learning entailment relations by global graph structure optimization. *Computational Linguistics*, 38:73–111.

Dmitry Davidov and Ari Rappoport. 2006. Efficient unsupervised discovery of word categories using symmetric patterns and high frequency words. In *Proceedings of the 21st International Conference on Computational Linguistics and the 44th annual meeting of the Association for Computational Linguistics*, pages 297–304. Association for Computational Linguistics.

Amaru Cuba Gyllensten and Magnus Sahlgren. 2018. Distributional term set expansion. *arXiv preprint arXiv:1802.05014*.

Zellig S Harris. 1954. Distributional structure. *Word*, 10(2-3):146–162.

Yeye He and Dong Xin. 2011. Seisa: set expansion by iterative similarity aggregation. In *Proceedings of the 20th international conference on World wide web*, pages 427–436. ACM.

Omer Levy and Yoav Goldberg. 2014. Dependency-based word embeddings. In *Proceedings of the 52nd Annual Meeting of the Association for Computational Linguistics (Volume 2: Short Papers)*, volume 2, pages 302–308.

Jonathan Mamou, Oren Pereg, Moshe Wasserblat, Ido Dagan, Yoav Goldberg, Alon Eirew, Yael Green, Shira Guskin, Peter Izsak, and Daniel Korat. 2018. Setexpander: End-to-end term set expansion based on multi-context term embeddings. In *Proceedings of the 27th International Conference on Computational Linguistics: System Demonstrations*, pages 58–62.

Tomas Mikolov, Ilya Sutskever, Kai Chen, Greg S Corrado, and Jeff Dean. 2013. Distributed representations of words and phrases and their compositionality. In *Advances in neural information processing systems*, pages 3111–3119.

Patrick Pantel, Eric Crestan, Arkady Borkovsky, Ana-Maria Popescu, and Vishnu Vyas. 2009. Web-scale distributional similarity and entity set expansion. In *Proceedings of the 2009 Conference on Empirical Methods in Natural Language Processing: Volume 2-Volume 2*, pages 938–947. Association for Computational Linguistics.

Brian Roark and Eugene Charniak. 1998. Noun-phrase co-occurrence statistics for semiautomatic semantic lexicon construction. In *Proceedings of the 36th Annual Meeting of the Association for Computational Linguistics and 17th International Conference on Computational Linguistics-Volume 2*, pages 1110–1116. Association for Computational Linguistics.

Xin Rong, Zhe Chen, Qiaozhu Mei, and Eytan Adar. 2016. Egoset: Exploiting word ego-networks and user-generated ontology for multifaceted set expansion. In *Proceedings of the Ninth ACM International Conference on Web Search and Data Mining*, pages 645–654. ACM.

Luis Sarmento, Valentin Jijkuon, Maarten de Rijke, and Eugenio Oliveira. 2007. More like these: growing entity classes from seeds. In *Proceedings of the sixteenth ACM conference on Conference on information and knowledge management*, pages 959–962. ACM.

Jiaming Shen, Zeqiu Wu, Dongming Lei, Jingbo Shang, Xiang Ren, and Jiawei Han. 2017. Setexpan: Corpus-based set expansion via context feature selection and rank ensemble. In *Joint European Conference on Machine Learning and Knowledge Discovery in Databases*, pages 288–304. Springer.

Shuming Shi, Huibin Zhang, Xiaojie Yuan, and Ji-Rong Wen. 2010. Corpus-based semantic class mining: distributional vs. pattern-based approaches. In *Proceedings of the 23rd International Conference on Computational Linguistics*, pages 993–1001. Association for Computational Linguistics.

Peter D Turney. 2012. Domain and function: A dual-space model of semantic relations and compositions. *Journal of Artificial Intelligence Research*, 44:533–585.

Richard C Wang and William W Cohen. 2007. Language-independent set expansion of named entities using the web. In *Data Mining, 2007. ICDM 2007. Seventh IEEE International Conference on*, pages 342–350. IEEE.

Manzil Zaheer, Satwik Kottur, Siamak Ravanbakhsh, Barnabas Poczos, Ruslan R Salakhutdinov, and Alexander J Smola. 2017. Deep sets. In *Advances in Neural Information Processing Systems*, pages 3394–3404.

MorAz: an Open-source Morphological Analyzer for Azerbaijani Turkish

Berke Özenç[†], Razieh Ehsani[††], Ercan Solak[†]
[†] Computer Engineering ,Işık University, Istanbul, Turkey
[††] Department of Modern Languages, University of Helsinki, Finland
{berke.ozenc, ercan.solak}@isikun.edu.tr
razieh.ehsani@helsinki.fi

Abstract

MorAz is an open-source morphological analyzer for Azerbaijani Turkish. The analyzer is available through both as a website for interactive exploration and as a RESTful web service for integration into a natural language processing pipeline. MorAz implements the morphology of Azerbaijani Turkish following a two-level approach using Helsinki finite-state transducer and wraps the analyzer with python scripts in a Django instance.

1 Introduction

Morphological analysis is a crucial part of processing languages with complex morphologies, such as the agglutinative Azerbaijani Turkish. The morphological analysis provides a number of "readings" or analysis for each word, as a part of the overall NLP task. Indeed, morphological analysis yields some properties of a word like "stem", "root" and morphological role of "suffixes" inside word. Naturally, when the number of suffixes and their combination increase, so does the number of possible analysis of a word.

Since its application to morphology by Koskenniemi [Koskenniemi, 1983], Finite State Transducer (FST) has become a favored computational tool for representing morphology and phonology. In the two-level approach developed in Koskenniemi [Koskenniemi, 1983], the morphotactics is represented as a separate FST in the first level. The output of the first level is then re-written by a sequence of phonological re-write rules.

The two-level approach to morphology has been successfully applied to many languages with several publicly available analyzers, [Karp et al., 1992], [Piskorski et al., 2009]. There are also a number of open-source toolkits that provide the underlying FST implementation, [Hulden, 2009], [Lindén et al., 2011], [Schmid, 2005].

In this paper, we present an open-source FST implementation of the full morphology of Azerbaijani Turkish (AT). Noun and Verb morphology were previously discussed in [Ehsani et al., 2017]. The source code is available for use as a local analyzer. It is also available as a RESTful web service.

The rest of the paper is organized as follows. In the next section, we review related work. In Section 3, we outline the structure of MorAz. Section 4 introduces the website and the web service of MorAz. In Section 5, we report some statistics on the performance of the analyzer. Finally, the paper finishes with some concluding remarks.

2 Related analyzers

MorAz is the first complete morphological analyzer for AT. There is also a partial implementation of AT morphology within the Apertium project [Forcada et al., 2011]. This analyzer is based upon the Trmorph [Çöltekin, 2010] with the assumption that the Azerbaijani Turkish and Anatolian Turkish are similar, whereas our analyzer was developed from scratch directly for the Azerbaijani Turkish. Apertiums coverage of the morphotactics and phonology and the extent of its lexicon are quite narrow compared with MorAz. So, Apertium Azerbaijani analyzer is not sufficient for testing. Moreover, the only way to use Apertium analyzer is through incorporating the code base into the NLP pipeline, with all its dependencies and libraries. The web service interface to MorAz does not require anything other than `json` constructors and parsers. The manually constructed lexicon of MorAz reduces the number of redundant analyses due to trivial derivations resulting from an automatic root lexicon such as the one used in Apertium. The coverage of morphotactics rules in MorAz is wider and thus results in correct anal-

Proceedings of the 2018 Conference on Empirical Methods in Natural Language Processing (System Demonstrations), pages 25–29
Brussels, Belgium, October 31–November 4, 2018. ©2018 Association for Computational Linguistics

yses where Apertium analyzer results in out-of-vocabulary analyses.

Morphological analyzers for other Turkic languages have varying levels of completeness and availability. Among these, the most widely studied language is Anatolian Turkish. [Oflazer, 1994] presented a two-level description and implementation of Turkish morphology. Their implementation uses `xfst` [Beesley and Karttunen, 2003] as the underlying FST implementation. Their analyzer is not available publicly. Following the same approach as Oflazer's, Şahin's [Şahin et al., 2013], re-implemented the analyzer on Xerox [Beesley and Karttunen, 2003]. Şahin's analyzer is available through a web interface and as a web service, though, the source is closed. TRMorph [Çöltekin, 2010] is an open-source analyzer for Anatolian Turkish, implemented over SFST. It is available as an interactive web tool but lacks a web service interface. Zemberek [Akın and Akın, 2007] is another open-source, Java-based analyzer for Anatolian Turkish.

For Kazakh, there is an open-source analyzer in Apertium project. There is also, the analyzer described in [Kessikbayeva and Cicekli, 2016], however, currently, the implementation is not publicly available. For Turkmen and Uighur, the analyzers described in [Tantug et al., 2006] and [Orhun et al., 2009] are not publicly available.

3 Structure of MorAz

Azerbaijani Turkish (AT) is a Turkic language spoken by about 30 million people, mainly in Iran and Azerbaijan. AT is an agglutinative language with a predominant SOV word order, although scrambling is common especially in spoken form. The phonology of AT has vowel harmony, devoicing, and apocope. Written AT uses Latin alphabet in Azerbaijan and Arabic alphabet in Iran. The current implementation of MorAz works with the Latin alphabet.

The FST description of the morphology of AT as implemented in MorAz consists of 4 main parts; nominal and verb inflections, nominal predicate, and derivation. Derivation FST is the bridge that connects the other 3 FSTs. In detail, the derivation FST has 36, nominal inflection has 36, nominal predicate has 22 and verb inflection has 145 rules. Morphotactics level which is also called level 1 has 239 rules and 67 states in total. Complete FST diagram of MorAz is shown in Figure 2. Since ad-

jectives in AT behave like nouns when their suffixation is concerned, we treat adjective and nouns as a single morphological class Nominal. At a morphosyntactic level, there will still be two distinct POS tags for adjectives and nouns. In MorAz, we used 8 morphological categories: Nominal, Verb, Predicate, Adverb, Number, Postposition and Interjection.

In MorAz we represent the abstract form of a morpheme either as a key-value pair or just as a key.

The key-value form is more suited for consistently representing the inflection paradigms where a zero surface realization of the abstract morpheme corresponds to a particular assignment of the inflection feature. For example, Number feature has zero surface form when Singular. When it is Plural, it is realized as -lar or -lər depending on vowel harmony. Since every Nominal has a Number feature, we reserve a number slot in Nominal Inflection.

We denote the key-value abstract morphemes as <Key_Mnemonic:Value>.

When a morphological feature is optional, we use just a mnemonic key to represent the corresponding morpheme in the form <Key>. For example, all derivational morphemes are optional.

The following example illustrates the use of abstract morphemes.

(1) xəstəlikdən

xəstə<NOM>
<State><NOM>
<Num:Sg><Poss:No><Case:Abl>

The documentation for all the mnemonic keys and their possible values are provided on the website of MorAz. There are a total of 38 keys in the key-value pair form and 40 optional keys, 20 of which correspond to derivational morphemes.

Figure 1 gives the FST for Nominal inflection as an illustration of the morphotactics of MorAz. The expansion of transition labels sn_1-sn_1 is given in full in the expanded diagrams on the MorAz website.

The root lexicon includes 2707 verb roots, 35547 nominal roots as well as 14937 person names and 929 adverbs. We obtained the root lexicon of MorAz, by reducing a large lexicon of roots. In the reduction, we manually eliminated the roots that can be trivially derived from other

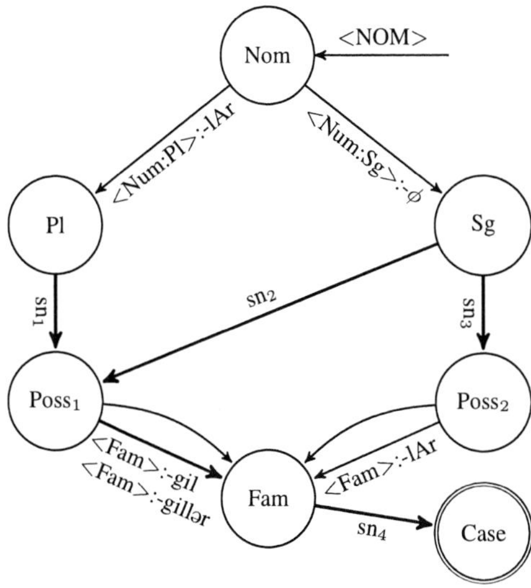

Figure 1: Nominal inflection

Archiphoneme	Surface forms
A	ə, a
I	ı, i, u, ü
K	k, y
Q	q, ğ
D	d, t
N	d, n

Table 1: Archiphonemes used at the first level output of MorAz

roots that are not eliminated. The cases where the derived form undergoes a meaning drift away from the one that the derivational morpheme nominally entails are distinguished. If the drift is so large that the meaning of the derivation cannot be inferred from those of the root and the suffixes, then a new word needs to be added to the dictionary [Ehsani et al., 2018]. For example, the large lexicon contains both

(2) xəstə
     xəstə<NOM>
     sick

and

(3) xəstəlik
     xəstə<NOM><State>
     sickness

where 3 is trivially derived from 2.

In AT, there are 4 distinct morphemes for Causative and 2 morphemes for Passive.

In order to handle the selection of Causative and Passive morphemes, we manually marked our verb lexicon of about 2700 verb roots with 15 verb classes. These include the classes representing the cases where a verb root cannot be suffixed with Causative for some intransitive verbs and the cases where a Passive is semantically impossible. For example, "öyren" (learn) has no Causative and "dol" (be filled) has no Passive form.

The second level of MorAz deals with the phonology. The first level output consists of base morphemes and archmorphemes. Archmorphemes use 5 archiphonemes which are given in Table 1.

The archiphoneme A maps to its surface form to satisfy back-front harmony. Similarly, I maps to its surface forms under back-front and roundedness harmony. K and Q choose their surface forms through palatalization and velarization, respectively. D chooses its surface form to adapt to the voicing feature of its context. Finally, N is a convenience archiphoneme that we use to unify two surface forms of the Ablative morpheme.

A common phonological phenomenon in AT is the insertion of epenthetic letters y, n, ş, and s. The choice of the epenthesis phoneme depends on the phonological and morphological context. In MorAz implementation, we consider epenthetic as optional phonemes attached to morphemes. So, the phonological rules in the second level drop the epenthetic depending only on the phonological context.

4 Website and API

MorAz uses Helsinki finite-state transducer (HSFT) for the implementation of the two-level morphology. We wrapped the compiled analyzer with python scripts in a Django web server. The source code for the analyzer is available in GitHub [1].

MorAz website includes an interactive query screen shown in Figure 3. It allows querying multiple tokens separated by line breaks.

The web service API [2] uses the `json` format for posting the list of tokens to be analyzed. The output is also in `json` format as an array of arrays where the innermost array contains the list of analyses for a single token.

[1] https://github.com/berkeozenc/MorAz
[2] http://ddil.isikun.edu.tr/morazws/

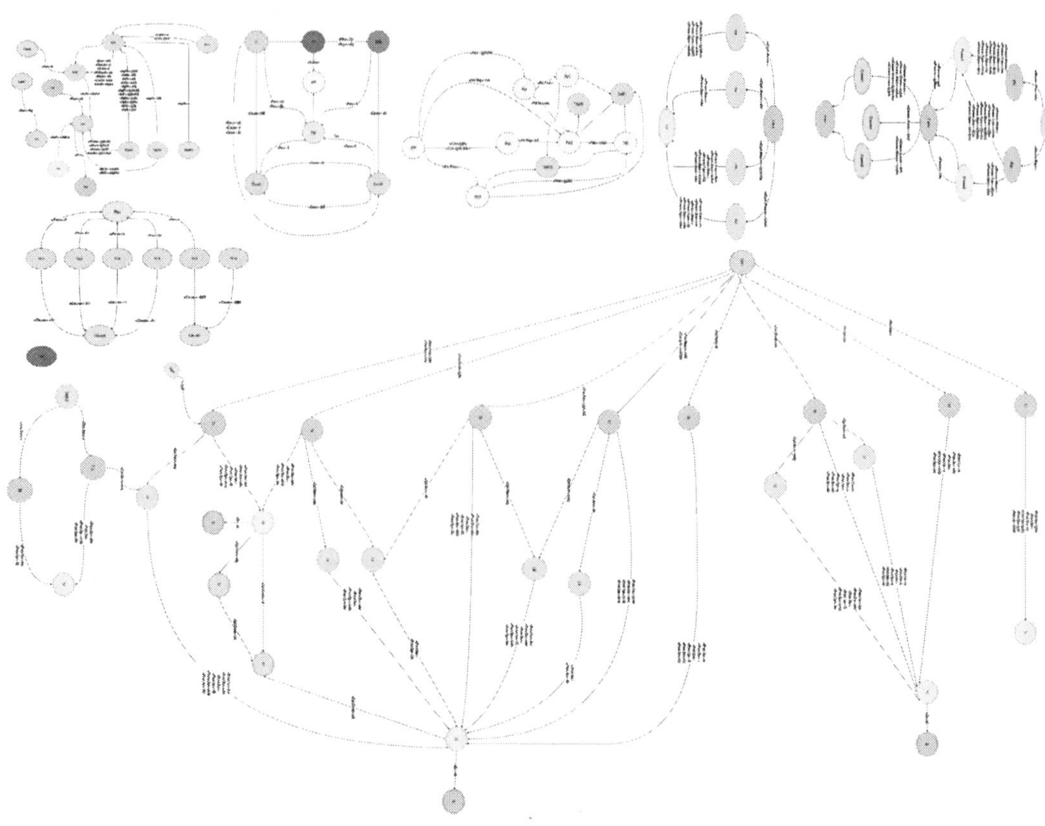

Figure 2: Complete FST Diagram of MorAz

5 Statistics

In order to measure the performance of MorAz, we ran it over an input text collected from BBC Azərbaycanca. Since MorAz lexicon is not complete in terms of named entities, we eliminated from the input all the tokens that start with capital letters. What remained was a test input is a list of 10890 distinct Azerbaijani words. We also eliminated punctuation marks.

Of all the tokens fed into the analyzer, MorAz did not return an analysis for %23.92 of total words. For the ones that it provided an analysis, on average there were 1.96 analyses per word. Since the token is Azerbaijani word, it is possible to use them to test other Azerbaijani morphological analyzers.

6 Conclusion

In this paper, we presented MorAz, an open-source morphological analyzer for Azerbaijani Turkish. MorAz provides an interactive query interface for short pieces of tokenized text through its website. For larger inputs, it exposes a simple RESTful web interface.

MorAz has a manually crafted minimal lexicon, with an aim to reduce the number of redundant analyses. Manual configuration is an ongoing process and we modify the lexicon by inspecting the results of analyses.

As a further development, we are planning to provide an interactive tool to generate surface forms out of abstract morphemes which will be useful for exploring the language.

References

Ahmet Afsin Akın and Mehmet Dündar Akın. Zemberek, an open source nlp framework for turkic languages. *Structure*, 10:1–5, 2007.

Kenneth R. Beesley and Lauri Karttunen. *Finite State Morphology*. CSLI Publications,, Stanford, CA, 2003.

Çağrı Çöltekin. A freely available morphological analyzer for Turkish. In *Proceedings of the 7th International Conference on Language Resources and Evaluation (LREC*

28

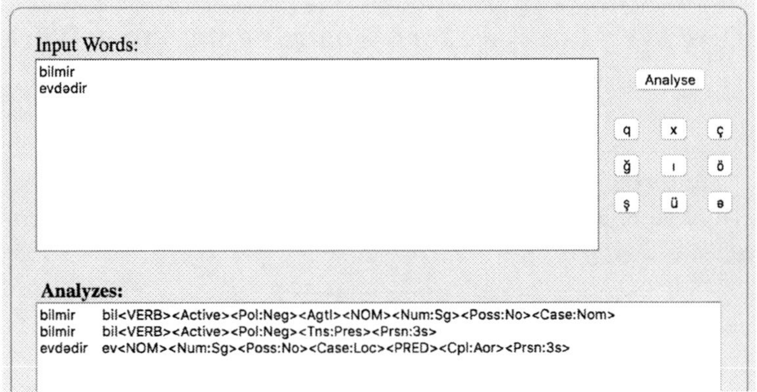

Figure 3: Interactive query in MorAz.

2010), pages 820–827, 2010. URL `http://www.lrec-conf.org/proceedings/lrec2010/summaries/109.html`.

Razieh Ehsani, Berke Özenç, and Ercan Solak. A fst description of noun and verb morphology of azarbaijani turkish. In *Proceedings of the 13th International Conference on Finite State Methods and Natural Language Processing (FSMNLP 2017)*, pages 62–68, 2017.

Razieh Ehsani, Ercan Solak, and Olcay Taner Yıldız. Constructing a wordnet for turkish using manual and automatic annotation. *ACM Transactions on Asian and Low-Resource Language Information Processing (TALLIP)*, 17(3), 2018.

Mikel L Forcada, Mireia Ginestí-Rosell, Jacob Nordfalk, Jim O'Regan, Sergio Ortiz-Rojas, Juan Antonio Pérez-Ortiz, Felipe Sánchez-Martínez, Gema Ramírez-Sánchez, and Francis M Tyers. Apertium: a free/open-source platform for rule-based machine translation. *Machine translation*, 25(2):127–144, 2011.

Mans Hulden. Foma: a finite-state compiler and library. In *Proceedings of the 12th Conference of the European Chapter of the Association for Computational Linguistics*, pages 29–32. Association for Computational Linguistics, 2009.

Daniel Karp, Yves Schabes, Martin Zaidel, and Dania Egedi. A freely available wide coverage morphological analyzer for english. In *Proceedings of the 14th conference on Computational linguistics-Volume 3*, pages 950–955. Association for Computational Linguistics, 1992.

Gulshat Kessikbayeva and Ilyas Cicekli. A Rule Based Morphological Analyzer and a Morphological Disambiguator for Kazakh Language. *Linguistics and Literature Studies*, 4(1):96–104, 2016.

Kimmo Koskenniemi. Two-level model for morphological analysis. In *IJCAI*, volume 83, pages 683–685, 1983.

Krister Lindén, Erik Axelson, Sam Hardwick, Miikka Silfverberg, and Tommi Pirinen. HFST–framework for compiling and applying morphologies. pages 67–85, 2011.

Kemal Oflazer. Two-level description of turkish morphology. *Literary and Linguistic Computing,*, 9(2): 137–148, 1994.

Murat Orhun, A. Cüneyd Tantug, and Esref Adali. Rule based analysis of the uyghur nouns. *Int. J. of Asian Lang. Proc.*, 19(1):33–44, 2009. URL `http://dblp.uni-trier.de/db/journals/jclc/jclc19.html#OrhunTA09`.

J Piskorski et al. Morphisto-an open source morphological analyzer for german. In *Finite-state Methods and Natural Language Processing: Postproceedings of the 7th International Workshop FSMNLP; Edited by Jakub Piskorski, Bruce Watson and Anssi Yli-Jyrä*, volume 7, page 224. IOS Press, 2009.

Muhammet Şahin, Umut Sulubacak, and Gülşen Eryiğit. Redefinition of turkish morphology using flag diacritics. In *Proceedings of The Tenth Symposium on Natural Language Processing (SNLP-2013)*, Phuket, Thailand, October 2013.

Helmut Schmid. A programming language for finite state transducers. In *FSMNLP*, volume 4002, pages 308–309, 2005.

A Cüneyd Tantug, Esref Adali, and Kemal Oflazer. Computer Analysis of the Turkmen Language Morphology. *FinTAL*, 4139:186–193, 2006.

An Interactive Web-Interface for Visualizing the Inner Workings of the Question Answering LSTM

Ekaterina Loginova
DFKI / Saarbrücken, Germany
ekaterina.loginova@dfki.de

Günter Neumann
DFKI / Saarbrücken, Germany
neumann@dfki.de

Abstract

Deep learning models for NLP are potent but not readily interpretable. It prevents researchers from improving a model's performance efficiently and users from applying it for a task which requires a high level of trust in the system. We present a visualisation tool which aims to illuminate the inner workings of a specific LSTM model for question answering. It plots heatmaps of neurons' firings and allows a user to check the dependency between neurons and manual features. The system possesses an interactive web-interface and can be adapted to other models and domains.

1 Introduction

Deep learning models have gained popularity in the last years due to their state-of-the-art performance combined with an end-to-end pipeline. However, even though these models do not require manual feature engineering, this advantage turns into a shortcoming when it comes to the interpretation of the model. Neural networks are considered black boxes by the majority of their users. Such low interpretability leads to a low level of trust in the system's decisions. Therefore, methods for interpreting neural networks are attracting increasing interest due to their need for practical applications.

Existing visualisation methods mainly focus on computer vision tasks. It raises the issue that not all of them can be easily adapted to the NLP domain since text preprocessing operates with noticeably different units. Furthermore, while some neural architectures such as CNNs, provide relatively clear feature illustrations, this is not the case for RNNs, which are dominant for many text processing tasks. Few researchers have addressed the issue of visualising the inner workings of RNNs, especially in an interactive way.

Our ultimate goal is to allow a researcher to check how interpretable the features in an RNN are automatically. The first step would be to check the dependency between a given manual feature and the features produced by the deep learning model. The next one is to develop a method to extract structural patterns from uninterpretable features. The last step would be to generate suggestions that would explain such patterns automatically. In this work, we address the first step and supply a visualisation tool for manually carrying out the second step.

This paper is a report on the visualisation system for LSTMs in the area of question answering. We present a new interactive web-interface which currently focuses on a specific system but can potentially be adapted to other models and domains. The proposed system aims to aid the development of deep learning models in NLP by providing a tool for data visualisation.

The paper is divided into three sections. The first section provides a brief overview of the related work. The system is described in the second section, and our conclusions are drawn in the final section.

2 Related work

A considerable amount of literature has been published on neural attention models (Vaswani et al., 2017; Li et al., 2015b). Most of them contain heat maps to illustrate the work of the attention mechanism. These plots provide insight into what the model sees as the more important parts of the sentence when making a prediction. For instance, self-attention might learn patterns related to syntactical properties of the text (Vaswani et al., 2017) or sentiment aspects (Li et al., 2015b). Recently researchers have also focused on illustrating the behaviour of machine translation sequence-to-

Proceedings of the 2018 Conference on Empirical Methods in Natural Language Processing (System Demonstrations), pages 30–35
Brussels, Belgium, October 31–November 4, 2018. ©2018 Association for Computational Linguistics

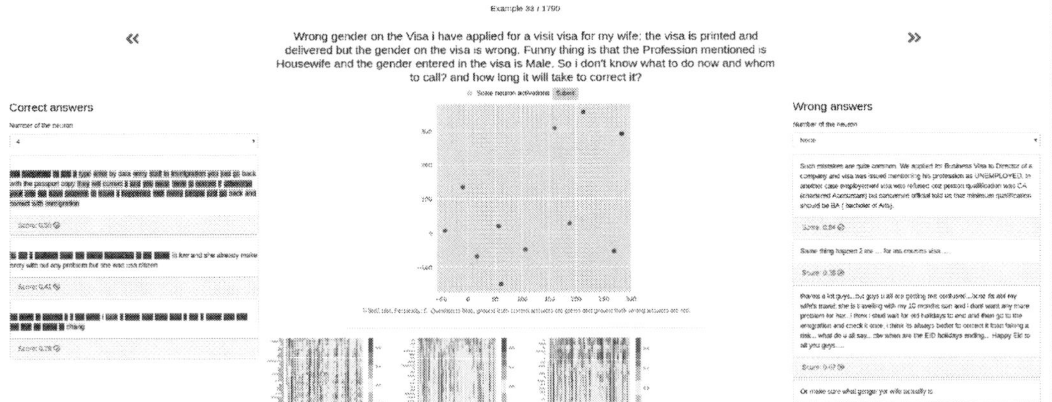

Figure 1: The second part of the interface. Left and right columns contain the ground truth correct and wrong answers respectively, highlighted according to a chosen neuron. The question is stated in the middle, a t-SNE plot is given under it. The heatmaps of neuron activations are placed below.

sequence architectures (Lee et al., 2017). Such systems include visualisations of the search tree for the beam search along with attention.

More recent research by (Karpathy et al., 2015) reveals that a small percentage of cells in LSTM learns interpretable patterns. For instance, a cell might correspond to the position in the line, indicate the depth of the nested structure or turn on inside quotes. Our system is greatly inspired by this research.

In (Li et al., 2015a) authors investigate visualisations of compositionality in NLP, basing their work on computer vision approaches. They provide t-SNE (van der Maaten and Hinton, 2008) plots for clause compositions and introduce saliency heatmaps. The latter indicates how neurons contribute to the final decision based on the first order derivatives.

Moreover, (Strobelt et al., 2016) demonstrated a system for visual analysis of hidden state dynamics in recurrent neural networks. The system, called LSTMVis, allows the researcher to check the hypothesis about local state changes against a similar pattern in the entire dataset, and align it with the textual annotations.

Finally, (Jia and Liang, 2017) show that a question answering system can be surprisingly unreliable when presented with artificial adversarial examples. They suggest that this can happen because a neural network learns heuristics, which are easy to fool. Hence, we hypothesise that a system which uses meaningful (from a human perspective) features might not only be more user-friendly but also demonstrate higher robustness.

3 System

Our system consists of two different interfaces. The first one visualises the scores and attention distribution produced by the model on answers to a user-defined question. The second one allows a user to iterate through fixed question-answer pairs to investigate the inner workings of a model. These inner workings are displayed in three separate views: General, Neuron and Correlation. In the General one, a user can observe t-SNE plots and heat maps for all neurons on the texts of the current question-answer pair from the dataset (see Figure 1 for the layout demonstration). In the Neuron view, the user can investigate the behaviour of one particular neuron further. Finally, in the Correlation part, the user can see the statistical measures for the dependency between a chosen manual feature and all neurons.

3.1 Deep learning model

Our system currently works with the Attentive (Bahdanau et al., 2014) QALSTM model. The method is essentially the same as (Tan et al., 2016) with some adjustments. Most importantly, we use two stacked shared LSTMs instead of a single one (the number of units is 96 and 64 respectively). We used Adam (Kingma and Ba, 2014) optimisation instead of SGD and cross entropy loss instead of margin ranking loss. Moreover, we modified the parameters: the embeddings are not trainable, dropout is not used, and the learning rate is set to 0.001. The main dataset used in the current stage is SemEval 2017 Task 3 Subtask A

(Nakov et al., 2017). The word embeddings are word2vec (Mikolov et al., 2013) of dimension 300 pre-trained on Google News. The texts are lower-cased and tokenised using built-in Keras functions.

Generally speaking, any pre-trained Keras model involving an attention mechanism and an LSTM can be loaded into the interface. The only requirement would be to provide the layer names to retrieve softmax attention scores and LSTM weights.

3.2 Key features

A pre-trained model is loaded from a Keras checkpoint: the weights are obtained from a .h5 file and the architecture from a .json. In case of an error, a message is shown to the user with the description. The dataset with the texts of question-answer pairs is loaded in either of two ways (denoted as D-I and D-II). It can be preloaded from a custom pickle file containing a pandas data frame. This method is suitable if the candidate answers are known at the test phase. Otherwise, the dataset can be saved into an index schema of documents which is compatible with the Whoosh (Chaput, 2007) library. This will allow the system to retrieve candidate answers based on a keyword match. It should be noted that it is relatively easy to modify the code to load other datasets as long as they have the fields pool (array of incorrect answer ids), answer_ids (array of correct answer ids), question (question text) and answer (candidate answer text). Lastly, pre-trained word embeddings and the tokeniser are loaded from pickled Keras objects.

Candidate answer retrieval and scoring. To begin with, the system receives a question from the user via a text field input. The question is filtered by length: too long or empty questions are discarded. Then, it is preprocessed to exclude out-of-vocabulary (OOV) words. In addition, it is spell-checked by the Whoosh library. If the question contains words which lemmata are not in the vocabulary of the system, a warning is displayed. As mentioned at the beginning of this section, our system is separated into two interfaces depending on whether the question can be formulated by the user or it is fixed in advance. The answers in the first part are sorted by their score. In case the question was present in the dataset, and we know the correct answer, we mark its text with a star icon for a quicker performance assessment by the user. The second interface allows the user to iterate through

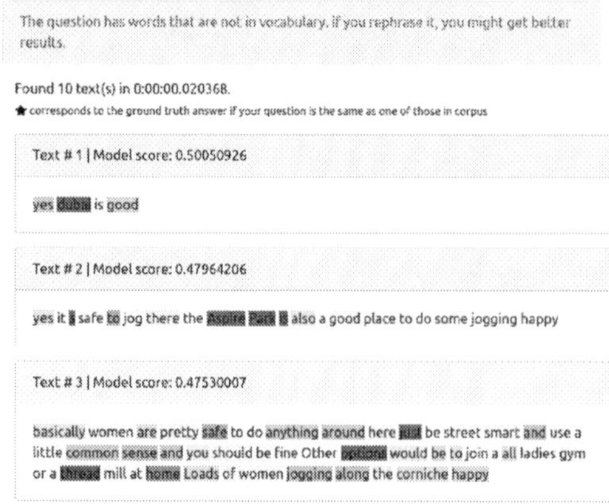

Figure 2: The heatmap of attention scores.

the fixed question-answer pairs to investigate the inner workings of the model. The answers in this part are separated into columns, where the left column contains the ground truth correct answers and the right one the ground truth incorrect answers. The prediction of the model is illustrated with an icon (cross mark for predicting the answer as incorrect, checkmark for the correct), and the original score is also displayed. This leads to a clearer picture of the mistakes the model makes, which will hopefully help researchers in eliminating possible sources of errors.

In D-II setting, after that, Whoosh's Multifield-Parser processes the question and attempts to retrieve candidate answers. If no candidates are found at this step, it extends the search by also checking the answer texts corresponding to the questions in the index. In other words, it checks not only the question-question similarity but also answer-question. If still no results are retrieved, the user receives an appropriate error message with a prompt to reformulate his question. If candidate answers were found, they are preprocessed. At this step, custom modifications, such as removing punctuation, can be added. In D-I setting, the candidate answers are provided and thus retrieved directly.

After that, the pre-trained deep learning model is applied to the texts of the question and the candidate answers to receive their scores. In our case, those are cosine similarities between LSTMs embeddings of the question and the candidate answer.

Attention visualisation. The next key feature of our system is the visualisation of the attention mechanism. In this part, we follow a traditional approach of using a heat map on the text. Words are highlighted in red based on their attention scores: the higher the score, the more intense the colour. The attention scores used in deciding the opacity of the colour are scaled to make them more visible. A user can still see the exact score of the word in a tooltip by hovering over it. Optionally, the user can adjust the attention threshold A to only highlight words with an attention score higher than A. Figure 2 shows an example of the attention visualisation.

t-SNE. Another part of the visualisations is specific to the model we currently use. The objective of this model is to learn a mapping to a new embedding space where the question has a smaller cosine distance to its correct answers than to the incorrect ones. In order to investigate the resulting space, we plot a t-SNE projection of the LSTM output embeddings on each QA-pair. The red dots correspond to the wrong answers, green - the correct ones and blue - the question. The perplexity parameter, which is known to affect the meaningfulness of t-SNE plots greatly, can be adjusted by the user with a corresponding text field input. The default value is 5.

Weights visualisation. Besides visualising attention, we develop an idea proposed by (Karpathy et al., 2015), as we suggest that the neuron behaviour in a question answering system might differ across the answers categories. The illustration is generated in two modes: heatmaps and highlighting the text. Figure 1 demonstrates the highlighted text mode and figure 3 - the corresponding heatmaps. The red colour corresponds to positive values and the blue to the negative ones. The brighter the colour, the larger the absolute value of the neuron output. The current model works on a word level as opposed to character level in (Karpathy et al., 2015). A researcher is encouraged to manually analyse whether the neurons align with easily interpretable patterns in the text. If a particular neuron is of interest, the user may see heatmaps in detail by navigating to the Neuron view. There the heatmaps spanning only this particular neuron on a subset of texts are plotted. Figure 4 illustrates this mode. The user can generate more heatmaps on random texts to check for the consistency of a pattern. It should be noted that for large systems or long texts the plots can

become difficult to analyse. We attempt to alleviate this by splitting the heatmaps into chunks by ten words and 32 neurons.

Correlation coefficients. We hypothesise that there is a dependency between a manual feature and a neuron. However, manually checking the heatmaps over a corpus for each neuron is time-consuming. Hence, we provide the researchers with additional information that might indicate promising pairs of features and neurons. The additional information consists of three statistical measures: the Pearson and the Spearman rank correlation coefficients and the Mutual Information score. As nature (discrete or continuous) of a user-defined manual feature is not known in advance, we provide all three scores by default. If the value of the coefficient is higher than a threshold of T, the text of the indicator will be highlighted in green. If the value is lower than $-T$, it will be highlighted in red. The user can adjust this threshold value with a corresponding text field input. The default value of T is 0.5. The user can input their own features. The format is a nested Python list of the features values for words in texts. Alternatively, the user can choose from one of the suggested features. The suggested features include the following: is the token a stopword? Does the token consist of alphabetic character? The length of the token in characters? Is the token a noun/a verb/an adjective? Is the token a named entity? Is the token a question word (what, how)?

The values for these features are computed with the SpaCy (Honnibal and Johnson, 2015) library. Besides, the user can see some numerical characteristics of neuron values: maximum, minimum, median and mean values. He can also choose the number of texts to use, and whether they are sampled randomly or sequentially from the dataset. In case the user would like to check the dependency on a particular subset, he may input the exact indices for the question-answer pairs from the dataset. By default, the first ten instances in the dataset are used to speed up the computation process.

3.3 Technical implementation

The visualisation application is a client-server system with a web interface. It uses JQuery on the client side and Python on the server side. The application is built with the Flask (Ronacher, 2018)

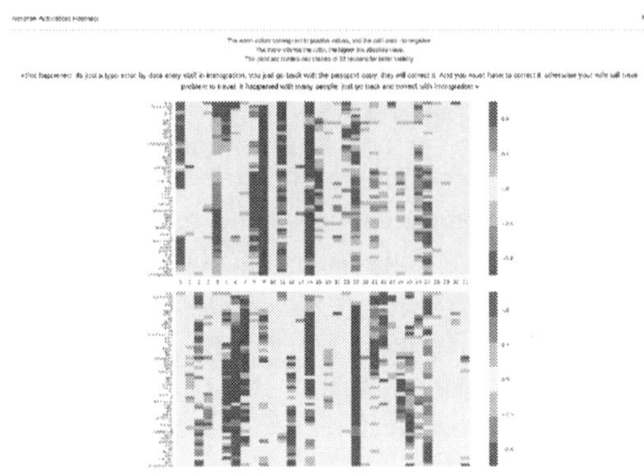

Figure 3: A heatmap of all the neuron's firings on a given text.

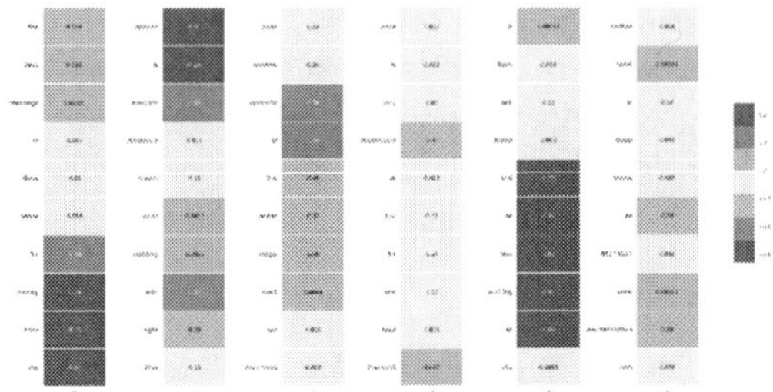

Figure 4: A heatmap of the given neuron's firings on a given text. Each cell corresponds to a word (in left to right order). The red colour corresponds to positive values and the blue to the negative ones. The more intense the colour, the larger the absolute value of the neuron output.

framework. For text preprocessing we use SpaCy (Honnibal and Johnson, 2015) and NLTK (Loper and Bird, 2002). Heatmaps and t-SNE results are plotted with the matplotlib (Hunter, 2007) library and sklearn (Pedregosa et al., 2011). The main deep learning framework is Keras (Chollet, 2015), but there is also a preliminary attempt to include PyTorch (Paszke et al., 2017) models. Statistical measures were calculated using scipy (Jones et al., 2001–).

3.4 Use cases

Regarding possible use cases, we can suggest at least five possible scenarios.

The first is to investigate possible sources of error by analysing the model's hidden vectors and attention scores.

The second promising application is to illustrate the difference between models. This can be done by loading two different models and comparing their heatmaps and attention distributions. For example, if two models with similar performance are given, the preference might go to the one with more explainable features.

The third scenario is a simplification of a model into a rule-based or machine learning approach. It can be seen as a compromise where we use a deep learning approach to extract features that might not be obvious for a human, and then transfer them to other models.

The fourth way to use the system is to try to interpret the features learnt by the network. For instance, while exploring the heatmaps, we noticed that the model seems to highlight words in the answers which are semantically relevant to the question (i.e., "money" when a person asks for a bank recommendation). It also often reacts to the question phrases ("how much", and so on).

Finally, we believe that interactive visualisations of LSTM hidden vectors might be enticing and helpful in education for students and beginner level practitioners.

4   Conclusion

Deep learning models for text processing are powerful, but not easily interpretable. This low interpretability leads to low trust in the systems decision and difficulties in improving its performance. Thus, there is a need for efficient visualisation tools that will illuminate the details of a neural network's decision making.

We have presented a prototype of a visualisation system for the RNN model in the question answering domain. This paper outlines the key features and structure of the system, along with the details of the technical implementation. The system displays heat maps for attention scores and firings of neurons and outputs correlation coefficients between the neurons and manual features. The approach we develop would lend itself well for use by machine comprehension researchers and developers.

Concerning possible improvements, there are five main directions. The first is to employ an automatic search for a structural pattern in neurons firing. The second is to transform neurons into transferable features which can be adapted to other models and tasks. For instance, if we see that the same type of a feature is extracted by several successful question answering systems, it might make sense to apply them in dialogue generation. The third is the need for more advanced statistical analysis. The fourth possible improvement is the incorporation of a direct comparison of two models in an interactive mode. Finally, the system can be extended to character-based models.

Future work will concentrate on extending the system to support other frameworks and visualisation techniques, such as saliency heatmaps. We also plan to include use cases for different domains, e.g. machine translation.

5 Acknowledgements

This work was partially supported by the German Federal Ministry of Education and Research (BMBF) through the project DEEPLEE (01IW17001).

References

Dzmitry Bahdanau, Kyunghyun Cho, and Yoshua Bengio. 2014. Neural machine translation by jointly learning to align and translate. *arXiv preprint arXiv:1409.0473*.

Matt Chaput. 2007. Whoosh. `https://bitbucket.org/mchaput/whoosh`.

Franois Chollet. 2015. keras. `https://github.com/fchollet/keras`.

Matthew Honnibal and Mark Johnson. 2015. An improved non-monotonic transition system for dependency parsing. In *Proceedings of the 2015 Conference on Empirical Methods in Natural Language Processing*, pages 1373–1378, Lisbon, Portugal. Association for Computational Linguistics.

J. D. Hunter. 2007. Matplotlib: A 2d graphics environment. *Computing In Science & Engineering*, 9(3):90–95.

Robin Jia and Percy Liang. 2017. Adversarial examples for evaluating reading comprehension systems. *CoRR*, abs/1707.07328.

Eric Jones, Travis Oliphant, Pearu Peterson, et al. 2001–. SciPy: Open source scientific tools for Python. [Online; accessed 29 May 2018].

Andrej Karpathy, Justin Johnson, and Li Fei-Fei. 2015. Visualizing and understanding recurrent networks. *arXiv preprint arXiv:1506.02078*.

Diederik P Kingma and Jimmy Ba. 2014. Adam: A method for stochastic optimization. *arXiv preprint arXiv:1412.6980*.

Jaesong Lee, Joong-Hwi Shin, and Jun-Seok Kim. 2017. Interactive visualization and manipulation of attention-based neural machine translation. In *Proceedings of the 2017 Conference on Empirical Methods in Natural Language Processing: System Demonstrations*, pages 121–126. Association for Computational Linguistics.

Jiwei Li, Xinlei Chen, Eduard Hovy, and Dan Jurafsky. 2015a. Visualizing and understanding neural models in nlp. *arXiv preprint arXiv:1506.01066*.

Jiwei Li, Xinlei Chen, Eduard H. Hovy, and Dan Jurafsky. 2015b. Visualizing and understanding neural models in NLP. *CoRR*, abs/1506.01066.

Edward Loper and Steven Bird. 2002. Nltk: The natural language toolkit. In *Proceedings of the ACL-02 Workshop on Effective Tools and Methodologies for Teaching Natural Language Processing and Computational Linguistics - Volume 1*, ETMTNLP '02, pages 63–70, Stroudsburg, PA, USA. Association for Computational Linguistics.

L.J.P. van der Maaten and G.E. Hinton. 2008. Visualizing high-dimensional data using t-sne.

Tomas Mikolov, Kai Chen, Greg Corrado, and Jeffrey Dean. 2013. Efficient estimation of word representations in vector space. *CoRR*, abs/1301.3781.

Preslav Nakov, Doris Hoogeveen, Lluís Màrquez, Alessandro Moschitti, Hamdy Mubarak, Timothy Baldwin, and Karin Verspoor. 2017. Semeval-2017 task 3: Community question answering. In *Proceedings of the 11th International Workshop on Semantic Evaluation (SemEval-2017)*, pages 27–48.

Adam Paszke, Sam Gross, Soumith Chintala, Gregory Chanan, Edward Yang, Zachary DeVito, Zeming Lin, Alban Desmaison, Luca Antiga, and Adam Lerer. 2017. Automatic differentiation in pytorch.

F. Pedregosa, G. Varoquaux, A. Gramfort, V. Michel, B. Thirion, O. Grisel, M. Blondel, P. Prettenhofer, R. Weiss, V. Dubourg, J. Vanderplas, A. Passos, D. Cournapeau, M. Brucher, M. Perrot, and E. Duchesnay. 2011. Scikit-learn: Machine learning in Python. *Journal of Machine Learning Research*, 12:2825–2830.

Armin Ronacher. 2018. Flask. `https://github.com/pallets/flask`.

Hendrik Strobelt, Sebastian Gehrmann, Bernd Huber, Hanspeter Pfister, and Alexander M Rush. 2016. Visual analysis of hidden state dynamics in recurrent neural networks. *arXiv preprint arXiv:1606.07461*.

Ming Tan, Cicero dos Santos, Bing Xiang, and Bowen Zhou. 2016. Improved representation learning for question answer matching. In *Proceedings of the 54th Annual Meeting of the Association for Computational Linguistics (Volume 1: Long Papers)*, volume 1, pages 464–473.

Ashish Vaswani, Noam Shazeer, Niki Parmar, Jakob Uszkoreit, Llion Jones, Aidan N. Gomez, Lukasz Kaiser, and Illia Polosukhin. 2017. Attention is all you need. *CoRR*, abs/1706.03762.

Visual Interrogation of Attention-Based Models for Natural Language Inference and Machine Comprehension

Shusen Liu[1], Tao Li[2], Zhimin Li[3], Vivek Srikumar[2], Valerio Pascucci[3], Peer-Timo Bremer[1]

Lawrence Livermore National Laboratory[1]
School of Computing, University of Utah[2]
SCI Institute, University of Utah[3]

Abstract

Neural networks models have gained unprecedented popularity in natural language processing due to their state-of-the-art performance and the flexible end-to-end training scheme. Despite their advantages, the lack of interpretability hinders the deployment and refinement of the models. In this work, we present a flexible visualization library for creating customized visual analytic environments, in which the user can investigate and interrogate the relationships among the input, the model internals (i.e., attention), and the output predictions, which in turn shed light on the model decision-making process.

1 Introduction

Deep neural networks have been successfully applied to various natural language processing tasks. As the design of neural networks evolves, there is a clear trend of increasing model complexity in terms of both the architecture and the parameter count. Although expressive models help improve the prediction performance, the fundamental lack of interpretability leads many researchers to consider neural network models black boxes. The ability to interpret model internals and reason about predictions is essential for understanding the limitation of the models and improving upon them.

Recently, the attention networks have recently become widely-adopted (Bahdanau et al., 2015; Seo et al., 2017; Parikh et al., 2016b; Vaswani et al., 2017). Attention not only improves the model performance but also yields interpretable intermediate representations (i.e., alignment among words). As a result, attention can provide a natural interface for analyzing the internals of neural networks. Conducting analysis directly on the raw attention values can be challenging for human users, and therefore, visual representations

that highlight word alignments between sentences have been proposed, such as the bipartite graph and the heatmap of the attention matrix (Li et al., 2015, 2016; Lee et al., 2017). However, many challenges remain. Firstly, for some NLP tasks, the word sequences pair for which the attention is computed can be highly asymmetrical (i.e., in machine comprehension, the context paragraph can be much longer than the question sentence), which the standard visual encoding cannot adequately handle. Also, many previous works present the attention in a static setting. However, the ability to provide an interactive environment in which the user can instantaneously look at how changes in the input affect the attention, and how small variations in the attention alter the prediction, is crucial for interpreting the model. Finally, many previous visualization efforts, despite revealing many exciting results, focus more on illustrating potentially useful visualization techniques than on providing a flexible software tool that can be easily integrated into an existing code base. As a result, applying these proposed techniques to real-world examples may involve substantial engineering effort, which could prevent wide adoption.

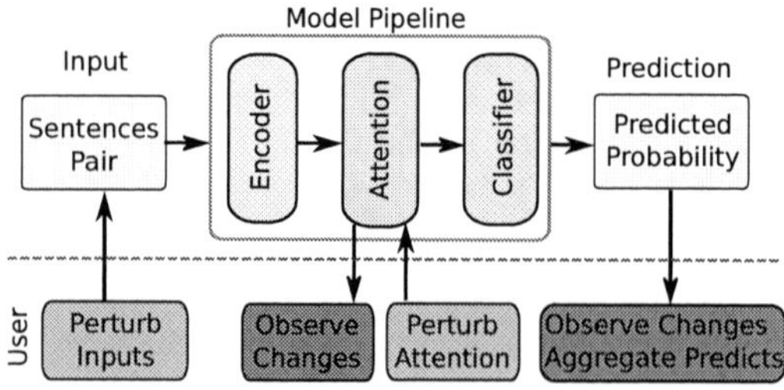

Figure 1: Perturbation-driven interrogation of the end-to-end models that follow the encoder, attention, and classifier structure. The user can generate a small perturbation of the input (i.e., replacing synonyms, paraphrasing), edit the attention, and observe the changes.

To address these challenges in interpreting

Proceedings of the 2018 Conference on Empirical Methods in Natural Language Processing (System Demonstrations), pages 36–41
Brussels, Belgium, October 31–November 4, 2018. ©2018 Association for Computational Linguistics

attention-based models, we introduce a Python library that allows users to create web-based interactive visual analytics environments, in which they can interrogate the model by perturbing the input text and observing the effects on the attention and prediction, or modifying the attention and studying how it affects predictions (see Figure 1). We demonstrate our library applied to two NLP tasks: natural language inference (NLI) and machine comprehension (MC).

2 Related Works

Due to the increasing demand for model interpretability, many previous works have been proposed for making sense of NLP models by examining individual predictions as well as the model mechanism as a whole. In recent work, Li et al. (2015) investigated the composability of the vector-based text representations using instance-level attribution techniques that originated from the vision community (e.g., Zeiler and Fergus, 2014). In a study of the representation of erasure, Li et al. (2016) explained neural model decisions by exploring the impact of altering or removing the components of the model (i.e., changing the dimension count of hidden units or input words) on the prediction performance.

Besides interpreting the model via carefully designed experiments, several interactive demo/visualization systems, such as AllenNLP's demos (`http://demo.allennlp.org/`), often rely on visual encodings to summarize the model predictions. These systems provide a flexible environment in which the user can experiment with the various inputs and perform error analysis. The hidden state properties of the LSTM are visualized and investigated in the LSTMvis visualization system (Strobelt et al., 2018). Lee et al. (2017) visualized the beam search and attention component in neural machine translation models, in which the user can dynamically change the probability for the next step of the search tree or change the weight of the attention. In the visualization work on question answering (Rücklé and Gurevych, 2017), the system shows the text context and highlights the critical phrase that is used to answer the question.

3 Visualization System

As illustrated in Figure 1, many recent end-to-end NLP models follow a similar encoder–attention–classifier structure. The attention stage provides a window to peek into the model decision-making process. However, the static attention alone does not tell the whole story. Our proposed system uses a perturbation-driven exploration strategy that allows the user to manually or automatically perturb part of the pipeline and observe the changes downstream. The system consists of several visualization components that can be selectively combined to form a functional interactive system for a given task. In the following section, we will cover some of the essential components; the usage of all components can be found in the accompanying video link.

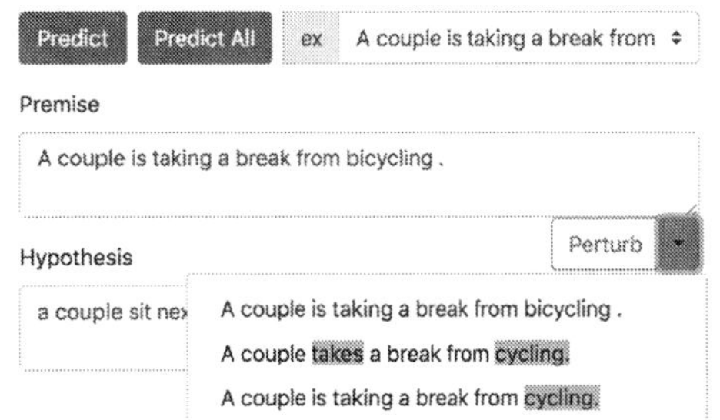

Figure 2: The interface for showing input sentences. The user can manually edit the words or apply automatic perturbation/paraphrasing of the inputs. In the "perturbed" drop-down menu, the blue background highlights words not in the original sentence.

3.1 Input Sentences Perturbation

Due to the discrete nature of natural language, automatically perturbing a sentence for sensitivity analysis can be particularly challenging (compared to other domains such as images) — small changes in words can lead to drastic differences in the semantics of the sentences. To reduce the potential semantic deviation, we allow for a straightforward perturbation method by replacing *nouns* and *verbs* by their synonyms in WordNet (Miller, 1995). However, synonym replacement does not guarantee that the meaning of the sentence remains the same. Furthermore, WordNet often produces rare words or obscure usages that may lead to less meaningful sentences.

To improve the perturbation quality, we also allow for a translation-based paraphrasing technique similar to that proposed by Mallinson et al. (2017). Here, we translate the original English sentence into several other languages and then pivot back to English. Provided the translation produces a good result (in our case, we use the Google Cloud

Translation Platform), we can obtain paraphrases of the original sentence (see Figure 2, where the drop-down menu shows some of the perturbed sentences).

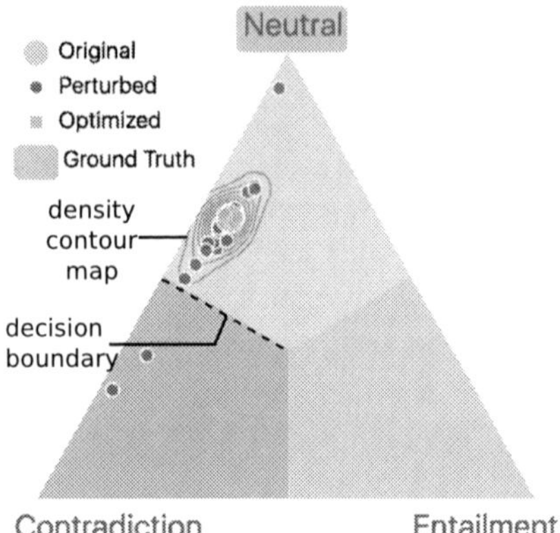

Figure 3: Summary of the prediction results of the perturbed input for the natural language inference model. The prediction is encoded as a point in the barycentric coordinate system of the triangle, in which each vertex corresponds to one prediction label.

3.2 Prediction Visualization

Efficient visual encoding for prediction is crucial for communicating the model behavior, and to fully support the input perturbation feature, the visual encoding should also allow multiple predictions to be shown in the same visualization.

For the natural language inference task, as illustrated in Figure 3, the predicted probabilities are encoded via a triangular barycentric coordinate system, where the vertices represent the three possible predictions (namely, *entailment*, *contradiction*, and *neutral*). The prediction for the original unperturbed input is illustrated by a larger yellow circle, whereas the prediction of perturbed inputs is represented by smaller gray circles.

A density contour of the prediction is computed to emphasize the highly cluttered areas and detect outliers.

3.3 Attention Visualization

As illustrated in Figures 4(a)(b), the most widely adopted visual encodings for attention are bipartite graphs (a) and heatmaps (b). In the graph attention view (Figure 4(a)), the edge thickness corresponds to the attention value of the word pairs. The graph view is suitable for highlighting the most dominant alignments. However, the edges may become cluttered if multiple attention values are high. The matrix attention view (Figure 4(b)) resolves these issues, despite being more verbose and less efficient in highlighting the most dominant alignments. We also enable the linkage between highlighted actions in both views (see Figure 4(a)(b), where one alignment relationship is highlighted).

We augment these standard visual encodings with grammar structure to address the challenge of long sentences. The text can be dynamically simplified based on the dependency tree (see Figure 4(a1)). We also show how the dependency information can potentially improve the prediction result in Section 4.1. To facilitate the perturbation of attention (see Figure 1), as illustrated in Figure 4(c), we implement an interface for directly manipulating the attention value.

However, when the text sequence becomes significantly longer, i.e., a full paragraph in the machine comprehension task, even the simplified sentence cannot be meaningfully represented in the graph or matrix visual encoding. To address this visualization challenge, as illustrated in Figure 4(d), we introduce a hierarchical representation. Here, a pure graphical encoding (the color bars marked by *att2*) is used to capture the aggregated attention information for the whole paragraph. The user can focus on localized attention information by selecting a pixel bar that represents a single sentence (the colored blocks in the bar correspond to individual works). We also link this attention representation with the matrix form, such that whenever a sentence is selected the local attention is shown in the matrix view (see Figure 6(a)).

3.4 Implementation

The initial setup cost and unnecessary learning curve are often the barriers to broad adaptation of a tool. Therefore, instead of designing a visualization system as a monolithic standalone application, we implement the proposed system as a Python library with modularity and ease of use in mind. The different pieces of the visualization (i.e., matrix-based attention encoding) can be accessed individually or combined with other components to fit one's workflow via a simple API. More importantly, the library-based design allows easy integration with the existing model implemented in Python. The code for creating an interactive exploration environment for a machine comprehension model is illustrated below.

```
from visPackage import MCModule
```

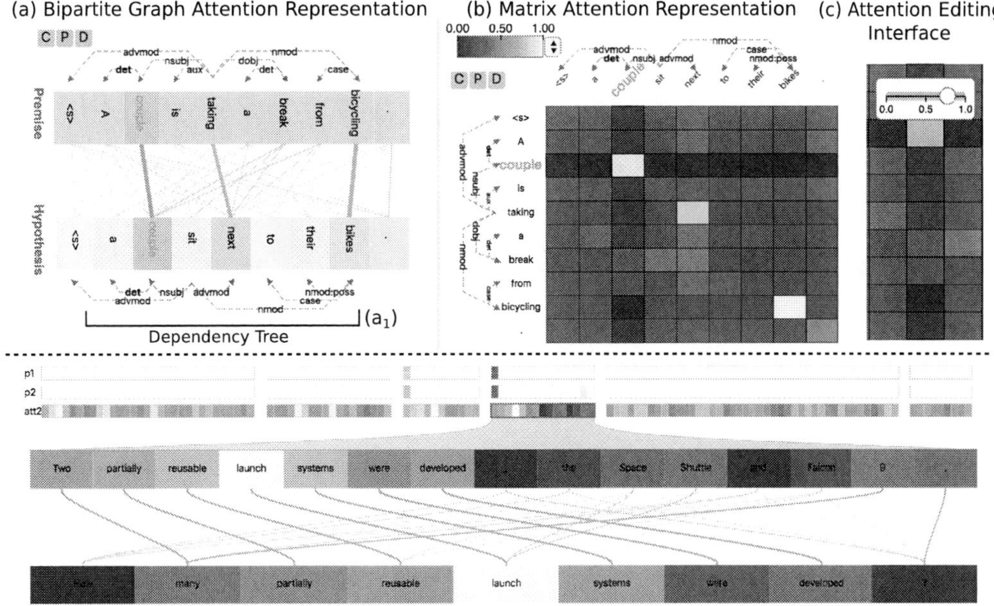

Figure 4: Attention visualization. A bipartite graph encoding is adopted in the graph attention view (a), in which the edge thickness corresponds to the attention value. The same attention values can also be directly visualized in the matrix form (b). The user can edit the attention values via the pop-up interface illustrated in (c). We overlay the dependency tree (a_1) grammar structure to highlight important words and allow simplification of complex sentences (shown in the video). For highly asymmetric attention, we utilize a zoomable hierarchical visual representation (d). The user can focus on the individual sentence by selecting the summary visualization.

```
from bidaf_src import bidafModelInterface
from NLPutility import translationPerturbation

#initialize machine comprehension model
model = bidafModelInterface(
    wordDict="data/bidaf/squad.word.dict",
    wordVec="data/bidaf/glove.hdf5",
    model="data/bidaf/bidaf.ema")
gen = translationPerturbation()
#visualization components
visLayout = {
    "column":[{"row": ["Paragraph",
                       "AttentionSubMatrix"]},
             {"row": ["AttentionAsymmetric"]}]
    }
#setup interface
modelVis = MCModule(visLayout)
modelVis.setPredictionHook(model.predict)
modelVis.setAttentionHook(model.attention)
modelVis.setSentenceHook(gen.perturbSentence)
#open browser for the web-based visualization
modelVis.show()
```

Listing 1: Code for setting up the visualization system shown in Figure 6(a).

4 Applications

We demonstrate the proposed visualization system on the decomposable attention network (Parikh et al., 2016a) for the NLI task and the BIDAF model (Seo et al., 2017) for the MC task.

4.1 Natural Language Inference

The NLI task predicts the entailment relationship between a premise sentence (P) and a hypothe-sis sentence (H). The attention matrix captures the alignment of words between these two sentences. Here we give an example of how a wrong prediction can be corrected by editing attention values.

As illustrated in Figure 5(a), the input sentence pair (P:"A woman in a green jacket is drinking tea." H:"A woman is drinking green tea.") is predicted to be *entailment*, which is incorrect. By examining the attention, we can see the word *green* in "*green* jacket" is aligned to the *green* in "*green* tea." However, these two *greens* modify different nouns, which potentially leads to the wrong prediction. The grammatical structure is visually shown in the form of the dependency tree. However, the model does not have access to the syntactic information and mistakenly assumes the two *greens* modify the same thing. To correct the mistake, we can edit the attention value and remove the align between these two "greens" (see (c)(b)). As expected, the prediction label is corrected (*neutral*).

4.2 Machine Comprehension

In the machine comprehension task, the goal is to select a span of text as the answer to a question sentence. The attention information is encoded

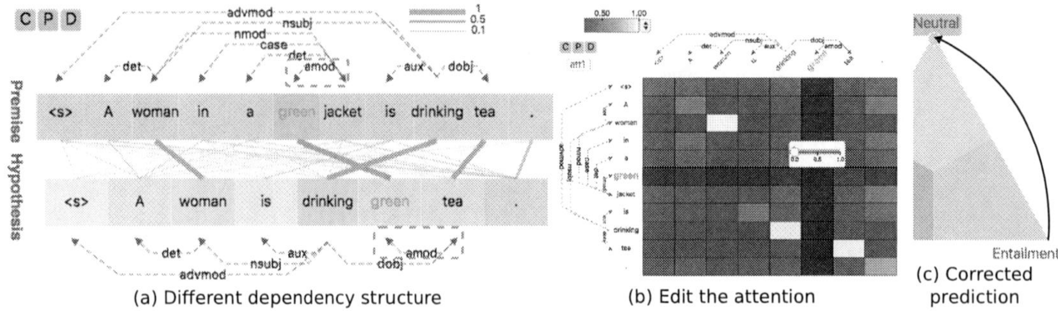

(a) Different dependency structure | (b) Edit the attention | (c) Corrected prediction

Figure 5: An illustration of the attention editing process. The dependency structure is shown in (a), where the two "greens" decorate different nouns. By removing the "wrong" alignment in (b), the original prediction *entailment* is corrected to *neutral* in (c).

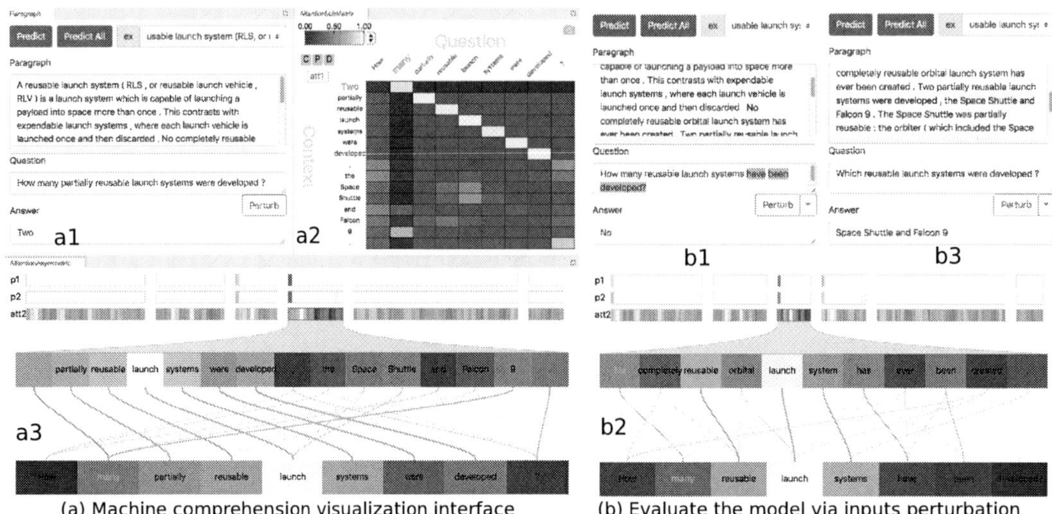

(a) Machine comprehension visualization interface | (b) Evaluate the model via inputs perturbation

Figure 6: In the machine comprehension visualization interface (a), the $p1$, $p2$ colored bar (in $a3$) illustrates the predicted start and end index of the answer in the context (the deeper the red, the higher the probability). The most likely answer is shown in ($a1$). The global attention and local attention are visualized by ($a2$, $a3$). We can evaluate the robustness of the prediction by perturbing the question sentence ($b1$, $b3$). As illustrated in ($b1$, $b2$), by removing the word "partial", the model still finds the correct answer (albeit different, as the sentence perturbation changes the exact meaning of the question).

as a bidirectional alignment (i.e., from context to question and vice versa). Here, we refer the context to question attention as *att1* and the question to context attention as *att2* (which is a vector instead of a matrix according to Seo et al. (2017)). In this demo, we apply a min max normalization for *att2* after the softmax layer to better distinguish different attention values.

As illustrated in Figure 6, we represent *att2* as colored bars with a *yellow-green-blue* colormap. Each rectangular bar corresponds to one sentence. The user can focus on individual sentences by clicking on the rectangular bar (see Figure 6). The $p1$, $p2$ colored bars (*white-red* colormap) illustrate the predicted probabilities of the start and the end

index for the answer (the deeper the higher). In Figure 6(a3), the sentence containing the answer exhibits good alignment with the question (e.g., "Two" with "many"). Interestingly, the number "9" (in "Falcon 9") is also aligned with "many", which may lead to problems.

The user can explore the robustness of the model by examining how the prediction varies when the question is perturbed. As illustrated in ($b1$, and $b2$), the perturbation removes the word "partial" in the original sentence, which leads the model to produce a different yet correct answer ("No"). Referring to ($a1$), we can see the word "No" exhibits the second highest probability for the original question. The user can also manually edit the text. As shown in ($b3$), the model still produces the correct answer when changing the question from "how many" to "which".

5 Discussion

In this work, we introduce a visualization library for creating customized environments that allows the user to interrogate the relationships among different parts of the model pipeline via interactive queries. We demonstrate the usability and flexibility of the tool by configuring the visual components to investigate models for different NLP tasks (e.g., NLI, MC). We also conducted a small-scale user evaluation, in which five Ph.D.-level students with an NLP background spent 30 minutes with the tool and then provided feedback. Most suggested the environment allowed them to refine queries iteratively and identify potential issues with the model, but some also mentioned the tool might not provide enough guidance for users who do not have an in-depth understanding of the model at hand.

Even though we designed the individual components with versatility in mind, due to a large number of variants of attention networks, we found it difficult to ensure compatibility with all the available configurations. In the future, we plan to improve upon the current attention interface, release the library as an open-source package, and expand the visualization components to handle tasks such as neural machine translation and more.

Acknowledgments

This work was performed under the auspices of the U.S. Department of Energy by Lawrence Livermore National Laboratory under Contract DE-AC52-07NA27344. This work is also supported in part by NSF: CGV: Award: 1314896, NSF: IIP: Award: 1602127, NSF: ACI: award: 1649923, DOE/SciDAC DESC0007446, CCMSC DE-NA0002375, PIPER: ER26142 DE-SC0010498, and NVIDIA Corporation. This material is based upon work supported by the Department of Energy, National Nuclear Security Administration, under Award Number(s) DE-NA0002375.

References

Dzmitry Bahdanau, Kyunghyun Cho, and Yoshua Bengio. 2015. Neural machine translation by jointly learning to align and translate. *ICLR*.

Jaesong Lee, Joong-Hwi Shin, and Jun-Seok Kim. 2017. Interactive visualization and manipulation of attention-based neural machine translation. In *Proceedings of the 2017 Conference on Empirical Methods in Natural Language Processing: System Demonstrations*, pages 121–126.

Jiwei Li, Xinlei Chen, Eduard Hovy, and Dan Jurafsky. 2015. Visualizing and understanding neural models in nlp. *arXiv preprint arXiv:1506.01066*.

Jiwei Li, Will Monroe, and Dan Jurafsky. 2016. Understanding neural networks through representation erasure. *arXiv preprint arXiv:1612.08220*.

Jonathan Mallinson, Rico Sennrich, and Mirella Lapata. 2017. Paraphrasing revisited with neural machine translation. In *Proceedings of the 15th Conference of the European Chapter of the Association for Computational Linguistics: Volume 1, Long Papers*, volume 1, pages 881–893.

George A Miller. 1995. Wordnet: a lexical database for english. *Communications of the ACM*, 38(11):39–41.

Ankur Parikh, Oscar Täckström, Dipanjan Das, and Jakob Uszkoreit. 2016a. A decomposable attention model for natural language inference. In *Proceedings of the 2016 Conference on Empirical Methods in Natural Language Processing*, pages 2249–2255, Austin, Texas. Association for Computational Linguistics.

Ankur P Parikh, Oscar Täckström, Dipanjan Das, and Jakob Uszkoreit. 2016b. A decomposable attention model for natural language inference. *arXiv preprint arXiv:1606.01933*.

Andreas Rücklé and Iryna Gurevych. 2017. End-to-end non-factoid question answering with an interactive visualization of neural attention weights. *Proceedings of ACL 2017, System Demonstrations*, pages 19–24.

Minjoon Seo, Aniruddha Kembhavi, Ali Farhadi, and Hannaneh Hajishirzi. 2017. Bidirectional attention flow for machine comprehension. *ICLR*.

Hendrik Strobelt, Sebastian Gehrmann, Hanspeter Pfister, and Alexander M Rush. 2018. Lstmvis: A tool for visual analysis of hidden state dynamics in recurrent neural networks. *IEEE transactions on visualization and computer graphics*, 24(1):667–676.

Ashish Vaswani, Noam Shazeer, Niki Parmar, Jakob Uszkoreit, Llion Jones, Aidan N Gomez, Łukasz Kaiser, and Illia Polosukhin. 2017. Attention is all you need. In *Advances in Neural Information Processing Systems*, pages 6000–6010.

Matthew D Zeiler and Rob Fergus. 2014. Visualizing and understanding convolutional networks. In *European conference on computer vision*, pages 818–833. Springer.

DERE: A Task and Domain-Independent Slot Filling Framework for Declarative Relation Extraction

Heike Adel, Laura Bostan, Sean Papay, Sebastian Padó, and **Roman Klinger**[*]
Institut für Maschinelle Sprachverarbeitung
University of Stuttgart, Germany
`{firstname.lastname}@ims.uni-stuttgart.de`
`dereproject@ims.uni-stuttgart.de`

Abstract

Most machine learning systems for natural language processing are tailored to specific tasks. As a result, comparability of models across tasks is missing and their applicability to new tasks is limited. This affects end users without machine learning experience as well as model developers. To address these limitations, we present DERE, a novel framework for declarative specification and compilation of template-based information extraction. It uses a generic specification language for the task and for data annotations in terms of spans and frames. This formalism enables the representation of a large variety of natural language processing challenges. The backend can be instantiated by different models, following different paradigms. The clear separation of frame specification and model backend will ease the implementation of new models and the evaluation of different models across different tasks. Furthermore, it simplifies transfer learning, joint learning across tasks and/or domains as well as the assessment of model generalizability. DERE is available as open-source software.

1   Introduction

A large number of tasks in natural language processing (NLP) are information extraction (IE) tasks, such as n-ary relation extraction (Doddington et al., 2004; Mintz et al., 2009; Hendrickx et al., 2010), semantic role labeling (Das et al., 2014) and event extraction (Kim et al., 2009; Doddington et al., 2004). Researchers address these tasks with a variety of different model paradigms, such as support vector machines (Rink and Harabagiu, 2010), convolutional neural networks (Collobert et al., 2011; Zeng et al., 2014) and recurrent neural networks (Tang et al., 2015; Nguyen et al., 2016).

This landscape of different tasks and models gives rise to four challenges: (C1) *Lack of gener-*

alizability: Most models are tailored to a specific task or setup, making it hard to transfer lessons learned between tasks; (C2) *Lack of comparability*: Although benchmark datasets are available for most tasks, end-to-end evaluation typically includes peripheral aspects, such as preprocessing components – thus, it is unclear to what extent reported improvements mark actual advances in the core models or model components; (C3) *Difficulty of reusability*: Given task-specific models inside complex systems, it is hard to reuse specific code or models; (C4) *Difficulty of usage*: Users typically have limited areas of expertise, but IE systems span a range of such areas. Thus, developers of IE tools may have trouble properly (re)training complex machine learning models, and end users without ML or CS background might even be unable to use existing tools.

To tackle these challenges, we develop the general framework DERE (Declarative Relation Extraction). It enables users to (i) specify (novel or established) IE tasks, (ii) compile models and transfer them across tasks without additional development effort, (iii) develop and evaluate models across tasks, (iv) formulate and address research questions, such as the investigation of model generalizability across tasks, transfer learning, or joint learning across tasks and/or domains, and (v) verify the generalizability of models by applying them to a large variety of tasks.

DERE achieves this by providing (a) a general mechanism to declaratively specify IE tasks and (b) a shared processing framework that decouples frontend and backend. This provides an attractive shared basis for modeling tasks which are typically perceived as being very different. In this paper, we use *BioNLP event extraction* and *aspect-based sentiment analysis (ABSA)* as examples. At the same time, the decoupling exposes accessible interfaces for different user groups (*cf.* Section 3).

---

*All authors contributed equally.

Proceedings of the 2018 Conference on Empirical Methods in Natural Language Processing (System Demonstrations), pages 42–47
Brussels, Belgium, October 31–November 4, 2018. ©2018 Association for Computational Linguistics

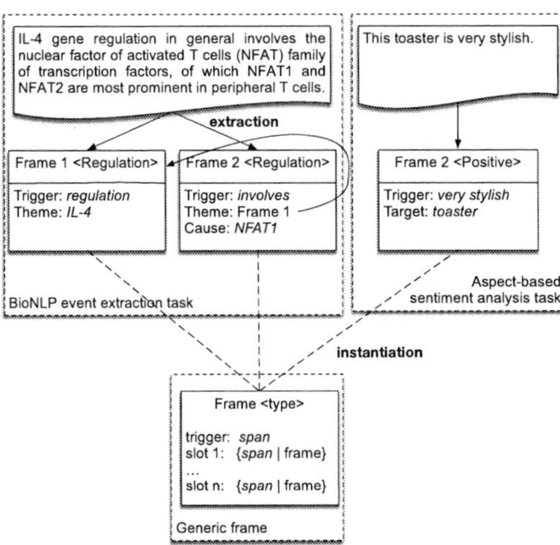

Figure 1: Example formalizations of two different tasks in terms of frames, slots, and spans.

The declarative specification of a task (which we call a *schema*) builds upon *spans* and *relations between spans* as basic concepts which are used by essentially all IE tasks. To model n-ary relations, we propose a *slot-filling* scheme in which *frames* model n-ary relations and their arguments. Figure 1 shows the general structure of frames (below) and two concrete instantiations for ABSA and BioNLP (above). Each frame is triggered (anchored) by a span, *e.g.,* a subjective evaluating phrase like "very stylish" or a BioNLP event trigger, such as "regulation" or "involves".

Frames hold a task-specific number of typed slots, filled by relation arguments. The frames for ABSA have a slot filled by the target (aspect) of the sentiment while the frames for the BioNLP regulation event hold a Theme slot and an optional Cause slot. While triggers are always textual spans, slots can be filled by either spans or frames, depending on the task specification. We argue that this simple setup can model most IE tasks. Note that the framework poses no theoretical restrictions to the window from which frames are extracted. Thus, it can model sentence-level, document-level as well as multi-document tasks.

2   Related Work

Several applications require the joint extraction of spans and relations between spans, such as the BioNLP shared task (Kim et al., 2009), semantic role labeling (Das et al., 2014) or (temporal) slot filling (Surdeanu, 2013). However, all sys-

tems we are aware of for solving these tasks are tailored to specific scenarios (Angeli et al., 2016; Adel et al., 2016, *i.a.*). As a result, it is not straightforward to apply them to other use cases. In contrast, our framework is designed to be task- and domain-independent.

Clarke et al. (2012) develop an NLP component manager which combines several existing NLP tools in a pipeline. Similarly, Curran (2003) aims at a general NLP infrastructure but only reports implementations of non-relational sequence-tagging tasks. Examples of the few available toolkits which are intended to provide users with the possibility of automatically extracting information from text data are Jet (Java Extraction Toolkit), GATE (General Architecture for Text Engineering, Cunningham et al., 2013), UIMA (Unstructured Information Management Architecture, Ferrucci and Lally, 2004), FACTORIE (McCallum et al., 2009) and Stanbol which integrates other NLP frameworks, *e.g.,* OpenNLP (Morton et al., 2005).

Stanbol and OpenNLP, however, focus on tagging tasks and do not provide tools for relation extraction. FACTORIE is a general approach to formulate factor graphs for arbitrary tasks. Our framework takes arbitrary model paradigms as a backend and is focused on IE, which enables the abstraction layers introduced earlier. Jet, on the other hand, is an IE engine developed specifically for the ACE task specification.

GATE is most similar to our framework in scope. It offers both a framework for programmers and an environment for language engineers and computational linguists. However, it is a very general framework and working with it requires both domain and machine learning knowledge. In contrast, our framework provides end users with an interface for training models on new tasks without requiring any specific knowledge.

3   Framework Design

Use Cases. We address the needs of the following three user groups with associated use cases: (1) Researchers/Model developers: Our framework helps researchers to formulate their models in a task-independent manner, such that they can be tested and compared across tasks. This addresses challenges C1, C2 and C3 mentioned in Section 1. (2) Developers of IE tools for a new use case: Our framework provides a common interface to models previously developed for other tasks. Those mod-

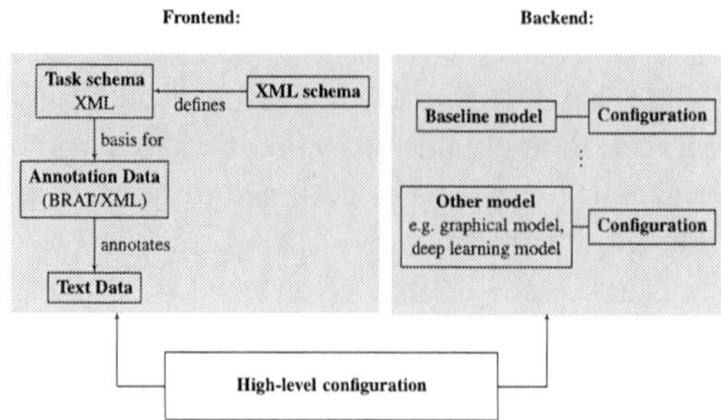

Figure 2: Structure of the DERE framework.

```
<deREschema name="BioNLP-ST 2009" ver="0.01" auth="Klinger">
  <spantypes>
    <span name="Protein" predict="False"/>
    <span name="Gene_expression" anchors="Gene_expression"
          predict="True"/>
    <span name="Binding" anchors="Binding" predict="True"/>
  </spantypes>
  <frames>
    <frame name="Gene_expression">
      <slot name="Theme" types="Protein" cardinality="1"/>
    </frame>
    <frame name="Binding">
      <slot name="Theme" types="Protein" mincardinality="0"/>
    </frame>
  </frames>
</deREschema>
```

Figure 3: A small but complete task schema for part of the BioNLP shared task. Three span types are specified: `Protein`, `Gene_expression`, and `Binding`. The latter two anchor frames of the same name. Both frames possess a single slot `Theme` which can be filled by `Protein` spans. `Gene_expression` frames always have exactly one `Theme`, while `Binding` frames may have zero or more `Themes`.

```
T1 Protein 1650 1655 IP-10
T2 Protein 951 955 PU.1
T3 Protein 1665 1670 ISG54
T4 Protein 978 992 CSF receptor
T5 Binding 932 937 binds
T6 Gene_expression 1634 1644 expression
E1 Binding:T5 Theme:T2 Theme2:T4
E2 Gene_expression:T6 Theme:T1
E3 Gene_expression:T6 Theme:T3
```

Figure 4: An example annotation in BRAT format, following the task specification from Figure 3. The text-bound annotations T are the span annotations, the event annotations E define our frames.

els can be integrated and interchanged for new use cases. This addresses challenges C3 and C4 from Section 1. (3) Users of IE tools: With the common interface our framework provides, end-users do not need to know theoretical details about models but can still use different models for their use case. This addresses challenge C4 from Section 1.

Framework Structure. Figure 2 illustrates the structure of the DERE framework. It is composed of two main components: The *frontend* comprises the user specification of the task ("task schema"), including the types of spans and entities to be identified, and the possible relations that can exist between them. It manages reading corpora and annotation files and provides an interface for users. The *backend* hosts the models that make actual predictions for spans, frames, and slots, given the task schema, and their configurations. DERE backends follow a modular design, wherein different backends, using different methods for prediction, can be used interchangeably with minimal changes to the frontend.

Task Schemata. DERE represents all relations $r \in \mathcal{R}$ in terms of two types of entities: *spans* and *frames*. A span $s \in \mathcal{S}$ is a contiguous span of text from the input corpus. Each span has a type $t \in \mathcal{T}_{\mathcal{S}}$, corresponding to the kind of entity that that span represents. The set of possible span types $\mathcal{T}_{\mathcal{S}}$ is specified by the user for the task. A frame $f \in \mathcal{F}$ represents a relationship between multiple spans or other frames. Each frame contains a number of named *slots* $l \in \mathcal{L}$. These slots can each be filled by zero or more other spans or frames. The set of frame types $\mathcal{T}_{\mathcal{F}}$, like span types, is task-specific. For each frame type, the user specifies a set of slots, and for each slot, what types of frames or spans can fill it, plus optional cardinality constraints.

We represent a task schema as an XML file. Figure 3 gives an example task schema file, for a sub-set of the BioNLP shared task (Kim et al., 2009). Note that this specification defines a directed graph with spans and frames as vertices $\mathcal{V} = \mathcal{S} \cup \mathcal{F}$ and relations as edges: $\mathcal{E} = \mathcal{R}$.

Data Files. Annotated data, needed for training models, are provided to DERE as annotation files. We currently support annotations in the BRAT (Stenetorp et al., 2012) format, *cf.* Figure 4.

4 Proof-of-Concept System

As a proof of concept, we present the following system consisting of a pipeline of traditional NLP formalizations: First, spans relevant for the task are identified. Then, a classifier decides for each pair of relevant spans which slots of which frame they are likely to fill. Finally, a heuristic decoding step compiles the results into frames. Figure 5 illustrates this pipeline. The proof-of-concept system only supports non-recursive structures: slots of frames cannot be filled by other frames, but must be filled by spans — *i.e.*, the right-hand BioNLP frame from Figure 1 could not be predicted in this

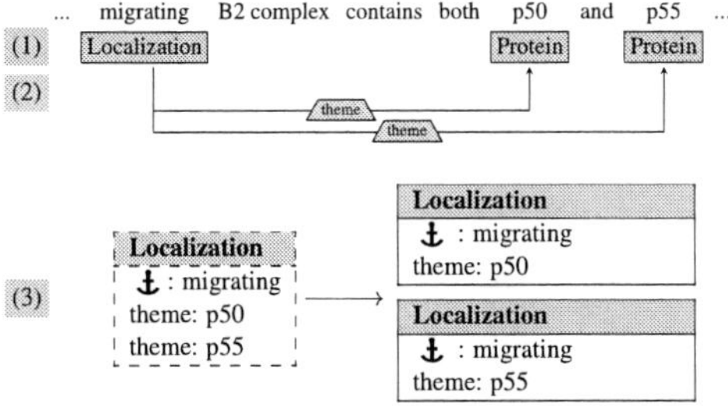

Figure 5: Proof-of-concept pipeline: span identification (1), slot classification (2), and decoding into frames (3). ⚓ : frame anchors (triggers)

implementation. Note that this is only a proof-of-concept baseline but the framework is not limited to pipeline models. In the future, we will develop joint models that can cope with recursive structures.

Span Identification. We cast the span identification problem as a BIO-style sequence-labeling task that predicts the span boundaries. To model overlapping spans, we train one model per span type which outputs all spans of that type. Our proof-of-concept system uses conditional random fields (CRF, Lafferty et al., 2001). The feature set consists of the lower-cased words, their stems, their shape (orthographic case, digits, punctuation), and a flag indicating whether the word is included in a task-specific gazetteer. All features (except the last one) are applicable to any NLP task. The gazetteer feature is based on a simple lexicon of label-specific words (*e.g.,* positive words for detecting positive spans for sentiment analysis) and can be instantiated without any technical knowledge.

Slot Classification. Once the spans are identified, the slot classifier is used to predict which slots of which frame they are likely to fill. We break this question down to a classification task at the level of span pairs – one anchor span representing a frame, and another span representing a potential argument. The search space is restricted to those pairs with compatible types according to the schema.

Formally, the classifier takes as input the set $\mathcal{S}$ of all spans identified previously, along with a task schema. For each pair $(s_i, s_j) \in \mathcal{S}^2$ of spans following the task schema, our classifier produces as output either a single relation label r_{ij}, or NR (no relation)[1] if the two spans are unrelated. Conceptually, two spans s_i and s_j are related iff s_i anchors a frame, and s_j fills a slot in that same frame. Relation labels r_{ij} are pairs $(f_i, l_j) \in \mathcal{T}_{\mathcal{F}} \times \mathcal{L}$, where f_i

is the frame type anchored by s_i and l_j is the slot type in f_i that s_j fills. This enables us to model, *e.g.,* in the task schema in Figure 3, BINDING.THEME and GENE_EXPRESSION.THEME as separate relations. A linear support vector machine is used to predict the most likely relation label (or NR). Users can enable subsampling of negative examples.

As outlined in the introduction, the features we take into account are included with the aim of being task-agnostic. Intra-span features are types of identified spans and the bag of words in both spans. Inter-span features take into account context. We use the bag of words of tokens between the spans, and of the tokens on the shortest path connecting the spans in a parsed dependency tree, which we assume to accurately capture the relationship expressed by the slot that links the two spans. Since spans can contain multiple tokens, there can be several shortest paths between tokens from the two spans. Under the assumption that tokens in a span are closely related to each other, we select the shortest of these paths. In addition, we also use a bag of bigrams of alternating label-token sequence on that same path. Finally, we measure the length of the shortest path and the token distance.

Decoding. Once the slot classifier identifies all related span pairs, the decoding step generates frames. Pairs of spans (s_i, s_j) that stand in a relation r are first partitioned into equivalence classes $\mathcal{C}_h$ according to their anchor span (i.e., $(s_i, s_j) \in \mathcal{C}_i$). It would be possible to produce one frame for each equivalence class $\mathcal{C}_h$, anchored by the common anchoring span s_h, and with slots filled according to each span pair's relation label r. However, as equivalence classes can be arbitrarily large, this would allow for each slot to be filled by arbitrarily many spans (as illustrated in the bottom-left of Figure 5). As the task schema might impose cardinality constraints, further processing is required to ensure that all produced frames are consistent with the task schema. For each equivalence class $\mathcal{C}_h$, we consider all possible *legal frames* – i.e., all frames that are consistent with the task schema and whose slots are filled according to some subset of $\mathcal{C}_h$. Of these legal frames, we retain all *maximally-filled legal frames* (see bottom-right of Figure 5).

Evaluation and Results. To prove the feasability of our proof of concept, we report results with this configuration on the 2009 BioNLP shared task, for which we re-use the original evaluation machin-

---

[1] We generate negative examples automatically.

Event Class	Precision	Recall	F1
Gene_expression	68.12	57.30	62.25
Transcription	70.59	14.63	24.24
Protein_catabolism	64.00	76.19	69.57
Phosphorylation	65.85	57.45	61.36
Localization	78.57	41.51	54.32
SVT-TOTAL	68.46	50.27	57.97

Table 1: Performance of the proof-of-concept system for biomedical relation extraction (BioNLP'09 dev set)

Sentiment Class	Precision	Recall	F1
Positive	41.07	24.19	28.57
Negative	26.68	7.15	11.00
Neutral	5.83	4.50	5.08

Table 2: Performance of the proof-of-concept system for aspect based sentiment analysis (10-fold cross-validation on USAGE corpus).

ery. The evaluation calculates the F_1 scores for the individual frames (events in the BioNLP task) using a soft matching for trigger boundaries and approximate recursive matching. Table 1 provides the results of our simple system on that task. Due to the restriction of our proof of concept to non-recursive structures (*cf.* Section 4), we only report on the BioNLP event types where all slots are filled by spans. In comparison to the second-ranked system, which also reports results on dev (Buyko et al., 2009), our performance is slightly lower (1 percentage point less for protein catabolism, 13pp less for gene expression and phosphorylation, but 11pp more for localization). This confirms the general usability of our general method.

Correspondingly, Table 2 provides the current results of the same model on the USAGE corpus for aspect based sentiment analysis (Klinger and Cimiano, 2014), with 10-fold crossvalidation on the English subset. In comparison to previous results, our numbers are very low. Previous work showed that this is tackled by joint inference, which we did not implement yet (Klinger and Cimiano, 2013; Yang and Cardie, 2013). However, this proof-of-concept implementation of the same model already shows the reusability of our framework by only changing the task schema specification. It motivates and enables further research on reusable models across tasks with different needs.

Technical Details and Availability. The framework is implemented in Python, following an object-oriented design for frontend and backends to support easy interchangeability of components.

The choice of Python will also help with future integration of neural network models. For the proof-of-concept backend, we use scikit-learn for feature extraction and training (Pedregosa et al., 2011) with crfsuite and liblinear. Tokenization and stemming is done with NLTK (Loper and Bird, 2002), dependency features are extracted with spacy (Honnibal and Johnson, 2015) and dependency graphs are stored and processed using NetworkX (Schult, 2008). The code is available under the Apache 2.0 License.[2]

5 Conclusion and Future Work

This paper presented DERE, a general framework for declarative specification and compilation of template-based slot filling. It addresses the needs of three groups of users: backend model developers, developers of information extraction tools for new use cases and end users of information extraction tools. vEspecially, it simplifies the evaluation and comparison of new information extraction models across tasks as well as the straightforward application of existing models to new tasks. By our general design of spans and frames, it is possible to apply DERE to a large variety of natural language processing tasks, such as unary, binary and n-ary relation extraction, event extraction, semantic role labeling, aspect-based sentiment analysis, etc.

As BRAT annotations are not as expressive as our task schema files, we plan to extend the frontend of DERE by supporting a native, XML-based annotation format in the future. For the backend, our goal is to develop a variety of state-of-the-art models with joint span identification, slot classification, and frame decoding, *e.g.,* neural networks with structured-prediction output layers (Lample et al., 2016; Adel and Schütze, 2017, *i.a.*). Given a variety of different models and tasks, we will be able to address interesting research questions, such a transfer learning and joint learning across tasks and domains. We plan to further analyze the usage of DERE and the possibilities it provides for integrating different model types and configurations in a multi-task oriented shared task.

Acknowledgments This work has been partially funded by the German Research Council (DFG), projects KL 2869/1-1 and PA 1956/4-1.

---

[2]http://www.ims.uni-stuttgart.de/forschung/ressourcen/werkzeuge/DeRE.en.html

References

H Adel, B Roth, and H Schütze. 2016. Comparing convolutional neural networks to traditional models for slot filling. In *NAACL-HLT*.

H Adel and H Schütze. 2017. Global normalization of convolutional neural networks for joint entity and relation classification. In *EMNLP*.

G Angeli, V Zhong, D Chen, A Chaganty, J Bolton, MJ Premkumar, P Pasupat, S Gupta, and CD Manning. 2016. Bootstrapped self training for knowledge base population. In *TAC*.

Ekaterina Buyko, Erik Faessler, Joachim Wermter, and Udo Hahn. 2009. Event extraction from trimmed dependency graphs. In *BioNLP'09 Shared Task on Event Extraction*.

J Clarke, V Srikumar, M Sammons, and D Roth. 2012. An NLP curator (or: How i learned to stop worrying and love NLP pipelines). In *LREC*.

R Collobert, J Weston, L Bottou, M Karlen, K Kavukcuoglu, and P Kuksa. 2011. Natural language processing (almost) from scratch. *Journal of Machine Learning Research*, 12:2493–2537.

H Cunningham, V Tablan, A Roberts, and K Bontcheva. 2013. Getting more out of biomedical documents with GATE's full lifecycle open source text analytics. *PLOS Computational Biology*, 9(2).

JR Curran. 2003. Blueprint for a high performance NLP infrastructure. In *Workshop on software engineering and architecture of language technology systems*.

D Das, D Chen, A Martins, N Schneider, and NA Smith. 2014. Frame-semantic parsing. *Computational Linguistics*, 40:9–56.

GR Doddington, A Mitchell, MA Przybocki, LA Ramshaw, S Strassel, and RM Weischedel. 2004. The automatic content extraction (ACE) program – tasks, data, and evaluation. In *LREC*.

D Ferrucci and A Lally. 2004. UIMA: An architectural approach to unstructured information processing in the corporate research environment. *Natural Language Engineering*, 10(3–4):327–348.

I Hendrickx, SN Kim, Z Kozareva, P Nakov, D Ó Séaghdha, S Padó, M Pennacchiotti, L Romano, and S Szpakowicz. 2010. Semeval-2010 task 8: Multi-way classification of semantic relations between pairs of nominals. In *SemEval*.

M Honnibal and M Johnson. 2015. An improved non-monotonic transition system for dependency parsing. In *EMNLP*.

J Kim, T Ohta, S Pyysalo, Y Kano, and J Tsujii. 2009. Overview of BioNLP'09 shared task on event extraction. In *BioNLP*.

R Klinger and P Cimiano. 2013. Joint and pipeline probabilistic models for fine-grained sentiment analysis: Extracting aspects, subjective phrases and their relations. In *ICDMW*.

R Klinger and P Cimiano. 2014. The USAGE review corpus for fine grained multilingual opinion analysis. In *LREC*.

JD Lafferty, A McCallum, and FCN. Pereira. 2001. Conditional random fields: Probabilistic models for segmenting and labeling sequence data. In *ICML*.

G Lample, M Ballesteros, S Subramanian, K Kawakami, and C Dyer. 2016. Neural architectures for named entity recognition. In *NAACL-HLT*.

E Loper and S Bird. 2002. Nltk: The natural language toolkit. In *Workshop on Effective Tools and Methodologies for Teaching NLP and CL*.

A McCallum, K Schultz, and S Singh. 2009. Factorie: Probabilistic programming via imperatively defined factor graphs. In *NIPS*.

M Mintz, S Bills, R Snow, and D Jurafsky. 2009. Distant supervision for relation extraction without labeled data. In *ACL-AFNLP*.

T Morton, J Kottmann, J Baldridge, and G Bierner. 2005. OpenNLP: A java-based NLP toolkit. http://opennlp.sourceforge.net.

TH Nguyen, K Cho, and R Grishman. 2016. Joint event extraction via recurrent neural networks. In *NAACL*.

F Pedregosa et al. 2011. Scikit-learn: Machine learning in Python. *Journal of Machine Learning Research*, 12:2825–2830.

B Rink and S Harabagiu. 2010. UTD: Classifying semantic relations by combining lexical and semantic resources. In *SemEval*.

DA Schult. 2008. Exploring network structure, dynamics, and function using networkx. In *Python in Science Conference*.

P Stenetorp, S Pyysalo, G Topić, T Ohta, S Ananiadou, and J Tsujii. 2012. brat: a web-based tool for NLP-assisted text annotation. In *EACL*.

M Surdeanu. 2013. Overview of the TAC2013 knowledge base population evaluation: English slot filling and temporal slot filling. In *TAC*.

D Tang, B Qin, and T Liu. 2015. Document modeling with gated recurrent neural network for sentiment classification. In *EMNLP*.

B Yang and C Cardie. 2013. Joint inference for fine-grained opinion extraction. In *ACL*.

D Zeng, K Liu, S Lai, G Zhou, and J Zhao. 2014. Relation classification via convolutional deep neural network. In *COLING*.

Demonstrating PAR4SEM -
A Semantic Writing Aid with Adaptive Paraphrasing

Seid Muhie Yimam   **Chris Biemann**

Language Technology Group
Department of Informatics
Universität Hamburg, Germany
`{yimam,biemann}@informatik.uni-hamburg.de`

Abstract

In this paper, we present PAR4SEM, a semantic writing aid tool based on adaptive paraphrasing. Unlike many annotation tools that are primarily used to collect training examples, PAR4SEM is integrated into a real word application, in this case a writing aid tool, in order to collect training examples from usage data. PAR4SEM is a tool, which supports an adaptive, iterative, and interactive process where the underlying machine learning models are updated for each iteration using new training examples from usage data. After motivating the use of ever-learning tools in NLP applications, we evaluate PAR4SEM by adopting it to a text simplification task through mere usage.

1 Introduction

Natural language processing and semantic applications that depend on a machine learning component require training data, i.e. examples from which the machine learning algorithm learns from. The training datasets require, most of the time, manual annotation. Usually, such annotations are conducted in a predefined cycle of annotation activities. Once the annotation problem is identified, a standalone annotation tool along with the annotation guideline is developed. At the end of the annotation cycle, the collected dataset is fed to the machine learning component, which produces a static model that can be used thereafter in an application.

Possible limitations of these annotation approaches are: 1) Developing a standalone annotation tool is costly, sometimes expert or specially trained annotators are required. 2) There is no direct way to evaluate the dataset towards its effectiveness for the real-world application. 3) It suffers from what is known as *concept drift*, as the annotation process is detached from the target application, the dataset might get obsolete over time.

In this regard, we have dealt specifically with the semantic annotation problem, using an adaptive, integrated, and personalized annotation process. By *adaptive*, we mean that target applications do not require pre-existing training data, rather it depends on the usage data from the user. The machine learning model then adapts towards the actual goal of the application over time. Instead of developing a standalone annotation tool, the collection of training examples is *integrated* inside a real-world application. Furthermore, our approach is *personalized* in a sense that the training examples being collected are directly related to the need of the user for the application at hand. After all, the question is not: how good is the system *today*? It is rather: how good will it be *tomorrow* after we use it today?

Thus, such adaptive approaches have the following benefits:

Suggestion and correction options: Since the model immediately starts learning from the usage data, it can start predicting and suggesting recommendations to the user immediately. Users can evaluate and correct suggestions that in turn help the model to learn from these corrections.

Less costly: As the collection of the training data is based on usage data, it does not need a separate annotation cycle.

Personalized: It exactly fits the need of the target application, based on the requirement of the user.

Model-Life-Long Learning: As opposed to static models that once deployed on the basis of training data, adaptive models incorporate more training data the longer they are used, which should lead to better performance over time.

We have developed PAR4SEM, a semantic writing aid tool using an adaptive paraphrasing component, which is used to provide context-aware lexical paraphrases while composing texts. The tool incorporates two adaptive models, namely target identification and candidate ranking. The adaptive target identification component is a clas-

Proceedings of the 2018 Conference on Empirical Methods in Natural Language Processing (System Demonstrations), pages 48–53
Brussels, Belgium, October 31–November 4, 2018. ©2018 Association for Computational Linguistics

sification algorithm, which learns how to automatically identify target units (such as words, phrases or multi-word expressions), that need to be paraphrased. When the user highlights target words (*usage data*), it is considered as a training example for the adaptive model.

The adaptive ranking model is a learning-to-rank machine learning algorithm, which is used to re-rank candidate suggestions provided for the target unit. We rely on existing paraphrase resources such as PPDB 2.0, WordNet, distributional thesaurus and word embeddings (see Section 2.1.1) to generate candidate suggestions.

Some other examples for adaptive NLP setups include: 1) online learning for ranking, example Yogatama et al. (2014) who tackle the pairwise learning-to-ranking problem via a scalable online learning approach, 2) adaptive machine translation (MT), e.g. Denkowski et al. (2014) describe a framework for building adaptive MT systems that learn from post-editor feedback, and 3) incremental learning for spam filtering, e.g. Sheu et al. (2017) use a window-based technique to estimate for the condition of concept drift for each incoming new email.

We have evaluated our approach with a lexical simplification task use-case. The lexical simplification task contains complex word identification (*adaptive target identification*) and simpler candidate selection (*adaptive ranking*) components.

As far as our knowledge concerned, PAR4SEM is the first tool in the semantic and NLP research community, where adaptive technologies are integrated into a real-world application. PAR4SEM is open source[1] and the associated data collected for the lexical simplification use-case are publicly available. The live demo of PAR4SEM is available at `https://ltmaggie.informatik.uni-hamburg.de/par4sem`.

2 System Architecture of PAR4SEM

The PAR4SEM system consists of backend, frontend, and API components. The backend component is responsible for NLP related pre-processing, adaptive machine learning model generation, data storage, etc. The frontend component sends requests to the backend, highlights target units, presents candidate suggestions, sends user interaction to the database and so on. The API component transforms the frontend requests to the backend and returns responses to the frontend. Figure 1 shows the three main components of PAR4SEM and their interactions.

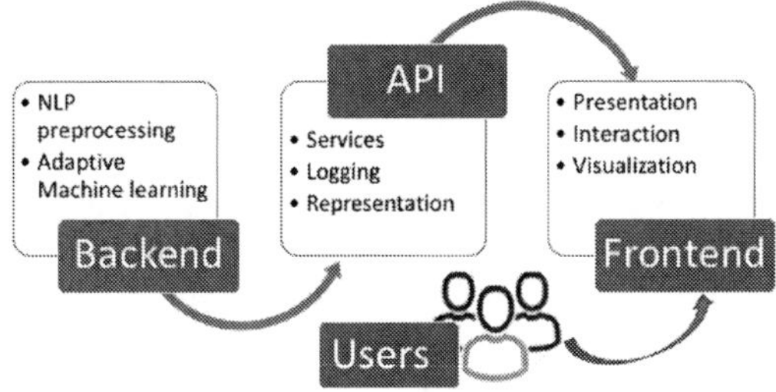

Figure 1: The main components of PAR4SEM

2.1 The Backend Component

The backend component consists of several modules. For the adaptive paraphrasing system, the first component is to identify possible target units (such as single words, phrases, or multi-word expressions). For our lexical simplification use-case, the target units identification component is instantiated with the datasets obtained from Yimam et al. (2017a,b, 2018). The adaptive target identification unit then keeps on learning from the usage data (when the user highlights portions of the text to get paraphrase candidate suggestions).

Once target units are marked or recognized (by the target unit identification system), the next step is to generate possible candidate suggestion for the target unit (paraphrase candidates). The candidate suggestion module includes candidate generation and candidate ranking sub-modules. Section 2.1.1 discusses our approaches to generating and ranking paraphrase candidates in detail.

2.1.1 Paraphrasing Resources

Paraphrase resources are datasets where target units are associated with a list of candidate units equivalent in meaning, possibly ranked by their meaning similarity. One can refer to the work of Ho et al. (2014) about the details on how paraphrase resources are produced, but we will briefly discuss the different types of paraphrase resources that are used in generating candidate suggestions for PAR4SEM.

PPDB 2.0: The Paraphrase Database (PPDB) is a collection of over 100 million paraphrases that was automatically constructed using a bilingual pivoting method. Recently released PPDB 2.0 includes improved paraphrase rankings, en-

---

[1] `https://uhh-lt.github.io/par4sem/`

tailment relations, style information, and distributional similarity measures for each paraphrase rule (Pavlick et al., 2015).

WordNet: We use WordNet synonyms, which are described as *words that denote the same concept and are interchangeable in many contexts* (Miller, 1995), to produce candidate suggestions for a given target unit.

Distributional Thesaurus – JoBimText: We use JoBimText, an open source platform for large-scale distributional semantics based on graph representations (Biemann and Riedl, 2013), to extract candidate suggestions that are semantically similar to the target unit.

Phrase2Vec: We train a Phrase2Vec model (Mikolov et al., 2013) using English Wikipedia and the AQUAINT corpus of English news text (Graff, 2002). Mikolov et al. (2013) pointed out that it is possible to extend the word based embeddings model to phrase-based model using a data-driven approach where each phrase or multi-word expressions are considered as individual tokens during the training process. We have used a total of 79,349 multiword expression and phrase resources as given in Yimam et al. (2016). We train the Phrase2Vec embeddings with 200 dimensions using skip-gram training and a window size of 5. We have retrieved the top 10 similar words to the target units as candidate suggestions.

2.1.2 Adaptive Machine Learning

PAR4SEM incorporates two adaptive machine learning models. The first one is used to identify target units (*target adaption*) in a text while the second one is used to rank candidate suggestions (*ranking adaption*). Both models make use of usage data as a training example. The target adaption model predicts target units based on the usage data (training examples) and sends them to the frontend component, which are then highlighted for the user. If the user replaced the highlighted target units, they are considered as positive training examples for the next iteration.

The ranking adaption model first generates candidate paraphrases using the paraphrase resource datasets (see Section 2.1.1). As all the candidates generated from the paraphrase resources might not be relevant to the target unit at a context, or as the number of candidates to be displayed might be excessively large (for example the PPDB 2.0 resource alone might produce hundreds of candidates for a target unit), we re-rank the candidate

suggestions using a learning-to-rank adaptive machine learning model. Figure 2 displays the process of the adaptive models while Figure 3 displays the pipeline (as a loop) used in the generations of the adaptive models.

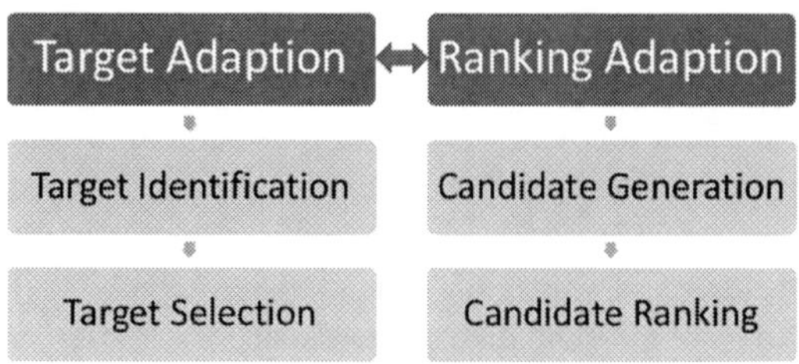

Figure 2: The main and sub-processes of target and ranking adaption components of PAR4SEM.

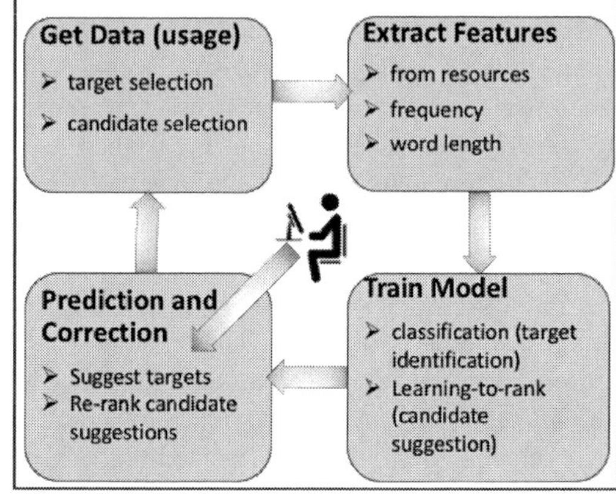

Figure 3: The loop for the generation of the adaptive models of PAR4SEM.

The whole process is iterative, interactive, and adaptive in a sense that the underlying models (both target adaption and ranking adaption) get usage data continuously from the user. The models get updated for each iteration, where n examples conducted in a batch mode without model update, and provide better suggestions (as target units or candidate suggestions) for the next iteration. The user interacts with the tool, probably accepting or rejecting tool suggestions, which is fed as a training signal for the next iterations model. Figure 4 shows the entirety of interactions, iterations, and adaptive processes of the PAR4SEM system. In the first iteration, the ranking is provided using a baseline language model while for the subsequent iterations, the usage data from the previous batches (t-1) is used to train a model that is used to rank the current batch (t).

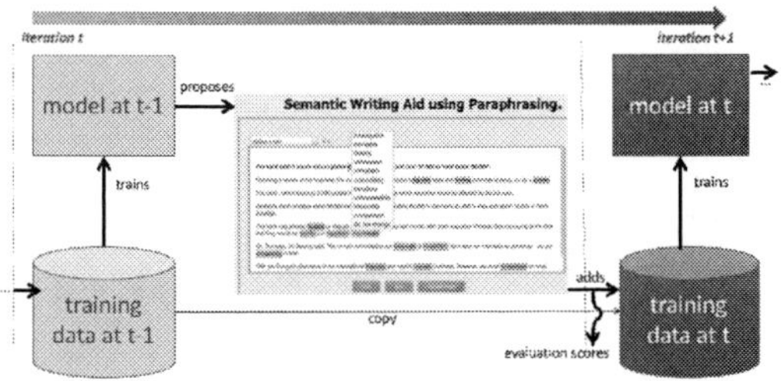

Figure 4: The iterative and adaptive interaction of PAR4SEM.

2.1.3 Backend Technologies

The backend components are fully implemented using the Java programming language. Text segmentation such as sentence splitting, tokenization, lemmatization, and parts of speech tagging is handled using the Apache OpenNLP[2] library.

For the target unit identification system, we have used *Datumbox*[3], a powerful open-source machine learning framework written in Java. We have used specifically the *Adaboost* classification algorithm.

For the ranking model, RankLib, which is the well-known library for the learning to rank algorithms from the Lemur[4] project is integrated. All the data related to PAR4SEM interactions (usage data, time, and user details) are stored in a MySQL database.

2.2 Frontend Components

The frontend component of PAR4SEM is designed where document composing with a semantic paraphrasing capability is integrated seamlessly. It is a web-based application allowing access either on a local installation or over the internet.

2.2.1 UI Components for Paraphrasing

The frontend part of PAR4SEM comprises different modules. The most important UI component is the text editing interface (Figure 5) that allows for adding text, highlighting target units, and displaying candidate suggestions. ① is the main area to compose (or paste) texts. The operational buttons (②) are used to perform some actions such as to undo and redo (composing, target unit highlighting, and paraphrase ranking), automatically highlighting target units, and clear the text area. Target

units are underlined in cyan color and highlighted in yellow background color as a link (③) which enables users to click, display, and select candidate suggestions for a replacement (④).

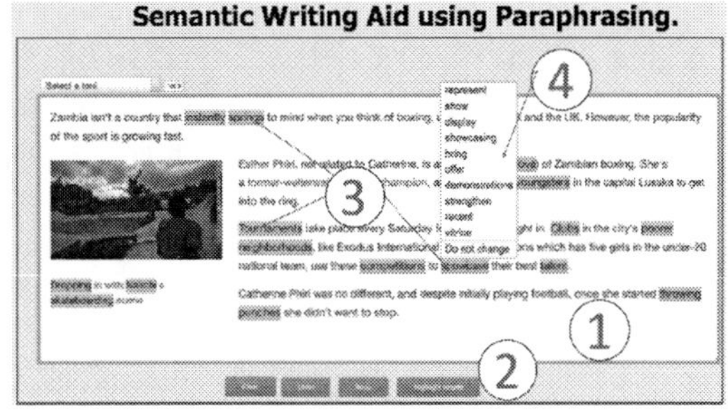

Figure 5: The PAR4SEM text editing component that is used to compose texts, highlight target units, and display candidate suggestions for the target units.

2.2.2 Frontend Technologies

The frontend components are implemented using HTML, CSS and JavaScript technologies. For the text highlighting and candidate suggestion replacement, the jQuery Spellchecker[5] module is slightly modified to incorporate the semantic highlighting (underline in cyan and a yellow background). The accompanied documentation and datasets of PAR4SEM[6] are hosted at Github pages.

2.3 RESTful API Component

Semantic technologies, those like PAR4SEM incorporates highly dynamic dimensions. One dimension is that the paraphrase resources can be varied depending on the need of the application. Another dimension is that the application can be in different languages. If the backend and the frontend technologies are highly coupled, it will be difficult to reuse the application for different languages, resources, and applications. To solve this problem, we have developed PAR4SEM using a RESTful API (aka. microservices) as a middleware between the backend and the frontend components.

The API component consumes requests (getting target units and candidate suggestions) or resources (saving usage data such as selection of new target units, user's preference for candidate ranking, user and machine information) from the frontend and transfers them to the backend. The

---

[2]https://opennlp.apache.org/

[3]http://www.datumbox.com/

[4]https://sourceforge.net/p/lemur/wiki/RankLib/

[5]http://jquery-spellchecker.badsyntax.co/

[6]https://uhh-lt.github.io/par4sem/

backend component translates the requests or resources and handles them accordingly. Spring Boot[7] is used to implement the API services.

2.3.1 Installation and Deployment

As PAR4SEM consists of different technologies, machine learning setups, resources, and configurations, we opted to provide a Docker-based installation and deployment options. While it is possible to fully install the tool on ones own server, we also provide an API access for the whole backend services. This allows users to quickly and easily install the frontend component and relay on our API service calls for the rest of the communications.

3 Use-case – Adaptive Text Simplification using Crowdsourcing

An appropriate use case for adaptive paraphrasing is lexical text simplification. Lexical simplification aims to reduce the complexity of texts due to difficult words or phrases in the text (Siddharthan, Advaith, 2014). We have used PAR4SEM particularly for text simplification task with an emphasis of making texts accessible for language learners, children, and people with disabilities.

We conducted the experiment by integrating the tool into the Amazon Mechanical Turk (MTurk)[8] crowdsourcing and employ workers to simplify texts using the integrated adaptive paraphrasing system. While PAR4SEM is installed and run on our local server, we make use of the MTurk's external HIT functionality to embed and conduct the text simplification experiment. Once workers have access to our embedded tool in the MTurk browser, they will be redirected to our local installation to complete the simplification task. Figure 5 shows the PAR4SEM user interface to perform text simplification task by the workers while Figure 7 shows the instructions as they appeared inside the MTurk's browser.

We asked workers to simplify the text for the target readers, by using the embedded paraphrasing system. Difficult words or phrases are automatically highlighted so that workers can click and see possible candidate suggestions. The experiment was conducted over 9 iterations, where the ranking model is updated using the training dataset (usage data) collected in the previous iterations. The first iteration does not use ranking model but

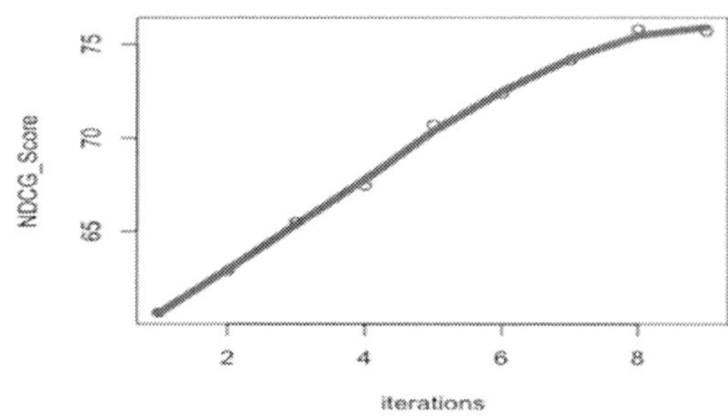

Figure 6: Learning curve showing the increase of NDCG@10 score over 9 iterations.

candidates are presented using a default language-model-based ranking. In (Yimam and Biemann, 2018) we have shown that the adaptive paraphrasing system adopts very well to text simplification, improving the NDCG (Wang et al., 2013) score from 60.66 to 75.70. Figure 6 shows the learning curve for the different iterations conducted in the experiment.

4 Conclusion

In this paper, we have described PAR4SEM, a semantic writing aid tool based on an embedded adaptive paraphrasing system. Unlike most annotation tools, which are developed exclusively to collect training examples for machine learning applications, PAR4SEM implements an adaptive paraphrasing system where training examples are obtained from usage data.

To the best of our knowledge, PAR4SEM is the first of its kind where machine learning models are improved based on usage data and user feedback (correction of suggestions) for semantic applications. PAR4SEM is used in a text simplification use-case. Evaluation of the system showed that the adaptive paraphrasing system for text simplification successfully adapted to the target task in a small number of iterations.

For future work, we would like to evaluate the system in an open task setting where users can paraphrase resp. simplify self-provided texts, and explore how groups of similar users can be utilized to provide adaptations for their respective sub-goals.

References

Chris Biemann and Martin Riedl. 2013. Text: Now in 2D! a framework for lexical expansion with contextual similarity. *JLM*, 1(1):55–95.

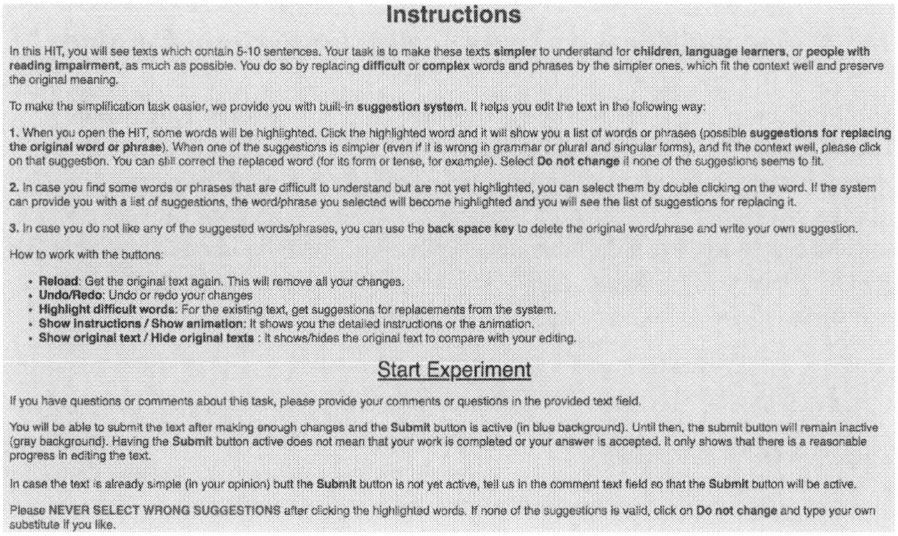

Figure 7: The instructions for the text simplification task using PAR4SEM

Michael Denkowski, Alon Lavie, Isabel Lacruz, and Chris Dyer. 2014. Real Time Adaptive Machine Translation for Post-Editing with cdec and TransCenter . In *Proc. EACL 2014 Workshop on HCAT*, pages 72–77, Gothenburg, Sweden.

David Graff. 2002. The AQUAINT Corpus of English News Text LDC2002T31. In *Web Download. Philadelphia: Linguistic Data Consortium.*

ChukFong Ho, Masrah Azrifah Azmi Murad, Shyamala Doraisamy, and Rabiah Abdul Kadir. 2014. Extracting lexical and phrasal paraphrases: a review of the literature. *Artificial Intelligence Review*, 42(4):851–894.

Tomas Mikolov, Ilya Sutskever, Kai Chen, Gregory S. Corrado, and Jeffrey Dean. 2013. Distributed Representations of Words and Phrases and their Compositionality. In *ANIPS/ACNIPS*, pages 3111–3119, Stateline, Nevada, USA.

George A. Miller. 1995. WordNet: A Lexical Database for English. *Commun. ACM*, 38(11):39–41.

Ellie Pavlick, Pushpendre Rastogi, Juri Ganitkevitch, Benjamin Van Durme, and Chris Callison-Burch. 2015. PPDB 2.0: Better paraphrase ranking, fine-grained entailment relations, word embeddings, and style classification. In *Proc. ACL/IJCNLP*, pages 425–430, Beijing, China.

Jyh-Jian Sheu, Ko-Tsung Chu, Nien-Feng Li, and Cheng-Chi Lee. 2017. An efficient incremental learning mechanism for tracking concept drift in spam filtering. *PLOS ONE*, 12(2):1–17.

Siddharthan, Advaith. 2014. A survey of research on text simplification. *IJAL*, 165(2):259–298.

Yining Wang, Liwei Wang, Yuanzhi Li, Di He, Wei Chen, and Tie-Yan Liu. 2013. A Theoretical Analysis of Normalized Discounted Cumulative Gain (NDCG) Ranking Measures. In *MLR*, pages 25–54, Princeton, New Jersey, USA.

Seid Muhie Yimam and Chris Biemann. 2018. Par4sim – adaptive paraphrasing for text simplification. In *Proc. of COLING 2018*, pages 331–342, Santa Fe, New Mexico, USA.

Seid Muhie Yimam, Chris Biemann, Shervin Malmasi, Gustavo Paetzold, Lucia Specia, Sanja Štajner, Anaïs Tack, and Marcos Zampieri. 2018. A report on the complex word identification shared task 2018. In *Proc. of the 13th BEA*, pages 66–78, New Orleans, Louisiana.

Seid Muhie Yimam, Héctor Martínez Alonso, Martin Riedl, and Chris Biemann. 2016. Learning Paraphrasing for Multiword Expressions. In *Proc. of the 12th Workshop on MWE*, pages 1–10, Berlin, Germany.

Seid Muhie Yimam, Sanja Štajner, Martin Riedl, and Chris Biemann. 2017a. CWIG3G2 - Complex Word Identification Task across Three Text Genres and Two User Groups. In *Proc. IJCNLP-17*, pages 401–407, Taipei, Taiwan.

Seid Muhie Yimam, Sanja Štajner, Martin Riedl, and Chris Biemann. 2017b. Multilingual and cross-lingual complex word identification. In *PROC. of RANLP*, pages 813–822, Varna, Bulgaria. INCOMA Ltd.

Dani Yogatama, Chong Wang, Bryan R. Routledge, Noah A. Smith, and Eric P. Xing. 2014. Dynamic language models for streaming text. *TACL*, 2:181–192.

Juman++: A Morphological Analysis Toolkit for Scriptio Continua

Arseny Tolmachev
Graduate School
of Informatics
Kyoto University
Yoshida-honmachi, Sakyo-ku
Kyoto, 606-8501, Japan
`arseny@kotonoha.ws`

Daisuke Kawahara
Graduate School
of Informatics
Kyoto University
Yoshida-honmachi, Sakyo-ku
Kyoto, 606-8501, Japan
`dk@i.kyoto-u.ac.jp`

Sadao Kurohashi
Graduate School
of Informatics
Kyoto University
Yoshida-honmachi, Sakyo-ku
Kyoto, 606-8501, Japan
`kuro@i.kyoto-u.ac.jp`

Abstract

We present a three-part toolkit for developing morphological analyzers for languages without natural word boundaries. The first part is a lattice-based morphological analysis library that uses a combination of linear and recurrent neural net language models for analysis. The other parts are a tool for exposing problems in the trained model and a partial annotation tool. Our morphological analyzer for Japanese achieves new SOTA on Jumandic-based corpora while being 250 times faster than the previous one. We also perform a small experiment and quantitive analysis of using our toolkit.

1 Introduction

Processing *scriptio continua* natural languages, or languages without natural word boundaries, like space in English, frequently requires performing tokenization into morphemes in the natural language processing pipeline. Usually, tokenization is done together with part of speech (POS) tagging, pronunciation estimation or other subtasks. This process is usually referred to as morphological analysis.

A morphological analyzer is useful from a practical point of view only if it is fast as well as highly accurate in its analysis. Because morphological analysis is very important to languages without word boundaries (like Japanese), there already exist many approaches and tools for performing it. Morphological analyzers usually use two kinds of resources: a dictionary which defines possible morphemes and an annotated corpus which is used to train an analysis model for connecting morphemes together.

Modern morphological analyzers achieve high accuracy (a segmentation F1 score of $> .99$ for Japanese) on established domains like newspaper. However, when using them on out-of-domain or open domain data (like web texts) the accuracy decreases, and it is difficult to improve that accuracy without creating costly annotations by trained experts.

The Juman++ Japanese morphological analyzer (Morita et al. 2015, referred to also as V1), which uses a combination of a linear model and a neural network-based language model (RNNLM) to compute a semantic plausibility of a segmentation. Juman++ has achieved state-of-the-art analysis accuracy on Jumandic (the JUMAN dictionary and segmentation standard (Kurohashi and Kawahara, 2012)) based corpora, and drastically reduced the number of intolerable analysis errors. Unfortunately, its execution speed was extremely slow and this has limited the practical usage of Juman++.

We have developed a morphological analysis toolkit consisting of three components: a morphological analyzer and two support tools which help with the development of analysis models. The analyzer is a complete rewrite of core ideas of Juman++, released as Juman++ V2[1] (Tolmachev and Kurohashi, 2018). Our reimplementation is **more than 250 times faster** than V1, reaching the speed of traditional analyzers, at the same time achieving better accuracy than V1.

We have also developed a tool which uses *raw, unannotated data* and gives an insight into problematic dictionary and grammar points, together with finding sentences which contain situations not present in training data by exploiting differences in the analysis that arise from using different beam search configurations. It is bundled with V2. Also, we have developed a partial annotation tool which makes it easy to review problematic sentences and create partial annotation data for improving the analysis[2]. To the best of our knowl-

---

[1] `https://github.com/ku-nlp/jumanpp`
[2] `https://github.com/eiennohito/nlp-tools-demo`

Proceedings of the 2018 Conference on Empirical Methods in Natural Language Processing (System Demonstrations), pages 54–59
Brussels, Belgium, October 31–November 4, 2018. ©2018 Association for Computational Linguistics

edge, a similar set of tools has never been developed before. Juman++ V2 and the development tools are language and segmentation standard independent and are released under the permissive Apache 2 open source license.

2 Related Work

KyTea (Neubig et al., 2011) is a similar tool that can perform morphological analysis for languages with the continuous script. It can also be trained using partial annotation data and output point-wise confidence scores for the analysis result which were used for creating partially annotated data in an active learning scenario. Still, by using a point-wise approach and estimating auxiliary tags (like POS) after computing segmentation, KyTea trades off accuracy for simplicity. Juman++ is faster, has better accuracy, does tag estimation jointly with segmentation, uses an online learning approach and can use longer contexts in forms of RNNLM and trigram features.

3 Juman++ Morphological Analyzer V2

Juman++ V2 is implemented with modern C++, with the intention to be used not only as a program, but also as an embeddable library, usable in a multi-threaded environment. Additionally, V2 is not hardwired to a particular dictionary and can use partially annotated data for training.

Juman++ is a lattice-based analyzer. For an input sentence, it looks up all possible morphemes from a dictionary, makes a lattice from them, and assigns a score s to each path going through the lattice. The path with the highest score is considered to be the analysis result. The score s consists of two components: a feature-based linear model score s^l and an RNNLM score s^{RNN}, which are combined as

$$s = s^l + \alpha(s^{\mathrm{RNN}} + \beta),$$

where α and β are scale and bias hyperparameters respectively. The RNNLM score is a log-probability score from the language model.

The linear score is defined as

$$s^l = \sum_{t \in p} \mathbf{f}(t, p)\mathbf{w},$$

where $\mathbf{f}(t, p)$ is an indicator vector which contains features, extracted for a node t in a path p, and $\mathbf{w}$ is a model weight vector. Features use dictionary information of the node t and at most two previous nodes and their surface surroundings. Weights are learned using the Soft Confidence Weighted algorithm (Wang et al., 2016).

In practice, it is intractable to compute scores for all paths through the lattice. Instead, we use beam search. Additionally, because the RNNLM is computationally-heavy, we compute the RNN score only for the paths which remain in the beam of the special end-of-string token. The overall design is to cut off improbable analysis results with a simple model and then re-rank by RNNLM.

3.1 Search Space Trimming

One of important optimizations of V2 is the reduction of search space by changing the beam search operation mode. Because the Juman++ linear model uses up to 3-gram features, the beam searching procedure has to deal with combinatorial explosion caused by higher order n-gram features. V1 uses *local beams* of width j, meaning that *each lattice node* keeps j incoming paths with top scores. The rest of the paths are discarded. The problem is that paths are discarded after evaluating their scores and the number of evaluations is still large. Most of the sentences have several boundaries which have 20-30 both left and right nodes. Because almost all these paths are useless, we do not want to consider them in the analysis at all.

The first improvement is to use only paths ending on left nodes with top k scores instead of using all left paths. Connections for the remaining paths are not considered. We refer to this process as *left global beam*. The application of the left global beam is shown in Figure 1a.

The second improvement is the *right global beam*, displayed in Figure 1b. As the first substep, we use top $l(\le k)$ paths ending at left nodes to compute scores of right nodes. After that, we evaluate the connections from the remaining $k - l$ left paths to the top-scored m right nodes. The rest of connections are not considered.

We call search using local beams as *full beam*. In comparison to that, a combination of left and right global beams is referred to as *trimmed beam* because it uses significantly smaller search space.

3.2 Partially Annotated Data

Juman++ V2 supports both training with partially annotated data and soft-constrainted analysis using partially annotated data as constraints.

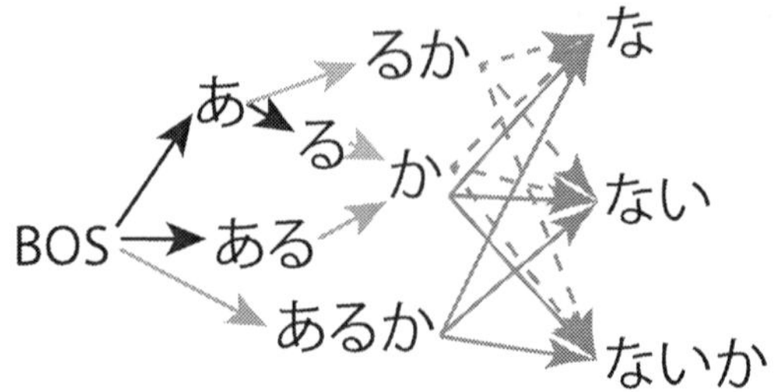

(a) Left global beam. $k = 2$. Top left paths are displayed in orange. Remaining left paths are displayed in solid gray. Non-considered paths are displayed as dashed blue arrows. Considered paths are solid blue.

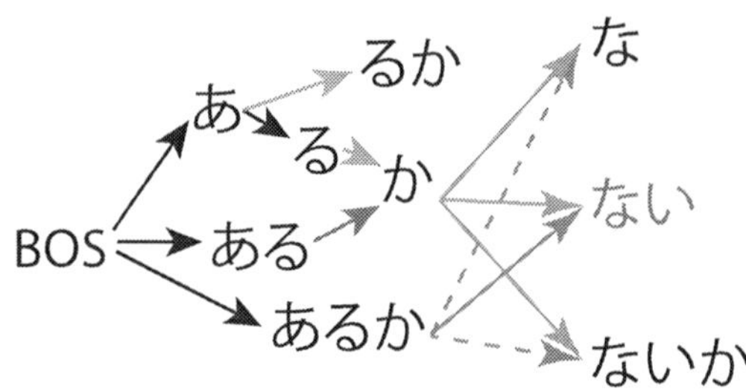

(b) Right global beam. $l = m = 1$. A top left path and a top right node are displayed in green. Orange paths via the boundary were used for scoring right nodes. Solid blue path via the boundary connects the remaining $k - l$ top left paths the top right nodes. Dashed blue paths are not considered.

Figure 1: Trimming the search space using the global beams

There exist three types of annotations: boundary (break here), non-boundary (no break here) and *word*. A word annotation means that a sequence of characters must not contain boundaries inside it; additionally, the word can have tags attached to it, meaning that the analysis result also must have these tags.

For training, we need to provide sets of correct and incorrect features for the training algorithm. A feature computed from the correct path would be correct, and a feature containing any lattice node that is not contained in the correct path would be incorrect.

When using the fully annotated data, there exist only a single correct path. However, for partial annotated data, there could exist multiple allowed paths through the lattice. Because of this, when training using the partially annotated data, we use several highly-scored candidates which do not violate annotation requirements instead of the only correct path as in the case of fully annotated data.

3.3 Performance Comparison

We compare both speed and accuracy of five different Japanese morphological analyzers: JUMAN[3], MeCab[4], KyTea, Juman++ (V1) and Juman++ (V2). For both versions of Juman++ we report results both using and not using RNNLM (noRNN).

Analysis speed We used a desktop computer with Intel i7-6850K CPU, 64GB of RAM and Ubuntu 16.04 Linux for analysis speed comparison. The models were trained from scratch us-

Analyzer	Speed (sents/s)	Ratio
JUMAN	8,802	1.00
MeCab	52,410	0.17
KyTea (Jumandic)	4,892	1.79
KyTea (Unidic)	1,995	4.41
V1 noRNN	27	328.82
V1 RNN	16	535.72
V2 noRNN	7,422	1.18
V2 RNN	4,803	1.83

Table 1: Morphological analysis speed comparison

ing the same Juman++ dictionary, the Kyoto University[5] (KU) and KWDLC[6] corpora for all morphological analyzers except JUMAN, which is not trainable. For KyTea we also report the throughput using the Unidic-based models, which are available for download from the KyTea website. A Jumandic-based model for KyTea was learned using default parameters. V1 uses the full beam of width $j = 5$. V2 uses trimmed beam with parameters $j = 5, k = 6, l = 1, m = 5$. All analyzers were using only a single thread.

Table 1 shows the analysis speed of the considered morphological analyzers and speed ratio as compared to JUMAN. The speed was measured by analyzing 50k sentences from a web corpus. Each analyzer was launched five times and the median time was used for computing the analysis speed. V2 noRNN is only 20% slower than JUMAN while having a considerably complex model. V2

[3] http://nlp.ist.i.kyoto-u.ac.jp/EN/index.php?JUMAN

[4] http://taku910.github.io/mecab/

[5] http://nlp.ist.i.kyoto-u.ac.jp/EN/index.php?Kyoto University Text Corpus

[6] http://nlp.ist.i.kyoto-u.ac.jp/EN/index.php?KWDLC

Analyzer	KU		KWDLC	
	Seg	+Pos	Seg	+Pos
JUMAN	98.41	97.20	98.10	97.01
KyTea	99.12	98.16	98.00	96.75
MeCab	99.14	98.58	98.28	97.61
V1 noRNN	98.94	98.42	97.66	96.95
V1 RNN	99.38	98.95	98.41	97.87
V2 noRNN	99.44	98.98	98.44	97.79
V2 RNN	**99.51**	**99.05**	**98.67**	**98.02**

Table 2: F1 scores of morphological analyzers on Jumandic-based corpora. Seg is segmentation; +Pos is correctly guessing the POS-tags after segmentation.

RNN has 1.8 times the execution speed of JUMAN and is more than 250 times faster than V1.

Accuracy Table 2 shows F1 scores for both the KU and KWDLC corpora. A concatenation of training sections of both corpora was used to train a combined model; the reported scores are for the test sections. MeCab and V2 have hyperparameters optimized using Spearmint (Snoek et al., 2012).

V2 RNN achieves a higher F1 score than the previous SOTA of V1 RNN. Even the scores of V2 noRNN are higher in some cases than those of V1 RNN. Note that the scores of V1 noRNN are one of the lowest, and thus we hypothesize that the number of training iterations of the V1 linear model was not sufficient. However, it was difficult to increase it because of very slow analysis speed.

With V2, we could find an optimal number of iterations for learning the linear model with the best accuracy. The other reason for the improved accuracy for V2 is that it uses surface character and character type features.

4 Beam Search Diffs as Active Learning

We compared the accuracy of the trimmed beam search to the full configuration in the in-domain setting. For this experiment, we trained the model using 1 pass of full beam search followed by 4 passes of trimmed beam search for the optimal number of iterations for different trimmed beam parameters. Figure 2 shows the F1 score average on 10-fold cross-validation over the KU corpus. It can be seen that the accuracy of the models does not fall even if using very small global beam sizes. Nevertheless, we noticed that there exist sentences

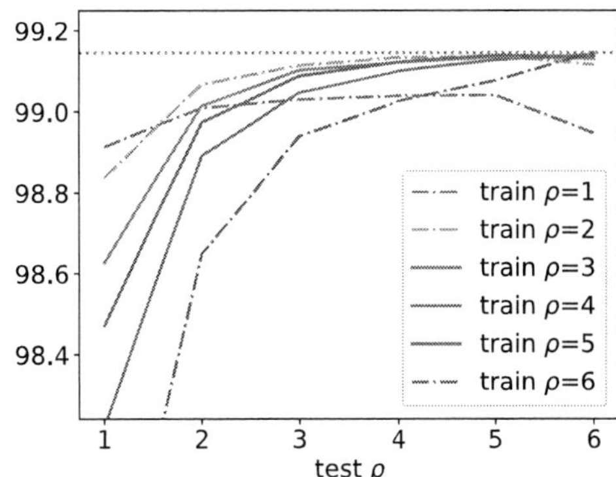

Figure 2: Cross-validation test F1 score average on the KU corpus for POS tags when using different global beam parameters $k = m = \rho, l = 1$. Red dotted line at the top is F1 score of a model without global beams.

when the full and trimmed search configurations do not agree on the top-scoring path when analyzing random web sentences and produce diffs.

To get a better picture, we analyzed a large number of sentences from a raw Japanese corpus, crawled from the web. On average, 0.38% (1969/510595) of sentences were diffs, a relatively small number. In contrary to our expectations, the full beam analysis was correct only in around 50% of the cases. The rest of sentences had both of analysis variants incorrect either because the dictionary did not support the language phenomena (20%) or lack of coverage by the training data (10%); the trimmed beam analysis was the correct one (10%); and other situations that were difficult to decide or impossible to analyze correctly like typos.

Based on these insights, we believe that the diffs can be treated as a result of selection by the Query-by-Committee active learning algorithm with two committee members (Settles and Craven, 2008; Seung et al., 1992). We think that diffs actually reveal problems not only with a training corpus (the goal of active learning) but also with an analysis dictionary as well. Note that we are using exactly the same model in both beam modes and the only difference is beam configuration. So, a diff can form only if trimmed beam ranking was not learned correctly either because the model capacity was not enough, features were not strong enough, or the situation was not present in the training data.

When the beam size at training is very small,

the model does not learn to rank for the trimmed case well enough, lowering the accuracy on larger beam sizes. Increasing the beam size above three makes the trimmed beam score indistinguishable with the full beam. On the other hand, the model loses accuracy on smaller beam sizes at test time, because the trimmed ranking fails in those situations. Thus we believe that the model capacity and the feature set should be enough to capture the ranking and the diffs are caused mostly by the lack of training data. The fact that the diffs include situations when it is *impossible* to produce the correct analysis at all, namely lack of dictionary words and typos, confirms our belief.

On the other hand, we also believe that the corrections of places pointed by diffs are not going to significantly improve benchmark scores exactly because of the same reason. The benchmark corpus will usually be relatively in-domain and not contain dictionary or grammar problems, because they would be fixed when creating the corpus. So we hope that this method would be useful to improve *real world* morphological analysis accuracy and for domain adaptation.

5   Partial Annotation Tool

Because the diffs must be reviewed by human annotators to be useful as training data, we have developed a partial annotation tool based on a simple idea: to allow annotators to select a correct analysis from two candidates. The output of the tool can be used as partially annotated training data.

5.1   Tool Description

The tool is a web application, implemented in Scala. As an input, it uses sentences with some parts being diffs, which are produced by a tool bundled with the Juman++ V2 distribution. For each sentence, annotators are asked to select a correct variant, correct an analysis if both are not correct, or report if it is impossible to select a correct analysis or there is a problem with the sentence itself.

A sentence diff view is shown in Figure 3. The annotation targets are diffs: we want annotators to choose a correct analysis from the possible variants, which are displayed side-by-side. A sentence can contain more than one annotation target in general and each variant can contain more than one morpheme. Non-diff parts form contexts and are displayed in grey. The tool shows diffs in an

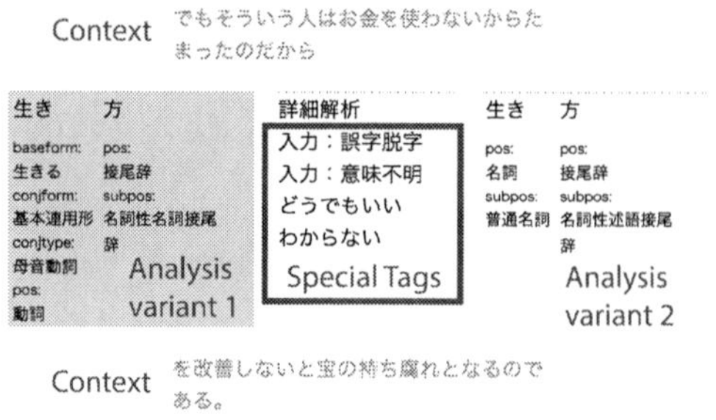

Figure 3: Annotation tool: diff view. UI explanations are in blue. Variant 1 is selected.

unspecified order. In the shown example, the left variant is selected as the correct one. The area in the middle of the target section contains a button which activates an interactive analysis mode and buttons for assigning special tags in the case when the mistake in the target part is due to a typo or a phenomenon that we do not want to support in the automatic analysis, such as netspeak.

In the case when both analyses are incorrect, an annotator can use the interactive analysis mode, shown in Figure 4, which performs constrained morphological analysis. Constraint nodes are shown in blue. A full beam analysis becomes initial constraints.

The interactive analysis mode uses lattice information from the Juman++ to provide morpheme candidates for constraints. It is possible to show either all morphemes containing a focused character or morphemes spanning exactly selected characters. The corrected analysis replaces the closest diff variant which was not selected by any annotator yet, or creates a new variant if replacing is not possible. Finally, if there are no variants, annotators can select a character span and report that it is impossible to choose a correct morpheme in this sentence for that span.

5.2   Annotation Experiment

We performed a small scale annotation experiment using the developed annotation tool. For the experiment, we trained a model on the concatenation of the training and test data from both benchmark corpora and the copy of data augmented by removing "ga", "ha" and "wo" case markers, which are often omitted in the spoken language so that the model would be more robust to case marker omission. Using this model we have collected sentences which contained diffs, as described in Sec-

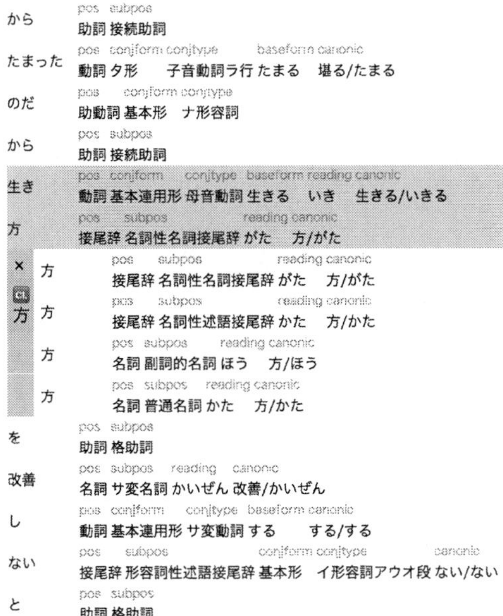

Figure 4: Annotation tool: interactive analysis. Constraint nodes background is blue. Other analysis variants for the last constraint node are displayed after the gray indent. The "CL" button removes a constraint.

tion 4. We asked two annotators to work for three hours each.

During the allocated time, the two annotators could review 111 and 112 sentences each. Both the annotators started annotating rather slowly, while gradually increasing their annotation speed. An inter-annotator agreement was 0.819. The annotators have selected at least one of analysis candidates in most (82%) cases; the rest were special tags.

We also checked sentences where the annotators did not agree on the correct analysis, but both the annotations were analysis results (9 in total). Each of them was difficult to decide even for us. We believe that the relatively large number of sentences which caused annotators to spend a long time on annotation is caused by the fact that the diff extractor selects difficult cases.

6 Conclusion and Future Work

We present Juman++ V2: a morphological analysis and tokenization toolkit for languages with the continuous script. Our current implementation focuses on Japanese and the Jumandic-based segmentation standard, but the core library is language independent. Juman++ V2 achieves a new state-of-the-art accuracy for both the Kyoto University and KWDLC corpora while drastically reducing the analysis time compared to Juman++ V1. Juman++ V2 can be used as a library and can use both fully and partially annotated data for training.

We also release a morphological analysis developer tool which reveals problematic places of a dictionary and segmentation standard using only unannotated data by comparing the analysis results in the two different beam search configurations. Also, we release the partial annotation tool for easily viewing and fixing these problems.

We plan to create a Unidic version of Juman++ V2 and use it to annotate readings of the Jumandic-based corpora, which are currently rather arbitrary, enabling the Jumandic-based models to estimate correct readings as well. We also plan to continue collecting partially annotated data and release a partially annotated web corpus.

References

Sadao Kurohashi and Daisuke Kawahara. 2012. Japanese morphological analysis system juman 7.0 users manual. *Kyoto University*.

Hajime Morita, Daisuke Kawahara, and Sadao Kurohashi. 2015. Morphological analysis for unsegmented languages using recurrent neural network language model. In *EMNLP*, pages 2292–2297.

Graham Neubig, Yosuke Nakata, and Shinsuke Mori. 2011. Pointwise prediction for robust, adaptable japanese morphological analysis. In *ACL*, pages 529–533.

Burr Settles and Mark Craven. 2008. An analysis of active learning strategies for sequence labeling tasks. In *EMNLP*, pages 1070–1079, Honolulu, Hawaii. Association for Computational Linguistics.

H. S. Seung, M. Opper, and H. Sompolinsky. 1992. Query by committee. In *Proceedings of the Fifth Annual Workshop on Computational Learning Theory*, COLT '92, pages 287–294, New York, NY, USA. ACM.

Jasper Snoek, Hugo Larochelle, and Ryan P Adams. 2012. Practical bayesian optimization of machine learning algorithms. In *NIPS*, pages 2951–2959.

Arseny Tolmachev and Sadao Kurohashi. 2018. Juman++ v2: A practical and modern morphological analyzer. In *ANLP*, pages 917–920, Okayama, Japan.

Jialei Wang, Peilin Zhao, and Steven CH Hoi. 2016. Soft confidence-weighted learning. *ACM TIST*, 8(1):15.

Visualization of the Topic Space of Argument Search Results in args.me

Yamen Ajjour [*]   Henning Wachsmuth [**]   Dora Kiesel [*]   Patrick Riehmann [*]
Fan Fan [*]   Giuliano Castiglia [*]   Rosemary Adejoh [*]   Bernd Fröhlich [*]   Benno Stein [*]
[*] Bauhaus-Universität Weimar, Weimar, Germany, `<first>.<last>@uni-weimar.de`
[**] Paderborn University, Paderborn, Germany, `henningw@upb.de`

Abstract

In times of fake news and alternative facts, pro and con arguments on controversial topics are of increasing importance. Recently, we presented *args.me* as the first search engine for arguments on the web. In its initial version, args.me ranked arguments solely by their relevance to a topic queried for, making it hard to learn about the diverse topical aspects covered by the search results. To tackle this shortcoming, we integrated a visualization interface for result exploration in args.me that provides an instant overview of the main aspects in a barycentric coordinate system. This *topic space* is generated ad-hoc from controversial issues on Wikipedia and argument-specific LDA models. In two case studies, we demonstrate how individual arguments can be found easily through interactions with the visualization, such as highlighting and filtering.

1 Introduction

For many controversial topics in life and politics, people disagree on what is the right stance towards them, be it the need for feminism, the influence of religion, or the assassination of dictators. Stance is affected by the subjective assessment and weighting of pro and con arguments on the diverse aspects of a topic (Kock, 2007). Building stance in a self-determined manner is getting harder and harder in times of fake news and alternative facts, due to the unclear reliability of many sources and their bias in stance and covered aspects. This was our societal motivation for the development of the first dedicated argument search engine, *args.me*.[1]

args.me allows querying for arbitrary controversial topics. As search results, it opposes pro and con arguments from the web, ranked by their computed relevance to the topic. args.me is non-commercial and aims to avoid bias towards either stance. In

(Wachsmuth et al., 2017b), we introduced the software framework and the initial argument index underlying args.me as well as its basic user interface.

In its first version, args.me presented arguments in textual form with linked sources, similar to the web page snippets of conventional search engines, but with color-encoded stance. Examples are given below in Figures 1 and 2. This is adequate for comprehending those arguments deemed most relevant. Unlike for many general information needs (Croft et al., 2009), however, reading the top results is not enough for building an informed stance. Rather, diverse aspects of a controversial topic need to be explored. In our recent study with 97 international users, *aspect coverage* was seen as the second most important ranking criterion — after *source reliability* but before *recency*, *user ratings*, and others.[2] A simple relevance ranking of possibly thousands of arguments provides weak support in that regard.

This paper shows a novel way of presenting argument search results, which we designed and integrated into args.me to support a rapid exploration of the aspects of a topic. In particular, we visualize this *topic space* in a barycentric coordinate system (Riehmann et al., 2018), representing the distribution of pro and con arguments over the main covered aspects (see Figure 3). Possible aspects were derived offline from the Wikipedia list of controversial issues[3] as well as from LDA topic models built based on the 291k arguments in our index, whereas the aspects actually visualized are derived ad-hoc from the search results. Through interactions with the visualization, a user can easily highlight and filter arguments on the aspects of interest. In two case studies, we demonstrate how the visualization speeds up argument search notably.

---

[1] Also known as just *args*, found at: `https://args.me`

[2] The user study, also including other questions related to argument search, is going to be published in another venue.

[3] Issue list: `https://en.wikipedia.org/wiki/Wikipedia:List_of_controversial_issues`

Proceedings of the 2018 Conference on Empirical Methods in Natural Language Processing (System Demonstrations), pages 60–65
Brussels, Belgium, October 31–November 4, 2018. ©2018 Association for Computational Linguistics

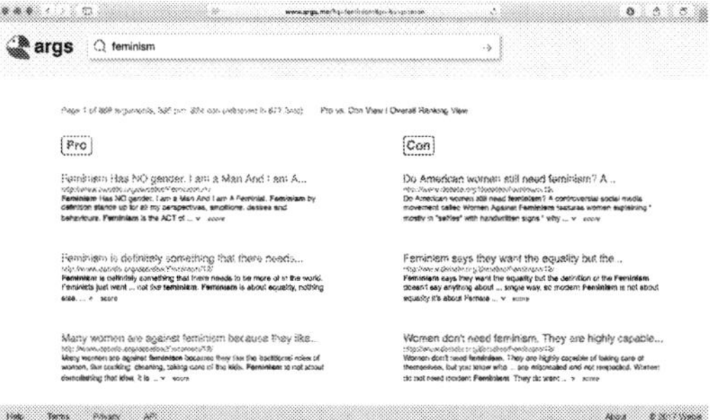

Figure 1: The *pro vs. con view* of args.me, showing the argument search results for the query "feminism".

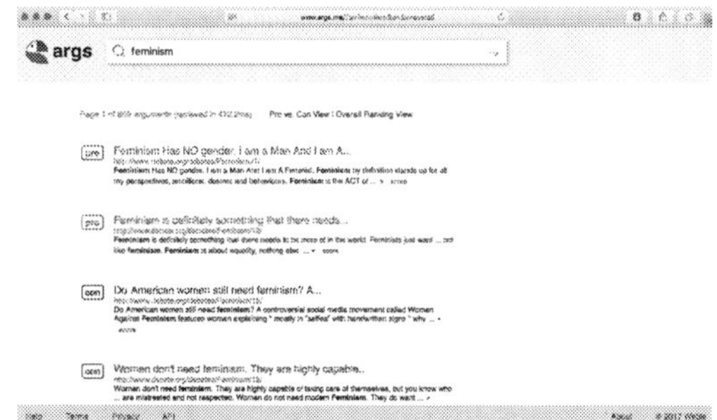

Figure 2: The *overall ranking view* of the initial version of args.me, showing results for the query "feminism".

2 Related Work

Different systems to visually create and analyze arguments have been introduced in the past. Some of their visualizations serve as a mind map to support ongoing discussions, such as *gIBIS* (Conklin and Begeman, 1988), *Belvedere* (Suthers et al., 1995), *ArgVis* (Karamanou et al., 2011), *Dicode* (Tzagarakis and Karacapilidis, 2013), and *Debate-Graph* (Baldwin and Price, 2018). Others allow for evaluating the structure and schemes of arguments, such as *Araucaria* (Reed and Rowe, 2004), *Rationale* (van Gelder, 2007), *ArgueApply* (Pührer, 2017), *Argunet* (Betz et al., 2018), and *Truthmapping* (Truthmapping, 2018).

To support achieving consensus in a discussion, *SEAS* (Lowrance et al., 2000), *VUE* (Baroni et al., 2015), and *Dialectic Map* (Niu, 2016) provide a combination of automatic argument analysis and visual argument summaries. With similar intentions, *Lexical Episode Plots* (Gold et al., 2015), *ConToVi* (El-Assady et al., 2016), *NEREx* (El-Assady et al., 2017), and Jentner et al. (2017) visualize specific aspects of transcribed discussions.

All these works focus on single arguments or the set of arguments within a single debate or text. In contrast, we present a visualization that summarizes arguments from many different texts. Unlike in (Wachsmuth et al., 2017a), where we illustrated *structural* argumentation patterns in the texts of a corpus, here we target the *content* of arguments. As the above-mentioned system ConToVi, we visualize the topic space covered by a set of arguments. While ConToVi provides insights into the flow of aspects during the discussion of a controversial topic, our visualization aims to make arguments on specific aspects easily findable. Moreover, we allow arguments to cover a weighted distribution of multiple aspects rather than only a single aspect.

3 Argument Search with args.me

As presented in (Wachsmuth et al., 2017b), the initial version of args.me follows approved concepts of conventional search engines (such as *Google* or *Bing*), but it adapts them to the specific goals of argument search. Via the interface of args.me, users can enter free text queries on controversial topics, such as "feminism" and "assassination of dictators". While conventional search engines return links to web pages along with short textual excerpts as results, args.me directly returns all arguments found to be relevant, linked to their source web pages.

Originally, args.me provided two views that displayed the found arguments in a textual result list with color-encoded stance, as shown in Figures 1 and 2: a *pro vs. con view* that opposes the most relevant pros and cons, and an *overall ranking view* that ranks all arguments by their relevance irrespective of stance. A fundamental question in this regard is what arguments are actually deemed *most relevant*? Argument search implies specific ranking criteria, such as recency, perceived quality, aspect coverage, and source reliability. Assessing these criteria is all but trivial and partly unsolved. In its current state (mid 2018), args.me therefore still relies on standard information retrieval measures (Robertson and Zaragoza, 2009), i.e., it ranks arguments higher the more they match the words in the query.

So far, however, for many queries the top-ranked arguments neither appear to be the strongest on the given topic, nor do they cover the whole diversity of the topic. Having only a textual result list can then make it hard to find the best arguments or specific arguments of interest. This is why we aimed for new ways to support an efficient search space exploration — one main goal of information visualization (Munzner, 2014). While our recent user study suggested that source reliability

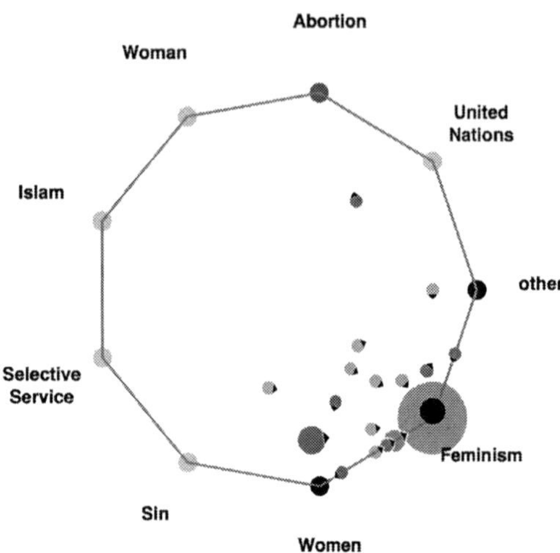

Figure 3: Topic space visualization for the query "feminism", positioning the retrieved arguments according to the eight main covered aspects and *other*.

is most important (see Section 1), the 291,440 arguments currently indexed by args.me anyway come from five selected sources only (Wachsmuth et al., 2017b). Instead, we thus focus on the second most important ranking criterion: aspect coverage.

4   Visualization of the Topic Space

For building an informed stance on a controversial topic, obtaining insights into the variety of aspects touched by the topic is crucial. We aid this process by accompanying the textual result list in args.me with a topic space visualization, which puts the aspects covered by the listed arguments into the focus, highlights the main aspect of each argument, and groups arguments covering similar aspects.

4.1   Determining Topical Aspects

The first step to develop the visualization was to build a topic model that can represent the aspects of each argument in the result list. We compared two alternative approaches for this purpose:

First, we computed the relative distribution of all the over 1000 terms from the Wikipedia list of controversial issues in each indexed argument. For instance, if "Women" occurs ten times, "Woman" six times, "Feminism" four times, and no other term, then we have *(Women 0.5, Woman 0.3, Feminism 0.2)* with implicit zeros for all others. Second, we performed LDA topic modeling (Blei et al., 2003) based on the words in all arguments from our index. With an interval size of 10, we tested all numbers of topics from 10 to 100 and chose the

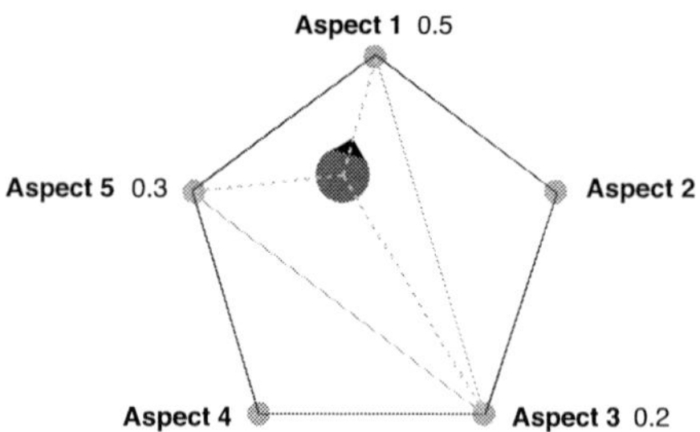

Figure 4: Positioning an argument glyph in the topic space: the black arrow shows the linear combination of weighted vertices (*Aspect 3* 0.2, *Aspect 5* 0.3, *Aspect 1* 0.5). The glyph itself points to the main covered aspect.

number that minimized perplexity: 40. Each aspect is then represented by all words of one LDA topic, and the relative aspect distribution is calculated by counting the occurrence of all associated words in each argument. We found the Wikipedia-based topic model to be more convincing, which is why it is set as the default in args.me.[4]

4.2   Visualizing Topical Aspects

To visualize the aspect-based topic space, we opted for *generalized barycentric coordinates* (Meyer et al., 2002), as they naturally fit our purpose: We represent an argument as a linear combination of weights for all aspects, while barycentric coordinates represent a point as a linear combination of the vertices of a polygon (both adding up to 1.0). Thus, the topic model can be used as input for the visualization without recalculation. Figure 3 shows the visualization of the results for the query "feminism", consisting of two main elements: the *topic space* and the *argument glyphs* within this space.

The topic space is depicted as a regular polygon with one vertex for each represented aspect. Both given topic model alternatives comprise too many aspects to depict them all. To reduce visual clutter in favor of a lean visualization, we limit the maximum number of visualized aspects, such that readability is not diminished. In particular, we keep only those eight aspects that are the most frequent in the argument search results. All other aspects are merged into a ninth aspect "other". The labels for the aspects are short terms in case of the Wikipedia-based topic model or visualized as word clouds in case of the LDA topic model.

Each argument glyph represents one argument in the form of a colored circle (green for pro, red

---

[4]The LDA alternative can be activated in args.me by changing the value of the *v*-parameter in the URL field to "lda".

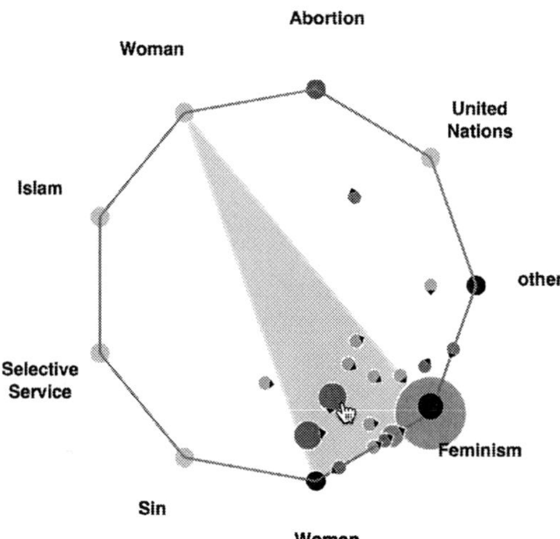
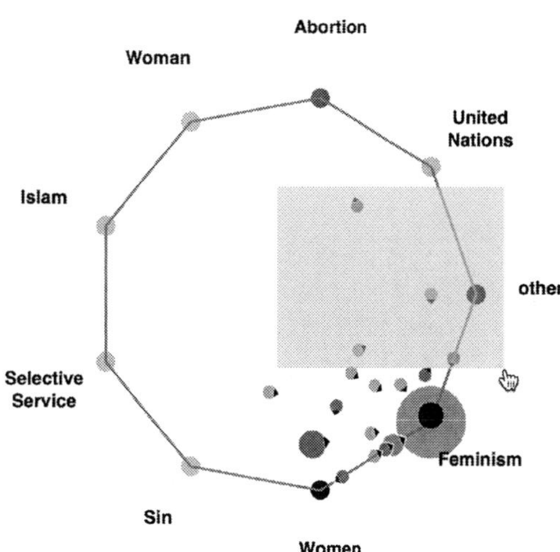

Figure 5: Hovering over an argument reveals the aspects it covers (main aspect marked by a small arrow).

Figure 6: Selecting arguments in the topic space visualization filters them in the textual result list of args.me.

for con) with a small arrow pointing to the main covered aspect. The glyphs are positioned based on their aspect distribution: the stronger one aspect, the stronger a glyph is "pulled" in that direction, as sketched in Figure 4. Accordingly, similar arguments are placed spatially near to each other. To ensure the visibility of all glyphs and to avoid over-plotting, arguments placed on top of each other are aggregated into a single glyph. The glyph size depends on a logarithmic mapping of the number of represented arguments. Since arguments with both stances may be grouped, the color of an aggregate glyph represents the majority stance of all arguments contained, from green (all pro), over gray (balanced pro/con), to red (all con).

4.3 Interacting with Topical Aspects

The integration of our visualization into args.me is shown below in Figures 7 and 8. This new *topic space view* replaces the old overall ranking view: it includes the textual argument ranking and adds the visualization to the right. At first, the visualization shows only the information outlined above, but it provides further details upon interaction.

Barycentric coordinates are ambiguous and may place arguments with different aspects at similar locations. For disambiguation, users can hover over a glyph to reveal all covered aspects, as exemplified in Figure 5. The represented arguments are also highlighted in the textual list, given that they appear on the current result page. Vice versa, hovering over a textual argument highlights the respective glyph with a wide green or red border.

In addition, the visualization enables a filtering of the textual results: A user can select one or more arguments by clicking or brushing (see Figure 6), in order to narrow down the list to the aspects of interest. All other arguments are grayed out.

5 Case Studies

To verify the benefit of our visualization, we finally explore two typical use cases of argument search: *topic space exploration* and *search refinement*.

5.1 Topic Space Exploration

First, we consider a query for "feminism". 659 arguments are returned by args.me for this topic, as shown in Figure 7. While the top-ranked arguments seem highly relevant in general, our visualization reveals that also some rather specific aspects are covered by the search results, such as "Abortion" and "United Nations". Interacting with the visualization helps explore the entire topic space.

In particular, hovering over the argument glyphs clarifies what aspects they exactly cover, such as "Woman", "Women", and "Feminism" itself for the highlighted argument in Figure 7. After a first exploration via hovering, a result subset of interest can be filtered through brushing, say, the four topmost glyphs (see Figure 6 above). The selected arguments are then shown at the top of the textual result list (all below are grayed out). From the selected arguments, we learn that Emma Watson has made the need for feminism a point at the United Nations, whereas the claimed necessity of abortion is used as an analogy to justify the necessity of

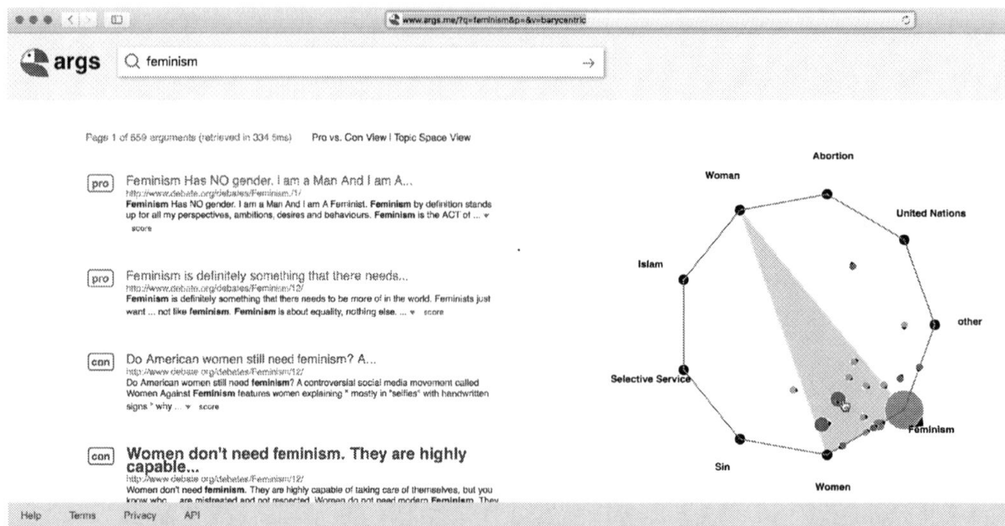

Figure 7: The args.me search results for the query "feminism", along with the integrated topic space visualization. The argument hovered over in the visualization is highlighted in the textual result list ("Women don't need...").

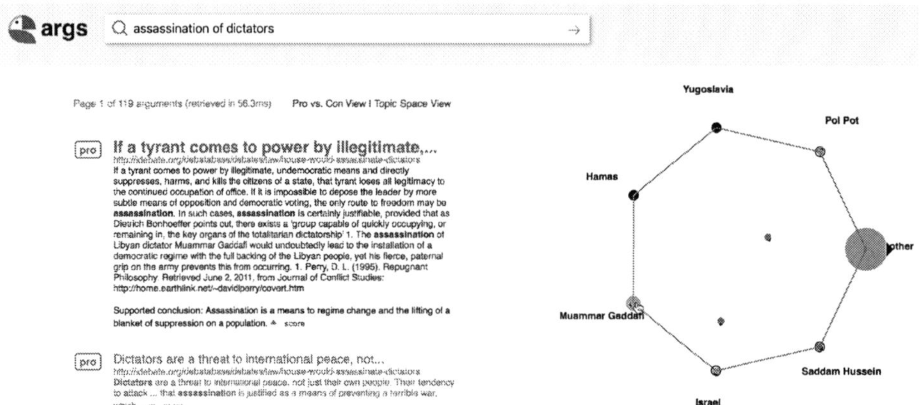

Figure 8: The single filtered args.me search result on the aspect *Muammar Gaddafi* for the query "assassination of dictators". The filtering is the result of clicking in the respective argument glyph in the topic space visualization.

feminism. Without the visualization, these insights would have been hard to gain; the two respective arguments were ranked at position #43 and #46.

5.2 Search Refinement

As a second example, we assume that a user looks for new arguments on the "assassination of dictators", for which args.me provides 119 results. If the user wants to refine a search to restrict it to a specific aspect of the topic only (e.g., to arguments covering *Muammar Gaddafi*), a simple click on the respective argument glyph in the topic space visualization suffices, as illustrated in Figure 8. The associated arguments are filtered and placed at the top of the result list (only one argument in the illustrated case). With the existing interaction methods of args.me, the argument text can be extended and its source web page shows up after clicking on it. In the old overall ranking view, the argument would have been ranked at position #34.

6 Conclusion

This paper has presented a new visual interface for our argument search engine, args.me. The visualization supports users in learning about the topical aspects covered by the arguments returned in response to a query. In two case studies, we have demonstrated how this topic space visualization enables an efficient exploration and refinement of argument search results. Future research on modeling the aspects of an argument can further enhance the usability of the visualization.

References

Peter Baldwin and David Price. 2018. Debategraph. `https://debategraph.org`.

Pietro Baroni, Marco Romano, Francesca Toni, Marco Aurisicchio, and Giorgio Bertanza. 2015. Automatic evaluation of design alternatives with quantitative argumentation. *Argument & Computation*, 6(1):24–49.

Gregor Betz, Sebastian Cacean, and Christian Voigt. 2018. Argunet. `http://www.argunet.org`.

David M. Blei, Andrew Y. Ng, and Michael I. Jordan. 2003. Latent dirichlet allocation. *Journal of Machine Learning Research*, 3:993–1022.

Jeff Conklin and Michael L. Begeman. 1988. gIBIS: A hypertext tool for exploratory policy discussion. *ACM Transactions on Information Systems*, 6(4):303–331.

Bruce Croft, Donald Metzler, and Trevor Strohman. 2009. *Search Engines: Information Retrieval in Practice*, 1st edition. Addison-Wesley Publishing Company, USA.

Mennatallah El-Assady, Valentin Gold, Carmela Acevedo, Christopher Collins, and Daniel Keim. 2016. ConToVi: Multi-party conversation exploration using topic-space views. *Computer Graphics Forum*.

Mennatallah El-Assady, Rita Sevastjanova, Bela Gipp, Daniel Keim, and Christopher Collins. 2017. NEREx: Named-entity relationship exploration in multi-party conversations. *Computer Graphics Forum*, 36(3):213–225.

Tim van Gelder. 2007. The rationale for rationale. *Law, Probability & Risk*, 6(1-4):23–42.

Valentin Gold, Christian Rohrdantz, and Mennatallah El-Assady. 2015. Exploratory text analysis using lexical episode plots. In *Eurographics Conference on Visualization (EuroVis) - Short Papers*. The Eurographics Association.

Wolfgang Jentner, Mennatallah El-Assady, Bela Gipp, and Daniel A. Keim. 2017. Feature alignment for the analysis of verbatim text transcripts. *EuroVis Workshop on Visual Analytics (EuroVA)*.

Areti Karamanou, Nikolaos Loutas, and Konstantinos Tarabanis. 2011. ArgVis: Structuring political deliberations using innovative visualisation technologies. *Electronic Participation*, pages 87–98.

Christian Kock. 2007. Dialectical obligations in political debate. *Informal Logic*, 27(3):233–247.

John D. Lowrance, Ian W. Harrison, and Andres C. Rodriguez. 2000. Structured argumentation for analysis. In *Proceedings of the 12th International Conference on Systems Research, Informatics, and Cybernetics: Focus Symposia on Advances in Computer-Based and Web-Based Collaborative Systems*, pages 47–57.

Mark Meyer, Alan Barr, Haeyoung Lee, and Mathieu Desbrun. 2002. Generalized barycentric coordinates on irregular polygons. *Journal of Graphics Tools*, 7(1):13–22.

Tamara Munzner. 2014. *Visualization Analysis and Design*. AK Peters Visualization Series. CRC Press.

Hui Niu. 2016. *Pedagogical Efficacy of Argument Visualization Tools*. Ph.D. thesis, Education: Faculty of Education.

Jörg Pührer. 2017. ArgueApply: A mobile app for argumentation. In *International Conference on Logic Programming and Nonmonotonic Reasoning*, pages 250–262. Springer.

Chris Reed and Glenn Rowe. 2004. Araucaria: Software for argument analysis, diagramming and representation. *International Journal on Artificial Intelligence Tools*, 13(04):961–979.

Patrick Riehmann, Dora Kiesel, Martin Kohlhaas, and Bend Fröhlich. 2018. Visualizing a thinker's life. *IEEE Transactions on Visualization and Computer Graphics*.

Stephen Robertson and Hugo Zaragoza. 2009. The probabilistic relevance framework: BM25 and beyond. *Foundations and Trends in Information Retrieval*, 3(4):333–389.

Daniel Suthers, Arlene Weiner, John Connelly, and Massimo Paolucci. 1995. Belvedere: Engaging students in critical discussion of science and public policy issues. In *Proceedings of the 7th World Conference on Artificial Intelligence in Education*, pages 266–273.

Truthmapping. 2018. Truthmapping. `https://www.truthmapping.com`.

Manolis Tzagarakis and Nikos Karacapilidis. 2013. On the exploitation of semantic types in the visualization of complex argumentative discourses. In *Proceedings of the 2nd International Workshop on Intelligent Exploration of Semantic Data*, page 3. ACM.

Henning Wachsmuth, Giovanni Da San Martino, Dora Kiesel, and Benno Stein. 2017a. The impact of modeling overall argumentation with tree kernels. In *Proceedings of the 2017 Conference on Empirical Methods in Natural Language Processing*, pages 2379–2389. Association for Computational Linguistics.

Henning Wachsmuth, Martin Potthast, Khalid Al Khatib, Yamen Ajjour, Jana Puschmann, Jiani Qu, Jonas Dorsch, Viorel Morari, Janek Bevendorff, and Benno Stein. 2017b. Building an argument search engine for the web. In *Proceedings of the 4th Workshop on Argument Mining*, pages 49–59. Association for Computational Linguistics.

SentencePiece: A simple and language independent subword tokenizer and detokenizer for Neural Text Processing

Taku Kudo **John Richardson**

Google, Inc.

{taku, johnri}@google.com

Abstract

This paper describes SentencePiece, a language-independent subword tokenizer and detokenizer designed for Neural-based text processing, including Neural Machine Translation. It provides open-source C++ and Python implementations for subword units. While existing subword segmentation tools assume that the input is pre-tokenized into word sequences, SentencePiece can train subword models directly from raw sentences, which allows us to make a purely end-to-end and language independent system. We perform a validation experiment of NMT on English-Japanese machine translation, and find that it is possible to achieve comparable accuracy to direct subword training from raw sentences. We also compare the performance of subword training and segmentation with various configurations. SentencePiece is available under the Apache 2 license at https://github.com/google/sentencepiece.

1 Introduction

Deep neural networks are demonstrating a large impact on Natural Language Processing. Neural machine translation (NMT) (Bahdanau et al., 2014; Luong et al., 2015; Wu et al., 2016; Vaswani et al., 2017) has especially gained increasing popularity, as it can leverage neural networks to directly perform translations with a simple end-to-end architecture. NMT has shown remarkable results in several shared tasks (Denkowski and Neubig, 2017; Nakazawa et al., 2017), and its effective approach has had a strong influence on other related NLP tasks such as dialog generation (Vinyals and Le, 2015) and automatic summarization (Rush et al., 2015).

Although NMT can potentially perform end-to-end translation, many NMT systems are still relying on language-dependent pre- and postprocessors, which have been used in traditional statistical machine translation (SMT) systems. Moses[1], a de-facto standard toolkit for SMT, implements a reasonably useful pre- and postprocessor. However, it is built upon hand-crafted and language dependent rules whose effectiveness for NMT has not been proven. In addition, these tools are mainly designed for European languages where words are segmented with whitespaces. To train NMT systems for non-segmented languages such as Chinese, Korean and Japanese, we need to run word segmenters independently. Such language-dependent processing also makes it hard to train multilingual NMT models (Johnson et al., 2016), as we have to carefully manage the configurations of pre- and postprocessors per language, while the internal deep neural architectures are language-independent.

As NMT approaches are standardized and moving forward to more language-agnostic architectures, it is becoming more important for the NLP community to develop a simple, efficient, reproducible and language independent pre- and postprocessor that can easily be integrated into Neural Network-based NLP systems, including NMT.

In this demo paper, we describe SentencePiece, a simple and language independent text tokenizer and detokenizer mainly for Neural Network-based text generation systems where the size of vocabulary is predetermined prior to the Neural model training. SentencePiece implements two subword segmentation algorithms, byte-pair-encoding (BPE) (Sennrich et al., 2016) and unigram language model (Kudo, 2018), with the extension of direct training from raw sentences. SentencePiece enables building a purely end-to-end system that does not depend on any language-specific processing.

---

[1] http://www.statmt.org/moses/

66

Proceedings of the 2018 Conference on Empirical Methods in Natural Language Processing (System Demonstrations), pages 66–71

Brussels, Belgium, October 31–November 4, 2018. ©2018 Association for Computational Linguistics

```
% spm_train --input=data/input.txt
    --model_prefix=spm --vocab_size=1000

% echo "Hello_world." | spm_encode
    --model=spm.model
_He ll o _world .

% echo "Hello_world." | spm_encode
    --model=spm.model --output_format=id
151 88 21 887 6

% echo "_He_ll_o__world_." |
    spm_decode --model=spm.model
Hello world.

% echo "151_88_21_887_6" |
    spm_decode --model=spm.model
        --input_format=id
Hello world.
```

Figure 1: Commandline usage of SentencePiece

2   System Overview

SentencePiece comprises four main components: **Normalizer**, **Trainer**, **Encoder**, and **Decoder**. Normalizer is a module to normalize semantically-equivalent Unicode characters into canonical forms. Trainer trains the subword segmentation model from the normalized corpus. We specify a type of subword model as the parameter of Trainer. Encoder internally executes Normalizer to normalize the input text and tokenizes it into a subword sequence with the subword model trained by Trainer. Decoder converts the subword sequence into the normalized text.

The roles of Encoder and Decoder correspond to preprocessing (tokenization) and postprocessing (detokenization) respectively. However, we call them encoding and decoding as SentencePiece manages the vocabulary to id mapping and can directly convert the text into an id sequence and vice versa. Direct encoding and decoding to/from id sequences are useful for most of NMT systems as their input and output are id sequences.

Figure 1 presents end-to-end example of SentencePiece training (spm_train), encoding (spm_encode), and decoding (spm_decode). We can see that the input text is reversibly converted through spm_encode and spm_decode.

3   Library Design

This section describes the design and implementation details of SentencePiece with command line and code snippets.

3.1   Lossless Tokenization

The following raw and tokenized sentences are an example of language-dependent preprocessing.

- **Raw text:** Hello world.
- **Tokenized:** [Hello] [world] [.]

One observation is that the raw text and tokenized sequence are not reversibly convertible. The information that no space exists between "world" and "." is not kept in the tokenized sequence. Detokenization, a process to restore the original raw input from the tokenized sequence, has to be language-dependent due to these irreversible operations. For example, while the detokenizer usually puts whitespaces between the primitive tokens in most European languages, no spaces are required in Japanese and Chinese.

- **Raw text:** こんにちは世界。 (*Hello world.*)
- **Tokenized:** [こんにちは] [世界] [。]

Such language specific processing has usually been implemented in manually crafted rules, which are expensive to write and maintain.

SentencePiece implements the Decoder as an inverse operation of Encoder, i.e.,

$$\mathrm{Decode}(\mathrm{Encode}(\mathrm{Normalize}(text))) = \mathrm{Normalize}(text).$$

We call this design **lossless tokenization**, in which all the information to reproduce the normalized text is preserved in the encoder's output. The basic idea of lossless tokenization is to treat the input text just as a sequence of Unicode characters. Even whitespace is handled as a normal symbol. For the sake of clarity, SentencePiece first escapes the whitespace with a meta symbol _ (U+2581), and tokenizes the input into an arbitrary subword sequence, for example:

- **Raw text:** Hello_world.
- **Tokenized:** [Hello] [_wor] [ld] [.]

As the whitespace is preserved in the tokenized text, we can detokenize the tokens without any ambiguities with the following Python code.

```
detok = ''.join(tokens).replace('_', ' ')
```

It should be noted that subword-nmt[2] adopts a different representation for subword units. It focuses on how the word is segmented into subwords and uses @@ as an intra-word boundary marker.

---

[2]https://github.com/rsennrich/subword-nmt

- **Tokenized:** [Hello] [wor] [@@ld] [@@.]

This representation can not always perform loss-less tokenization, as an ambiguity remains in the treatment of whitespaces. More specifically, it is not possible to encode consecutive whitespaces with this representation.

3.2 Efficient subword training and segmentation

Existing subword segmentation tools train subword models from pre-tokenized sentences. Such pre-tokenization was introduced for an efficient subword training (Sennrich et al., 2016). However, we can not always assume that pre-tokenization is available, especially for non-segmented languages. In addition, pre-tokenization makes it difficult to perform lossless tokenization.

SentencePiece employs several speed-up techniques both for training and segmentation to make lossless tokenization with a large amount of raw data. For example, given an input sentence (or word) of length N, BPE segmentation requires $O(N^2)$ computational cost when we naively scan the pair of symbols in every iteration. SentencePiece adopts an $O(N \log(N))$ algorithm in which the merged symbols are managed by a binary heap (priority queue). In addition, the training and segmentation complexities of unigram language models are linear to the size of input data.

3.3 Vocabulary id management

SentencePiece manages the vocabulary to id mapping to directly convert the input text into an id sequence and vice versa. The size of vocabulary is specified with the `--vocab_size=<size>` flag of `spm_train`. While subword-nmt specifies the number of merge operations, Sentence-Piece specifies the final size of vocabulary, as the number of merge operations is a BPE specific parameter and can not be applicable to other segmentation algorithms, e.g., unigram language model (Kudo, 2018).

SentencePiece reserves vocabulary ids for special meta symbols, e.g., unknown symbol (`<unk>`), BOS (`<s>`), EOS (`</s>`) and padding (`<pad>`). Their actual ids are configured with command line flags. We can also define custom meta symbols to encode contextual information as virtual tokens. Examples include the language-indicators, `<2ja>` and `<2de>`, for multilingual

```
U+41 U+302 U+300 <tab> U+1EA6
U+41 U+302 U+301 <tab> U+1EA4
...
```

Figure 2: Custom normalization rule in TSV

models (Johnson et al., 2016).

3.4 Customizable character normalization

Character normalization is an important preprocessing step for handling real world text, which consists of semantically-equivalent Unicode characters. For example, Japanese fullwidth Latin characters can be normalized into ASCII Latin characters. Lowercasing is also an effective normalization, depending on the application.

Character normalization has usually been implemented as hand-crafted rules. Recently, Unicode standard Normalization Forms, e.g., NFC and NFKC, have been widely used in many NLP applications because of their better reproducibility and strong support as Unicode standard.

By default, SentencePiece normalizes the input text with the Unicode NFKC normalization. The normalization rules are specified with the `--normalization_rule_name=nfkc` flag of `spm_train`. The normalization in Sentencepiece is implemented with string-to-string mapping and leftmost longest matching. The normalization rules are compiled into a finite state transducer (Aho-Corasick automaton) to perform an efficient normalization[3].

SentencePiece supports custom normalization rules defined as a TSV file. Figure 2 shows an example TSV file. In this example, the Unicode sequence [U+41 U+302 U+300] is converted into U+1EA6[4]. When there are ambiguities in the conversion, the longest rule is applied. User defined TSV files are specified with the `--normalization_rule_tsv=<file>` flag of `spm_train`. Task-specific rules can be defined by extending the default NFKC rules provided as a TSV file in SentencePiece package.

3.5 Self-contained models

Recently, many researchers have provided pre-trained NMT models for better reproduciblity of

---

[3]The original NFKC normalization requires CCC (Canonical Combining Class) reordering, which is hard to model in a finite state transducer. SentencePiece does not handle the full CCC reordering and only implements a subset of NFKC normalization.

[4]Note that tabs are used as the delimiter for source and target sequence and spaces are used as the delimiter for individual characters.

their experimental results. However, it is not always stated how the data was preprocessed. (Post, 2018) reported that subtle differences in preprocessing schemes can widely change BLEU scores. Even using the Moses toolkit, it is not guaranteed to reproduce the same settings unless the configurations of Moses (e.g., version and command line flags) are clearly specified. Strictly speaking, NFKC normalization may yield different results depending on the Unicode version.

Ideally, all the rules and parameters for preprocessing must be embedded into the model file in a self-contained manner so that we can reproduce the same experimental setting as long as we are using the same model file.

The SentencePiece model is designed to be purely self-contained. The model file includes not only the vocabulary and segmentation parameters, but also the pre-compiled finite state transducer for character normalization. The behavior of SentencePiece is determined only by the model file and has no external dependencies. This design guarantees a perfect reproducibility as well as allowing to distribute the SentencePiece model file as part of an NMT model. In addition, the developers of SentencePiece can refine the (default) normalization rules without having to worry about breaking existing preprocessing behaviors.

The SentencePiece model is stored as a binary wire format Protocol buffer[5], a platform neutral and extensible mechanism for serializing structured data. Protocol buffers help to safely serialize structured data while keeping backward compatibility as well as extensibility.

3.6 Library API for on-the-fly processing

Text preprocessing is usually considered as offline processing. Prior to the main NMT training, raw input is preprocessed and converted into an id sequence with a standalone preprocessor.

Such off-line preprocessing has two problems. First, standalone tools are not directly integrated into the user-facing NMT applications which need to preprocess user input on-the-fly. Second, off-line preprocessing makes it hard to employ sub-sentence level data augmentation and noise injection, which aim at improving the accuracy and robustness of the NMT models. There are several studies to inject noise to input sen-

```
#include <sentencepiece_processor.h>
#include <sentencepiece_trainer.h>

SentencePieceTrainer::Train(
  "--input=input.txt "
  "--model_prefix=spm "
  "--vocab_size=1000");

SentencePieceProcessor sp;
sp.Load("spm.model");

std::vector<std::string> pieces;
sp.Encode("Hello world.", &pieces);

std::vector<int> ids;
sp.Encode("Hello world.", &ids);

std::string text;
sp.Decode({151, 88, 21, 887, 6}, &text);
```

Figure 3: C++ API usage (The same as Figure 1.)

```
import sentencepiece as spm

params = ('--input=input.txt '
          '--model_prefix=spm '
          '--vocab_size=1000')
spm.SentencePieceTrainer.Train(params)

sp = spm.SentencePieceProcessor()
sp.Load('spm.model')

print(sp.EncodeAsPieces('Hello world.'))
print(sp.EncodeAsIds('Hello world.'))
print(sp.DecodeIds([151, 88, 21, 887, 6]))
```

Figure 4: Python API usage (The same as Figure 1.)

tences by randomly changing the internal representation of sentences. (Kudo, 2018) proposes a subword regularization that randomly changes the subword segmentation during NMT training. (Lample et al., 2017; Artetxe et al., 2017) independently proposed a denoising autoencoder in the context of sequence-to-sequence learning, where they randomly alter the word order of the input sentence and the model is trained to reconstruct the original sentence. It is hard to emulate this dynamic sampling and noise injection only with the off-line processing.

SentencePiece not only provides a standalone command line tool for off-line preprocessing but supports a C++, Python and Tensorflow library API for on-the-fly processing, which can easily be integrated into existing NMT frameworks. Figures 3, 4 and 5 show example usages of the C++, Python and TensorFlow API[6]. Figure 6 presents example Python code for subword regularization where one subword sequence is sampled according to the unigram language model. We can find that the text "New York" is tokenized differently

---

[5] https://developers.google.com/protocol-buffers/

[6] As the Python and TensorFlow wrappers call the native C++ API, there is no performance drop in their interfaces.

```
import tensorflow as tf
import tf_sentencepiece as tfs

model = tf.gfile.GFile('spm.model', 'rb').read()

input_text = tf.placeholder(tf.string, [None])
ids, lens = tfs.encode(input_text, model_proto=model,
        out_type=tf.int32)
output_text = tfs.decode(ids, lens, model_proto=model)

with tf.Session() as sess:
  text = ['Hello world.', 'New York']
  ids_, lens_, output_text_ = sess.run([ids, lens,
      output_text], feed_dict={input_text:text})
```

Figure 5: TensorFlow API usage

The SentencePiece model (model proto) is an attribute of
the TensorFlow operation and embedded into the TensorFlow
graph so the model and graph become purely self-contained.

```
>>> sp.Load('spm.model')
>>> for n in range(5):
... sp.SampleEncodeAsPieces('New York', -1, 0.1)
['_', 'N', 'e', 'w', '_York']
['_', 'New', '_York']
['_', 'New', '_Y', 'o', 'r', 'k']
['_', 'New', '_York']
['_', 'New', '_York']
```

Figure 6: Subword sampling with Python API

on each `SampleEncodeAsPieces` call. Please
see (Kudo, 2018) for the details on subword regularization and its sampling hyperparameters.

4   Experiments

4.1   Comparison of different preprocessing

We validated the performance of the different
preprocessing on English-Japanese translation of
Wikipedia articles, as specified by the Kyoto Free
Translation Task (KFTT) [7]. The training, development and test data of KFTT consist of 440k, 1166
and 1160 sentences respectively.

We used GNMT (Wu et al., 2016) as the implementation of the NMT system in our experiments.
We generally followed the settings and training
procedure described in (Wu et al., 2016), however,
we changed the node and layer size of LSTM to be
512 and 6 respectively.

A word model is used as a baseline system.
We compared to SentencePiece (unigram language model) with and without pre-tokenization.
SentencePiece with pre-tokenization is essentially
the same as the common NMT configuration
with subword-nmt. SentencePiece without pre-
tokenization directly trains the subword model
from raw sentences and does not use any external resources. We used the Moses tokenizer[8] and

---

[7]http://www.phontron.com/kftt
[8]http://www.statmt.org/moses/

Lang pair	setting (source/target)	# vocab.	BLEU
ja→en	Word model (baseline)	80k/80k	28.24
	SentencePiece	8k (shared)	29.55
	SentencePiece w/ pre-tok.	8k (shared)	29.85
	Word/SentencePiece	80k/8k	27.24
	SentencePiece/Word	8k/80k	29.14
en→ja	Word model (baseline)	80k/80k	20.06
	SentencePiece	8k (shared)	21.62
	SentencePiece w/ pre-tok.	8k (shared)	20.86
	Word/SentencePiece	80k/8k	21.41
	SentencePiece/Word	8k/80k	19.94

Table 1: Translation Results (BLEU(%))

KyTea[9] for English and Japanese pre-tokenization
respectively. The same tokenizers are applied to
the word model.

We used the case-sensitive BLEU score
(Papineni et al., 2002) as an evaluation metric.
As the output sentences are not segmented in
Japanese, we segmented them with KyTea for be-
fore calculating BLEU scores.

Table 1 shows the experimental results. First,
as can be seen in the table, subword segmen-
tations with SentencePiece consitently improve
the BLEU scores compared to the word model.
This result is consistent with previous work
(Sennrich et al., 2016). Second, it can be seen
that the pre-tokenization is not always necessary
to boost the BLEU scores. In Japanese to English,
the improvement is marginal and has no significant difference. In English to Japanese, the BLEU
score is degraded with pre-tokenization.

We can find larger improvements in BLEU
when 1) SentencePiece is applied to Japanese, and
2) the target sentence is Japanese. As Japanese is
a non-segmented language, pre-tokenization acts
as a strong constraint to determine the final vocabulary. It can be considered that the positive effects of unsupervised segmentation from raw input
worked effectively to find the domain-specific vocabulary in Japanese.

4.2   Segmentation performance

Table 2 summarizes the training and segmentation
performance of various configurations.

We can see that the training and segmentation
speed of both SentencePiece and subword-nmt is
almost comparable on English data set regardless
of the choice of pre-tokenization. This is expected,
as English is a segmented language and the search
space for the vocabulary extraction is largely restricted. On the other hand, SentencePiece shows

---

[9]http://www.phontron.com/kytea

Task	Tool	Pre-tok.	time (sec.)	
			Japanese	English
Train	subword-nmt	yes	56.9	54.1
	SentencePiece	yes	10.1	16.8
	subword-nmt	no	528.0	94.7
	SentencePiece	no	217.3	21.8
Seg.	subword-nmt	yes	23.7	28.6
	SentencePiece	yes	8.2	20.3
	subword-nmt	no	216.2	36.1
	SentencePiece	no	5.9	20.3
Pre-tokenizaion KyTea(ja)/Moses(en)			24.6	15.8

Table 2: Segmentation performance. KFTT corpus (440k sentences) is used for evaluation. Experiments are executed on Linux with Xeon 3.5Ghz processors. The size of vocabulary is 16k. Moses and KyTea tokenizers are used for English and Japanese respectively. Note that we have to take the time of pre-tokenization into account to make a fair comparison with and without pre-tokenization. Because subword-nmt is based on BPE, we used the BPE model in SentencePiece. We found that BPE and unigram language models show almost comparable performance.

larger performance improvements when applying it to raw Japanese data (w/o pre-tok). The segmentation speed of SentencePiece is about 380 times faster than that of subword-nmt in this setting. This result strongly supports our claim that SentencePiece is fast enough to be applied to raw data and the pre-tokenization is not always necessary. Consequently, SentencePiece helps to build a purely data-driven and language-independent system. The segmentation speed of SentencePiece is around 21k and 74k sentences/sec. in English and Japanese respectively, which is fast enough to be executed on-the-fly.

5 Conclusions

In this paper, we introduced SentencePiece, an open-source subword tokenizer and detokenizer designed for Neural-based text processing. SentencePiece not only performs subword tokenization, but directly converts the text into an id sequence, which helps to develop a purely end-to-end system without replying on language specific resources. The model file of SentencePiece is designed to be self-contained to guarantee perfect reproducibility of the normalization and subword segmentation. We hope that SentencePiece will provide a stable and reproducible text processing tool for production use and help the research community to move to more language-agnostic and multilingual architectures.

References

Mikel Artetxe, Gorka Labaka, Eneko Agirre, and Kyunghyun Cho. 2017. Unsupervised neural machine translation. *arXive preprint arXiv:1710.11041*.

Dzmitry Bahdanau, Kyunghyun Cho, and Yoshua Bengio. 2014. Neural machine translation by jointly learning to align and translate. *arXiv preprint arXiv:1409.0473*.

Michael Denkowski and Graham Neubig. 2017. Stronger baselines for trustable results in neural machine translation. *Proc. of Workshop on Neural Machine Translation*.

Melvin Johnson, Mike Schuster, et al. 2016. Google's multilingual neural machine translation system: enabling zero-shot translation. *arXiv preprint arXiv:1611.04558*.

Taku Kudo. 2018. Subword regularization: Improving neural network translation models with multiple subword candidates. In *Proc. of ACL*.

Guillaume Lample, Ludovic Denoyer, and Marc'Aurelio Ranzato. 2017. Unsupervised machine translation using monolingual corpora only. *arXive preprint arXiv:1711.00043*.

Minh-Thang Luong, Hieu Pham, and Christopher D Manning. 2015. Effective approaches to attention-based neural machine translation. In *Proc of EMNLP*.

Toshiaki Nakazawa, Shohei Higashiyama, et al. 2017. Overview of the 4th workshop on asian translation. In *Proceedings of the 4th Workshop on Asian Translation (WAT2017)*.

Kishore Papineni, Salim Roukos, Todd Ward, and Wei-Jing Zhu. 2002. Bleu: a method for automatic evaluation of machine translation. In *Proc. of ACL*.

Matt Post. 2018. A call for clarity in reporting bleu scores. *arXiv preprint arXiv:1804.08771*.

Alexander M Rush, Sumit Chopra, and Jason Weston. 2015. A neural attention model for abstractive sentence summarization. In *Proc. of EMNLP*.

Rico Sennrich, Barry Haddow, and Alexandra Birch. 2016. Neural machine translation of rare words with subword units. In *Proc. of ACL*.

Ashish Vaswani, Noam Shazeer, Niki Parmar, Jakob Uszkoreit, Llion Jones, Aidan N. Gomez, Lukasz Kaiser, and Illia Polosukhin. 2017. Attention is all you need. *arXive preprint arXiv:1706.03762*.

Oriol Vinyals and Quoc V. Le. 2015. A neural conversational model. In *ICML Deep Learning Workshop*.

Yonghui Wu, Mike Schuster, et al. 2016. Google's neural machine translation system: Bridging the gap between human and machine translation. *arXiv preprint arXiv:1609.08144*.

CogCompTime: A Tool for Understanding Time in Natural Language

Qiang Ning,[1] **Ben Zhou,**[1] **Zhili Feng,**[2] **Haoruo Peng,**[1] **Dan Roth**[1,3]
Department of Computer Science
[1]University of Illinois at Urbana-Champaign, Urbana, IL 61801, USA
[2]University of Wisconsin-Madison, Madison, WI 53706, USA
[3]University of Pennsylvania, Philadelphia, PA 19104, USA
{qning2,xzhou45,hpeng7}@illinois.edu, zfeng49@cs.wisc.edu, danroth@seas.upenn.edu

Abstract

Automatic extraction of temporal information is important for natural language understanding. It involves two basic tasks: (1) Understanding time expressions that are mentioned explicitly in text (e.g., *February 27, 1998* or *tomorrow*), and (2) Understanding temporal information that is conveyed implicitly via relations. This paper introduces CogCompTime, a system that has these two important functionalities. It incorporates the most recent progress, achieves state-of-the-art performance, and is publicly available.[1] We believe that this demo will provide valuable insight for temporal understanding and be useful for multiple time-aware applications.

1 Introduction

Time is an important dimension when we describe the world because many facts are time-sensitive, e.g., one's place of residence, one's employment, or the progress of a conflict between countries. Consequently, many applications can benefit from temporal understanding in natural language, e.g., timeline construction (Do et al., 2012; Minard et al., 2015), clinical events analysis (Jindal and Roth, 2013; Bethard et al., 2015), question answering (Llorens et al., 2015), and causality inference (Ning et al., 2018a).

Temporal understanding from natural language requires two basic components (Verhagen et al., 2007, 2010; UzZaman et al., 2013). The first, also known as the Timex component, requires extracting explicit time expressions in text (i.e., "Timex") and normalize them to a standard format. In Example 1, the Timex is ***February 27, 1998*** and its *normalized* form is '1998-02-27'. Note that normalization may also require a reference time for Timexes like "tomorrow", for which we need to

---

[1]http://cogcomp.org/page/publication_view/844

know the document creation time (DCT). In addition to DATE, there are also other Timex types including TIME (e.g., ***8 am***), DURATION (e.g., ***3 years***), and SET (e.g., ***every Monday***).

Timexes carry temporal information *explicitly*, but temporal information can also be conveyed *implicitly* via temporal relations (i.e., "TempRel"). In Example 2, there are two events: ***e1:exploded*** and ***e2:died***. The text does not tell us when they happened, but we do know that there is a TempRel between them, i.e., ***e1:exploded*** happened *before* ***e2:died***. The second basic component of temporal understanding is thus the TempRel component, which extracts TempRels automatically from text. While the Timex component provides absolute time anchors, the TempRel component provides the relative order of events. These two together provide a complete picture of the temporal dimension of a story, so they are naturally the most important building blocks towards temporal understanding.

> **Example 1:** Presidents Leonid Kuchma of Ukraine and Boris Yeltsin of Russia signed an economic cooperation plan on (***t1:February 27, 1998***).
> **Example 2:** A car (***e1:exploded***) in the middle of a group of men playing volleyball. More than 10 people have (***e2:died***), police said.

In this paper, we present CogCompTime (see Fig. 1), a tool with both the Timex and TempRel components, which are conceptually built on Zhao et al. (2012) and Ning et al. (2017), respectively. CogCompTime is a new implementation that integrates both components and also incorporates the most recent advances in this area (Ning et al., 2018a,b,c). Two highlights are: First, CogCompTime achieves comparable performance to state-of-the-art Timex systems, but is almost two times faster than the second fastest, HeidelTime (Strötgen and Gertz, 2010). Second, CogCompTime improves the performance of the

Proceedings of the 2018 Conference on Empirical Methods in Natural Language Processing (System Demonstrations), pages 72–77
Brussels, Belgium, October 31–November 4, 2018. ©2018 Association for Computational Linguistics

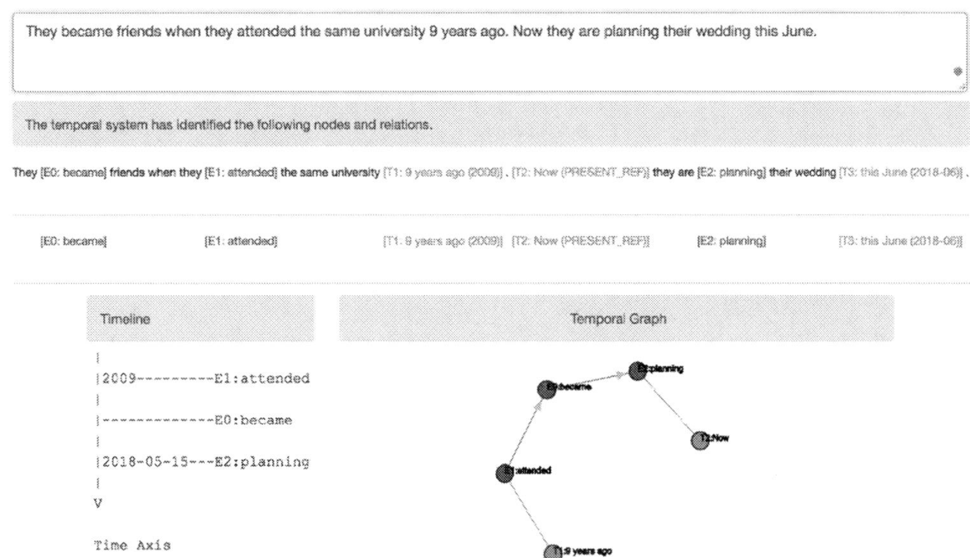

Figure 1: **A snapshot of the interface of CogCompTime.** From top to bottom: Input box, event and Timex highlight, and two visualizations (timeline and graph). The document creation time was chosen to be 2018-05-15.

TempRel component by a large margin, from the literature's $F_1 \approx 50$ (UzZaman et al., 2013) to $F_1 \approx 70$ (see details in Sec. 3). Given these two contributions, we believe that CogCompTime is a good demonstration of the state-of-the-art in temporal understanding. In addition, since CogCompTime is publicly available, it will provide easy access to users working on time-aware applications, as well as valuable insight to researchers seeking further improvements.

We briefly review the literature and explain in detail the processing pipeline of CogCompTime in Sec. 2: the Timex component, the Event Extraction component, and the TempRel component. Following that, we provide a benchmark evaluation in Sec. 3 on the TempEval3 and the MATRES datasets (UzZaman et al., 2013; Ning et al., 2018c). Finally, we point out directions for future work and conclude this paper.

2 System

The system pipeline of CogCompTime is shown in Fig. 2: It takes raw text as input and uses CogCompNLP (Khashabi et al., 2018) to extract features such as lemmas, part-of-speech (POS) tags, and semantic role labelings (SRL). Then CogCompTime sequentially applies the Timex component, the event extraction component, and the TempRel component. Finally, both a graph visualization and a timeline visualization are provided for the users. In the following, we will ex-

plain these main modules in detail.

2.1 Timex Component

Existing work on Timex extraction and normalization falls into two categories: rule-based and learning-based. Rule-based systems use regular expressions to extract Timex in text and then deterministic rules to normalize them (e.g., HeidelTime (Strötgen and Gertz, 2010) and SUTime (Chang and Manning, 2012)). Learning-based systems use classification models to chunk out Timexes in text and normalize them based on grammar parsing (e.g., UWTime (Lee et al., 2014) and ParsingTime (Angeli et al., 2012)). CogCompTime adopts a mixed strategy: we use machine learning in the Timex extraction step and rule parsing in the normalization step. This mixed strategy, while maintaining a state-of-the-art performance, significantly improves the computational efficiency of the Timex component, as we show in Sec. 3.

Technically, the Timex extraction step can be formulated as a generic text chunking problem and the standard B(egin), I(nside), and O(utside) labeling scheme can be used. CogCompTime proposes TemporalChunker, by retraining Illinois-Chunker (Punyakanok and Roth, 2001) on top of the Timex chunk annotations provided by the TempEval3 workshop (UzZaman et al., 2013). Here a machine learning based extraction algorithm significantly improves the computational efficiency by quickly sifting out impossible text chunks, as com-

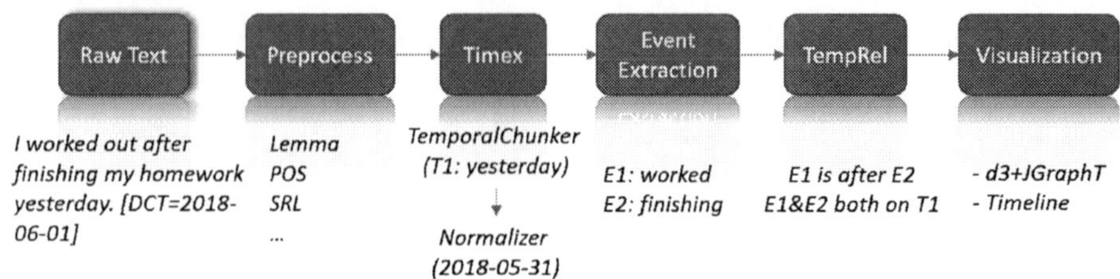

Figure 2: **System pipeline of CogCompTime**: It preprocesses raw text input using CogCompNLP and then applies Timex, Event Extraction, and TempRel components sequentially, with two user-friendly visualizations (i.e., graph-type visualization and timeline-type visualization) provided at the end.

pared to regular expression matching, which has to check every substring of text against regular expressions and is often slow. However, we do admit that learning-based extraction handles corner cases not as well as rule-based systems because of the limited training examples.

After Timexes are extracted, we apply rules to normalize them. We think rule-based methods are generally more natural for normalization: On one hand, the desired formats of various types of Timexes are already defined as rules by corresponding annotation guidelines; on the other hand, the intermediate steps of how one Timex is normalized are not annotated in any existing datasets (it is inherently hard to do so), so learning-based methods usually have to introduce latent variables and need more training instances as a result. Therefore, we have adopted a rule-based normalization method. However, we admit that an obvious drawback is that the rule set needs to be redesigned for every single language.

2.2 Event Extraction Component

Event extraction is closely related to how events are defined. Generally speaking, an event is considered to be an action associated with the corresponding participants. In the context of temporal understanding, events are usually represented by their head verb token, so unlike the generic chunking problem in Timex extraction, event extraction can be formulated as a classification problem for each token. Specifically, CogCompTime only considers those *main-axis* events, so event extraction is simply a binary classification problem (i.e., whether or not a token is a main-axis event or not). As defined by the MATRES annotation scheme (Ning et al., 2018c), main-axis events are those events that form the primary timeline of a story and approximately 60%-70% of the verbs are on the main-axis in MATRES. We extract lemmas and POS tags within a fixed window, SRL,

and prepositional phrase head, and train a sparse averaged perceptron for event extraction.

2.3 TempRel Component

Temporal relations can be generally modeled by a graph (called temporal graph), where the nodes represent events and Timexes, and the edges represent TempRels. With all the nodes extracted (by previous steps), the TempRel component is to make predictions on the labels of those edges. In this paper, the label set for Event-Event TempRels is *before*, *after*, *equal*, and *vague* and for Event-Timex TempRels is *equal* and *not-equal*.[2] State-of-the-art methods include, e.g., ClearTK (Bethard, 2013), CAEVO (Chambers et al., 2014), and Ning et al. (2017). The TempRel task is known to be very difficult. Ning et al. (2018c) attributes the difficulty partly to the low inter-annotator agreement (IAA) of existing TempRel datasets and proposes a new Multi-Axis Temporal RElations dataset of Start-points (MATRES) with significantly improved IAA, so for the TempRel task, we have chosen MATRES as the benchmark in this paper.[3]

We also incorporate the recent progress of Ning et al. (2017, 2018a,b). The feature set used for TempRel is shown in Fig. 3, which contains features derived individually from each node and jointly from a node pair. Since a node can be either an event or a Timex, an edge can also be either an Event-Event edge or an Event-Timex edge and the features have to vary a bit, as detailed by Fig. 3. Note that for Event-Event edges, we incorporate features from TemProb,[4] which encodes prior knowledge of typical temporal orders

---

[2]The simplification of Event-Timex label set is due to our observation that other labels have very low accuracies. As a demo paper, we have chosen not to use them. However, we think it is interesting and worth further investigation.

[3]Specifically, we only need to replace the TempRel annotations in TempEval3 by the new annotations in MATRES.

[4]`http://cogcomp.org/page/resource_view/114`

of events (Ning et al., 2018b). With these features, we also adopt the constraint-driven learning algorithm for TempRel classification proposed in Ning et al. (2017) with sparse averaged perceptron. Then our TempRel component assigns local prediction scores (i.e., soft-max scores) to each edge and solves an integer linear programming (ILP) problem via Gurobi (Gurobi Optimization, 2015) to achieve globally consistent temporal graphs (please refer to Ning et al. (2018a) for details). CogCompTime is a unique package so far that incorporates all the recent progress.

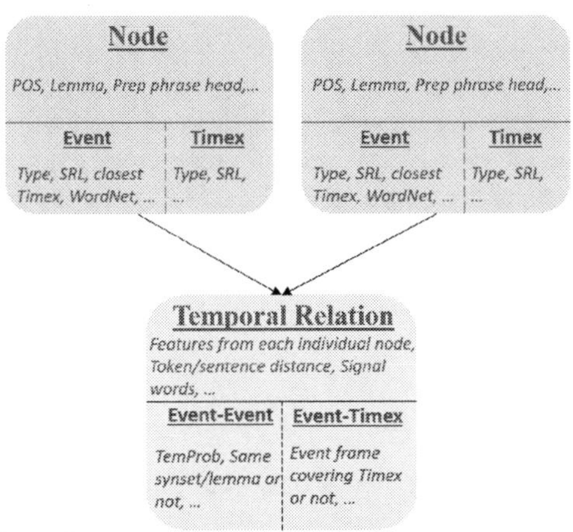

Figure 3: **The primary features used in the TempRel component** (also standard features used in the literature). Since there are two types of nodes (i.e., event and Timex), and two types of TempRels (i.e., Event-Event and Event-Timex), we put the common features above and split specific feature sets below. Conjunctive features are not listed exhaustively here.

2.4 Visualization

As shown in Fig. 1, we highlight the extracted Timexes and events in the text. Specifically for Timexes, we also annotate their normalized values along with their chunks. We provide two forms of visualization for the extracted TempRels. Since TempRels can be naturally modeled by a graph, a graph visualization is an obvious choice and we use d3 (https://d3js.org/) in CogCompTime. Additionally, we provide a more compact visualization to those graphs via timeline construction. Since a graph is only partially ordered (as opposed to a timeline which is fully ordered), we resort to the appearance order of events in timeline construction when the temporal order is *vague* according to its graph.

3 Benchmark Experiment

We used the dataset provided by the TempEval3 workshop, with the original train/test split in

our experiment: TimeBank and AQUAINT were for training (256 articles), and Platinum was for testing (20 articles). Note that we replaced the TempRel annotations in the original TempEval3 datasets by MATRES due to its higher IAA. In the Timex component, TemporalChunker by default takes 10% of the train set as the development set, and in other components, 5-fold cross-validation was used for parameter tuning.

Table 1 evaluates the Timex component of CogCompTime, comparing with state-of-the-art systems. The "normalization" and "end-to-end" columns were evaluated based on gold Timex extraction and system Timex extraction, respectively. The fact that CogCompTime had the best extraction F_1 and normalization accuracy but not the best end-to-end performance is due to our mixed strategy: Timexes extracted by our learning-based TemporalChunker sometimes cannot be normalized correctly by our rule-based normalizer. This phenomenon is relatively more severe in CogCompTime comparing to systems that are consistently rule-based or learning-based in both extraction and normalization. However, the computational efficiency is improved significantly by reducing the runtime of the second fastest, HeidelTime, by more than 50%.

Table 2 shows the performance of the Event Extraction and TempRel components. We also copied the Timex extraction performance from Table 1. Note that CogCompTime only extracts those main-axis events as defined by MATRES. Since Ning et al. (2018c) did not propose an event extraction method, Table 2 is in fact the first reported performance of event extraction on MATRES and as we see, both the precision and recall are better than those numbers reported in TempEval3. Note that since CogCompTime works on different annotations, this does not indicate that our event extraction algorithm is better than those participants in TempEval3; instead, this indicates that the event extraction problem in MATRES is a better-defined machine learning task.

The performance of TempRel extraction is further evaluated in Table 2, both when the gold event and Timex extraction is used and when system extraction is used. As for Event-Event TempRels, we also introduce a new relaxed metric[5], where predictions of *before/after* are not penalized when the gold label is *vague*. This is based on the definition

---

[5]This relaxed metric does not apply to Event-Timex TempRels since the label set is only *equal* and *not-equal*, .

Timex Systems	Extraction			Normalization	End-to-end	Runtime
	P	R	F_1	Accuracy	F_1	Seconds
HeidelTime (Strötgen and Gertz, 2010)	84.0	79.7	81.8	78.1[†]	78.1	18
SUTime (Chang and Manning, 2012)	80.0	81.1	80.6	69.8[†]	69.8	16
UWTime (Lee et al., 2014)	**86.7**	80.4	83.5	84.4	**82.7**	400
CogCompTime	86.5	**83.3**	**84.9**	**84.7**	76.8	7

Table 1: **Performance of our Timex component** compared with state-of-the-art systems on a benchmark dataset, the Platinum dataset from the TempEval3 workshop (UzZaman et al., 2013). The "extraction" and "normalization" columns are the two intermediate steps. "Normalization" was evaluated given gold extraction, while "end-to-end" means system extraction was used. Runtimes were evaluated under the same setup.

[†]HeidelTime and SUTime have no clear-cut between extraction and normalization, so even if gold Timex chunks are fed in, their extraction step cannot be easily skipped.

of *vague* in MATRES, i.e., to assign *vague* labels when either *before* or *after* is reasonable. We think this relaxed metric is more suitable when creating timelines from temporal graphs, where an order must be picked anyhow when two events have a *vague* relation. When system extraction was used, the TempRel performance saw a large drop. However, the performance here, although it is perhaps still not sufficiently good for some applications, is already a significant step forward in temporal understanding. As a reference point, the best system in TempEval3, ClearTK (Bethard, 2013), had P=34.08, R=28.40, F_1=30.98 (using system extraction) and P=37.32, R=35.25, F_1=36.26 (using gold extraction). Again, given the dataset difference, these numbers are not directly comparable, but it indicates that the MATRES dataset used here probably has the TempRel task better defined and we hope this demo paper will be a good showcase of the new state-of-the-art.

	P	R	F_1
Event Extraction	83.5	87.0	85.2
Timex Extraction	86.5	83.3	84.9
Gold Extraction			
Event-Event	61.6	70.9	65.9
Event-Event (Relaxed)	75.2	74.8	75.0
Event-Timex	84.6	84.6	84.6
System Extraction			
Event-Event	48.4	58.0	52.8
Event-Event (Relaxed)	75.6	61.8	68.0
Event-Timex	79.5	61.1	69.0

Table 2: **Performance of the Event/Timex Extraction and TempRel components** when gold/system extraction is used. The relaxed metric does not penalize the system if a *be-fore/after* prediction is made on a *vague* relation. Please also refer to the text about this metric.

4   Future Work

We plan to further improve CogCompTime in the following directions. First, the MATRES dataset (Ning et al., 2018c) only considers verb events, but nominal events are also very common and important, so we plan to incorporate nominal event extraction and corresponding TempRel extraction. Second, CogCompTime currently does not incorporate an event coreference component. Since coreference is important for bridging long-distance event pairs, it is a desirable feature. We can adopt existing event coreferencing techniques such as Peng et al. (2016) in the next step. Third, CogCompTime currently only works on the main-axis events as defined in MATRES. How to incorporate other axes, e.g., intention axis, opinion axis, and hypothesis axis, requires further investigation.

5   Conclusion

This paper presents CogCompTime, a new package that, given raw text, (1) extracts time expressions (Timex) and normalizes them to a standard format, and (2) extracts events on the main time axis of a story and the temporal relations between events and Timexes. CogCompTime takes advantage of many recent advances and achieves state-of-the-art performance in both tasks. We think this demo will be interesting for a broad audience because it is useful not only for identifying the shortcomings of existing methods, but also for applications that depend on the temporal understanding of natural language text.

Acknowledgements

This research is supported in part by a grant from the Allen Institute for Artificial Intelligence (allenai.org); the IBM-ILLINOIS Center for Cognitive Computing Systems Research (C3SR) - a research collaboration as part of the IBM AI Horizons Network; and by the Army Research Laboratory (ARL) and was accomplished under Cooperative Agreement Number W911NF-09-2-0053 (the ARL Network Science CTA). The views and conclusions contained in this document are those of the authors and should not be interpreted as representing the official policies, either expressed or implied, of the Army Research Laboratory or the

References

Gabor Angeli, Christopher D. Manning, and Daniel Jurafsky. 2012. Parsing time: Learning to interpret time expressions. In *Proc. of the Annual Meeting of the North American Association of Computational Linguistics (NAACL)*.

Steven Bethard. 2013. ClearTK-TimeML: A minimalist approach to TempEval 2013. In *Second Joint Conference on Lexical and Computational Semantics (* SEM)*, volume 2, pages 10–14.

Steven Bethard, Leon Derczynski, Guergana Savova, James Pustejovsky, and Marc Verhagen. 2015. SemEval-2015 Task 6: Clinical TempEval. In *Proc. of the 9th International Workshop on SemEval*.

Nathanael Chambers, Taylor Cassidy, Bill McDowell, and Steven Bethard. 2014. Dense event ordering with a multi-pass architecture. *TACL*, 2:273–284.

Angel X. Chang and Christopher D. Manning. 2012. SUTIME: A library for recognizing and normalizing time expressions. In *LREC*.

Quang Do, Wei Lu, and Dan Roth. 2012. Joint inference for event timeline construction. In *Proc. of the Conference on Empirical Methods in Natural Language Processing (EMNLP)*.

Inc. Gurobi Optimization. 2015. Gurobi optimizer reference manual.

Prateek Jindal and Dan Roth. 2013. Extraction of events and temporal expressions from clinical narratives. *Journal of Biomedical Informatics (JBI)*.

Daniel Khashabi, Mark Sammons, Ben Zhou, Tom Redman, Christos Christodoulopoulos, and Vivek Srikumar et al. 2018. CogCompNLP: Your swiss army knife for NLP. In *LREC*.

Kenton Lee, Yoav Artzi, Jesse Dodge, and Luke Zettlemoyer. 2014. Context-dependent semantic parsing for time expressions. In *Proc. of the Annual Meeting of the Association for Computational Linguistics (ACL)*, pages 1437–1447.

Hector Llorens, Nathanael Chambers, Naushad UzZaman, Nasrin Mostafazadeh, James Allen, and James Pustejovsky. 2015. SemEval-2015 Task 5: QA TempEval - evaluating temporal information understanding with question answering. In *Proc. of the 9th International Workshop on SemEval*.

Anne-Lyse Minard, Manuela Speranza, Eneko Agirre, Itziar Aldabe, Marieke van Erp, Bernardo Magnini, German Rigau, Ruben Urizar, and Fondazione Bruno Kessler. 2015. SemEval-2015 Task 4: TimeLine: Cross-document event ordering. In *Proc. of the 9th International Workshop on SemEval*.

Qiang Ning, Zhili Feng, and Dan Roth. 2017. A structured learning approach to temporal relation extraction. In *Proc. of the Conference on Empirical Methods in Natural Language Processing (EMNLP)*, pages 1038–1048, Copenhagen, Denmark.

Qiang Ning, Zhili Feng, Hao Wu, and Dan Roth. 2018a. Joint reasoning for temporal and causal relations. In *Proc. of the Annual Meeting of the Association for Computational Linguistics (ACL)*, pages 2278–2288, Melbourne, Australia.

Qiang Ning, Hao Wu, Haoruo Peng, and Dan Roth. 2018b. Improving temporal relation extraction with a globally acquired statistical resource. In *Proc. of the Annual Meeting of the North American Association of Computational Linguistics (NAACL)*, pages 841–851, New Orleans, Louisiana.

Qiang Ning, Hao Wu, and Dan Roth. 2018c. A multi-axis annotation scheme for event temporal relations. In *Proc. of the Annual Meeting of the Association for Computational Linguistics (ACL)*, pages 1318–1328, Melbourne, Australia.

Haoruo Peng, Yangqiu Song, and Dan Roth. 2016. Event detection and co-reference with minimal supervision. In *Proc. of the Conference on Empirical Methods in Natural Language Processing (EMNLP)*.

Vasin Punyakanok and Dan Roth. 2001. The use of classifiers in sequential inference. In *Proc. of the Conference on Neural Information Processing Systems (NIPS)*, pages 995–1001. MIT Press.

Jannik Strötgen and Michael Gertz. 2010. HeidelTime: High quality rule-based extraction and normalization of temporal expressions. In *Proc. of the 5th International Workshop on SemEval*.

Naushad UzZaman, Hector Llorens, James Allen, Leon Derczynski, Marc Verhagen, and James Pustejovsky. 2013. SemEval-2013 Task 1: TEMPEVAL-3: Evaluating time expressions, events, and temporal relations. *SEM*, 2:1–9.

Marc Verhagen, Robert Gaizauskas, Frank Schilder, Mark Hepple, Graham Katz, and James Pustejovsky. 2007. SemEval-2007 Task 15: TempEval temporal relation identification. In *Proc. of the 4th International Workshop on SemEval*, pages 75–80.

Marc Verhagen, Roser Sauri, Tommaso Caselli, and James Pustejovsky. 2010. SemEval-2010 Task 13: TempEval-2. In *Proc. of the 5th international workshop on SemEval*, pages 57–62.

Ran Zhao, Quang Do, and Dan Roth. 2012. A robust shallow temporal reasoning system. In *Proc. of the Annual Conference of the North American Chapter of the Association for Computational Linguistics (NAACL)*.

A Multilingual Information Extraction Pipeline for Investigative Journalism

Gregor Wiedemann   **Seid Muhie Yimam**   **Chris Biemann**

Language Technology Group
Department of Informatics
Universität Hamburg, Germany
`{gwiedemann, yimam, biemann}@informatik.uni-hamburg.de`

Abstract

We introduce an advanced information extraction pipeline to automatically process very large collections of unstructured textual data for the purpose of investigative journalism. The pipeline serves as a new input processor for the upcoming major release of our *New/s/leak 2.0* software, which we develop in cooperation with a large German news organization. The use case is that journalists receive a large collection of files up to several Gigabytes containing unknown contents. Collections may originate either from official disclosures of documents, e.g. Freedom of Information Act requests, or unofficial data leaks. Our software prepares a visually-aided exploration of the collection to quickly learn about potential stories contained in the data. It is based on the automatic extraction of entities and their co-occurrence in documents. In contrast to comparable projects, we focus on the following three major requirements particularly serving the use case of investigative journalism in cross-border collaborations: 1) composition of multiple state-of-the-art NLP tools for entity extraction, 2) support of multi-lingual document sets up to 40 languages, 3) fast and easy-to-use extraction of full-text, metadata and entities from various file formats.

1 Support Investigative Journalism

Journalists usually build up their stories around entities of interest such as persons, organizations, companies, events, and locations in combination with the complex relations they have. This is especially true for investigative journalism which, in the digital age, more and more is confronted to find such relations between entities in large, unstructured and heterogeneous data sources.

Usually, this data is buried in unstructured texts, for instance from scanned and OCR-ed documents, letter correspondences, emails or protocols. Sources typically range from 1) official disclosures of administrative and business documents,

2) court-ordered revelation of internal communication, 3) answers to requests based on Freedom of Information (FoI) acts, and 4) unofficial leaks of confidential information. Well-known examples of such disclosed or leaked datasets are the *Enron* email dataset (Keila and Skillicorn, 2005) or the *Panama Papers* (O'Donovan et al., 2016).

To support investigative journalism in their work, we have developed *New/s/leak* (Yimam et al., 2016), a software implemented by experts from natural language processing and visualization in computer science in cooperation with journalists from *Der Spiegel*, a large German news organization. Due to its successful application in the investigative research as well as continued feedback from academia, we further extend the functionality of *New/s/leak*, which now incorporates better pre-processing, information extraction and deployment features. The new version *New/s/leak 2.0* serves four central requirements that have not been addressed by the first version or other existing solutions for investigative and forensic text analysis:

Improved NLP processing: We use stable and robust state-of-the-art natural language processing (NLP) to automatically extract valuable information for journalistic research. Our pipeline combines extraction of temporal entities, named entities, key-terms, regular expression patterns (e.g. URLs, emails, phone numbers) and user-defined dictionaries.

Multilingualism: Many tools only work for English documents or a few other 'big languages'. In the new version, our tool allows for automatic language detection and information extraction in 40 different languages. Support of multilingual collections and documents is specifically useful to foster cross-country collaboration in journalism.

Multiple file formats: Extracting text and metadata from various file formats can be a daunting task, especially in journalism where time is a very

Proceedings of the 2018 Conference on Empirical Methods in Natural Language Processing (System Demonstrations), pages 78–83
Brussels, Belgium, October 31–November 4, 2018. ©2018 Association for Computational Linguistics

scarce resource. In our architecture, we include a powerful data wrangling software to automatize this process as much as possible. We further put emphasis on scalability in our pipeline to be able to process very large datasets. For easy deployment, *New/s/leak 2.0* is distributed as a Docker setup.

Keyword graphs: We have implemented keyword network graphs, which is build based on the set of keywords representing the current document selection. The keyword network enables to further improve the investigation process by displaying entity networks related to the keywords.

2   Related Work

There are already a handful of commercial and open-source software products to support investigative journalism. Many of the existing tools such as OpenRefine[1], Datawrapper[2], Tabula[3], or Sisense[4] focus solemnly on structured data and most of them are not freely available. For unstructured text data, there are costly products for forensic text analysis such as Intella[5]. Targeted user groups are national intelligence agencies. For smaller publishing houses, acquiring a license for those products is simply not possible. Since we also follow the main idea of openness and freedom of information, we concentrate on other open-source products to compare our software to.

DocumentCloud[6] is an open-source tool specifically designed for journalists to analyze, annotate and publish findings from textual data. In addition to full-text search, it offers named entity recognition (NER) based on OpenCalais[7] for person and location names. In addition to automatic NER for multiple languages, our pipeline supports the identification of keyterms as well as temporal and user-defined entities.

Overview (Brehmer et al., 2014) is another open-source application developed by computer scientists in collaboration with journalists to support investigative journalism. The application supports import of PDF, MS Office, and HTML documents, document clustering based on topic similarity, a simple location entity detection, full-text search, and document tagging. Since this tool is already mature and has successfully been used in a number of published news stories, we adapted some of its most useful features such as document tagging, full-text search and a keyword-in-context (KWIC) view for search hits.

The Jigsaw visual analytics (Görg et al., 2014) system is a third tool that supports analyzing and understanding of textual documents. The Jigsaw system focuses on the extraction of entities using Gate tool suite for NLP (Cunningham et al., 2013). Hence, support for multiple languages is somewhat limited. It also lacks sophisticated data import mechanisms.

The new version of *New/s/leak* was built targeting these drawbacks and challenges. With *New/s/leak 2.0* we aim to support the journalist throughout the entire process of collaboratively analyzing large, complex and heterogeneous document collections: data cleaning and formatting, metadata extraction, information extraction, interactive filtering, visualization, close reading and tagging, and providing provenance information.

3   Architecture

Figure 1 shows the overall architecture of *New/s/leak*. In order to allow users to analyze a wide range of document types, our system includes a document processing pipeline, which extracts text and metadata from a variety of document types into a unified representation. On this unified text representation, a number of NLP pre-processing tasks are performed as a UIMA pipeline (Ferrucci and Lally, 2004), e.g. automatic identification of the document language, segmentation into paragraph, sentence and token units, and extraction of named entities, keywords and metadata. ElasticSearch is used to store the processed data and create aggregation queries for different entity types to generate network graphs. The user interface is implemented with a RESTful web service based on the Scala Play framework in combination with an AngularJS browser app to present information to the journalists. Visualizations are realized with D3 (Bostock et al., 2011).

In order to enable a seamless deployment of the tool by journalists with limited technical skills, we have integrated all of the required components of the architecture into a Docker[8] setup. Via docker-compose, a software to orchestrate Docker con-

---

[1]http://openrefine.org
[2]https://www.datawrapper.de
[3]http://tabula.technology
[4]https://www.sisense.com
[5]https://www.vound-software.com
[6]https://www.documentcloud.org
[7]http://www.opencalais.com
[8]https://www.docker.com

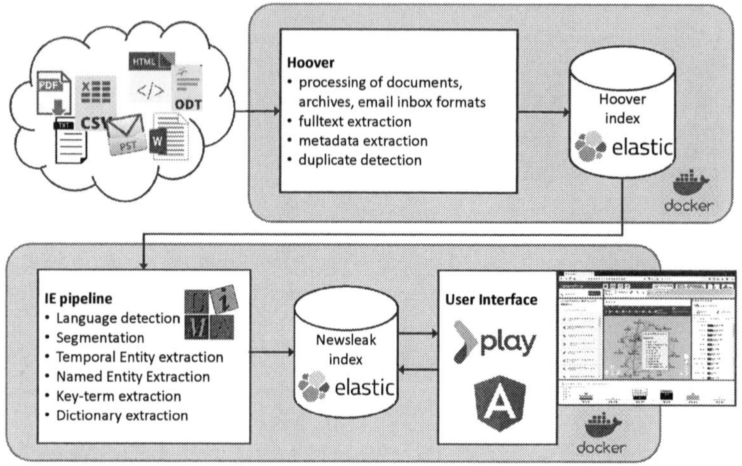

Figure 1: Architecture of *New/s/leak 2.0*

tainers for complex architectures, end-users can download and run locally a preconfigured version of *New/s/leak* with one single command. Being able to process data locally and even without any connection to the internet is a vital prerequisite for journalists when they work with sensitive data. All necessary source code and installation instructions can be found on our Github project page.[9]

4 Data Wrangling

Extracting text and metadata from various formats into a format readable by a specific analysis tool can be a tedious task. In an investigative journalism scenario, it can even be a deal breaker since time is an especially scarce resource and file format conversion might not be a task journalists are well trained in. To offer access to as many file formats as possible in *New/s/leak*, we opted for a close integration with *Hoover*,[10] a set of open-source tools for text extraction and search in large text collections. Hoover is developed by the European Investigative Collaborations (EIC) network with a special focus on large data leaks and heterogeneous datasets. It can extract data from various text file formats such as txt, html, docx, pdf, zip, tar, pst, mbox, eml, etc. The text is extracted along with metadata from files (e.g. file name, creation date, file hash) and header information (e.g. subject, sender, and receiver). In the case of emails, attachments are processed automatically, too.

New/s/leak connects directly to Hoover's index to read full-texts and metadata for its own information extraction pipeline. Through this close integration with Hoover, *New/s/leak* can offer information extraction to a wide variety of data formats. In many cases, this drastically limits or even completely eliminates the amount of work needed to clean and preprocess large datasets beforehand.

5 Multilingual Information Extraction

The core functionality of *New/s/leak* is the automatic extraction of various kinds of entities from text to facilitate the exploration and sense-making process from large collections. Since a lot of steps in this process involve language-dependent resources, we put an emphasis on the work to support as many languages as possible.

5.1 Preprocessing

Information extraction in *New/s/leak* is implemented as a configurable UIMA pipeline (Ferrucci and Lally, 2004). Text documents and metadata from a Hoover collection (see Section 4) are read in parallelized manner and put through a chain of annotators. In a final step of the chain, results from annotation processes are indexed in an ElasticSearch index for later retrieval and visualization.

First, we identify the language of each document. Alternatively, language can also be determined on a paragraph level to support multi-language documents, which can occur quite often, for instance in email leaks or bilingual con-

---

[9]https://uhh-lt.github.io/newsleak-frontend
[10]https://hoover.github.io

tracts. Second, we separate sentences and tokens in each text. To guarantee compatibility with various Unicode scripts in different languages, we rely on the ICU4J library[11] for this task. ICU4J provides locale-specific sentence and word boundary detection relying on a simple rule-based approach. While the quality of the segmentation and tokenization results might be better when using specifically trained segmentation models, the advantage of the rule-based approach in ICU4J is that it works robustly not only for many languages but also for noisy data, which we expect to be abundant in real-life datasets.

5.2 Dictionaries and RE-patterns

In many cases, journalists follow some hypothesis to test for their investigative work. Such a proceeding can involve looking for mentions of already known terms or specific entities in the data. This can be realized by lists of dictionaries provided to the initial information extraction process. *New/s/leak* annotates every mention of a dictionary term with the respective list type. Dictionaries can be defined in a language-specific fashion, but also applied across documents of all languages in the corpus. Extracted dictionary entities are displayed along with extracted named entities in the visualization.

In addition to self-defined dictionaries, we annotate email addresses, telephone numbers, and URLs with regular expression patterns. This is useful, especially for email leaks to reveal communication networks of persons and filter for specific email account related content.

5.3 Temporal Expressions

Tracking documents across the time of their creation or by temporal events they mention can provide valuable information during investigative research. Unfortunately, many document sets (e.g. collections of scanned pages) do not come with a specific document creation date as structured metadata. To offer a temporal selection of contents to the user, we extract mentions of temporal expressions. This is done by integrating the Heidel-Time temporal tagger (Strötgen and Gertz, 2015) in our UIMA workflow. HeidelTime provides automatically learned rules for temporal tagging in more than 200 languages. Extracted timestamps can be used to select and filter documents.

5.4 Named Entity Recognition

We automatically extract person, organization and location names from all documents to allow for an entity-centric exploration of the data collection. Named entity recognition is done using the *polyglot-NER* library (Al-Rfou et al., 2015). Polyglot-NER contains sequence classification for named entities based on weakly annotated training data automatically composed from Wikipedia[12] and Freebase[13]. Relying on the automatic composition of training data allows polyglot-NER to provide pre-trained models for 40 languages.[14]

5.5 Keyterm Extraction

To further summarize document contents in addition to named entities, we automatically extract keyterms and phrases from documents. For this, we implemented a keyterm extraction library for the 40 languages also supported in the previous step.[15] Our approach is based on a statistical comparison of document contents with generic reference data. Reference data for each language is retrieved from the Leipzig Corpora Collection (Goldhahn et al., 2012), which provides large representative corpora for language statistics. We employ log-likelihood significance as described in (Rayson et al., 2004) to measure the overuse of terms (i.e. keyterms) in our target documents compared to the generic reference data. Ongoing sequences of keyterms in target documents are concatenated to key phrases if they occur regularly in that exact same order. Regularity is determined with the Dice coefficient. This simple method allows to reliably extract multiword units such as "stock market" or "machine learning" in the documents. Since this method also extracts named entities if they occur significantly often in a document, there can be a substantial overlap between both types. To allow for a separate display of named entities and keywords, we filter keyterms if they already have been annotated as a named entity. The remaining top keyterms are used to create a brief summary of each document for the user and to generate keyterm networks for document browsing.

---

[11] http://icu-project.org/apiref/icu4j

[12] https://wikipedia.org
[13] https://developers.google.com/freebase
[14] A list of the 40 languages covered by Polyglot-NER can be found at https://tinyurl.com/yaju7bf7
[15] https://github.com/uhh-lt/lt-keyterms

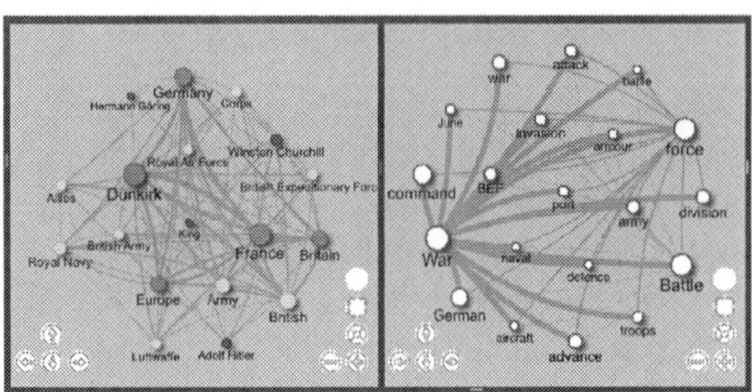

Figure 2: The entity and keyword graphs of *New/s/leak* based on the WW2 collection (see Section 7). Networks are visualized based on the current document selection, which can be filtered by full-text search, entities or metadata. Visualization parameters such as the number of nodes per type or minimum edge strength can be set by the user. Hovering over nodes and edges in one graph highlights information present in the respective another graph to show which entities and keywords frequently co-occur with each other in documents.

6 User Interface

Browsing entity networks: Access to unstructured text collections via named entities is essential for journalistic investigations. To support this, we included two types of graph visualization, as it is shown in Figure 2. The first graph, called entity network, displays entities in a current document selection as nodes and their joint occurrence as edges between nodes. Different node colors represent different types such as person, organization or location names. Furthermore, mentions of entities that are annotated based on dictionary lists are included in the entity network graph. The second graph, called keyword network, is build based on the set of keywords representing the current document selection. The keyword network also includes tags that can be attached to documents by journalists during work with the collection.

Journalist in the loop: In addition to the automatic annotation of entities and keyterms, we further enable journalists to: 1) annotate new entity types that are not in the system at all, 2) correct automatic annotations provided by the pipeline, e.g. to remove false positives or false entity type labels annotated by the NER process, 3) merge identical entities which have different forms (e.g. last names to full names, or spelling variants in different languages), and 4) label documents with user-defined terms called *tags*. The tags are mainly used to annotate the document either for later reading or to share with collaborators.

7 Case Study

To illustrate analysis capabilities of the new version of *New/s/leak*, we present an exemplary case study at `https://ltdemos.informatik. uni-hamburg.de/newsleak/` (login with "user" and "password"). Since we refrain from publishing any confidential leak data, we created an artificial dataset from publicly available documents that share certain characteristics with the data from intended use cases in investigative journalism. It contains documents written in multiple languages, roughly centered on one topic and is full of references to entities.

Ca. 27.000 documents in our sample set are Wikipedia articles related to the topic of World War II. Articles were crawled from the encyclopedia in four languages (English:en, Spanish:es, Hungarian:hu, German:de) as a link network starting from the article "Second World War" in each respective language. Preprocessing and data extraction took around 75 minutes on a moderately fast server with 12 parallel CPU threads.

Analysis: From a perspective of national history discourses and education, a certain common knowledge about WW2 can be expected. But, the topic becomes quickly a novel unexplored terrain for most people when it comes to aspects outside of the own region, e.g. the involvement of Asian powers. In our test case, we strive to fill gaps in our knowledge by identifying interesting details regarding this question. First, we start with a visualization of entities from the entire collection which highlights central actors of WW2 in general. In the list of extracted location entities, we can filter for ca. 2,000 articles referencing to Asia (en, es), Ázsia (hu) or Asien (de). In this subselection, we find most references to China as a political power of the region followed by India and Japan. Further refinement of the collection by references to China highlights a central person name in the network, Chiang Kai-shek, who raises our interest. To find out more, we start the filter process all over again, subselecting all articles referencing this name. The resulting entity network reveals a close connection to the organization Kuomintang (KMT). Filtering for this organization, too, we can quickly identify articles centrally referencing to both entities by looking at their titles and extracted keywords. From the corresponding keyterm network and a KWIC view into the article full-texts, we learn that KMT is the national party of China and Kai-Shek as their leader ruled the country during the period of WW2. A second central actor, Mao Zedong, is strongly connected with both, KMT and Chiang Kai-shek in our entity network. From articles also prominently referencing Zedong, we learn from sections highlighting both person names that Kaishek and Zedong, also a member of KMT and later leader of the Chinese Communists, shared a complicated relationship. By filtering for both names, we can now explore the nature of this relationship in more detail and compare its display across the four languages in our dataset.[16]

8 Discussion and Future Work

In this paper, we introduced the completely renewed information extraction pipeline of *New/s/leak 2.0*, an open-source software to support investigative journalism. As major requirements based on prior experiences, we identified the automatic annotation of various entity types in very large, multi-lingual document sets contained in heterogeneous file formats. Our solution involves a combination of powerful NLP libraries for temporal and named entities, own developments for keyterm and pattern extraction, and a powerful data wrangling suite for text and metadata extraction. The pipeline is capable to process information extraction in 40 languages.

New/s/leak has been in use successfully at the German news organization *Der Spiegel*. It recently has also been introduced as an open-source tool to the community of investigative journalists at respective conferences. We expect to collect more user feedback and experiences from case studies in the near future to further improve the software.

As a new main feature, we plan to extend the information extraction pipeline for user-defined categories into the direction of adaptive and active machine learning approaches. Currently, while reading the full-texts, users can manually annotate new entity types in the text or tag the entire documents. In combination with an adaptive and active learning approach, users will be able to train automatic tagging of documents and extraction of information while working with the data in the user interface.

---

[16]A video of the proceeding can be found at: `http://youtu.be/96f_4Wm5BoU`

References

Rami Al-Rfou, Vivek Kulkarni, Bryan Perozzi, and Steven Skiena. 2015. Polyglot-NER: Massive Multilingual Named Entity Recognition. In *Proc. SIAM/ICDM-2015*, pages 586–594.

Michael Bostock, Vadim Ogievetsky, and Jeffrey Heer. 2011. D3 Data-Driven Documents. *IEEE Trans. Visualization & Comp. Graphics*, 17(12):2301–2309.

M. Brehmer, S. Ingram, J. Stray, and T. Munzner. 2014. Overview: The Design, Adoption, and Analysis of a Visual Document Mining Tool for Investigative Journalists. *IEEE Trans. Visualization & Comp. Graphics*, 20(12):2271–2280.

Hamish Cunningham, Valentin Tablan, Angus Roberts, and Kalina Bontcheva. 2013. Getting more out of biomedical documents with GATE's full lifecycle open source text analytics. *PLoS computational biology*, 9(2):e1002854.

David Ferrucci and Adam Lally. 2004. UIMA: An architectural approach to unstructured information processing in the corporate research environment. *Natural Language Engineering*, 10(3-4):327–348.

Dirk Goldhahn, Thomas Eckart, and Uwe Quasthoff. 2012. Building large monolingual dictionaries at the Leipzig corpora collection: From 100 to 200 languages. In *Proc. LREC 2012*, pages 759–547.

Carsten Görg, Zhicheng Liu, and John Stasko. 2014. Reflections on the evolution of the Jigsaw visual analytics system. *Information Visualization*, 13(4):336–345.

P. S. Keila and D. B. Skillicorn. 2005. Detecting unusual email communication. In *Proc. CASCON 2005*, pages 117–125.

James O'Donovan, Hannes F. Wagner, and Stefan Zeume. 2016. The value of offshore secrets evidence from the panama papers. *SSRN Electronic Journal*.

Paul Rayson, Damon Berridge, and Brian Francis. 2004. Extending the Cochran rule for the comparison of word frequencies between corpora. In *Proc. JADT '04*, pages 926–765.

Jannik Strötgen and Michael Gertz. 2015. A Baseline Temporal Tagger for all Languages. In *Proc. EMNLP 2015*, pages 541–547.

Seid Muhie Yimam, Heiner Ulrich, Tatiana von Landesberger, Marcel Rosenbach, Michaela Regneri, Alexander Panchenko, Franziska Lehmann, Uli Fahrer, Chris Biemann, and Kathrin Ballweg. 2016. new/s/leak – Information Extraction and Visualization for Investigative Data Journalists. In *Proc. ACL 2016 System Demonstrations*, pages 163–168.

Sisyphus, a Workflow Manager Designed for
Machine Translation and Automatic Speech Recognition

Jan-Thorsten Peter, Eugen Beck, and Hermann Ney
RWTH-Aachen University
Templergraben 55, 52062 Aachen, Germany
{lastname}@cs.rwth-aachen.de

Abstract

Training and testing many possible parameters or model architectures of state-of-the-art machine translation or automatic speech recognition system is a cumbersome task. They usually require a long pipeline of commands reaching from pre-processing the training data to post-processing and evaluating the output.

This paper introduces Sisyphus, a tool that aims at managing scientific experiments in an efficient way. After defining the workflow for a given task, Sisyphus runs all required steps and ensures that all commands finish successfully. It avoids unnecessary computations by reusing tasks that are needed for multiple parts of the workflow and saves the user time by determining the order in which the tasks are to be performed. Since the program and workflow are written in Python they can be easily extended to contain arbitrary code. This makes it possible to use the rich collection of Python tools for editing, debugging, and documentation. It only has few requirements on the underlying server or cluster, and has been successfully tested in many large scale setups and can handle thousands of tasks inside the workflow.

1 Introduction

Building competitive machine learning systems requires the correct execution of many different commands and components.

For example, a machine translation system needs to pre-process the data, train a neural network, and its performance evaluated. Each of these steps can contain a large number of separate steps. Running and later replicating all steps by hand is cumbersome and error-prone.

A common approach to reduce these problems is to create ad-hoc scripts for each given task. Although this can be a solution for some parts of the process, it is inflexible when changing workflows as often as required in research. Additionally, er-

rors are easily overlooked when running a large number of scripts in parallel.

Sisyphus is written to ensure that tasks can be easily repeated and offers an overview of large experiment setups with a vast number of steps. Organizing the work this way also allows the user to easily reconfigure experiment and reuse tested sub-tasks in other workflows. It is designed to handle large and complicated workflows, containing ten thousands of tasks in practice.

Finding a good naming scheme for multiple related experiments is also hard, since initially good choices often turn out to grow into strange constructs as new experiments are added over time resulting in names like "ExperimentA-withB-withoutC-D=6-version3". Sisyphus maps all jobs to a unique path and can create links bearing descriptive names. This allows the user to rename everything without violating any dependencies.

1.1 Basic Assumption

In Sisyphus, workflows are broken down into sub-tasks called "Jobs". A job performs a specific function, e.g. evaluating a translation, it often requires an external script or program. Sisyphus is built on one main assumption: Any job only relies on a given list of parameters. e.g. evaluating a translation depends on the hypothesis, the reference, and optionally a script.

This property is used to avoid multiple computations of the same job. Randomness is best modeled using seeds that are given via the job parameters to allow for reliable reproducible results. If this is not possible, e.g. for asynchronous neural network training, Sisyphus still works, but cannot be guaranteed to to reproduce the exact same result.

This means that the automatic handling of changing input files is beyond the scope of Sisyphus. If an input file changes, it is necessary to manually tell Sisyphus to invalidate all jobs that

Proceedings of the 2018 Conference on Empirical Methods in Natural Language Processing (System Demonstrations), pages 84–89
Brussels, Belgium, October 31–November 4, 2018. ©2018 Association for Computational Linguistics

depend on it. Since a reliable test, e.g. hashing, would be too costly to run for each startup, since it can take a long time on large files like the training data.

1.2 Design Goals

The design of Sisyphus is mainly guided by the problems that we encounter while building statistical machine translation and automatic speech recognition systems. Sisyphus aims to address the following problems:

- Separation of the workflow description of an experiment and the place where the experiment is run: This allows the user to store the small description on an expensive but safe file server with backups, while the outputs of an experiment are stored on a larger, but less reliable file system (Section 4.1 and 4.3).

- Reusability of jobs: Once a job is defined, it should be easy to use at a different position within the workflow.

- Minimal requirements on the underlying server structure: Sisyphus only requires Python 3^1 with a few basic packages and a Unix-type operating system.

- Work definition independent of underlying queuing engine: Moving it to a different engine should be easy, e.g. testing the workflow on a local computer before moving it to a grid engine.

- Avoid redundant computations to save time and disk space by grouping jobs with the same input arguments.

- Start all needed jobs automatically in the correct order and, if no blocking dependencies are found, in parallel.

- Automatically check for errors and, if possible, recover. Errors that occur silently somewhere in the pipeline can cause strange results and are hard to find. (Section 3.3)

- Be as general as possible and easy to extend: The whole workflow definition is written in standard conforming Python. This allows for a lot of flexibility in defining a workflow and to use external tools written for Python e.g. to check and edit the workflow.

- The ability to integrate any external tool that has a command line interface into a job.

---

[1] https://www.python.org/

2 Related Work

A large variety of heavyweight workflow management systems exist, e.g. Pegasus (Deelman et al., 2015), Taverna (Wolstencroft et al., 2013), and Kepler (Ludäscher et al., 2006). They can cover a large variety of use-cases (Liew et al., 2016), but their use is hindered by strict requirements on the users computing nodes.

The toolkit that seems to be most similar to our approach is Ducttape[2], the successor of LonnyBin (Clark and Lavie, 2010). It is well designed and covers many useful points. However, we miss a more flexible configuration of the workflow e.g. workflows that adjust to the outputs of finished jobs are not supported. This does not allow to trigger parts of the workflow only if current computations show that they are required.

Ducttape uses branch points to distinguish between different experiment settings. This creates a fairly intuitive directory structure, but does not depend on the true value given to each parameter. If a parameter of a step is changed, it still maps to the same directory. Additionally, long names collapse to a hash value, losing the benefit of intuitively named directories. Interruptions of Ducttape automatically stop all current computations, which makes it problematic to add additional experiments to a running workflow.

Sisyphus contains an experimental script to convert Ducttape workflows into Sisyphus recipes.

3 Basic Elements

Every workflow can be modeled as a series of jobs. The output of a job can be either files or parameters (parameters can be seen as special case of files). This can be mapped to a directed acyclic graph where each node is a job and each edge is a file or parameter. The latter are either passed on to another job or returned as result of the workflow.

The user can request the necessary files and Sisyphus executes all jobs that are needed to compute them. All jobs that are part of the graph but are not required for the desired output are ignored. This graph structure, as shown in Figure 1, is similar to the approach followed by (Clark and Lavie, 2010).

3.1 Jobs

Jobs are the core element of Sisyphus, and are represented by the nodes in the dependency graph. Every Job has specified inputs and outputs. When

---

[2] https://github.com/jhclark/ducttape

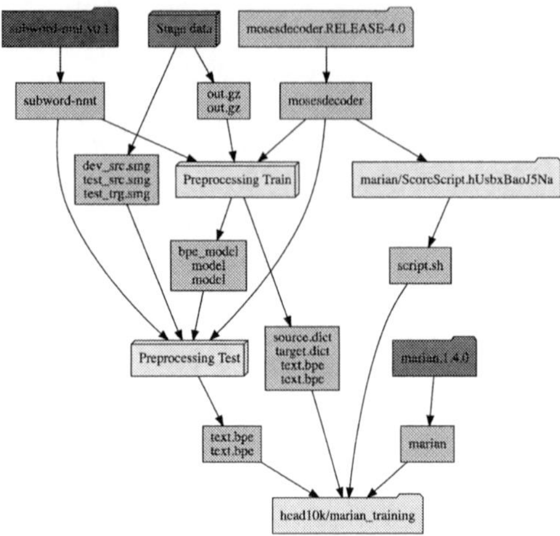

Figure 1: Example of a workflow as it is drawn by the web interface. Jobs can be grouped to blocks for a better visualization as it is done here with the stage data block and the pre-processing blocks. If a Job finishes successfully it is marked dark-green, running Jobs are marked in green-yellow, Jobs that are runnable but not running yet are marked blue, Jobs that have to wait for other Jobs to finish are marked yellow, and Jobs that failed are marked red. A block takes always the status of the most problematic Job, e.g. if one Job failed it is red, if all Jobs are finished it is green. Files that are shared between Jobs are colored aquamarine.

an instance of a Job is created all inputs need to be specified. However, they can be the output of another Job. Once a Job is completed, all of its outputs are guaranteed to be available for future computations.

After a Job is created, a hash value is computed based on the given input parameters. This hash is used to ensure that only one node is used to represent the same computation. Additionally, it is used as part of the path inside the work directory (Section 4.3) associated with the Job. This directory contains log files, status files, the work directory and the output directory. All commands will be run in the work directory, which is initially empty.

A Job is executed as soon as all inputs are ready, meaning all Jobs that compute inputs are finished. Before its execution, a Job has the opportunity to request additional inputs. This can happen as a response to the content of the previously specified inputs, e.g. to implement an automatic parameter optimization. If the Job does not specify additional inputs, it is scheduled for execution in the configured queueing system.

An example Job definition is shown in Figure 2.

3.2 Tasks

Each Job must have one or more Tasks in which the actual command is specified. All Tasks that belong to the same Job share the same work directory, and are executed in a fixed linear order.

A Task object is the combination of a method of the Job class, a set of requirements, and optionally a set of parameters that will be passed to the method when executed. It is submitted to the grid engine and once it is scheduled Sisyphus executes the given method. It is also possible to create arrays of Jobs by providing a list of parameter-sets. These are executed in parallel (to the extent supported by the queue). A common approach is to have a setup Task using one worker, a Task with multiple parallel running instances, and finally a Task to collect the outputs of all parallel Tasks and to write them into the Jobs output file.

3.3 Error Handling

Sisyphus uses strict error checking to avoid errors in which a step causes problems down the line. This makes it easier to track down the problem that caused the error. By default, a Job switches into an error state if:

- a shell command returns a non-zero value, which is also true for any command inside a pipeline,

- an uninitialized variable is called, or

- the Python code throws an exception, which can be used in combination with assertions.

This means the execution of this Job is stopped to give the user a chance to fix the problem. Afterwards, the user can either delete or move the Job directory by himself, or let Sisyphus do it for him. If a Task is known to fail spontaneously, it can be set to retry multiple times.

If a Task is interrupted before it is finished executing all commands, it switches into the interrupted state. The Task can be marked as resumeable, if executing the same code multiple times results in the same outputs. In this case, Sisyphus automatically tries to determine if the Task got interrupted due to a time or memory limit. It increases the requested requirements automatically and resubmits the Task. Resuming is not performed automatically by default, since some programs behave differently if they find files from previous runs in their work directory. If a Job can be resumed, meaning restarting the script will always result in the same output, the user can mark

```python
1  from sisyphus import * # import all Sisyphus related classes, mainly job and task
2
3  class ParallelPipeline(Job):
4      #Example how to distibute a slow pipeline command to multiple machines
5      def __init__(self, text, command, parallel_processe=8):
6          self.text = text # Text that will be split and piped though command
7          self.command = command # The actuall command
8          self.parallel_processe = parallel_processe # Split into that many parallel processes
9          self.out = self.output_path('out.gz') # Name of the output path
10
11     def split(self):
12         #Count lines, capture_output gives stdout of command back as string
13         lines = int(self.sh('zcat -f {text} | wc -l', capture_output=True))
14         self.batch_size = (lines // self.parallel_processe) + 1 # compute batch size
15         self.sh('zcat -f {text} | split -d -l {batch_size}') # Split file
16
17     def run(self, pos):   # pos will be given by task
18         self.sh('cat x%02i | {command} > tmp.%02i' % (pos, pos)) # Run the command for each batch
19
20     def collect(self):
21         self.sh('cat tmp.* | gzip > {out}')   # collect all outputs
22         # Additional manual sanity check
23         output_lines = int(self.sh('zcat {out} | wc -l', capture_output=True))
24         print("Number of output lines: %i" % output_lines)
25         assert output_lines > 0, "No output created"
26
27     def tasks(self):
28         yield Task('split', rqmt={'cpu': 1, 'mem': 1}) # Run split task first
29         # Continue with the main task and starting a worker for each element in args list
30         yield Task('run', rqmt={'cpu': 2, 'mem': 4}, args=list(range(self.parallel_processe)))
31         yield Task('collect', rqmt={'cpu': 1, 'mem': 1}) # Finish with the collect task
```

Figure 2: Example of a job containing multiple task and running the one task on multiple computers

it as such. If not it stops executing further steps and waits for a manual fix by the user.

3.4 Paths and Variables

Jobs are connected by Path and Variable objects, representing the edges in the dependency graph. A Variable is a subclass of the Path object which can store arbitrary pickleable Python objects to be passed between Jobs.

A Job checks all Path objects that are given as inputs and start a Job only once all inputs are available. There are multiple ways for a Path to become available. If it is created as an output of a Job, it is available either once the Job is finished or it is marked as available by the Job earlier. This can be used for example if a neural network training creates save points of the current training state which can be evaluated before the whole training is finished. If a Path object is used to add an input file to the graph, Sisyphus marks it as available if the file exists and alerts the user otherwise.

3.5 Engine

An engine defines how to execute and schedule the given tasks. Currently supported engines are the Son Grid Engine (SGE) with its closely related forks, Platform Load Sharing Facility (LSF), and a local engine running on the same node as Sisyphus. It is also possible to combine different engines. A common setup is to have a local engine for small Jobs, e.g. counting the number of lines in a file, and a cluster-based engine for everything else. The choice which engine to use can be given via the requirement argument of a Task. Currently all engine implementations require that all nodes have access to a shared file system.

4 Directory Structure

A Sisyphus experiment directory usually consists of:

- a recipe directory, containing the source code for the Jobs (Section 4.1),

- a config directory, which defines the Jobs to run and the order of their execution (Section 4.2),

- a work directory, each Job will create a directory here to run its code, store its output, and save log files (Section 4.3),

- a output directory containing links the finished outputs (Section 4.4),

- an aliases directory, containing links to running Jobs with given aliases (Section 4.4), and

- a settings files, that holds global settings, e.g. which engines are available (Section 4.5).

4.1 Recipe Directory

The recipes are a collection of files that contain the code describing the Jobs that can be executed to run an experiment. Recipe files are valid Python files and can be imported similarly to any other Python modules. This allows the users to manage their experiments like a regular Python project, creating dependencies between different Jobs similar to Python module imports. The only thing that separates the recipe directory from a regular module directory is that it can contain Jobs descriptions.

Beside placing Jobs in the recipe directory, it is also common to place functions encapsulating re-occurring workflows here. Any valid Python code can be placed here.

4.2 Config Directory

The configuration directory is used to actually create the graph and select which outputs has to be computed. Similar to the recipe directory, it contains regular Python files that can be imported like any other Python module. It has to import the needed modules from the recipe directory and create the appropriate Jobs. When starting Sisyphus the user selects which configuration should be loaded to construct the graph.

4.3 Work Directory

The work directory stores the realization of the graph. Each Job gets its own directory. Its path is constructed from the recipe module, the Job name and the hash value of the given inputs. This yields a compromise between structured file names, brevity and the individuality of these names. The work directory can be linked to a different file system with sufficient disk space.

4.4 Output and Aliases Directory

Outputs that are computed by Sisyphus are linked to the output directory. Similarly, it is possible to give important Jobs one or more meaningful aliases to make it trivial to find them.

4.5 Settings File

The settings file is used for global parameters. This is the place to define which engine should be used, if and how the requirements of interrupted Jobs are changed, if the Job directory is cleaned automatically after it finishes, what the default environment of an executed shell command should looks like, and various delays to allow networked file systems to synchronize.

5 Helpers

Sisyphus provides a few tools to help with reoccurring tasks.

5.1 Web Server

The web server provides a list with all Jobs and their current states. Alternatively, it is also possible to show all Jobs in a graph structure, as shown in Figure 1. Each Job can be selected to show more detailed information about its status, dependencies and possible error messages.

5.2 Console

It is possible to start an interactive Python shell to analyze the graph or test different functions directly. It also serves to call the team import (Section 5.3) and clean up helper (Section 5.5).

5.3 Team Import

If multiple people work on the same task, it is helpful to avoid rerunning computations that have been already carried out by others. Sisyphus can automatically check other work directories and import finished Jobs. This saves one from manually linking finished computations, as it is usually the case when using scripts.

5.4 Virtual File System

An alternative way to have a structured access to all Job work directories and attributes is the virtual file system using fuse. This allows one to use any console or script to navigate the graph.

5.5 Clean Up

After the experiments are finished it is time to clean up. Sisyphus supports a few options to do this depending how harsh the clean up has to be. This is mainly a trade-off between how much space is used on disk vs. how many steps are needed to re-run the experiments.

The least invasive method is to delete the work directory of each Job to remove temporary data created during the execution of the Job and to pack all log files into a tar archive. This can be set to run automatically in the background after a Job has finished successfully.

The second method is to remove lost Job directories from Jobs that are not in the final graph. This usually happens if the workflow changed over time and some steps had to be re-run due to changed inputs. The now obsolete directories remain on disk until they are removed. A alternative source for lost data in the work directories are Jobs that have been restarted after an error which causes Sisyphus to move the old directory aside in case later debugging is necessary. This step keeps all the data used in the current workflow.

A more invasive option to free space is the clean-up of the current graph by removing Jobs that are not needed for further computations of the workflow anymore. This only keeps Jobs which produce outputs that are marked as targets or Jobs that are still needed to reach unfinished targets. In addition Jobs can be saved from deletion by defining a score, Jobs with a score higher than the chosen threshold will be kept. These are typically Jobs that are expensive to recompute, e.g. the training of a neural networks.

6 Real-World Usage

Sisyphus is extensively used by the machine translation and the automatic speech recognition teams at the RWTH Aachen University. All WMT and IWSLT submissions by the RWTH Aachen University since 2015 until now have been created using Sisyphus (Peter et al., 2015b,a). It was used for speech recognition in Zeyer et al. (2017). AppTek[3] also uses Sisyphus internally.

7 Conclusion

We presented overview of our novel workflow manager Sisyphus. Features like automatic error detection, efficient usage of computational resources, scalability, easy of reproducibility, ability to share work with others have been proven to be extremely helpful for our research. The large collection of tools for Python can be used without modification for editing, debugging, and documenting the workflow, since it is written in Python. It is freely available online[4] under the Mozilla License v2.0 to encourage the adoption by other groups.

Acknowledgements

This work has received funding from the European Research Council (ERC) (under the European Union's Horizon 2020 research and innovation programme, grant agreement No 694537, project "SEQ-CLAS") and the Deutsche Forschungsgemeinschaft (DFG; grant agreement NE 572/8-1, project "CoreTec"). The GPU computing cluster was supported by DFG (Deutsche Forschungsgemeinschaft) under grant INST 222/1168-1 FUGG. The work reflects only the authors' views and none of the funding agencies is responsible for any use that may be made of the information it contains.

We want to thank explicitly Wilfried Michel, Nick Rossenbach, Arne Nix, Jan Rosendahl, Weiyue Wang, Henrik Rosendahl, and Julian Schamper for using and testing Sisyphus early on. We also really appreciate the detailed feedback from our reviewers.

References

Jonathan H. Clark and Alon Lavie. 2010. Loony-Bin: Keeping Language Technologists Sane through Automated Management of Experimental (Hyper)Workflows. In *Proceedings of the International Conference on Language Resources and Evaluation, LREC 2010, 17-23 May 2010, Valletta, Malta.*

Ewa Deelman, Karan Vahi, Gideon Juve, Mats Rynge, Scott Callaghan, Philip J. Maechling, Rajiv Mayani, Weiwei Chen, Rafael Ferreira da Silva, Miron Livny, and Kent Wenger. 2015. Pegasus, a Workflow Management System for Science Automation. *Future Gener. Comput. Syst.*, 46(C):17–35.

Chee Sun Liew, Malcolm P. Atkinson, Michelle Galea, Tan Fong Ang, Paul Martin, and Jano I. Van Hemert. 2016. Scientific Workflows: Moving Across Paradigms. *ACM Comput. Surv.*, 49(4):66:1–66:39.

Bertram Ludäscher, Ilkay Altintas, Chad Berkley, Dan Higgins, Efrat Jaeger, Matthew Jones, Edward A. Lee, Jing Tao, and Yang Zhao. 2006. Scientific Workflow Management and the Kepler System: Research Articles. *Concurr. Comput. : Pract. Exper.*, 18(10):1039–1065.

Jan-Thorsten Peter, Farzad Toutounchi, Stephan Peitz, Parnia Bahar, Andreas Guta, and Hermann Ney. 2015a. The RWTH Aachen German to English MT System for IWSLT 2015. In *International Workshop on Spoken Language Translation*, pages 15–22, Da Nang, Vietnam.

Jan-Thorsten Peter, Farzad Toutounchi, Joern Wuebker, and Hermann Ney. 2015b. The RWTH Aachen German-English Machine Translation System for WMT 2015. In *EMNLP 2015 Tenth Workshop on Statistical Machine Translation*, page 158163, Lisbon, Portugal.

Katherine Wolstencroft, Robert Haines, Donal Fellows, Alan Williams, David Withers, Stuart Owen, Stian Soiland-Reyes, Ian Dunlop, Aleksandra Nenadic, Paul Fisher, Jiten Bhagat, Khalid Belhajjame, Finn Bacall, Alex Hardisty, Abraham Nieva de la Hidalga, Maria P. Balcazar Vargas, Shoaib Sufi, and Carole Goble. 2013. The Taverna workflow suite: designing and executing workflows of Web Services on the desktop, web or in the cloud. *Nucleic Acids Research*, 41(W1):W557–W561.

Albert Zeyer, Eugen Beck, Ralf Schlüter, and Hermann Ney. 2017. CTC in the Context of Generalized Full-Sum HMM Training. In *Interspeech*, pages 944–948, Stockholm, Sweden.

---

[3] http://www.apptek.com/
[4] https://github.com/rwth-i6/sisyphus

KT-Speech-Crawler: Automatic Dataset Construction for Speech Recognition from YouTube Videos

Egor Lakomkin   Sven Magg   Cornelius Weber   Stefan Wermter

Department of Informatics, Knowledge Technology
University of Hamburg
Vogt-Koelln Str. 30, 22527 Hamburg, Germany
`{lakomkin, magg, weber, wermter}@informatik.uni-hamburg.de`

Abstract

In this paper, we describe KT-Speech-Crawler: an approach for automatic dataset construction for speech recognition by crawling YouTube videos. We outline several filtering and post-processing steps, which extract samples that can be used for training end-to-end neural speech recognition systems. In our experiments, we demonstrate that a single-core version of the crawler can obtain around 150 hours of transcribed speech within a day, containing an estimated 3.5% word error rate in the transcriptions. Automatically collected samples contain reading and spontaneous speech recorded in various conditions including background noise and music, distant microphone recordings, and a variety of accents and reverberation. When training a deep neural network on speech recognition, we observed around 40% word error rate reduction on the Wall Street Journal dataset by integrating 200 hours of the collected samples into the training set. The demo[1] and the crawler code[2] are publicly available.

1   Introduction

End-to-end neural networks significantly simplified the development of automatic speech recognition (ASR) systems (Graves and Jaitly, 2014). Traditionally, ASR systems are based on Gaussian Mixture Models (GMM) or Deep Neural Networks (DNN) for acoustic state representations followed by the Hidden Markov Model (HMM) for sequence-level learning. Though such systems are successful and achieve high performance (Hinton et al., 2012), they require word- or phoneme-level alignments between the acoustic signal and the transcription. As a result, dataset preparation for such hybrid systems is a labor-intensive

---

[1] `http://emnlp-demo.lakomkin.me/`
[2] `https://github.com/EgorLakomkin/KTSpeechCrawler`

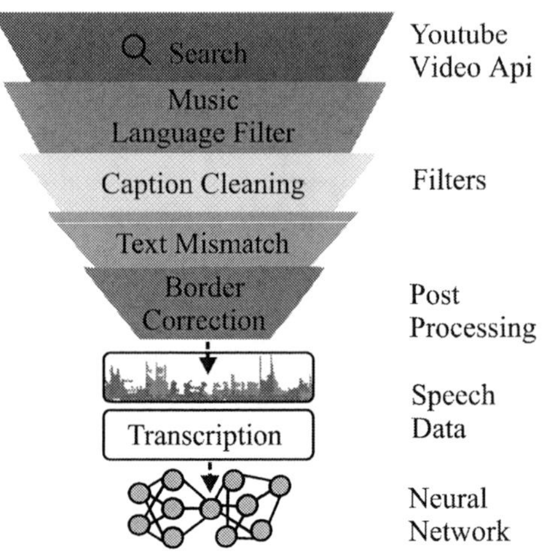

Figure 1:   Architecture of the proposed system crawling YouTube to find videos with closed captions. Several filtering and post-processing steps are applied to select high-quality speech candidates. As a result, pairs of speech and corresponding transcriptions are collected.

and error-prone process as the performance of the whole system is sensitive to the quality of the alignment. Also, each component is trained individually, which makes the whole process complex and difficult to maintain. Recently, Connectionist Temporal Classification (CTC) loss (Graves et al., 2006) has been introduced, which allows relaxing the constraint of having alignment between the spoken text and audio by introducing a sequence-level criterion. Also, recurrent neural network-based architectures that are state-of-the-art models in machine translation have been applied to speech recognition (Chan et al., 2016). Consequently, neural networks can be trained end-to-end via backpropagation (Graves and Jaitly, 2014).

Proceedings of the 2018 Conference on Empirical Methods in Natural Language Processing (System Demonstrations), pages 90–95
Brussels, Belgium, October 31–November 4, 2018. ©2018 Association for Computational Linguistics

CTC maximizes the log-likelihood of the ground truth transcription and thus only the spoken text is required without an explicit alignment, which is easier and cheaper to obtain.

Previous work outlined the importance of having large amounts of annotated data to train deep neural networks. For example, a ten times increase of the training data size from 1,200 hours to 12,000 hours resulted in improving the word error rate from 13.9% to 8.46% for clean and from 22.99% to 13.59% for noisy speech (Amodei et al., 2016). Collecting such large datasets is an expensive and labor-intensive process, which requires a significant amount of resources, usually not available for the research community compared to large industrial companies. For example, Baidu's internal speech dataset (Amodei et al., 2016) contains around 10,000 hours of speech, while the largest dataset available for the research community does not exceed 2,000 hours (David et al., 2004). We propose to utilize a vast amount of videos available on YouTube with user-provided closed captions as a source to extract speech datasets comparable in size to the ones available in the industry.

Our contribution in this paper is two-fold: 1) we provide a crawler that automatically extracts speech samples with transcriptions from YouTube and filters high-quality samples with several heuristic measures, and 2) we extend the training data of two benchmark datasets with the extracted samples and validate the benefit of the collected data by training a deep neural network on the original and the combined data to measure test performance difference. We also evaluate the amount of noise in transcriptions by manually checking the word error rate of a random subset of the dataset. We hope that our developed tool will foster research of large-scale automatic speech recognition systems[3].

2   Related work

Crowdsourcing has been successfully used to construct speech datasets like VoxForge[4] or Mozilla's Common Voice[5], where users recorded themselves through the provided web-interface, and uploaded samples can be checked by other partic-

ipants. While such an approach, in theory, can be a viable strategy to acquire a large number of diverse speech samples, it has several drawbacks. The main limitation of this approach is the difficulty of engaging and acquiring users to donate samples to achieve a large and diverse dataset in terms of the number of different speakers, accents, environments and recording conditions. Another approach, which is widely adopted by the research community, is to make use of a vast amount of available multi-modal data which contains transcribed speech. For example, TED talks (Rousseau et al., 2014) are carefully transcribed and contain around 200 hours of speech from around 1,500 speakers (TED-LIUM v2 dataset). LibriSpeech (Panayotov et al., 2015) is composed of a large number of audiobooks and is the largest freely available dataset: around 960 hours of English read speech. Google released their Speech Commands dataset[6] containing around 65,000 one-second-long utterances.

It has already been demonstrated that YouTube captions can be successfully used as a ground truth spoken text transcription to train large-scale ASR systems (Liao et al., 2013; Lecouteux et al., 2012). Users upload closed captions for various reasons: to make video accessible for people having some degree of hear loss, or to help non-native speakers, or to increase the number of views (YouTube search ranking algorithm indexes closed captions content[7]). Nevertheless, some videos contain inaccurate or even unrelated to speech captions, for example, advertisements. Several heuristics were proposed to remove low-quality samples: removing captions containing advertisements, language mismatch detection and using forced alignment to detect confident alignment regions between the caption and the audio. In addition, YouTube has been used previously in multiple ways to automatically collect multi-modal datasets, e.g. emotion recognition datasets by Barros et al. (2018) and Zadeh et al. (2016), or opinion mining (Marrese-Taylor et al., 2017), or video classification (YouTube-8M[8], or human action recognition (Kay et al., 2017)).

In this work, we combine several known heuris-

---

[3]The code and the Dockerfile are available by this link   https://github.com/EgorLakomkin/KTSpeechCrawler

[4]http://www.voxforge.org

[5]https://voice.mozilla.org/

[6]https://ai.googleblog.com/2017/08/launching-speech-commands-dataset.html

[7]https://www.3playmedia.com/customers/case-studies/discovery-digital-networks/

[8]https://research.google.com/youtube8m/

tics and propose some additional ones to select high quality samples in an automatic way. We integrate it into an easy to use tool *KT-Speech-Crawler*, which can continuously scan new videos uploaded to YouTube and update the speech database. To our knowledge, this is the first open-source tool available for automatic speech dataset construction.

3 Crawler

In this section, we describe the sample selection strategy, followed by several filtering and post-processing heuristics to locate high-quality samples and discard noisy ones from YouTube.

3.1 Candidate selection

Firstly, we download candidate videos with English closed captions, which are usually uploaded by the channel owner. To reach as many videos as possible we use the YouTube Search API, where one of the top 100 most common English words is used as a search keyword to match the video title (for example, *the, but, have, not, and, ...*). Such frequent keywords allow us to match many videos, even though, as a side effect, non-English videos with closed captions in English might be captured. The YouTube Search API allows to download the 600 most recent videos for each keyword, and since many videos are constantly being uploaded to YouTube it is possible to continuously collect speech samples. Also, we memorize YouTube channels containing samples that passed all the filtering steps (see section 3.2) and use other videos from this channel. This leads to many diverse candidates coming from TV shows and TV series, video blogs, news, and live recordings.

3.2 Filtering steps

We perform several filtering steps to select suitable candidates:

- we discard a caption if it overlaps with another caption, which sometimes happens due to incorrectly closed caption auto syncing,

- we filter out captions that indicate that there is music content in this sample and captions containing non-ASCII characters or URLs,

- we remove text chunks which do not correspond to the actual spoken text, like the information of the speaker name (*Speaker 1: ...*),

annotations (*[laughs], *laughs*, (laughs)*), and punctuation,

- we spell out numbers which are within the range from 1 to 100 as they have non-ambiguous pronunciation (in contrast, for example, *1,500* can be uttered as *fifteen hundred* or *one thousand and five hundred*),

- we discard captions if they contain any character that is not an English letter, apostrophe or a white space,

- we filter segments which have less than one second duration or more than ten seconds,

- in addition, we select randomly three phrases from the video and measure the Levenshtein similarity between the provided closed caption and the transcription generated by the Google ASR API. If the similarity is below a 70% threshold, we discard all the samples in this video. This step allows filtering videos which have English subtitles for non-English spoken text or videos with a bad alignment. Also, this filter removes videos with completely misaligned captions.

3.3 Post-processing steps

During our experiments on evaluating the quality of the extracted samples, we spotted that one of the major problems is imprecise alignments between caption and audio. For example, the first or the last word can be omitted on the recording due to incorrect caption timings. One possible way to reduce the number of samples with mis-aligned borders is to group together nearby captions if they are at a distance of less than one second. We stop grouping adjacent utterances if the overall length exceeds ten seconds. In addition, we perform a forced alignment[9] between the caption and the corresponding audio using Kaldi (Povey et al., 2011) and if the first or the last word is not successfully mapped, we try to extend the caption boundaries (up to 500 milliseconds) until the border word becomes mapped. If we cannot align the border word, we keep the caption boundaries unchanged.

4 Experiments and analysis

To evaluate the usefulness of the collected samples we conducted three types of experiments. We

---

[9]https://github.com/lowerquality/gentle

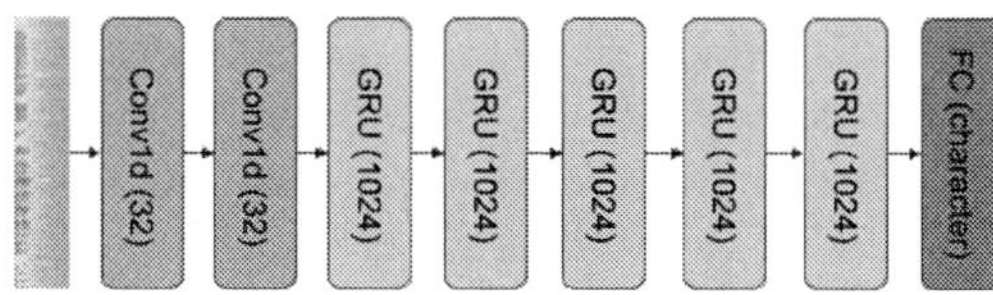

Figure 2: Architecture of the ASR model used in this work, following the DeepSpeech 2 architecture.

trained the deep neural network-based model on different training datasets:

- on the original training data,

- on the mix of the original and with the crawled samples,

- only on the crawled samples.

For benchmarking, we selected two well-known datasets for training ASR systems: The Wall Street Journal and TED-LIUM v2. In all experiments, we kept the same size and architecture of the neural model and its hyperparameters. In this section, we outline the details of benchmark data used in our experiments, neural model architecture and the evaluation protocol and metrics, followed by the evaluation results and comparisons.

4.1 ASR model

Our ASR model (see Figure 2) is a combination of convolutional and recurrent layers inspired by the DeepSpeech 2 (Amodei et al., 2016) architecture. Our model contains two 2D convolutional layers for feature extraction from power FFT spectrograms. Power spectrograms are extracted using a Hamming window of 20ms width and 10ms stride, resulting in 161 features for each speech frame. Convolutional layers are followed by five recurrent bi-directional Gated Recurrent Units (Chung et al., 2014) layers with a size of 1,024 followed by a softmax layer on top, predicting the character distribution for each speech frame. Overall, our model has around 61 million parameters. Connectionist Temporal Classification (CTC) loss (Graves et al., 2006) is used as a loss criterion to measure how good the alignment produced by the network is compared to the ground truth transcription.

The Stochastic Gradient Descent optimizer is used in all experiments with a learning rate of 0.0003, clipping the norm of the gradient at the

Table 1: Evaluation results. We evaluated the effect of adding samples extracted from YouTube by our tool on two benchmarking datasets: WSJ and TED-LIUM v2. We trained the deep neural network on the original training data, then combined the data with YouTube samples (*WSJ+YouTube*, for example), and, finally, only on the YouTube samples. We report word and character error rate.

Train	Test	WER	CER
WSJ	WSJ	27.4%	7.2%
WSJ + YouTube (200h)	WSJ	**15,8%**	**4.2%**
YouTube (200h)	WSJ	31.5%	8.3%
TED	TED	32.6%	10.4%
TED + YouTube (300h)	TED	**28.1%**	**8.2%**
YouTube (300h)	TED	36.6%	10.6%

level of 400 with a batch size of 32. During the training, we apply learning rate annealing with a factor of 1.1. We apply the SortaGrad algorithm (Amodei et al., 2016) during the first epoch by sorting utterances by their duration (Hannun et al., 2014a). We select the model with the best word error rate measured on the validation set to prevent model overfitting.

4.2 Data and evaluation measure

4.2.1 WSJ

The Wall Street Journal (WSJ) dataset is a well-known dataset for evaluating ASR systems, containing utterances of read speech coming from the news domain. The WSJ training set (*train-si284*) consists of 81 hours containing 37,318 sentences from 284 speakers (142 male and 142 female). We used the dev93 development set for validation and report the word error rate on the eval92 test set.

4.2.2 TED talks

We also evaluated our approach on the TED-LIUM v2 dataset, which contains around 200 hours of transcribed TED[10] talks of 1,495 speakers. In contrast to the WSJ dataset, it contains spontaneous speech rather than read speech.

4.3 Results

We summarize our results in Table 1. Note that we did not use a language model for decoding in our experiments but used greedy decoding, where the most probable character at each timestep was emitted. It is well known that decoding with the

---

[10] https://www.ted.com/

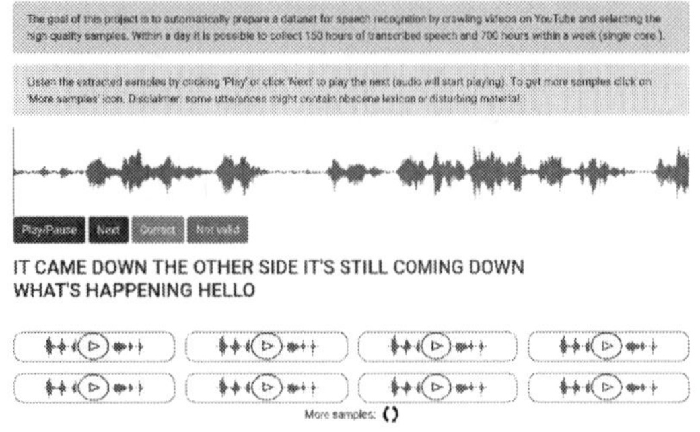

Figure 3: A screenshot of the web-based demo to browse the collected samples, presenting the extracted utterance and the corresponding transcription.

language model and beam search significantly improves the performance on the test set of character-based end-to-end models (Hannun et al., 2014b), but as our goal was to demonstrate the impact of adding extracted samples within the same neural model and test set, we left it out. We observed that adding samples from YouTube positively contributed to the overall performance in both metrics: word (WER) and character error rates (CER). For example, the word error rate improved from 34.2% to 15.8% on the WSJ test set by adding 200 hours of samples (108,617 utterances) to the WSJ training set. Similar results can be observed on the TED talks dataset: WER and CER improved from 32.6% to 28.1% and 10.4% to 8.2% by adding 300 hours of YouTube samples. To be sure that none of the TED videos appeared in the YouTube set, which could lead to overestimation of the performance, we excluded videos that contain a *TED* token in the title or in the description. Interestingly, if only YouTube samples were used as the training set, we observed CER values of 8.3% and 10.6% for the WSJ and the TED datasets, respectively (compared to 7.2% and 10.4% using original training data), indicating that having a domain-specific training set plays an important role and there is a room for improvement in designing better filtering and post-processing steps.

4.4 Transcriptions quality

We manually investigated samples by using developed a web-based demo, see Fig. 3 and analyzed the quality of the collected samples and their transcriptions. Our developed web-service presents random eight utterances and their corresponding transcriptions to the user and allows to load more

samples if necessary. We also integrated a simple functionality to validate the extracted samples: a user can confirm that the caption is correct or if not enter the right transcription.

$$WER = \frac{S + D + I}{S + D + C} \qquad (1)$$

We computed the word error rate using equation 1, where S, I, D, C is number of substitutions, insertions, deletions and correct words, respectively. We estimated 3.5% word error rate on the small randomly selected subset of 600 samples. The most common type of error was missing or wrongly added one or two words at the beginning or at the end of the utterance.

5 Conclusions and future work

In this work, we presented an open-source system that automatically constructs datasets for training end-to-end neural speech recognition systems. We demonstrated the usefulness of the collected samples on the WSJ and TED datasets. We provide the code for the crawler and metadata and a script to easily construct a dataset of 500 hours.

Future work includes extending the script to support other languages. A more sophisticated approach to identify wrongly added or missing words in transcriptions could also be used by using attention-based neural networks like pointer networks. We are also aware that some collected samples may contain automatically generated utterances with Text-To-Speech software, which may require performing speaker recognition to balance the dataset. Furthermore, domain-specific speech datasets can be collected by selecting samples after analyzing captions and video metadata (for example, in the financial domain). In addition, samples with several people talking at the same time and noisy samples with low signal-to-noise ratio need to be filtered, which could be implemented as neural network-based modules.

We believe that having large, free and high-quality speech datasets available to the research community will foster the development of new architectures and applications for speech understanding, and we hope that our presented tool will contribute to that.

Acknowledgments

This project has received funding from the European Union's Horizon 2020 research and innovation programme under the Marie Sklodowska-Curie grant agreement No 642667 (SECURE) and partial support from the German Research Foundation DFG under project CML (TRR 169).

References

Dario Amodei, Rishita Anubhai, Eric Battenberg, Carl Case, Jared Casper, Bryan Catanzaro, Jingdong Chen, Mike Chrzanowski, Adam Coates, and et al. 2016. Deep Speech 2: End-to-End Speech Recognition in English and Mandarin. *Proceedings of The 33rd International Conference on Machine Learning*, 48:173–182.

Pablo Barros, Nikhil Churamani, Egor Lakomkin, Henrique Siqueira, Alexander Sutherland, and Stefan Wermter. 2018. The OMG-Emotion Behavior Dataset. *To appear in International Joint Conference on Neural Networks*.

William Chan, Navdeep Jaitly, Quoc Le, and Oriol Vinyals. 2016. Listen, attend and spell: A neural network for large vocabulary conversational speech recognition. In *2016 IEEE International Conference on Acoustics, Speech and Signal Processing (ICASSP)*, pages 4960–4964. IEEE.

Junyoung Chung, Caglar Gulcehre, KyungHyun Cho, and Yoshua Bengio. 2014. Empirical Evaluation of Gated Recurrent Neural Networks on Sequence Modeling. *Deep Learning and Representation Learning Workshop*.

Christopher Cieri David, Christopher Cieri David, David Miller, and Kevin Walker. 2004. The Fisher Corpus: a Resource for the Next Generations of Speech-to-Text. *In Proceedings 4th International Conference On Language Resources and Evaluation*, pages 69–71.

Alex Graves, Santiago Fernández, Faustino Gomez, and Jrgen Schmidhuber. 2006. Connectionist temporal classification. In *Proceedings of the 23rd international conference on Machine learning - ICML '06*, pages 369–376, New York, New York, USA. ACM Press.

Alex Graves and Navdeep Jaitly. 2014. Towards end-to-end speech recognition with recurrent neural networks. *Proceedings of the 31st International Conference on International Conference on Machine Learning - Volume 32*, pages II–1764.

Awni Hannun, Carl Case, Jared Casper, Bryan Catanzaro, Greg Diamos, Erich Elsen, Ryan Prenger, Sanjeev Satheesh, Shubho Sengupta, Adam Coates, and Andrew Y Ng. 2014a. Deep Speech: Scaling up end-to-end speech recognition. *CoRR*, abs/1412.5567.

Awni Y. Hannun, Andrew L. Maas, Daniel Jurafsky, and Andrew Y. Ng. 2014b. First-Pass Large Vocabulary Continuous Speech Recognition using Bi-Directional Recurrent DNNs. *CoRR*, abs/1408.2873.

Geoffrey Hinton, Li Deng, Dong Yu, George Dahl, Abdel-rahman Mohamed, Navdeep Jaitly, Andrew Senior, Vincent Vanhoucke, Patrick Nguyen, Tara Sainath, and Brian Kingsbury. 2012. Deep Neural Networks for Acoustic Modeling in Speech Recognition: The Shared Views of Four Research Groups. *IEEE Signal Processing Magazine*, 29(6):82–97.

Will Kay, Joao Carreira, Karen Simonyan, Brian Zhang, Chloe Hillier, Sudheendra Vijayanarasimhan, Fabio Viola, Tim Green, Trevor Back, Paul Natsev, Mustafa Suleyman, and Andrew Zisserman. 2017. The Kinetics Human Action Video Dataset.

Benjamin Lecouteux, Georges Linarès, and Stanislas Oger. 2012. Integrating imperfect transcripts into speech recognition systems for building high-quality corpora. *Computer Speech & Language*, 26(2):67–89.

Hank Liao, Erik McDermott, and Andrew Senior. 2013. Large scale deep neural network acoustic modeling with semi-supervised training data for YouTube video transcription. In *2013 IEEE Workshop on Automatic Speech Recognition and Understanding*, pages 368–373.

Edison Marrese-Taylor, Jorge Balazs, and Yutaka Matsuo. 2017. Mining fine-grained opinions on closed captions of YouTube videos with an attention-RNN. In *Proceedings of the 8th Workshop on Computational Approaches to Subjectivity, Sentiment and Social Media Analysis*, pages 102–111, Stroudsburg, PA, USA. Association for Computational Linguistics.

Vassil Panayotov, Guoguo Chen, Daniel Povey, and Sanjeev Khudanpur. 2015. Librispeech: An ASR corpus based on public domain audio books. In *2015 IEEE International Conference on Acoustics, Speech and Signal Processing (ICASSP)*, pages 5206–5210. IEEE.

Daniel Povey, Daniel Povey, Arnab Ghoshal, Gilles Boulianne, Nagendra Goel, Mirko Hannemann, Yanmin Qian, Petr Schwarz, and Georg Stemmer. 2011. The kaldi speech recognition toolkit. *In IEEE Automatic Speech Recognition and Understanding Workshop*.

Anthony Rousseau, Anthony Rousseau, Paul Deléglise, and Yannick Estève. 2014. Enhancing the TED-LIUM corpus with selected data for language modeling and more TED talks. *In Proceedings 9th International Conference On Language Resources and Evaluation*, pages 26–31.

Amir Zadeh, Rowan Zellers, Eli Pincus, and Louis-Philippe Morency. 2016. MOSI: Multimodal Corpus of Sentiment Intensity and Subjectivity Analysis in Online Opinion Videos. *IEEE Intelligent Systems*, 31.6:82–88.

Visualizing Group Dynamics based on Multiparty Meeting Understanding

Ni Zhang[1], Tongtao Zhang[1], Indrani Bhattacharya[2], Heng Ji[1] and Richard J. Radke[2]
[1]Department of Computer Science
[2]Department of Electrical, Computer, and Systems Engineering
Rensselaer Polytechnic Institute
{zhangn5, zhangt13, bhatti, jih}@rpi.edu rjradke@ecse.rpi.edu

Abstract

Group discussions are usually aimed at sharing opinions, reaching consensus and making good decisions based on group knowledge. During a discussion, participants might adjust their own opinions as well as tune their attitudes towards others' opinions, based on the unfolding interactions. In this paper, we demonstrate a framework to visualize such dynamics; at each instant of a conversation, the participants' opinions and potential influence on their counterparts is easily visualized. We use multi-party meeting opinion mining based on bipartite graphs to extract opinions and calculate mutual influential factors, using the Lunar Survival Task as a study case.

1 Introduction

Group meetings are pervasive in modern workplaces, consuming workers' time and energy. Reaching consensus and making decisions more efficiently are major challenges. For example, during a meeting, some of the participants might insist on their own opinions towards the discussed items or topics, while others might rapidly change opinions and attitudes. As a meeting unfolds, we can observe developing leadership characteristics among the participants; for example, some participants may speak more assertively to drive decisive conclusions and steer the meeting, while others may follow the crowd and merely deliver tiny ideas.

In order to track the dynamics that reflect the change of opinions and the procedure of decision making, we require a meeting assistant that works in real time. That is, the assistant should keep track of the agenda and discussion process as a minute or note-taker, as well as record and assess the influence and contribution of each participant.

In this paper, using the NASA Lunar Survival Task [1] as a study case, we present an automatic meeting assistant with the following functionalities:

- The assistant detects and extracts participants' opinions from their speech and visualizes the groups' instantaneous state (ranking of items) based on current and previous utterances.
- The assistant visualizes an influence factor for each participant using current and previous utterances in real time. Using this information, emerging leadership in the group can be visualized.

The proposed assistant begins with speech recognition output, and detects the opinions from the speakers with Natural Language Processing (NLP) tools. We propose a bipartite graph formalism to assess participants' influence.

2 System Overview

2.1 Study Case Introduction

The NASA Lunar Survival Task is a widely used group consensus exercise that helps encourage the development of communication, cooperation, and decision making skills (Hall and Watson, 1970). In small groups of 3–4, participants discuss a hypothetical survival scenario and rank the value of supplies that may aid in their survival and safe rendezvous with their mothership. Before the discussion, each participant is asked to independently rank the items. Next, the participants are asked to reach consensus on the ranking with active verbal interaction. Each member of the group must agree upon the final ranking, which acts as the group decision.

---

[1]https://t.co/5e56cHayji

96

Proceedings of the 2018 Conference on Empirical Methods in Natural Language Processing (System Demonstrations), pages 96–101
Brussels, Belgium, October 31–November 4, 2018. ©2018 Association for Computational Linguistics

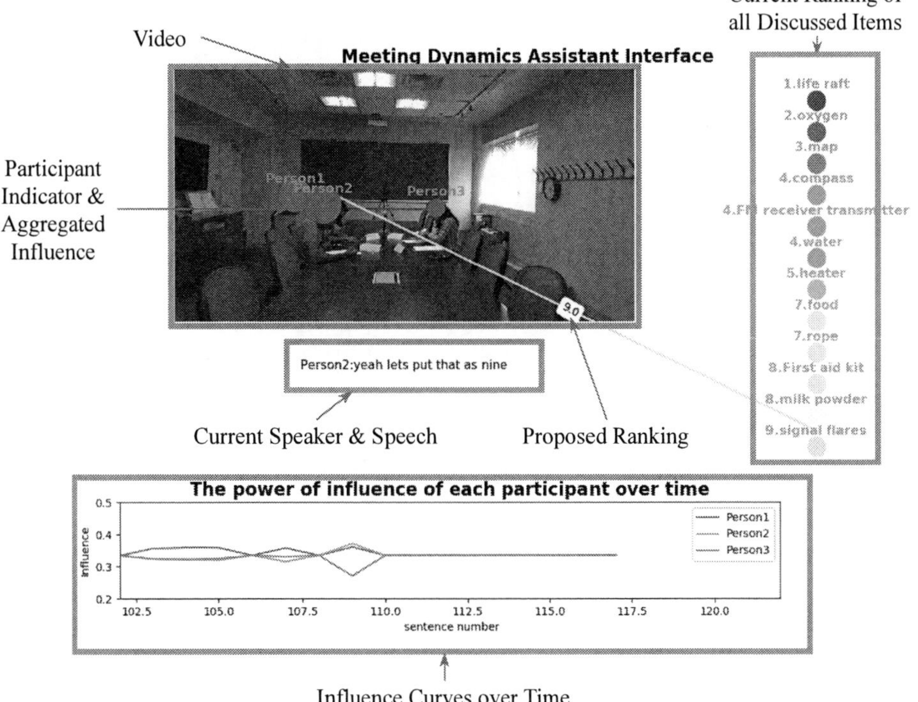

Figure 1: Main interface of our proposed meeting assistant.

2.2 Interface Details

Figure 1 illustrates the interface of the meeting assistant[2].

A video window shows the meeting scene. In this window, we use red circles to denote the participants. The sizes of the circles denote the aggregated influence factors of participants; the larger the circle is, the more influence (i.e., contribution to the conversation) the participant possesses.

Beneath the video window we provide the current speaker and speech. The raw speech is processed by IBM Watson's Speech to Text System [3], and we use the text output to detect discussion/focus items and extract speakers' opinions as detailed further below.

On the right side, we place a real-time ranking list for items that have been discussed. As the discussion proceeds, the ranking list expands with newly involved items. We also illustrate the current focus item of each participant and her/his proposed rank of the focused item with a colored edge. The colors of item circles and opinion edges denote different rankings; greener items have higher rankings and redder items have lower rankings.

At the bottom, we illustrate curves indicating instantaneous influence factors from each participant in real time based on the current speech.

Figure 2 illustrates a series of screenshots from our proposed meeting assistant. Three participants attend the meeting and start the discussion about several items. In Figure 2a and 2b, the meeting was in an early stage, and there is no difference among the participants in terms of influence. As the discussion continues in Figure 2c and 2d, where more items have been discussed, the curves of influence fluctuate and imply differences in activity among participants. Moreover, the rankings of discussed items are adjusted according to the speech and extracted opinions as mentioned above.

Finally, as shown in Figure 2f, from the size of the red circles representing aggregated influences and the historical record of the curves, we can conclude that `Person 1` and `Person 2` are contributing more in the discussion, while `Person 3` is less active.

---

[2]A short video clip illustrating the meeting assistant can be viewed at `https://youtu.be/3_YS0ZGQNQo`.

[3]`https://www.ibm.com/watson/services/speech-to-text/`

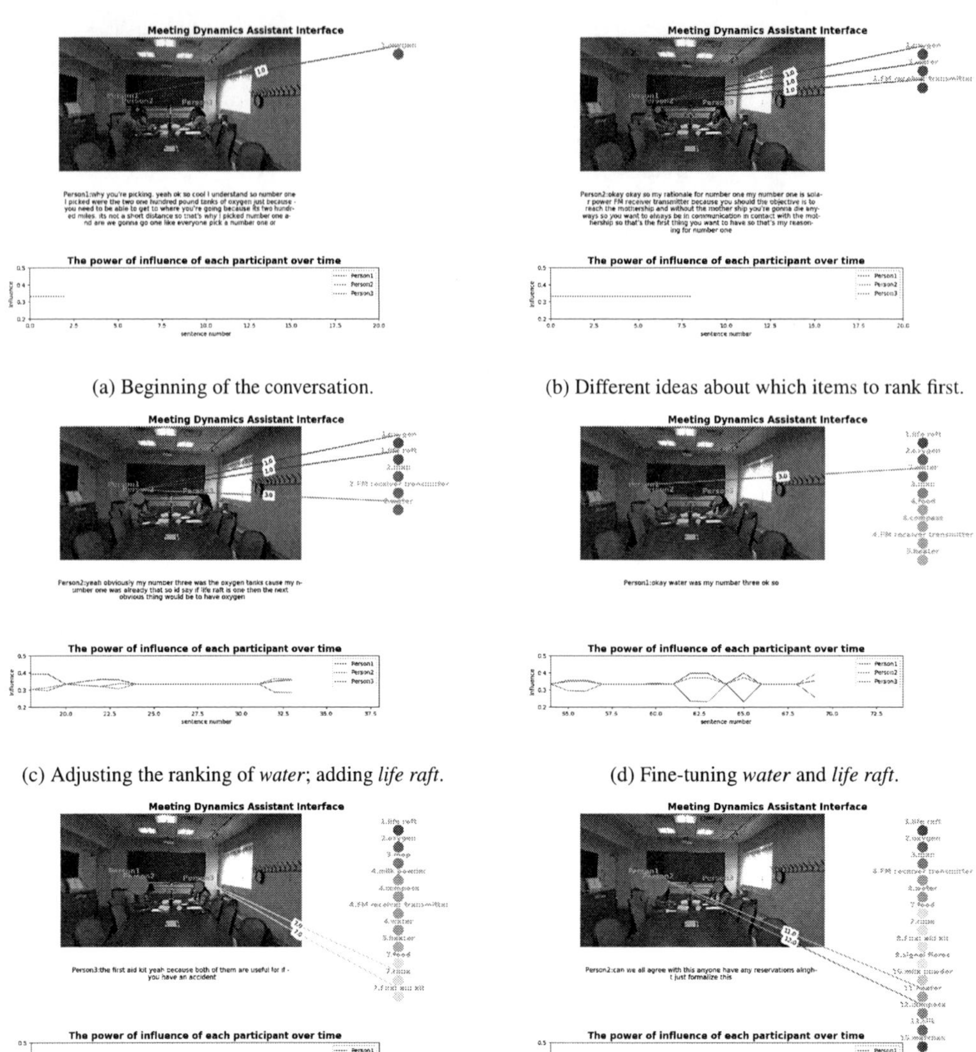

(a) Beginning of the conversation.

(b) Different ideas about which items to rank first.

(c) Adjusting the ranking of *water*; adding *life raft*.

(d) Fine-tuning *water* and *life raft*.

(e) Proceeding with other items.

(f) A substantially complete list at the end of discussion.

Figure 2: Screenshots of the meeting assistant at different points in time.

3 Opinion Detection and Extraction

Our system takes as input transcribed meeting speech, sentence by sentence, and outputs real-time rankings (opinion words) of the items after each participant expresses her/his thoughts.

3.1 Opinion Word Identification

In the context of the Lunar Survival Task discussion, we observed that participants express their opinions of item rankings in multiple ways, including

1. Explicitly mentioning an item with its rank-ing(e.g., *"In my opinion, we should put water as the second most important."*)
2. Agreement or disagreement (e.g., *"Yeah, I agree."*)
3. Comparison of the items by relative ranking (e.g., *"Matches are less important than signal flares because they don't work on the moon."*)

In the first scenario of a participant proposing an item ranking, we use the Stanford CoreNLP (Manning et al., 2014) name tagger to extract the NUMBERs and ORDINALs mentioned in the discussion (Finkel et al., 2005). We also eliminated numbers beyond 15 and numbers that are parts of pronouns such "this one". Additionally, in this specific discussion, people use "last" or "least" to imply they are ranking the item at 15 and we also implemented this rule.

As for the second scenario, people typically express agreement/disagreement with the person who talked immediately before them (Abu-Jbara et al., 2012). For agreement, we assume the current speaker accepts the previous speaker's stated opinion, which means we pass the weights captured for the previous person to the current speaker if we find the expression of agreement in the current sentence. We found that expressions of disagreement are not useful since people typically express their own opinion following their disagreement.

We currently do not deal with the third scenario of relative rankings, because no definitive ranking can be extracted from such statements.

3.2 Target Identification and Ranking

In this step, we identify discussed items in the discussion. As participants must have a very condensed discussion of these 15 items in a relatively short time, they usually mention the items with the exact words from the list they are given. Thus, we take the nouns and noun phrases as chunks and if any word matches with the nouns in the given list, it is recognized as the item in the given list.

So far, we have the opinion words and potential targets annotated in the conversation, and we want to pair them up and find the target of the ranking. It has been shown in previous work on relation extraction that the shortest dependency path between any two entities captures the information required to assert a relationship between them (Bunescu and Mooney, 2005). Based on the observation that people tend to mention items and their related ranks close to each other, we pair the item with the rank found in its shortest dependency path.

4 Bipartite Graph Construction

We propose an assessment method of the influence factors among participants based on bipartite graphs.

4.1 Dynamic Update of Weights and Vertices

We construct a directed bipartite graph $G = (U \cup V, E)$, where the vertices U represent the participants in the discussion, the vertices V represent the items, and E denotes the edges between these vertices. u_i denotes the ith vertex or participants' cumulative informative score in U. v_j is the jth vertex or item ranking in V.

In the Lunar Survival scenario, we observed that the information given in the conversation is very helpful in getting the right result and reaching consensus. To reflect this observation, we have total number of sentences so far for each speaker in the conversation as an informativeness indicator. The edges of the bipartite graph carry weights w_{ij}, representing the relationship between vertices u_i and v_j, i.e., u_i's current ranking of v_j. Thus, we can represent all the edge weights of the graph as a $|U| \times |V|$ matrix $W = [w_{ij}]$. With the item-rank pair extracted, we dynamically update W, and calculate v_j as $\frac{\sum_i w_{ij}}{i}$.

4.2 Influence Model

We implemented an influence model (IM) (Basu et al., 2001) to track and understand the participants' opinion behaviors. We model the participants' opinion shifts as a Markov chain with each state representing a user's opinion on the item. We use the coupled HMM to correlate the influence of the opinions among multiple participants. Each participant i has a chain of rankings on the items at time t denoted S_t^i. We assume that

$$P(S_t^i|S_{t-1}^1, ..., S_{t-1}^N) = \sum_j \alpha_{ij} P(S_t^i|S_{t-1}^j), \quad (1)$$

where α_{ij} (calculated from the model) can tell us how much the state transition of person i is influenced by the given neighbor j.

This observed IM is characterized by (Φ, A), where Φ is the state transition probability matrix, and A is the influence strength vector. At any time t, we calculate the pairwise transition probability matrix $P(S_t^i|S_{t-1}^j)$ by counting, and determine α_{ij} using the constrained gradient ascent method to maximize per-chain likelihood.

5 Experiments

5.1 Dataset Construction

We curated 5 meetings and transferred the recorded voice to the texts using IBM Watson's Speech-to-Text API (Saon et al., 2017). The conversations are 10–15 minutes long and have an average of 412 sentences. we collected the initial and final rankings of the items from each person using pre- and post-discussion questionnaires. We

Team ID	Precision	Recall	F1 score
Team 1	0.53	0.21	0.31
Team 2	0.65	0.55	0.6
Team 3	0.71	0.62	0.66
Team 4	0.65	0.33	0.44
Team 5	0.59	0.70	0.64

Table 1: Information extraction measures

performed the opinion extraction and target pairing as described in Section 3 for the 5 meetings. The extraction precision and accuracy compared to human annotated ground truth is summarized in Table 1. The precision is defined as the fraction of correct ranks among all ranks retrieved from the conversation, and recall is the fraction of correct ranks that have been retrieved over all the ranks supposed to be retrieved as in ground truth.

5.2 Meeting Dynamics Analysis

We see that groups have very distinct opinions on the 15 items before each meeting, and that they all achieved consensus at the final stage of the meeting. From the playback of the meeting assistant videos, we have a very clear view of the unfolding speech content that influences the participants' state of mind.

We observed the following patterns that correlate with a participant's influence:

1. Approval of other people first, followed by stating clearly the opinion on an item (e.g., Figure 3)
2. Detailed explanation of the reason to choose a specific rank (e.g., *"It's a two hundred mile trek so you need some sort of sustenance for the human body."*)
3. Drawing attention before a statement (e.g., *"OK so proposition hear me out. We're at nine now right? If we're going forward so what if we put milk powder as ten?"*)

6 Related Work

Opinion target extraction and pairing: In our context, the targets are constrained to 15 items given beforehand, but they appear in different forms in the conversation. In the context of product review mining, (Hu and Liu, 2004) extracted frequent nouns and noun phrases as product feature candidates. Following that method, (Abu-Jbara et al., 2012) extracted frequent noun phrases

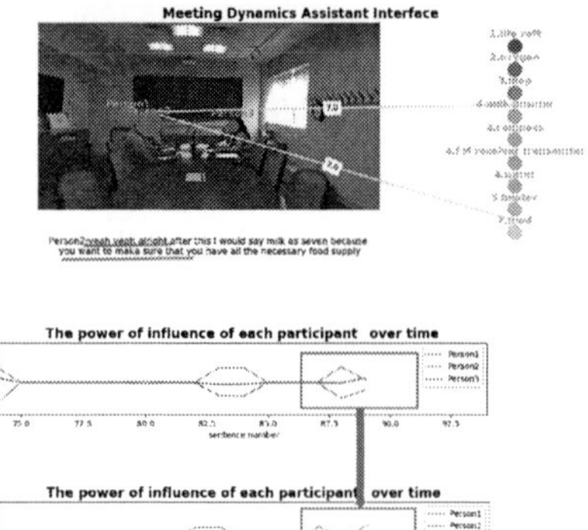

Figure 3: Example of arguments with stronger influence.

and named entities mentioned by different discussants.

As for opinion extraction, various methods were used in different contexts. (Kim and Hovy, 2006) collected opinion-bearing words and classified them into 3 classes. (Ortigosa et al., 2014) also studied opinion from 3 classes. Since in our case, the opinion on an item is restricted to a ranking of 1–15, we used name tagging results to identify the ordinals and numbers mentioned in the conversation.

Group dynamics studies: Most group dynamics studies to date of role recognition or influence studies are based on non-linguistic features. (Rienks and Heylen, 2005) used audio-only features including a collection of nonverbal and verbal cues to perform three-way classification of the participants dominance level. (Beyan et al., 2018) acquired audio and visual features and predicted emergent leadership with multiple kernel learning. Our group has extended the system proposed here to include non-verbal and visual cues to accurately predict emergent leadership and contribution (Bhattacharya et al., 2018).

When modeling opinion shifts, we referred to (Chen et al., 2017) but noticed that these are less complicated in face-to-face conversation than in a social network. (Asavathiratham, 2001) first proposed a simplified coupled-HMM influence model to understand the behaviors of a large number of interacting components. (Basu et al., 2001) expanded the theory and proposed a gradient ascent method to learn the influence model.

7 Conclusion and future work

In this paper we demonstrate a system for meeting assistance, visualizing real-time opinion extraction and group dynamics. We use the Lunar Survival Task to observe how people gradually change their opinions and make decisions. With the current meeting assistant tool, we have a closed set of 15 items given in advance and a fixed set of ranks. In future work, we plan to develop information extraction systems that handle open sets and detect multiple topics in a meeting. The opinions extracted could be used to study group dynamics and recognize roles in meetings, extending the scope of the meeting assistant to more general scenarios.

8 Acknowledgements

Thanks to Mike Foley, Christoph Riedl and Brooke Foucault Welles at Northeastern University for the experimental design. This work was supported by the U.S. National Science Foundation No. IIP-1631674. The views and conclusions contained in this document are those of the authors and should not be interpreted as representing the official policies, either expressed or implied, of the U.S. Government. The U.S. Government is authorized to reproduce and distribute reprints for Government purposes notwithstanding any copyright notation here on.

References

Amjad Abu-Jbara, Mona Diab, Pradeep Dasigi, and Dragomir Radev. 2012. Subgroup detection in ideological discussions. In *50th Annual Meeting of the Association for Computational Linguistics: Long Papers-Volume 1*, pages 399–409.

Chalee Asavathiratham. 2001. *The Influence Model: A Tractable Representation for the Dynamics of Networked Markov Chains*. Ph.D. thesis, Massachusetts Institute of Technology.

Sumit Basu, Tanzeem Choudhury, Brian Clarkson, Alex Pentland, et al. 2001. Learning human interactions with the influence model. NIPS.

Cigdem Beyan, Francesca Capozzi, Cristina Becchio, and Vittorio Murino. 2018. Prediction of the leadership style of an emergent leader using audio and visual nonverbal features. *IEEE Transactions on Multimedia*, 20(2):441–456.

Indrani Bhattacharya, Michael Foley, Ni Zhang, Tongtao Zhang, Christine Ku, Cameron Mine, Heng Ji, Christoph Riedl, Brooke Foucault Welles, and Richard J. Radke. 2018. A multimodal-sensor-enabled room for unobtrusive group meeting analysis. In *ACM International Conference on Multimodal Interaction*.

Razvan C Bunescu and Raymond J Mooney. 2005. A shortest path dependency kernel for relation extraction. In *Conference on Human Language Technology and Empirical Methods in Natural Language Processing*, pages 724–731. Association for Computational Linguistics.

Chengyao Chen, Wenjie Li, Dehong Gao, and Yuexian Hou. 2017. Exploring interpersonal influence by tracking user dynamic interactions. *IEEE Intelligent Systems*, 32(3):28–35.

Jenny Rose Finkel, Trond Grenager, and Christopher Manning. 2005. Incorporating non-local information into information extraction systems by Gibbs sampling. In *43rd Annual Meeting on Association for Computational Linguistics*, pages 363–370. Association for Computational Linguistics.

Jay Hall and Wilfred Harvey Watson. 1970. The effects of a normative intervention on group decision-making performance. *Human Relations*, 23(4):299–317.

Minqing Hu and Bing Liu. 2004. Mining and summarizing customer reviews. In *ACM SIGKDD International Conference on Knowledge Discovery and Data Mining*, pages 168–177. ACM.

Soo-Min Kim and Eduard Hovy. 2006. Extracting opinions, opinion holders, and topics expressed in online news media text. In *Proceedings of the Workshop on Sentiment and Subjectivity in Text*.

Christopher Manning, Mihai Surdeanu, John Bauer, Jenny Finkel, Steven Bethard, and David McClosky. 2014. The Stanford CoreNLP natural language processing toolkit. In *52nd Annual Meeting of the Association for Computational Linguistics: System Demonstrations*, pages 55–60.

Alvaro Ortigosa, José M Martín, and Rosa M Carro. 2014. Sentiment analysis in Facebook and its application to e-learning. *Computers in Human Behavior*, 31:527–541.

Rutger Rienks and Dirk Heylen. 2005. Dominance detection in meetings using easily obtainable features. In *International Workshop on Machine Learning for Multimodal Interaction*, pages 76–86. Springer.

George Saon et al. 2017. English conversational telephone speech recognition by humans and machines. In *Proceedings of INTERSPEECH 2017*.

An Interface for Annotating Science Questions

Michael Boratko, Harshit Padigela, Divyendra Mikkilineni, Pritish Yuvraj,
Rajarshi Das, Andrew McCallum
College of Information and Computer Sciences
University of Massachusetts, Amherst MA

Maria Chang, Achille Fokoue, Pavan Kapanipathi, Nicholas Mattei,
Ryan Musa, Kartik Talamadupula, Michael Witbrock
IBM Research, Yorktown Heights NY

Abstract

Recent work introduces the AI2 Reasoning Challenge (ARC) and the associated ARC dataset that partitions open domain, complex science questions into an Easy Set and a Challenge Set. That work includes an analysis of 100 questions with respect to the types of knowledge and reasoning required to answer them. However, it does not include clear definitions of these types, nor does it offer information about the quality of the labels or the annotation process used. In this paper, we introduce a novel interface for human annotation of science question-answer pairs with their respective knowledge and reasoning types, in order that the classification of new questions may be improved. We build on the classification schema proposed by prior work on the ARC dataset, and evaluate the effectiveness of our interface with a preliminary study involving 10 participants.

1   Introduction

Recent work by Clark et al. (2018) introduces the AI2 Reasoning Challenge (ARC)[1] and the associated ARC dataset. This dataset contains science questions from standardized tests that are separated into an Easy Set and a Challenge Set. The Challenge Set comprises questions that are answered incorrectly by two solvers based on Pointwise Mutual Information (PMI) Information Retrieval (IR). In addition to this division, a survey of the various types of knowledge as well as the types of reasoning that are required to answer various questions in the ARC dataset was presented. This survey was based on an analysis of 100 questions chosen at random from the Challenge Set. However, very little detail is provided about the questions chosen, the annotations provided, or the methodology used. These questions surround the

very core of the paper, since the main contribution is a dataset that contains complex questions.

In this work, in order to overcome some of the limitations of Clark et al. (2018) described above, we present a detailed annotation interface for the ARC dataset that allows a distributed set of annotators to label the knowledge and reasoning types (Boratko et al., 2018). Following an annotation round involving over ten people at two institutions, we measure and report statistics such as inter-rater agreement, and the distribution of knowledge and reasoning type labels in the dataset.

2   Annotation Interface

The annotation interface introduced in this paper is shown in Figure 1. The text of the science question is displayed at the top of the left side, followed by the answer options. Each of the answer options is preceded by a radio button: each button is initially transparent, but the annotator can click on a button to check whether the corresponding option is the answer to the question. This facility is to help annotators with extra information if it is needed in labeling the question; however, we leave it blank initially to avoid biasing the annotations.

Clicking on a specific answer option executes a search on the ARC corpus, with the query text of that search set to be the last sentence of the question appended with the entire text of the clicked answer option. The retrieved search results are shown in the bottom left half of the interface. Annotators have the option of labeling retrieved search results as *irrelevant* or *relevant* to answering the question at hand. The query box also accepts free text, and annotators who wish to craft more specific queries are free to do so. We collect all the queries executed, as well as the annotations pertaining to the relevance of the returned results.

---

[1] http://data.allenai.org/arc/

Proceedings of the 2018 Conference on Empirical Methods in Natural Language Processing (System Demonstrations), pages 102–107
Brussels, Belgium, October 31–November 4, 2018. ©2018 Association for Computational Linguistics

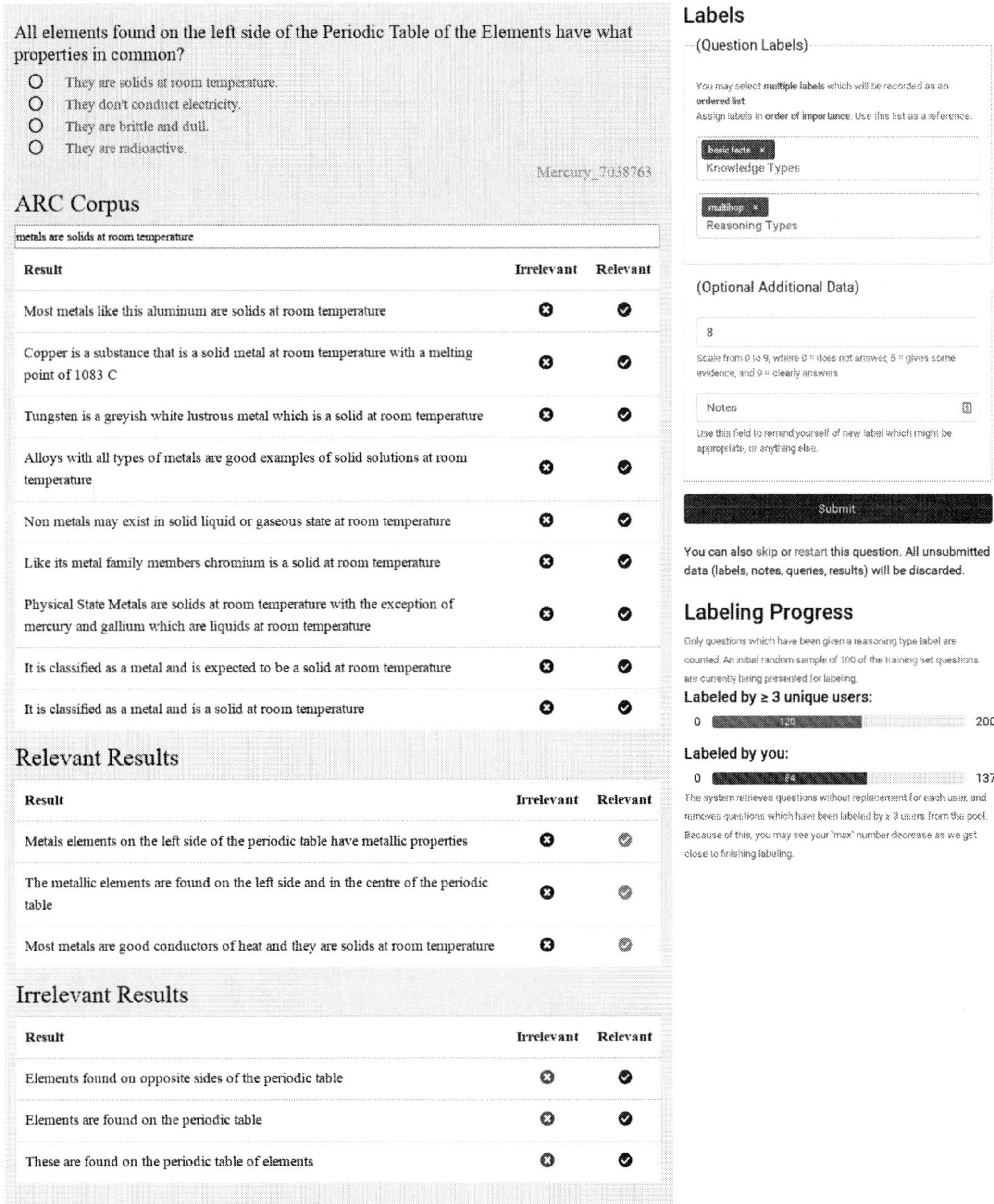

Figure 1: A screenshot of the interface to our annotation system, described in Section 2.

2.1 Question Annotation

The right hand side of the interface deals with the annotation of a given question. There are two boxes for annotating knowledge and reasoning types respectively. The labels are populated from the knowledge and reasoning type tables in Boratko et al. (2018) (more on these types in Section 3). The annotator can also provide optional information on the quality of the retrieved search results if they choose to run a query. Finally, the annotator can use the optional field below quality to enter additional notes about the question; these notes are stored and can be retrieved for subsequent discussion and refinement of the labels.

2.2 Search Result Retrieval & Annotation

In addition to labeling the knowledge and reasoning types systematically, we demonstrate yet another capability of our interface: given a corpus of knowledge, we are able to retrieve and display search results that may be relevant to the question (and its corresponding options) at hand. This is useful because it gives a solution technique an additional signal as it tries to identify the correct answer to a given question. In open-domain question answering, the retriever plays as important a role as the machine reader (Chen et al., 2017). In the past few years, there has been a lot of effort in designing sophisticated neural architectures for reading a small piece of text (e.g. paragraph) (Wang and Jiang, 2016; Xiong et al., 2016; Seo et al., 2016; Lee et al., 2016, inter alia). However, most work in open domain settings (Chen et al., 2017; Clark and Gardner, 2017; Wang et al., 2018) only uses simple retrievers (such as TF-IDF based ones). As a result, there is a notable decrease in the performance of the QA system. One roadblock for training a sophisticated retriever is the lack of available training data which annotates the relevance of a retrieved context with respect to the question. We believe our annotated retrieval data can be used to train a better ranker/retriever without obliging annotators to explicitly connect the supporting passages (Jansen et al., 2018).

The underlying retriever in our interface is a simple Elasticsearch, similar to the one used by Clark et al. (2018). The interface is populated by default with the top ranked sentences that are retrieved with the given question as the input query. However, we noticed that results thus retrieved were often irrelevant to answering the question. To address this, our labeling interface also allows annotators to input their own custom queries. We found that reformulating the initial query significantly improved the quality of the retrieved context (results). We encouraged the annotators to mark the contexts (results) that they thought were relevant to answering the question at hand. For example, in Figure 1, the annotator came up with a novel query – `metals are solid at room temperatures` – and also marked the relevant sentences which are needed to answer this question. Note that sometimes we need to reason over multiple sentences to arrive at the answer. For example, the question in Figure 1 can be answered by combining the first and third sentences in the `Relevant Results` tab.

3   Knowledge & Reasoning Types

In previous work (Clark et al., 2018), the standardized test questions under consideration were split into various categories based on the kinds of *knowledge* and *reasoning* that are needed to answer those questions. The idea of classifying questions by these two types is central to the notion of standardized testing, which endeavors to test students on various kinds of knowledge, as well as various problem types and solution techniques. These categories allow for the classification of questions, which makes it easier to partition them into subsets to measure performance and improve solution strategies.

3.1   Knowledge Types

In most question-answering (QA) scenarios, the knowledge that is present with the system (or the agent) determines whether a given question can be answered. The full list of the revised knowledge labels (types) – along with the instructions given to annotators and respective exemplars from the ARC question set – can be found in our complementary work (Boratko et al., 2018). For the annotation of knowledge types using our interface, annotators were given the following instructions:

> *You are to answer the question, "In a perfect world given an ideal knowledge source, what types of knowledge would you as a human need to answer this question?" You are allowed to select **multiple labels** for this type which will be recorded as an ordered list. You are to assign labels **in the order of importance** to answering the questions at hand.*

In order to level the field among annotators, we included phrasing about an *ideal knowledge source*. Additionally, displaying the retrieved search results in the interface provides another way for the annotators to share some common ground with respect to the typical kind of knowledge that is likely to be available. We also provide instruction-based definitions for each class, as opposed to the single exemplars provided previously. We believe this greatly simplifies the annotation task for new annotators, since they no longer need to perform a preliminary manual analysis of the QA set in order to understand the distinctions between the classes.

3.2   Reasoning Types

The annotation instructions for reasoning types follow a similar pattern to the knowledge types described in the previous section. The annotators

were given the following instructions when annotating the reasoning types:

Notice that the instructions in this case refer to being able to access a specific knowledge corpus,
and allow for the selection of multiple labels in
decreasing order of applicability. We also provide
specific instructions on the order of precedence
as relates to *linguistic* and *multi-hop* reasoning
types: this is based on our empirical observation
that many questions can be classified trivially into
these reasoning categories, and we would prefer
(for downstream application use) a clean split into
as many distinct categories as possible.

4 Results

Members of the annotation group were given access to the annotation interface (which includes
the question, answers, query search results and
more information as described above). Each annotator was shown the questions in a random order,
and was allowed to skip or pass any question.

Statistics. We collected labels from at least 3
unique annotators (out of the possible 10) for 192
distinct questions. This annotation process produced 1.42 knowledge type labels and 1.7 reasoning type labels per question. Figure 2 and Figure 3
shows the distribution of annotation labels by all
raters at any position. While *Basic Facts* domi-
nates the knowledge type labels, there is no clear
cut consensus for the reasoning type. Indeed, *qn
logic*, *linguistic*, and *explanation* occur most frequently.

4.1 Inter-Rater Agreement

A comprehensive look at the labels and inter-rater
agreement can be found in Table 1 and Table 2.
Fleiss' κ is often used to measure inter-rater agreement (Cohen, 1995). Informally, this measures the

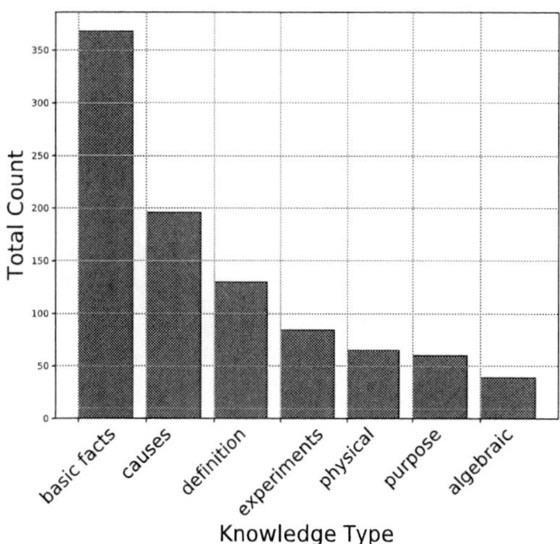

Figure 2: Histogram of the first (most important) knowledge label for each question; the Y-axis refers to annotations.

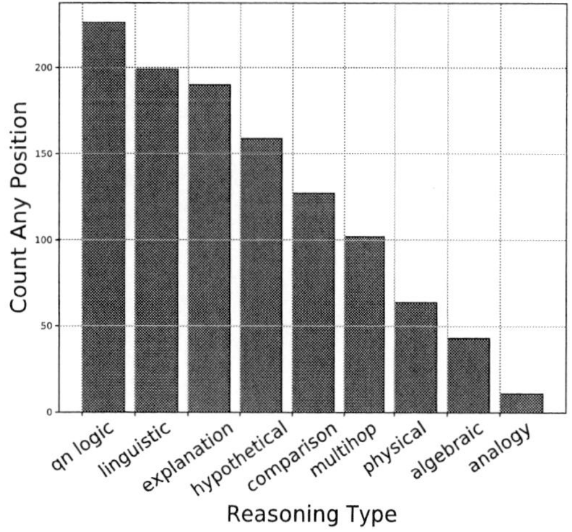

Figure 3: Histogram of the first (most important) reasoning label for each question; the Y-axis refers to annotations.

amount of agreement, beyond chance, based on
the number of raters, objects and classes. $\kappa > 0.2$
is typically taken to denote good agreement between raters, while a negative value means that
there was little to no agreement. Since Fleiss' κ
is only defined for a single set of labels, we consider only the first (most important) label for each
question in the statistic we report.

In addition to Fleiss' κ we also use the Kemeny
voting rule (Kemeny, 1959) to measure the consensus by the annotators. The Kemeny voting rule
minimizes the Kendall Tau (Kendall, 1938) (flip)
distance between the output ordering and the ordering of all annotators. One theory of voting (aggregation) is that there is a true or correct ordering
and all voters provide a noisy observation of the

ground truth. This method of thinking is largely credited to Condorcet (de Caritat, 1785; Young, 1988) and there is recent work in characterizing other voting rules as maximum likelihood estimators (MLEs) (Conitzer et al., 2009). The Kemeny voting rule is the MLE of the Condorcet Noise Model, in which pairwise inversions of the preference order happen uniformly at random (Young, 1988, 1995). Hence, if we assume all annotators make pairwise errors uniformly at random then Kemeny is the MLE of label orders they report.

Label	Appears	Majority	Consensus
basic facts	125	69	28
algebraic	13	5	2
definition	52	16	5
causes	78	33	15
experiments	35	19	13
purpose	30	13	0
physical	21	3	1
Fleiss' $\kappa = 0.342$			

Table 1: Pairwise inter-rater agreement for Knowledge Labels, along with the mean and Fleiss' κ for survey responses.

Label	Appears	Majority	Consensus
linguistic	66	31	8
algebraic	15	8	3
explanation	80	22	4
hypothetical	62	21	6
multihop	45	6	0
comparison	46	13	3
qn logic	78	33	2
physical	18	3	0
analogy	4	1	1
Fleiss' $\kappa = -0.683$			

Table 2: Pairwise inter-rater agreement for Reasoning Labels, along with the mean and Fleiss' κ for survey responses.

4.1.1 Knowledge Labels

We achieve $\kappa = 0.342$, which means that our raters did a reasonable job of independently agreeing on the types of knowledge required to answer the questions. The mean Kemeny score of the consensus ranking for each question is 2.57, meaning that on average there are less than three flips required to get from the consensus ranking to each of the annotators' rankings. The most frequent label in the first position was *basic facts*, followed by *causes*. Overall, there was a reasonable amount of consensus between the raters for knowledge type: $64/192$ questions had a consensus amongst all the raters. Taken together, our results on knowledge type indicate that most questions deal with *basic facts*, *causes*, and *definitions*; and that labeling can be done reliably.

4.1.2 Reasoning Labels

The inter-rater agreement score for the reasoning labels tells a very different story from the knowl-

edge labels. The agreement was $\kappa = -0.683$, which indicates that raters did not agree above chance on their labels. Strong evidence for this comes from the fact that only $27/192$ questions had a consensus label. This may be due to the fact that we allow multiple labels, and the annotators simply disagree on the *order* of the labels. However, the score of the consensus ranking for each question is 6.57, which indicates that on average the ordering of the labels is quite far apart.

Considering the histogram in Figure 3, we see that *qn logic*, *linguistic*, and *explanation* are the most frequent label types; this may indicate that getting better at understanding the questions themselves could lead to a big boost for reasoners. For Figure 4, we have merged the first and second label (if present) for all annotators. Now, the set of all possible labels is all singletons as well as all pairs of labels. Comparing this histogram to the one in Figure 3, we see that while *linguistic* and *explanation* remain somewhat unchanged, the *qn logic* label becomes very spread out across the types. This is more support for our hypothesis that annotators may be disagreeing on the ordering of the labels, rather than the content itself.

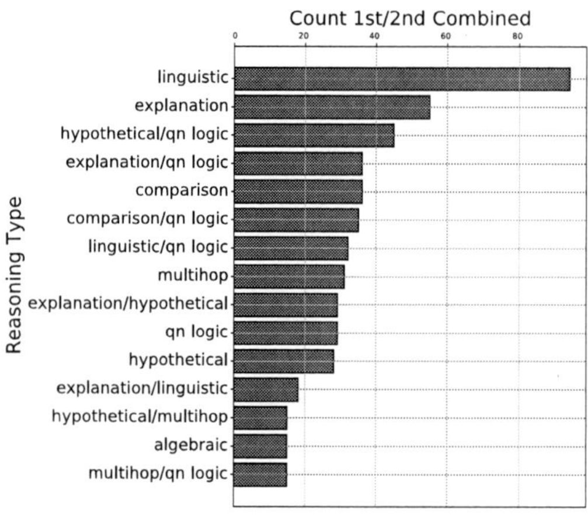

Figure 4: Histogram of the reasoning labels when we combine the first and (if present) second label of every annotator. The count refers to annotations.

4.2 Search Results

To quantitatively measure the efficacy of the annotated context (search results) from the interface, we evaluated 47 questions and their respective human-annotated relevant sentences with a pretrained `DrQA` model (Chen et al., 2017). We compared this to a baseline which only returned the sentences retrieved by using the text of the question plus given options as input queries. Since `DrQA` returns a span from the input sentences, we picked the multiple choice option that maximally overlapped with the returned answer span. Our baseline results are 7 correct out of 47 questions. With the annotated context, the performance increased to 27 correctly answered questions - a 42% increase in accuracy. Encouraged by these results, we posit that the community should focus a lot of attention on improving the retrieval portions of the various QA systems available; we think that annotated context will certainly help in training a better ranker. We conclude that the community should focus on improving the retrieval portion of their QA system and we think that the annotated context would help in training a better ranker.

5 Conclusion & Future Work

In this paper, we introduce a novel annotation interface and define annotation instructions for the knowledge and reasoning type labels that are used for question analysis for standardized tests. We annotate approximately 200 questions from the ARC Challenge Set shared by AI2 with the types of knowledge and reasoning required to answer the respective questions. Each question has at least 3 annotators, with high agreement on the requirements for knowledge type. We will leverage the knowledge and reasoning type annotations, as well as the search annotations, to improve the performance of QA systems. We will also release these annotations to the community to complement the ARC Dataset, and make our annotation interface available to interested researchers for use with other question-answering (QA) tasks.

References

Michael Boratko, Harshit Padigela, Divyendra Mikkilineni, Pritish Yuvraj, Rajarshi Das, Andrew McCallum, Maria Chang, Achille Fokoue-Nkoutche, Pavan Kapanipathi, Nicholas Mattei, Ryan Musa, Kartik Talamadupula, and Michael Witbrock. 2018. A Systematic Classification of the Knowledge, Reasoning, and Context within the ARC Dataset. In *Proceedings of the ACL 2018 Workshop on Machine Reading for Question Answering (MRQA)*. Association for Computational Linguistics.

M. J. A. N. de Caritat. 1785. *Essai sur l'application de l'analyse à la probabilité des décisions: rendues à la pluralité des voix*. Paris: L'Imprimerie Royale.

Danqi Chen, Adam Fisch, Jason Weston, and Antoine Bordes. 2017. Reading wikipedia to answer open-domain questions. *arXiv preprint arXiv:1704.00051*.

Christopher Clark and Matt Gardner. 2017. Simple and effective multi-paragraph reading comprehension. *arXiv preprint arXiv:1710.10723*.

P. Clark, I. Cowhey, O. Etzioni, T. Khot, A. Sabharwal, C. Schoenick, and O. Tafjord. 2018. Think you have solved question answering? Try ARC, the AI2 Reasning Challenge. In *ArXiv e-prints 1803.05457*.

P. R. Cohen. 1995. *Empirical Methods for Artificial Intelligence*. MIT Press.

V. Conitzer, M. Rognlie, and L. Xia. 2009. Preference functions that score rankings and maximum likelihood estimation. In *Proceedings of the 21st International Joint Conference on Artificial Intelligence (IJCAI)*, pages 109–115.

Peter Jansen, Elizabeth Wainwright, Steven Marmorstein, and Clayton Morrison. 2018. WorldTree: A Corpus of Explanation Graphs for Elementary Science Questions supporting Multi-hop Inference. In *Proceedings of the Eleventh International Conference on Language Resources and Evaluation (LREC 2018)*.

J. G. Kemeny. 1959. Mathematics without numbers. *Daedalus*, 88(4):577–591.

M. G. Kendall. 1938. A new measure of rank correlation. *Biometrika*, 30(1/2):81–93.

Kenton Lee, Shimi Salant, Tom Kwiatkowski, Ankur Parikh, Dipanjan Das, and Jonathan Berant. 2016. Learning recurrent span representations for extractive question answering. *arXiv preprint arXiv:1611.01436*.

Minjoon Seo, Aniruddha Kembhavi, Ali Farhadi, and Hannaneh Hajishirzi. 2016. Bi-directional attention flow for machine comprehension. *arXiv preprint arXiv:1611.01603*.

Shuohang Wang and Jing Jiang. 2016. Machine comprehension using match-lstm and answer pointer. *arXiv preprint arXiv:1608.07905*.

Shuohang Wang, Mo Yu, Xiaoxiao Guo, Zhiguo Wang, Tim Klinger, Wei Zhang, Shiyu Chang, Gerald Tesauro, Bowen Zhou, and Jing Jiang. 2018. R3: Reinforced ranker-reader for open-domain question answering.

Caiming Xiong, Victor Zhong, and Richard Socher. 2016. Dynamic coattention networks for question answering. *arXiv preprint arXiv:1611.01604*.

H. P. Young. 1988. Condorcet's theory of voting. *The American Political Science Review*, 82(4):1231 – 1244.

H. P. Young. 1995. Optimal voting rules. *The Journal of Economic Perspectives*, 9(1):51–64.

APLenty: annotation tool for creating high-quality datasets using active and proactive learning

Minh-Quoc Nghiem, Sophia Ananiadou
National Centre for Text Mining
School of Computer Science, The University of Manchester, United Kingdom
{minh-quoc.nghiem, sophia.ananiadou}@manchester.ac.uk

Abstract

In this paper, we present APLenty, an annotation tool for creating high-quality sequence labeling datasets using active and proactive learning. A major innovation of our tool is the integration of automatic annotation with active learning and proactive learning. This makes the task of creating labeled datasets easier, less time-consuming and requiring less human effort. APLenty is highly flexible and can be adapted to various other tasks.

1 Introduction

Labeled data play a critical role in many machine learning problems. Obtaining such data is difficult, time-consuming, and require a lot of human effort. Many researchers have utilized *active learning* or *proactive learning*, in which a learning algorithm is allowed to choose the data from which it learns (Settles, 2009). The annotators, in this scenario, only have to annotate a reasonable-size set of representative and informative data. It helps reduce the human labeling effort and at the same time reduces the cost of training the machine learning models.

In recent years, there has been an increasing amount of libraries and systems that focus on active learning, such as the JCLAL (Reyes et al., 2016), the Active-Learning-Scala (Santos and Carvalho, 2014), or the LibAct (Yang et al., 2017) libraries. They implement several state-of-the-art active learning strategies in single-label and multi-label learning paradigms. These libraries, however, have not treated sequence labeling tasks (part-of-speech tagging, information extraction, ...) in much detail. Due to the nature of sequence labeling tasks, the learning algorithm usually gets not a single label but a sequence of labels from the annotators. Besides, to the best of our knowledge, no system offers support for proactive learning.

Up to now, far too little attention has been paid to the interaction between the annotators and the active learning algorithm. The main point of active learning is that a learning algorithm must be able to interactively query the annotators to obtain the desired outputs at new data points. The available systems fail to deliver this by providing over-simplified user-interfaces for the annotators (i.e., showing the feature vector of an instance and asking for the label). Such user-interfaces are not suitable for the task since the annotators need to know the context of every instance to provide accurate annotations. Some tools provide excellent visualization front end, such as brat (Stenetorp et al., 2012), PubAnnotation (Kim and Wang, 2012) or WebAnno (Yimam et al., 2013), but unfortunately these tools provide no support for active learning.

To compensate for the lack of learning environment in the well-known annotation tool, we develop **APLenty** (Active Proactive Learning System), a web-based system for creating annotated data using active/proactive learning. The main innovation of APLenty is the combination of a well-known annotation tool (brat) with active/proactive learning. Specifically:

1. Proactive learning integration: APLenty makes annotation easy, time-efficient, and require less human effort by offering automatic and proactive learning.

2. An easy-to-use interface for annotators: APLenty adapts the interface of the brat rapid annotation tool, making annotation intuitive and easy to use.

3. Suitable for sequence labeling: APLenty is best used for sequence labeling tasks, although it can be used for other classification problems.

108

Proceedings of the 2018 Conference on Empirical Methods in Natural Language Processing (System Demonstrations), pages 108–113
Brussels, Belgium, October 31–November 4, 2018. ©2018 Association for Computational Linguistics

The remainder of this paper is organized as follows. Section 2 provides a brief overview of the related work. Section 3 presents details of APLenty. Section 4 describes a case study of using APLenty for named-entity recognition task. Section 5 concludes the paper and points to avenues for future work.

2   Related work

There are many tools available for active learning, such as the JCLAL (Reyes et al., 2016), the Active-Learning-Scala (Santos and Carvalho, 2014), or the LibAct (Yang et al., 2017) libraries. Among those, JCLAL includes the most state-of-the-art strategies for active learning. Other tools such as Vowpal Wabbit[1] or TexNLP (Baldridge and Palmer, 2009) also include some active learning methods. These tools, however, do not focus on the interaction with the annotators (the user-interface).

BRAT (Stenetorp et al., 2012) is one of the most well-known annotation tools that offer easy-to-use user-interfaces. BRAT has been developed for rich structured annotation and uses a vector graphics-based visualization component for rendering. BRAT can, at the same time, display many annotation layers. WebAnno (Yimam et al., 2013) improves the annotation interface of BRAT by letting the annotators choose the annotation layer(s) for rendering. WebAnno offers a purely web-based generic annotation tool and supports distributed annotation. PubAnnotation (Kim and Wang, 2012) also offers a web-based annotation interface but its main focus is to improve the reusability of corpora and annotations. These tools do not support active/proactive learning.

DUALIST (Settles, 2011; Settles and Zhu, 2012) and Prodigy[2] are most closely related to APLenty. DUALIST is an active learning annotation paradigm that offers annotation interface for semi-supervised active learning. Prodigy is a commercial product which provides an annotation tool powered by active learning. Unfortunately, both DUALIST and Prodigy do not support proactive learning.

3   APLenty

APLenty is a web-based tool implemented in Java using Apache Wicket web framework and

---

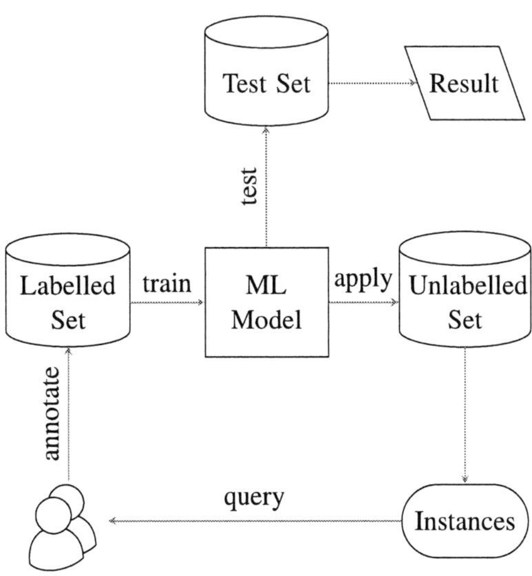

Figure 1: System architecture

JavaScript. The overall architecture of APLenty is depicted in Figure 1. The user interface consists of a project management page and an annotation page. Below, this section describes APLenty in detail.

3.1   Project management

In APLenty system, we have two main types of user: annotator and project manager. The annotators can only annotate text assigned to them while a project manager can create and customize annotation projects. The interface lets the project manager to:

1. create a project

2. upload the training, test, and unlabelled data to the web server

3. define the tagset

4. assign annotators to a project

5. choose the active/proactive learning strategy.

The system predefines some common tags, but the manager can override these by uploading a tagset file.

There are three types of data that the project manager can upload. The first one is the training data, which will be used to train the machine learning model. The second one is the testing data, which will be used to test the performance of the system after each annotation step. The last one is

---

[1] http://hunch.net/~vw/
[2] https://prodi.gy/

the unlabelled data, on which the annotators will work. Training and testing data is not required, but unlabelled data is mandatory. When there is no training data, the active learning algorithm will choose the longest sentences for annotation.

APLenty currently supports data using CoNLL-2003 format and XML Metadata Interchange (XMI) format. Since APLenty is based on the Apache Unstructured Information Management Architecture (UIMA) framework[3], new formats can be supported easily. UIMA enables the application to be decomposed into components. Out of which, a collection reader component is responsible for reading documents in a specific format. By swapping the collection reader component, one can allow APLenty to support data in different format.

The test set is optionally used to evaluate the annotation process. By providing the test set, the project manager can see the learning curve of the active learning method. This evaluation step is skipped if there is no test set.

3.2 Annotation interface

For annotation and visualization of annotated documents, we adapted the WebAnno annotation interface, which in turn, adapted the brat rapid annotation tool. Since the initial purpose of APLenty is sequence labeling, the smallest unit we consider is a sentence. The annotation interface only displays one sentence to the annotator at a time. It helps the annotator to focus on the current sentence. Figure 2 shows the annotation interface.

When working on APLenty, the annotator selects a span of text on the displayed sentence and chooses a tag for that span. The annotator does not need to save the annotation since every annotation is automatically sent to the web server (via Ajax using JSON format). The annotator has the possibility to skip annotating a sentence. By choosing skip, the algorithm marks the sentence as "skipped" and does not consider that sentence in the next annotation round for this specific annotator. When the annotator completed an active learning iteration step, APLenty will trigger the training process with newly annotated data and update the sentences for the next annotation batch.

The annotation ends when stopping criteria are met. A project manager can have several ways to define the stopping criteria: the algorithm reaches

---

a predefined number of iteration, or the dataset reaches a predefined number of instances, or the result on the test set reaches a predefined amount. The learning process has been completed when the stopping criteria are met. The annotators, however, can stop anytime they want and resume the process later.

The project manager can increase the annotation speed by turning on automation. APLenty, in this case, automatically annotates certain spans of text (based on the model available from the previous active learning iteration round). The annotators are then required to label only uncertain sequences. This approach was proved to reduce the number of tokens to be manually annotated about 60% compared to its fully supervised counterpart, and over 80% compared to a totally passive learning (Tomanek and Hahn, 2009). The project manager can set a threshold θ for automatic annotation. If the probability of an output sequence from the machine learning model is larger than θ, the output sequence is accepted as valid annotation and is used as a training instance for later active learning iterations.

3.3 Active learning

Depending on the project manager's settings, the system will choose a query strategy for active learning. Generally, a machine learning algorithm uses the instances in the labeled set (training set) to train a model. The system then uses the model to label the instances in the unlabeled set. Every instance now has a score indicating how informative or representative it is. Finally, the system aggregates these scores to get the score of the whole sentence. The system sends the most informative sentences to the annotators, based on the sentences' scores. When the system receives the annotations, a new iteration round starts.

Active learning for sequence labeling can use different query strategies. Most common query strategies are Least Confidence (Culotta and McCallum, 2005), Margin Sampling (Scheffer et al., 2001), Entropy Sampling (Mann and McCallum, 2007), Vote Entropy (Dagan and Engelson, 1995), Kullback Leibler Divergence (Settles and Craven, 2008), Expected Gradient Length (Settles et al., 2008), Information Density (Settles and Craven, 2008) strategies. Among which, no query strategy is completely outperformed other strategies (Settles and Craven, 2008). APLenty cur-

---

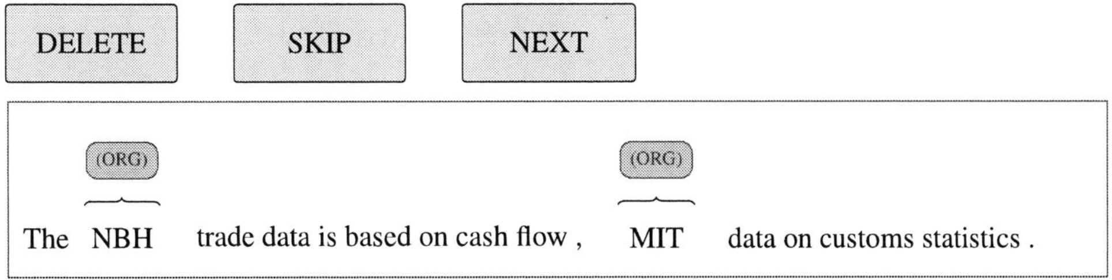

Figure 2: Annotation interface

rently employs the least confidence uncertainty-based strategy for sequence models based on the sequence outputs from a Conditional Random Fields model (Okazaki, 2007).

3.4 Proactive learning

Active learning assumes that annotators have similar level of expertise and nobody is fallible. But in reality, different annotators have different levels of expertize in a specific domain. Proactive learning has been proposed to model many types of annotators (Donmez and Carbonell, 2010; Li et al., 2017). Proactive learning assumes that there is at least one expert and one inexperienced annotator (fallible). The expert always provides correct annotations while the fallible annotator might provide incorrect annotations in certain cases.

At each iteration step, the proactive learning algorithm selects the sentences for the annotators based on the probabilities that the annotator will provide correct labels for a sequence in a sentence. A recent study by Li et al. (2017) estimated the performance of each annotator based on a benchmark dataset. The system calculates the probability that an annotator provides a correct label when annotating a sentence by combining the class probability and the likelihood that the annotator provides a correct label for the tokens in the sentence.

In the real-time annotation scenario where speed is one of the most important factors, APLenty uses a simple threshold ϱ to distribute sentences to annotators. If the probability of an output sequence from the machine learning model is smaller than ϱ, APLenty considers the sentence a hard case and sends it to the expert annotator. Otherwise, the sentence is sent to the fallible annotator. This reduces the cost of annotation since the time of the expert is more expensive than the time of the fallible annotator.

4 Case study

One use case that describes the best use of APLenty is the named entities annotation. This is a multiple span annotation task.

We used the English CoNLL-2003 named entity dataset (Tjong Kim Sang and De Meulder, 2003) for the case study. The dataset contains newswire articles annotated with four entities: LOC (locations), MISC (miscellaneous names), ORG (organizations), and PER (persons). In the experiment, we used 1,200 sentences as the initial training data, 3,622 sentences as test data, and the rest for unlabelled data. θ is set to 0.8, ϱ is set to 0.2, batch size is set to 100.

We compare four settings in this case study. The first one is Random Sampling: the system randomly chooses the next sentences for annotation. The second one is Active Learning: the system uses the output of CRF model to assign sentences to an expert. The third one is Proactive Learning: same as Active Learning, but we have two annotators, one expert, and one fallible annotator. The last one is Active Learning with Automation: the system automatically assigns labels for sequences based on the threshold θ.

Figure 3 shows the learning curves of the four settings. In all cases, active/proactive learning setting outperformed Random Sampling setting. It can be seen that the last three settings achieved peak performance when we reached 50th iteration. Combining active learning and automation lead to best performance. This result may be explained by the fact that the system got more reliable data for training after every iteration.

5 Conclusion and future work

We introduced APLenty, a web-based open environment for constructing annotated datasets using active and proactive learning while leveraging the functionalities of the popular annotation edi-

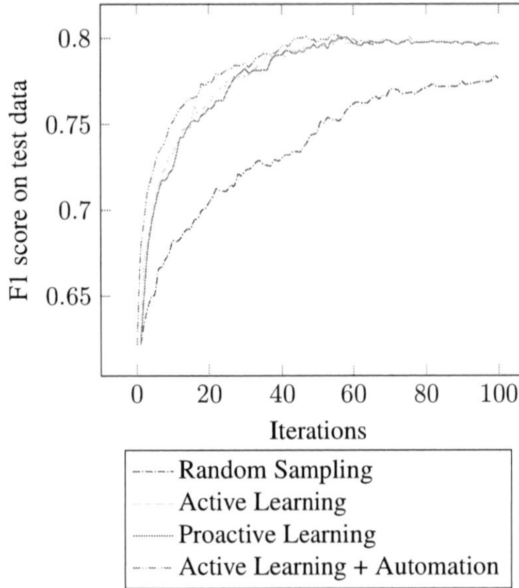

Figure 3: Learning curve

tor brat. APLenty can support the quick development of high-quality labeled data needed to train and evaluate text mining tools for different applications. Existing annotation editors do not provide such an integrated environment which can quickly produce labeled data while at the same time taking into account different levels of expertise of annotators.

A key feature of APLenty is how it supports the automation for sequences with high confidence to be included (certain sequences), thus allowing the annotators to focus only on the uncertain ones. We have demonstrated that this feature enables annotators to create high-quality labeled datasets in less time than other settings.

Considerably more work will need to be done to: 1. extend our work for link annotation; 2. further enhance APLenty to work with other active/proactive learning criteria; 3. evaluate APLenty in a complete data creation; 4. enhance centralize repository of annotation such as PubAnnotation.

Acknowledgments

This research has been carried out with funding from BBSRC BB/P025684/1 and BB/M006891/1. We would like to thank the anonymous reviewers for their helpful comments.

References

Jason Baldridge and Alexis Palmer. 2009. How well does active learning actually work?: Time-based evaluation of cost-reduction strategies for language documentation. In *Proceedings of the 2009 Conference on Empirical Methods in Natural Language Processing: Volume 1-Volume 1*, pages 296–305. Association for Computational Linguistics.

Aron Culotta and Andrew McCallum. 2005. Reducing labeling effort for structured prediction tasks. In *AAAI*, volume 5, pages 746–751.

Ido Dagan and Sean P Engelson. 1995. Committee-based sampling for training probabilistic classifiers. In *Machine Learning Proceedings 1995*, pages 150–157. Elsevier.

Pinar Donmez and Jaime G Carbonell. 2010. From active to proactive learning methods. In *Advances in Machine Learning I*, pages 97–120. Springer.

Jin-Dong Kim and Yue Wang. 2012. Pubannotation: a persistent and sharable corpus and annotation repository. In *Proceedings of the 2012 Workshop on Biomedical Natural Language Processing*, pages 202–205. Association for Computational Linguistics.

Maolin Li, Nhung Nguyen, and Sophia Ananiadou. 2017. Proactive learning for named entity recognition. *BioNLP 2017*, pages 117–125.

Gideon S Mann and Andrew McCallum. 2007. Efficient computation of entropy gradient for semi-supervised conditional random fields. In *Human Language Technologies 2007: The Conference of the North American Chapter of the Association for Computational Linguistics; Companion Volume, Short Papers*, pages 109–112. Association for Computational Linguistics.

Naoaki Okazaki. 2007. CRFsuite: a fast implementation of Conditional Random Fields (CRFs).

Oscar Reyes, Eduardo Pérez, María Del Carmen Rodríguez-Hernández, Habib M Fardoun, and Sebastián Ventura. 2016. JCLAL: a Java framework for active learning. *The Journal of Machine Learning Research*, 17(1):3271–3275.

Davi P Santos and André CPLF Carvalho. 2014. Comparison of active learning strategies and proposal of a multiclass hypothesis space search. In *Hybrid Artificial Intelligence Systems*, pages 618–629. Springer.

Tobias Scheffer, Christian Decomain, and Stefan Wrobel. 2001. Active hidden Markov models for information extraction. In *International Symposium on Intelligent Data Analysis*, pages 309–318. Springer.

Burr Settles. 2009. Active learning literature survey. Computer Sciences Technical Report 1648, University of Wisconsin–Madison.

Burr Settles. 2011. Closing the loop: Fast, interactive semi-supervised annotation with queries on features and instances. In *Proceedings of the conference on empirical methods in natural language processing*, pages 1467–1478. Association for Computational Linguistics.

Burr Settles and Mark Craven. 2008. An analysis of active learning strategies for sequence labeling tasks. In *Proceedings of the conference on empirical methods in natural language processing*, pages 1070–1079. Association for Computational Linguistics.

Burr Settles, Mark Craven, and Soumya Ray. 2008. Multiple-instance active learning. In *Advances in neural information processing systems*, pages 1289–1296.

Burr Settles and Xiaojin Zhu. 2012. Behavioral factors in interactive training of text classifiers. In *Proceedings of the 2012 Conference of the North American Chapter of the Association for Computational Linguistics: Human Language Technologies*, pages 563–567. Association for Computational Linguistics.

Pontus Stenetorp, Sampo Pyysalo, Goran Topić, Tomoko Ohta, Sophia Ananiadou, and Jun'ichi Tsujii. 2012. BRAT: a web-based tool for NLP-assisted text annotation. In *Proceedings of the Demonstrations at the 13th Conference of the European Chapter of the Association for Computational Linguistics*, pages 102–107. Association for Computational Linguistics.

Erik F Tjong Kim Sang and Fien De Meulder. 2003. Introduction to the CoNLL-2003 shared task: Language-independent named entity recognition. In *Proceedings of the seventh conference on Natural language learning at HLT-NAACL 2003-Volume 4*, pages 142–147. Association for Computational Linguistics.

Katrin Tomanek and Udo Hahn. 2009. Semi-supervised active learning for sequence labeling. In *Proceedings of the Joint Conference of the 47th Annual Meeting of the ACL and the 4th International Joint Conference on Natural Language Processing of the AFNLP: Volume 2-Volume 2*, pages 1039–1047. Association for Computational Linguistics.

Yao-Yuan Yang, Shao-Chuan Lee, Yu-An Chung, Tung-En Wu, Si-An Chen, and Hsuan-Tien Lin. 2017. libact: Pool-based active learning in Python. Technical report, National Taiwan University. Available as arXiv preprint `https://arxiv.org/abs/1710.00379`.

Seid Muhie Yimam, Iryna Gurevych, Richard Eckart de Castilho, and Chris Biemann. 2013. WebAnno: A flexible, web-based and visually supported system for distributed annotations. In *Proceedings of the 51st Annual Meeting of the Association for Computational Linguistics: System Demonstrations*, pages 1–6.

Interactive Instance-based Evaluation of
Knowledge Base Question Answering

Daniil Sorokin and **Iryna Gurevych**

Ubiquitous Knowledge Processing Lab (UKP) and Research Training Group AIPHES
Department of Computer Science, Technische Universität Darmstadt
www.ukp.tu-darmstadt.de

Abstract

Most approaches to Knowledge Base Question Answering are based on semantic parsing. In this paper, we present a tool that aids in debugging of question answering systems that construct a structured semantic representation for the input question. Previous work has largely focused on building question answering interfaces or evaluation frameworks that unify multiple data sets. The primary objective of our system is to enable interactive debugging of model predictions on individual instances (questions) and to simplify manual error analysis. Our interactive interface helps researchers to understand the shortcomings of a particular model, qualitatively analyze the complete pipeline and compare different models. A set of sit-by sessions was used to validate our interface design.

1 Introduction

Knowledge base question answering (QA) is an important natural language processing problem. Given a natural language question, the task is to find a set of entities in a knowledge base (KB) that constitutes the answer. For example, for a question "Who played Princess Leia?" the answer, "Carrie Fisher", could be retrieved from a general-purpose KB, such as Wikidata[1]. A successful KB QA system would ultimately provide a universally accessible natural language interface to factual knowledge (Liang, 2016).

KB QA requires a precise modeling of the question semantics through the entities and relations available in the KB in order to retrieve the correct answer. It is common to break down the task into three main steps: entity linking, semantic parsing or relation disambiguation and answer retrieval. We show in Figure 1 how the outlined steps lead to an answer on an example question and how the

---

[1] https://www.wikidata.org/

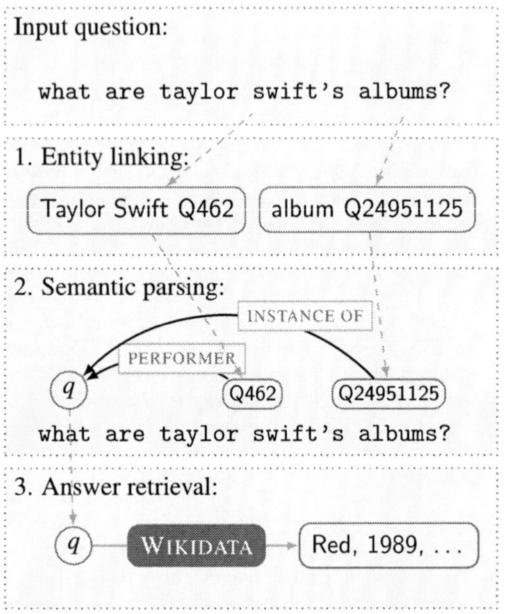

Figure 1: Typical steps undertaken by a QA system. Gray dashed arrows show how the output of the previous step is passed into the next one. Qxxx stands for a KB identifier

output of each step is re-used in the next one. This approach has been exhibited by the most of the recent works on the KB QA (Berant and Liang, 2014; Reddy et al., 2016; Yih et al., 2015; Peng et al., 2017; Sorokin and Gurevych, 2018b). The multi-step pipeline poses particular challenges for error analysis, since many unique errors can arise at different processing stages. With our tool, we aim at supporting the evaluation of QA systems and helping to identify problems that do not necessarily form generalisable error patterns, but hinder the overall system performance nonetheless.

Some frameworks have been introduced recently to streamline the evaluation of KB QA systems. The ParlAI framework focuses on building a uni-

Proceedings of the 2018 Conference on Empirical Methods in Natural Language Processing (System Demonstrations), pages 114–119
Brussels, Belgium, October 31–November 4, 2018. ©2018 Association for Computational Linguistics

fied interface for multiple QA data sets (Miller et al., 2017), while GerbilQA[2] introduces evaluation of individual steps of a QA pipeline. However, none of them addresses an interactive debugging scenario, that can be used by the researchers to do instance-base error analysis. This is especially relevant in the context of such benchmarks as QALD, where each individual question is meant to test a particular aspect of the system and debugging individual instances is crucial for understanding of the system performance (Unger et al., 2016).

Another set of tools have focused on building an infrastructure to support the development for KB QA. Ask Wikidata[3] offers an easy way to post queries to Wikidata via a web-based interface, though the tool relies on manual disambiguation to understand a question. The WDAqua project[4] has produced a speech-based plug-in interface (Kumar et al., 2017) and the Qanary specification for QA systems (Singh et al., 2016). These tools follow the described steps of the QA pipeline, but do not facilitate the interactive instance-based evaluation that is the main aspect of this work.

Main contribution In this paper, we present a modular debugging application for KB QA that can be used to manually evaluate the main steps of a QA pipeline. Our system focuses on the analysis of individual examples and a detailed view of possible causes of errors, so that individual error propagation cases can be identified.

Demo system and the code A demo instance with the default QA model is running at the following url: `http://semanticparsing.ukp.informatik.tu-darmstadt.de:5000/question-answering/`. Our system is freely available: `https://github.com/UKPLab/emnlp2018-question-answering-interface`.

2 A prototypical QA pipeline and the requirements

The first stage of every QA approach is entity linking (EL), that is the identification of entity mentions in the question and linking them to entities in KB. In Figure 1, two entity mentions are detected and linked to the KB referents. According to multiple error analyses, entity linking is a common source of errors in a QA system (Berant and Liang, 2014; Reddy et al., 2016).

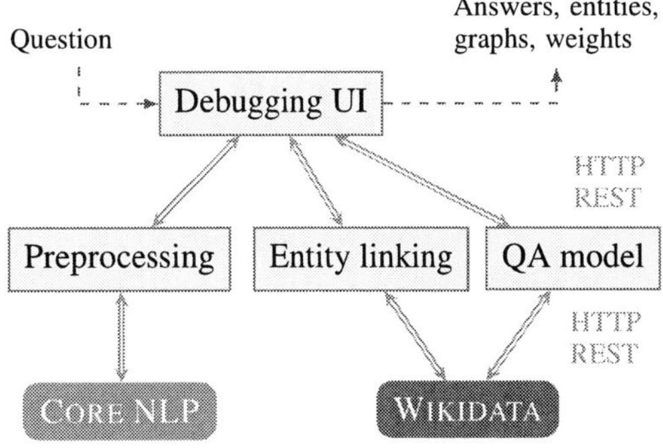

Figure 2: Overview of the system architecture

The entity linking stage is followed by semantic parsing that consists of combining the extracted entities into a single structured meaning representation. The entities are connected with semantic relations to a special question variable that denotes the answer to the question (Yih et al., 2015).

Given the ambiguity of the natural language, a semantic parsing model constructs multiple representations that can match the question and assigns probabilities to them (Liang, 2016). It is common to learn a vector encoding for the question and the structured representations and then use a similarity function to compute the probabilities (Yih et al., 2015; Reddy et al., 2016). The most probable structured representation is then translated into a query and used to extract the answer from the KB.

Some approaches circumvent building a structured representation and instead directly compose vector encodings of the potential answers (Dong et al., 2015). Since this is a less common architecture type for KB QA, we focused on semantic parsing approaches while developing our interface.

The described pipeline lets us outline the main requirements for an interactive debugging tool:

1. It needs to represent all stages of the QA pipeline in a sequential manner to let the user identify where the error occurs and how it propagates.

2. It needs to account for the specific properties of semantic parsing approaches to KB QA, such as structured semantic representations.

3. It needs to include an analysis block that shows if the model has learned meaningful vector representations.

115

```
1    entity.linking:
2      model: models/elmodel.pkl
3      max.entity.options: 5
4      max.ngram.len: 4
5
6    model:
7      model.file: models/qamodel.pkl
8
9    evaluation:
10     max.num.entities: 3
11     beam.size: 10
12     ...
13
14   wikidata:
15     backend: localhost:8890/sparql
16     timeout: 10
17     ...
```

Listing 1: A snippet of the YAML configuration file with the main modules and settings

3 System overview

Our system consists of a web-based front-end and a set of back-end services that communicate through HTTP REST API (see Figure 2). The front-end contains the interactive debugging user interface (Section 4). A separate request is sent to the back-end service for each processing step of the QA pipeline. Thus, we are able to show the results to the user as they are being delivered by the back-end services. The front-end is responsible for aggregating and visualizing the information after each step. In case any service fails, a partial result from the previous steps would be available to the user.

The back-end services include the pre-processing, the entity linking and the semantic parsing modules. The pre-processing module performs tokenization and part-of-speech tagging using the Stanford CoreNLP toolkit (Manning et al., 2014). The entity linking module recognizes mentions of the KB entities in the input question. We provide a default model for entity linking on Wikidata that is freely available feature-based implementation of Sorokin and Gurevych (2018a).

The semantic parsing module includes the construction of structured semantic representations and a learned model that selects the correct representation. The integrated model uses a convolutional neural network architecture to learn vector encodings for questions and semantic representations (Sorokin and Gurevych, 2017). We provide an integrated model for demonstartion purposes, while the main purpose of the tool is to enable manual evaluation and comparison of new models. We define an interface that a user needs to implement in

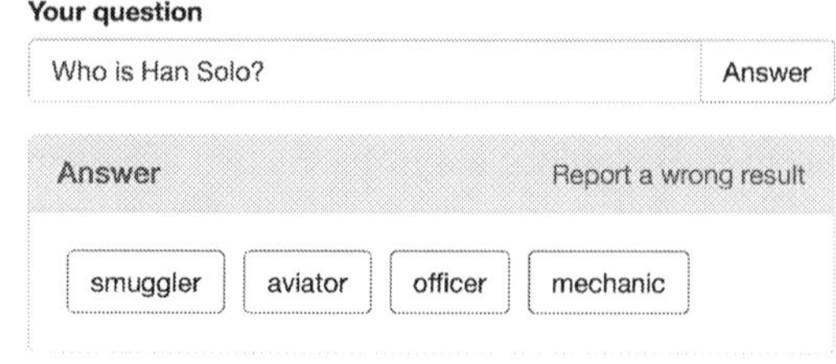

Figure 3: The main input field and the answer block

order to integrate their own model into the tool.

Finally, using the KB query provided by the semantic parsing module, the front-end retrieves the answers from the KB. The back-end modules can be configured using a YAML properties file (see Listing 1 for an example configuration).

3.1 Implementation details

We implement the user interface and the back-end services with modern web technologies, such as JQuery, D3.js and Bootstrap. The back-end services are implemented in Python with Flask. It is configurable and can be further easily extended with other models for entity linking and QA.

A new QA model can be integrated either as a Python module or as a separate REST service. To communicate the results to the front-end, the service has to send the response in the defined JSON format. We refer to the published code repository for additional details on the implementation.

4 User interface

The interactive web-based user interface (UI) is the central element of our system. We have designed the interface for an expert user and have considered the following user traits (Raskin, 2000): a background in KB QA, a knowledge of programming languages, an interest in manual error analysis.

The UI is modeled after the prototypical QA pipeline as described in Section 2. Each step of the pipeline is represented as a separate block in the interface (see the complete UI depicted in Figure 5). That is, the represented model of the UI directly corresponds to the implementation model of the prototypical QA system. Such design choice is appropriate for tools aimed at domain experts who already have a clear mental model of the underlying processes and it makes the UI understandable for the first time (expert) users (Cooper et al., 2007).

Consequently, the interface is divided into blocks

that correspond to the steps of the QA pipeline. There are several base blocks that are fixed and can not be removed, such as the input question block, while the other ones can be hidden if needed.

Input question and answer block The first block consists of the input question field and the answer area (Figure 3). When the user first loads the interface, only the input question field is presented. This avoids the confusion as to what is the starting point of the interactions with the system. Further elements appear only when the corresponding results are returned. For example, the answers area is only shown when the processing is finished.

Although the answer retrieval from the KB is the last step of the pipeline, we put the answer area right below the input question field. This design choice makes it easy to see right away if the system has processed the question correctly.

Entity linking block In this block, we list all identified entity mentions in the input question and the top 5 entity disambiguation candidates. The entity candidate with the highest score is automatically selected and forwarded to the QA model.

The list of entity disambiguation candidates is interactive and the user can select all or none candidates for each entity mention. In case multiple candidates are selected, all of them are sent to the QA system as separate entities. This lets the user correct potential entity linker mistakes by selecting some other than the top disambiguation candidate and continue to debug the rest of the pipeline.

Semantic graphs We visualize the structured semantic representations that the QA model generates as graphs. That is the most common way to visually depict structured representations (Yih et al., 2015; Reddy et al., 2016; Sorokin and Gurevych, 2018b). A semantic graph consists of a question variable node that denotes the answer to the question, KB entities and KB relation types.

We use circles to depict entities and solid lines between them to show relations. In each graph the question variable node is represented with a high-contrast blue circle. Since most relations are attached to the question node, this makes it easier to parse the structure of the graph. Additionally, since each graph has only one high contrast node, the user can identify at the first sight how many graphs have been composed for the input question. For example, Figure 4 shows four semantic graphs for a question "Who played Princess Leia in Star

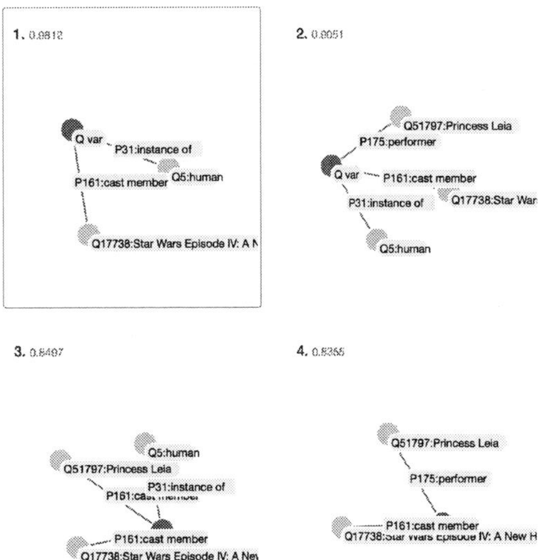

Figure 4: The semantic graphs block for the question "Who played Princess Leia in Star Wars?"

Wars?", that are clearly visible. In this instance, the model selects an incorrect graph (highlighted in green) and retrieves all cast members of the Star Wars movie. The correct graph would be the second one, that also uses the entity Princess Leia.

Representation analysis The visual inspection of the learned vector representation in the two final blocks makes it possible to identify implementation or training errors in the QA model. Once the error is attributed to the learned model, a researcher can continue to inspect the model in the tool that would be the most appropriate to inspect the weights of a particular model architecture (e.g. TensorBoard[5]).

The token-level representations block visualizes the weights computed by the model for each input token of the question. This kind of visual analysis is helpful to identify if the model is learning meaningful word representations. We rely on the shade and saturation visual variables to encode the computed vectors. Each vertical line corresponds to a vector dimension and the darker saturated colors denote a higher numerical value. In Figure 5, one can see that the model is assigning the highest weights to the main entity in the question.

The second representation analysis block places the vector representation of the question and of the semantic relations on a 2D-plane using

---

[5]`https://www.tensorflow.org/programmers_guide/summaries_and_tensorboard`

t-SNE (van der Maaten and Hinton, 2008). The vectors of the relations that appear in the generated semantic graphs are rendered as red circles. The user can zoom in and out to compare the position of the question vector to the surrounding relations.

5 User study

The interface was designed with the requirements that were outlined in Section 2. As domain experts, we were personally interested in applying the developed tool to QA systems. To verify that the interface and the designed interactions are in line with expectations of the first-time users, we have conducted a set of brief sit-by testing sessions. Sit-by sessions are usually used for exploratory situations and gathering first impressions about the design of a product (Rubin and Chisnell, 2008).

In the user study, we aimed to evaluate: can a person familiar with KB QA use the tool independently? Does the developed tool make it possible to manually identify errors in a QA pipeline? Two participants with background in natural language processing and linguistics were asked to perform a simple analysis task while a moderator was sitting near them and monitoring the progress. The participants were asked to input a list of three questions into the tool and tell if the model succeeded in answering them. In case of an incorrect answer, we have expected participants to be able to identify the stage of the pipeline that caused the error. During the sit-by sessions, we were able to confirm that the interface is intuitive and easy to use. All the participants were able to complete the task in under 10 minutes and could point out at what stage an error has occurred for all input questions. The representation analysis instruments, on the contrary, have proven to be the least intuitive element of the interface. Although the participants could attribute the error to the model, they were unable to say if the learned vector representations were meaningful based on the provided visualization.

6 Conclusions

In this work, we have presented an interactive debugging tool for semantic parsing approaches to KB QA. We have started by defining the main requirements for an instance-based evaluation tool and then demonstarted how the different aspects of the designed interface fulfill them. Our tool enables researchers to explore and qualitatively analyse a developed QA pipeline. We used sit-by sessions to verify the design choices and to assess the usability of the tool. Our architecture includes default models for entity linking and question answering, which makes it easy to replace only one of the components with a new module.

Acknowledgments

This work has been supported by the German Research Foundation as part of the Research Training Group AIPHES (grant No. GRK 1994/1), and via the QA-EduInf project (grant GU 798/18-1 and RI 803/12-1). We gratefully acknowledge the support of NVIDIA Corporation with the donation of the Titan X GPU.

References

Jonathan Berant and Percy Liang. 2014. Semantic Parsing via Paraphrasing. In *Proceedings of 52nd Annual Meeting of the Association for Computational Linguistics (ACL)*, pages 1415–1425, Baltimore, MD, USA.

Alan Cooper, Robert Reimann, and David Cronin. 2007. *About Face 3: The Essentials of Interaction Design*. John Wiley & Sons.

Li Dong, Furu Wei, Ming Zhou, and Ke Xu. 2015. Question Answering over Freebase with Multi-Column Convolutional Neural Networks. In *Proceedings of the 53rd Annual Meeting of the Association for Computational Linguistics and the 7th International Joint Conference on Natural Language Processing (ACL-IJCNLP)*, pages 260–269.

Ashwini Jaya Kumar, Christoph Schmidt, and Joachim Khler. 2017. A knowledge graph based speech interface for question answering systems. *Speech Communication*, 92:1–12.

Percy Liang. 2016. Learning Executable Semantic Parsers for Natural Language Understanding. *Communications of the ACM*, 59(9):68–76.

Laurens van der Maaten and Geoffrey Hinton. 2008. Visualizing High-Dimensional Data using t-SNE. *Journal of Machine Learning Research*, 9:2579–2605.

Christopher D. Manning, John Bauer, Jenny Finkel, Steven J. Bethard, Mihai Surdeanu, and David McClosky. 2014. The Stanford CoreNLP Natural Language Processing Toolkit. In *Proceedings of 52nd Annual Meeting of the Association for Computational Linguistics (ACL): System Demonstrations*, pages 55–60, Baltimore, MD, USA.

A. H. Miller, W. Feng, A. Fisch, J. Lu, D. Batra, A. Bordes, D. Parikh, and J. Weston. 2017. ParlAI: A Dialog Research Software Platform. *arXiv preprint arXiv:1705.06476*.

Haoruo Peng, Ming-Wei Chang, and Wen-Tau Yih. 2017. Maximum Margin Reward Networks for Learning from Explicit and Implicit Supervision. In *Proceedings of the 2017 Conference on Empirical Methods in Natural Language Processing (EMNLP)*, pages 2358–2368, Copenhagen, Denmark.

J Raskin. 2000. *The Humane Interface: New Directions for Designing Interactive Systems*. Addison-Wesley.

Siva Reddy, Oscar Täckström, Michael Collins, Tom Kwiatkowski, Dipanjan Das, Mark Steedman, and Mirella Lapata. 2016. Transforming Dependency Structures to Logical Forms for Semantic Parsing. *Transactions of the Association for Computational Linguistics*, 4:127–140.

J Rubin and D Chisnell. 2008. *Handbook of Usability Testing: Howto Plan, Design, and Conduct Effective Tests*, 2nd edition. Wiley Publishing.

Kuldeep Singh, Andreas Both, Dennis Diefenbach, Saedeeh Shekarpour, Didier Cherix, and Christoph Lange. 2016. Qanary – The Fast Track to Creating a Question Answering System with Linked Data Technology. In *The Semantic Web*, pages 183–188, Cham. Springer International Publishing.

Daniil Sorokin and Iryna Gurevych. 2017. End-to-end representation learning for question answering with weak supervision. In *Semantic Web Challenges: 4th SemWebEval Challenge at ESWC 2017*, volume 769 of *Communications in Computer and Information Science*, pages 70–83, Cham. Springer International Publishing.

Daniil Sorokin and Iryna Gurevych. 2018a. Mixing Context Granularities for Improved Entity Linking on Question Answering Data across Entity Categories. In *Proceedings of the Seventh Joint Conference on Lexical and Computational Semantics (*SEM)*, pages 65–75, New Orleans, LA, USA. Association for Computational Linguistics.

Daniil Sorokin and Iryna Gurevych. 2018b. Modeling semantics with gated graph neural networks for knowledge base question answering. In *Proceedings of COLING 2018, the 27th International Conference on Computational Linguistics*, pages 3306–3317. Association for Computational Linguistics.

Christina Unger, Axel-Cyrille Ngonga Ngomo, and Elena Cabrio. 2016. 6th Open Challenge on Question Answering over Linked Data (QALD-6). In *Semantic Web Challenges*, pages 171–177, Cham. Springer International Publishing.

Wen-tau Yih, Ming-Wei Chang, Xiaodong He, and Jianfeng Gao. 2015. Semantic Parsing via Staged Query Graph Generation: Question Answering with Knowledge Base. In *Proceedings of the 53rd Annual Meeting of the Association for Computational Linguistics and the 7th International Joint Conference on Natural Language Processing (ACL-IJCNLP)*, pages 1321–1331, Beijing, China.

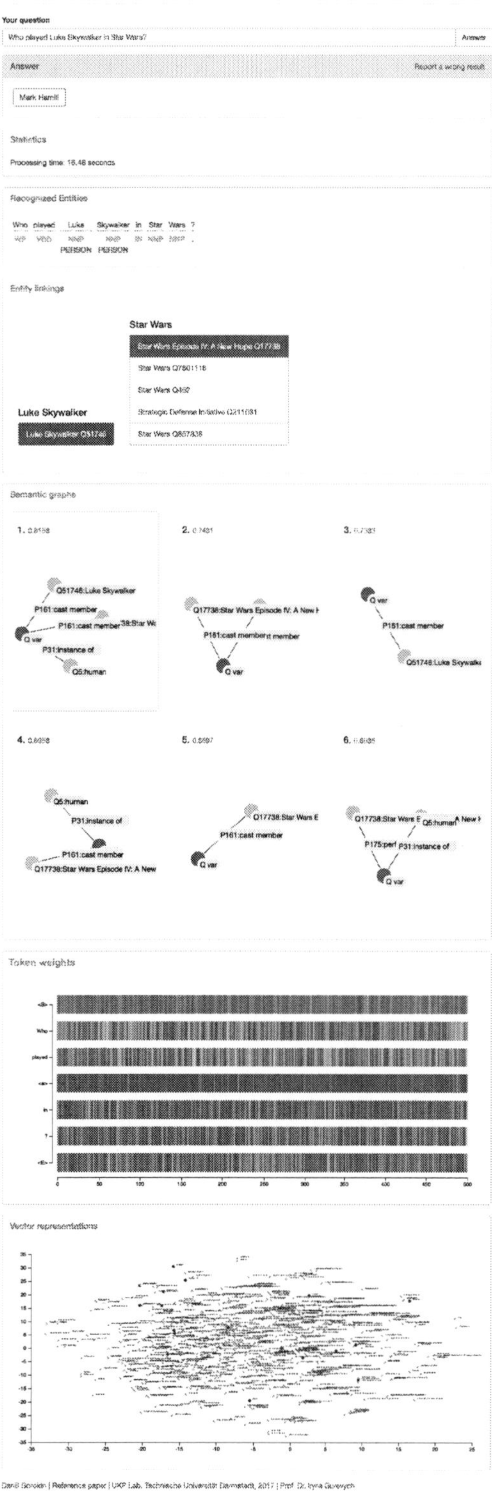

Figure 5: The complete unrolled UI for the question "Who played Luke Skywalker in Star Wars?"

Magnitude: A Fast, Efficient Universal Vector Embedding Utility Package

Ajay Patel
Plasticity Inc.
San Francisco, CA
ajay@plasticity.ai

Alexander Sands
Plasticity Inc.
San Francisco, CA
alex@plasticity.ai

Chris Callison-Burch
Computer and Information
Science Department
University of Pennsylvania
ccb@upenn.edu

Marianna Apidianaki
LIMSI, CNRS
Université Paris-Saclay
91403 Orsay, France
marapi@seas.upenn.edu

Abstract

Vector space embedding models like word2vec, GloVe, fastText, and ELMo are extremely popular representations in natural language processing (NLP) applications. We present Magnitude, a fast, lightweight tool for utilizing and processing embeddings. Magnitude is an open source Python package with a compact vector storage file format that allows for efficient manipulation of huge numbers of embeddings. Magnitude performs common operations up to 60 to 6,000 times faster than Gensim. Magnitude introduces several novel features for improved robustness like out-of-vocabulary lookups.

1   Introduction

Magnitude is an open source Python package developed by Ajay Patel and Alexander Sands (Patel and Sands, 2018). It provides a full set of features and a new vector storage file format that make it possible to use vector embeddings in a fast, efficient, and simple manner. It is intended to be a simpler and faster alternative to current utilities for word vectors like Gensim (Řehůřek and Sojka, 2010).

Magnitude's file format (".magnitude") is an efficient universal vector embedding format. The Magnitude library implements on-demand lazy loading for faster file loading, caching for better performance of repeated queries, and fast processing of bulk key queries. Table 1 gives speed benchmark comparisons between Magnitude and Gensim for various operations on the Google News pre-trained word2vec model (Mikolov et al., 2013). Loading the binary files containing the word vectors takes Gensim 70 seconds, versus 0.72 seconds to load the corresponding Magnitude

Metric	Cold	Warm
Initial load time	97x	–
Single key query	1x	110x
Multiple key query (n=25)	68x	3x
k-NN search query (k=10)	1x	5,935x

Table 1: Speed comparison of Magnitude versus Gensim for common operations. The 'cold' column represents the first time the operation is called. The 'warm' column indicates a subsequent call with the same keys.

file, a 97x speed-up. Gensim uses 5GB of RAM versus 18KB for Magnitude.

Magnitude implements functions for looking up vector representations for misspelled or out-of-vocabulary words, quantization of vector models, exact and approximate similarity search, concatenating multiple vector models together, and manipulating models that are larger than a computer's main memory. Magnitude's ease of use and simple interface combined with its speed, efficiency, and novel features make it an excellent tool for cases ranging from applications used in production environments to academic research to students in natural language processing courses.

2   Motivation

Magnitude offers solutions to a number of problems with current utilities.

Speed: Existing utilities are prohibitively slow for iterative development. Many projects use Gensim to load the Google News word2vec model directly from a ".bin" or ".txt" file multiple times. It can take between a minute to a minute and a half to load the file.

Proceedings of the 2018 Conference on Empirical Methods in Natural Language Processing (System Demonstrations), pages 120–126
Brussels, Belgium, October 31–November 4, 2018. ©2018 Association for Computational Linguistics

Memory: A production web server will run multiple processes for serving requests. Running Gensim, in the same configuration, will consume >4GB of RAM usage per process.

Code duplication: Many developers duplicate effort by writing commonly used routines that are not provided in current utilities. Namely, routines for concatenating embeddings, bulk key lookup, out-of-vocabulary search, and building indexes for approximate k-nearest neighbors.

The Magnitude library uses several well-engineered libraries to achieve its performance improvements. It uses SQLite[1] as its underlying data store, and takes advantage of database indexes for fast key lookups and memory mapping. It uses NumPy[2] to achieve significant performance speedups over native Python code using computations that follow the Single Instruction, Multiple Data (SIMD) paradigm. It uses spatial indexes to perform fast exact similarity search and Annoy[3] to perform approximate k-nearest neighbors in the vector space. To perform feature hashing, it uses xxHash[4], an extremely fast non-cryptographic hash algorithm, working at speeds close to RAM limits. Magnitude's file format uses LZ4 compression[5] for compact storage.

3 Design Principles

Several design principles guided the development of the Magnitude library:

- The API should be intuitive and beginner friendly. It should have sensible defaults instead of requiring configuration choices by the user. The option to configure every setting should still be provided to power users.

- The out of the box configuration should be fast and memory efficient for iterative development. It should be suitable for deployment in a production environment. Using the same configuration in development and production reduces bugs and makes deployment easier.

- The library should use lazy loading whenever possible to remain fast, responsive, and memory efficient during development.

- The library should aggressively index, cache, and use memory maps to be fast, responsive, and memory efficient for production.

- The library should be able to process data that is too large to fit into a computer's main memory.

- The library should be thread-safe and employ memory mapping to reduce duplicated memory resources when multiprocessing.

- The interface should act as a generic key-vector store and remain agnostic to underlying models (like word2vec, GloVe, fastText, and ELMo) and remain useable for other domains that use vector embeddings like computer vision (Babenko and Lempitsky, 2016).

Gensim offers several speed ups of its operations, but these are largely only accessible through advanced configuration. For example, by re-exporting a ".bin", ".txt", or ".vec" file into its own native format that can be memory-mapped. Magnitude makes this easier by providing a default configuration and file format that requires no extra configuration to make development and production workloads run efficiently out of the box.

4 Getting Started with Magnitude

The system consists of a Python 2.7 and Python 3.x compatible package (accessible through the PyPI index[6] or GitHub[7]) with utilities for using the ".magnitude" format and converting to it from other popular embedding formats.

4.1 Installation

Installation for Python 2.7 can be performed using the `pip` command:

```
pip install pymagnitude
```

Installation for Python 3.x can be performed using the `pip3` command:

```
pip3 install pymagnitude
```

4.2 Basic Usage

Here is how to construct the Magnitude object, query for vectors, and compare them:

---

[1] https://www.sqlite.org/
[2] http://www.numpy.org/
[3] https://github.com/spotify/annoy
[4] https://xxhash.org/
[5] http://www.lz4.org/

[6] https://pypi.org/project/pymagnitude/
[7] https://github.com/plasticityai/magnitude

```
from pymagnitude import *
vectors = Magnitude("w2v.magnitude")
k = vectors.query("king")
q = vectors.query("queen")
vectors.similarity(k,q) # 0.6510958
```

Magnitude queries return almost instantly and are memory efficient. It uses lazy loading directly from disk, instead of having to load the entire model into memory. Additionally, Magnitude supports nearest neighbors operations, finding all words that are closer to a key than another key, and analogy solving (optionally with Levy and Goldberg (2014)'s 3CosMul function):

```
vectors.most_similar(k, topn=5)
#[('king', 1.0), ('kings', 0.71),
# ('queen', 0.65), ('monarch', 0.64),
# ('crown_prince', 0.62)]

vectors.most_similar(q, topn=5)
#[('queen', 1.0), ('queens', 0.74),
#('princess', 0.71), ('king', 0.65),
# ('monarch', 0.64)]

vectors.closer_than("queen", "king")
#['queens', 'princess']

vectors.most_similar(
        positive = ["woman", "king"],
        negative = ["man"]
) # queen
vectors.most_similar_cosmul(
        positive = ["woman", "king"],
        negative = ["man"]
) # queen
```

In addition to querying single words, Magnitude also makes it easy to query for multiple words in a single sentence and multiple sentences:

```
vectors.query("play")
# Returns: a vector for the word
vectors.query(["play", "music"])
# Returns: an array with two vectors
vectors.query([
  ["play", "music"],
  ["turn", "on", "the", "lights"],
]) # Returns: 2D array with vectors
```

4.3 Advanced Features

OOVs: Magnitude implements a novel method for handling out-of-vocabulary (OOV) words. OOVs frequently occur in real world data since pre-trained models are often missing slang, colloquialisms, new product names, or misspellings. For example, while *uber* exists in Google News word2vec, *uberx* and *uberxl* do not. These products were not available when Google News corpus was built. Strategies for representing these words include generating random unit-length vectors for each unknown word or mapping all unknown words to a token like "UNK" and representing them with the same vector. These solutions are not ideal as the embeddings will not capture semantic information about the actual word. Using Magnitude, these OOV words can be simply queried and will be positioned in the vector space close to other OOV words based on their string similarity:

```
"uber" in vectors # True
"uberx" in vectors # False
"uberxl" in vectors # False
vectors.query("uberx")
  # Returns: [ 0.0507, -0.0708, ...]
vectors.query("uberxl")
  # Returns: [ 0.0473, -0.08237, ...]
vectors.similarity("uberx", "uberxl")
  # Returns: 0.955
```

A consequence of generating OOV vectors is that misspellings and typos are also sensibly handled:

```
"missispi" in vectors # False
"discrimnatory" in vectors # False
"hiiiiiiiiii" in vectors # False
vectors.similarity(
    "missispi",
    "mississippi"
) # Returns: 0.359
vectors.similarity(
    "discrimnatory",
    "discriminatory"
) # Returns: 0.830
vectors.similarity(
    "hiiiiiiiiii",
    "hi"
) # Returns: 0.706
```

The OOV handling is detailed in Section 5.

Concatenation of Multiple Models: Magnitude makes it easy to concatenate multiple types of vector embeddings to create combined models.

```
w2v = Magnitude("w2v.300d.magnitude")
gv = Magnitude("glove.50d.magnitude")
vectors = Magnitude(w2v, gv) # concat
vectors.query("cat")
# Returns: 350d NumPy array
# 'cat' from w2v and 'cat' from gv
vectors.query(("cat", "cats"))
# Returns: 350d NumPy array
# 'cat' from w2v and 'cats' from gv
```

Adding Features for Part-of-Speech Tags and Syntax Dependencies to Vectors: Magnitude can directly turn a set of keys (like a POS tag set) into vectors. Given an approximate upper bound on the number of keys and a namespace, it uses the hashing trick (Weinberger et al., 2009) to create an appropriate length dimension for the keys.

```
pos_vecs = FeaturizerMagnitude(
  100, namespace = "POS")
pos_vecs.dim # 4
# number of dims automatically
# determined by Magnitude from 100
pos_vecs.query("NN")
dep_vecs = FeaturizerMagnitude(
  100, namespace = "Dep")
dep_vecs.dim # 4
dep_vecs.query("nsubj")
```

Metric	Speed
Exact k-NN	0.9155s
Approx. k-NN (k=10, effort = 1.0)	0.1873s
Approx. k-NN (k=10, effort = 0.1)	0.0199s

Table 2: Approximate nearest neighbors significantly speeds up similarity searches compared to exact search. Reducing the amount of allowed effort further speeds the approximate k-NN search.

This can be used with Magnitude's concatenation feature to combine the vectors for words with the vectors for POS tags or dependency tags. Homonyms show why this may be useful:

```
vectors = Magnitude(vecs, pos_vecs,
                    dep_vecs)
vectors.query([
    ("Buffalo", "JJ", "amod"),
    ("buffalo", "NNS", "nsubj"),
    ("Buffalo", "JJ", "amod"),
    ("buffalo", "NNS", "nsubj"),
    ("buffalo", "VBP", "rcmod"),
    ("buffalo", "VB", "ROOT"),
    ("Buffalo", "JJ", "amod"),
    ("buffalo", "NNS", "dobj")
]) # array of 8 x (300 + 4 + 4)
```

Approximate k-NN We support approximate similarity search with the `most_similar_approx` function. This finds the approximate nearest neighbors more quickly than the exact nearest neighbors search performed by the `most_similar` function. The method accepts an `effort` argument which accepts the range $[0.0, 1.0]$. A lower `effort` will reduce accuracy, but increase speed. A higher `effort` does the reverse. This trade-off works by searching more- or less-indexed trees. Our approximate k-NN is powered by Annoy, an open source library released by Spotify. Table 2 compares the speed of various configurations for similarity search.

5 Details of OOV Handling

Facebook's fastText (Bojanowski et al., 2016) provides similar OOV functionality to Magnitude's. Magnitude allows for OOV lookups for any embedding model, including older models like word2vec and GloVe (Mikolov et al., 2013; Pennington et al., 2014), which did not provide OOV support. Magnitude's OOV method can be used with existing embeddings because it does not require any changes to be made at training time like fastText's method does. For ELMo vectors, Magnitude will use ELMo's OOV method.

Constructing vectors from character n-grams: We generate a vector for an OOV word w based on the character n-gram sequences in the word. First, we pad the word with a character at the beginning of the word and at the end of the word. Next, we generate the set of all character-ngrams in w (denoted with the fuction CGRAM_w) between length 3 and 6, following Bojanowski et al. (2016), although these parameters are tunable arguments in the Magnitude converter. We use the set of character n-grams C to construct a vector $\text{OOV}_d(w)$ with d dimensions to represent the word w. Each unique character n-gram c from the word contributes to the vector through a **p**seudorandom vector **g**enerator function PRVG. Finally, the vector is normalized.

$$C = \text{CGRAM}_w(3, 6)$$
$$\text{oov}_d(w) = \sum_{c \in C} \text{PRVG}_{\text{H}(c)}(-1.0, 1.0, d)$$
$$\text{OOV}_d(w) = \frac{\text{oov}_d(w)}{|\text{oov}_d(w)|}$$

PRVG's random number generator is seeded by the value "seed", which generates uniformly random vectors of dimension size d, with values in the range of -1 to 1. The hashing function H produces a 32 bit hash of its input using xxHash. $\text{H} : \{0, 1\}^* \rightarrow \{0, 1\}^{32}$. Since the PRVG's seed is only conditioned upon the word w, the output is deterministic across different machines.

This character n-gram-based method will generate highly similar vectors for a pair of OOVs with similar spellings, like *uberx* and *uberxl*. However, they will not be embedded close to similar in-vocabulary words like *uber*.

Interpolation with in-vocabulary words To handle matching OOVs to in-vocabulary words, we first define a function $\text{MATCH}_k(a, b, w)$. $\text{MATCH}_k(a, b, w)$ returns the normalized mean of the vectors of the top k most string-similar in-vocabulary words using the full-text SQLite index. In practice, we use the top 3 most string-similar words. These are then used to interpolate the values for the vector representing the OOV word. 30% of the weight for each value comes from the pseudorandom vector generator based on the OOV's n-grams, and the remaining 70% comes from the values of the 3 most string similar in-vocabulary words:

$$\mathrm{oov}_d(w) = [0.3 * \mathrm{OOV}_d(w)$$
$$+ 0.7 * \mathrm{MATCH}_3(3, 6, w)]$$

Morphology-aware matching For English, we have implemented a nuanced string similarity metric that is prefix- and suffix-aware. While *uberification* has a high string similarity to *verification* and has a lower string similarity to *uber*, good OOV vectors should weight stems more heavily than suffixes. Details of our morphology-aware matching are omitted for space.

Other matching nuances We employ other techniques when computing the string similarity metric, such as shrinking repeated character sequences of three or more to two (*hiiiiiiii → hii*), ranking strings of a similar length higher, and ranking strings that share the same first or last character higher for shorter words.

6   File Format

To provide efficiency at runtime, Magnitude uses a custom ".magnitude" file format instead of ".bin", ".txt", ".vec", or ".hdf5" that word2vec, GloVe, fastText, and ELMo use (Mikolov et al., 2013; Pennington et al., 2014; Joulin et al., 2016; Peters et al., 2018). The ".magnitude" file is a SQLite database file. There are 3 variants of the file format: Light, Medium, Heavy. Heavy models have the largest file size but support all of the Magnitude library's features. Medium models support all features except approximate similarity search. Light models do not support approximate similarity searches or interpolated OOV lookups, but they still support basic OOV lookups. See Figure 1 for more information about the structure and layout of the ".magnitude" format.

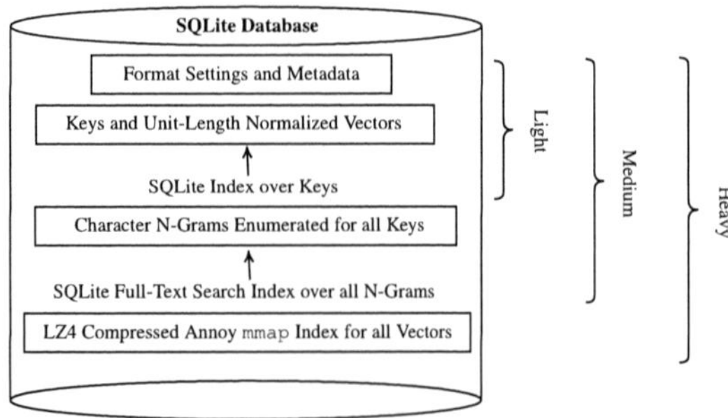

Figure 1: Structure of the ".magnitude" file format and its Light, Medium, and Heavy variants.

Converter The software includes a command-line converter utility for converting word2vec (".bin", ".txt"), GloVe (".txt"), fastText (".vec"), or ELMo (".hdf5") files to Magnitude files. They can be converted with the command:

```
python -m pymagnitude.converter
   -i "./vecs.(bin|txt|vec|hdf5)"
   -o "./vecs.magnitude"
```

The input format will automatically be determined by the extension and the contents of the input file. When the vectors are converted, they will also be unit-length normalized. This conversion process only needs to be completed once per model. After converting, the Magnitude file format is static and it will not be modified or written to in order to make concurrent read access safe.

By default, the converter builds a Medium ".magnitude" file. Passing the `-s` flag will turn off encoding of subword information, and result in a Light flavored file. Passing the `-a` flag will turn on building the Annoy approximate similarity index, and result in a Heavy flavored file. Refer to the documentation[8] for more information about conversion configuration options.

Quantization The converter utility accepts a `-p` `<PRECISION>` flag to specify the decimal precision to retain. Since underlying values are stored as integers instead of floats, this is essentially quantization[9] for smaller model footprints. Lower decimal precision will create smaller files, because SQLite can store integers with either 1, 2, 3, 4, 6, or 8 bytes.[10] Regardless of the precision selected, the library will create `numpy.float32` vectors. The datatype can be changed by passing `dtype=numpy.float16` to the `Magnitude` constructor.

7   Conclusion

Magnitude is a new open source Python library and file format for vector embeddings. It makes it easy to integrate embeddings into applications and provides a single interface and configuration that is suitable for both development and production workloads. The library and file format also

---

[8]https://github.com/plasticityai/magnitude#file-format-and-converter

[9]https://www.tensorflow.org/performance/quantization

[10]https://www.sqlite.org/datatype3.html

enable novel features like OOV handling that allow models to be more robust to noisy data. The simple interface, ease of use, and speed of the library, compared to other utilities like Gensim, will enable use by beginners to NLP and individuals in educational environments, such as university NLP and AI courses.

Pre-trained word embeddings have been widely adopted in NLP. Researchers in computer vision have started using pre-trained vector embedding models like Deep1B (Babenko and Lempitsky, 2016) for images. The Magnitude library intends to stay agnostic to various domains, instead providing a generic key-vector store and interface that is useful for all domains and for research that crosses the boundaries between NLP and vision (Hewitt et al., 2018).

8   Software and Data

We release the Magnitude package under the permissive MIT open source license. The full source code and pre-converted ".magnitude" models are on GitHub. The full documentation for all classes, methods, and configurations of the library can be found at `https://github.com/plasticityai/magnitude`, along with example usage and tutorials.

We have pre-converted several popular embedding models (Google News word2vec, Stanford GloVe, Facebook fastText, AI2 ELMo) to ".magnitude" in all its variants (Light, Medium, and Heavy). You can download them from `https://github.com/plasticityai/magnitude#pre-converted-magnitude-formats-of-popular-embeddings-models`.

Acknowledgments

We would like to thank Erik Bernhardsson for the useful feedback on integrating Annoy indexing into Magnitude and thank the numerous contributors who have opened issues, reported bugs, or suggested technical enhancements for Magnitude on GitHub.

This material is funded in part by DARPA under grant number HR0011-15-C-0115 (the LORELEI program) and by NSF SBIR Award #IIP-1820240. The U.S. Government is authorized to reproduce and distribute reprints for Governmental purposes. The views and conclusions contained in this publication are those of the authors and should not be interpreted as representing official policies or endorsements of DARPA, the NSF, and the U.S. Government. This work has also been supported by the French National Research Agency under project ANR-16-CE33-0013.

References

Artem Babenko and Victor Lempitsky. 2016. Efficient Indexing of Billion-Scale Datasets of Deep Descriptors. In *Proceedings of the IEEE Conference on Computer Vision and Pattern Recognition*, pages 2055–2063, Las Vegas, NV.

Piotr Bojanowski, Edouard Grave, Armand Joulin, and Tomas Mikolov. 2016. Enriching word vectors with subword information. *CoRR*, abs/1607.04606.

John Hewitt, Daphne Ippolito, Brendan Callahan, Reno Kriz, Derry Tanti Wijaya, and Chris Callison-Burch. 2018. Learning Translations via Images with a Massively Multilingual Image Dataset. In *Proceedings of ACL*, pages 2566–2576, Melbourne, Australia.

Armand Joulin, Edouard Grave, Piotr Bojanowski, and Tomas Mikolov. 2016. Bag of Tricks for Efficient Text Classification. *CoRR*, abs/1607.01759.

Omer Levy and Yoav Goldberg. 2014. Linguistic regularities in sparse and explicit word representations. In *Proceedings of CoNLL*, pages 171–180, Ann Arbor, Michigan.

Tomas Mikolov, Kai Chen, Greg Corrado, and Jeffrey Dean. 2013. Efficient Estimation of Word Representations in Vector Space. *CoRR*, abs/1301.3781.

Ajay Patel and Alex Sands. 2018. plasticityai/magnitude: Release 0.1.22. `https://doi.org/10.5281/zenodo.1255637`.

Jeffrey Pennington, Richard Socher, and Christopher Manning. 2014. Glove: Global vectors for word representation. In *Proceedings of EMNLP*, pages 1532–1543, Doha, Qatar.

Matthew E. Peters, Mark Neumann, Mohit Iyyer, Matt Gardner, Christopher Clark, Kenton Lee, and Luke Zettlemoyer. 2018. Deep contextualized word representations. *CoRR*, abs/1802.05365.

Radim Řehůřek and Petr Sojka. 2010. Software Framework for Topic Modelling with Large Corpora. In *Proceedings of the Workshop on New Challenges for NLP Frameworks*, pages 45–50, Valletta, Malta.

Kilian Weinberger, Anirban Dasgupta, John Langford, Alex Smola, and Josh Attenberg. 2009. Feature Hashing for Large Scale Multitask Learning. In *Proceedings of ICML*, pages 1113–1120, New York, NY.

A Benchmark Comparisons

All benchmarks[11] were performed on the Google News pre-trained word vectors, "GoogleNews-vectors-negative300.bin" (Mikolov et al., 2013) for Gensim and on the "GoogleNews-vectors-negative300.magnitude"[12] for Magnitude, with a MacBook Pro (Retina, 15-inch, Mid 2014) 2.2GHz quad-core Intel Core i7 @ 16GB RAM on a SSD over an average of trials where feasible. We are explicitly not using Gensim's memory-mapped native format as it requires extra configuration from the developer and is not provided out of the box from Gensim's data repository [13].

Metric	Gensim (Řehůřek and Sojka, 2010)	Magnitude Light	Magnitude Medium	Magnitude Heavy
Initial load time	70.26s	**0.7210s**	—[a]	—[a]
Cold single key query	**0.0001s**	**0.0001s**	—[a]	—[a]
Warm single key query *(same key as cold query)*	0.0044s	**0.00004s**	—[a]	—[a]
Cold multiple key query *(n=25)*	3.0050s	**0.0442s**	—[a]	—[a]
Warm multiple key query *(n=25) (same keys as cold query)*	**0.0001s**	0.00004s	—[a]	—[a]
First `most_similar` search query *(n=10) (worst case)*	**18.493s**	247.05s	—[a]	—[a]
First `most_similar` search query *(n=10) (average case) (w/ disk persistent cache)*	18.917s	**1.8217s**	—[a]	—[a]
Subsequent `most_similar` search *(n=10) (different key than first query)*	0.2546s	**0.2434s**	—[a]	—[a]
Warm subsequent `most_similar` search *(n=10) (same key as first query)*	0.2374s	**0.00004s**	**0.00004s**	**0.00004s**
First `most_similar_approx` search query *(n=10, effort=1.0) (worst case)*	N/A [b]	N/A	N/A	**29.610s**
First `most_similar_approx` search query *(n=10, effort=1.0) (average case) (w/ disk persistent cache)*	N/A	N/A	N/A	**0.9155s**
Subsequent `most_similar_approx` search *(n=10, effort=1.0) (different key than first query)*	N/A	N/A	N/A	**0.1873s**
Subsequent `most_similar_approx` search *(n=10, effort=0.1) (different key than first query)*	N/A	N/A	N/A	**0.0199s**
Warm subsequent `most_similar_approx` search *(n=10, effort=1.0) (same key as first query)*	N/A	N/A	N/A	**0.00004s**
File size	**3.64GB**	4.21GB	5.29GB	10.74GB
Process memory (RAM) utilization	4.875GB	**18KB**	—[a]	—[a]
Process memory (RAM) utilization after 100 key queries	4.875GB	**168KB**	—[a]	—[a]
Process memory (RAM) utilization after 100 key queries + similarity search	8.228GB [c]	**342KB** [d]	—[a]	—[a]

[a] Denotes the same value as the previous column.

[b] Gensim does support approximate similarity search, but not out of the box as the index must be built manually with `gensim.similarities.index` first which is a slow operation.

[c] Gensim has an option to not duplicate unit-normalized vectors in memory, but still requires up to 8GB of memory allocation while processing, before dropping down to half the memory. Moreover, this option is not on by default.

[d] Magnitude uses `mmap` to read from the disk, so the OS will still allocate pages of memory, when memory is available, in its file cache, but it can be shared between processes and is not managed within each process for extremely large files which is a performance win.

Table 3: Benchmark comparisons between Gensim, Magnitude Light, Magnitude Medium, and Magnitude Heavy.

---

[11] `https://github.com/plasticityai/magnitude/blob/master/tests/benchmark.py`
[12] `http://magnitude.plasticity.ai/word2vec+approx/GoogleNews-vectors-negative300.magnitude`
[13] `https://github.com/RaRe-Technologies/gensim-data`

Integrating Knowledge-Supported Search
into the INCEpTION Annotation Platform

Beto Boullosa   **Richard Eckart de Castilho**   **Naveen Kumar**
Jan-Christoph Klie   **Iryna Gurevych**
Ubiquitous Knowledge Processing Lab
Technische Universität Darmstadt, Germany
`https://www.ukp.tu-darmstadt.de`

Abstract

Annotating entity mentions and linking them
to a knowledge resource are essential tasks
in many domains. It disambiguates mentions,
introduces cross-document coreferences, and
the resources contribute extra information, e.g.
taxonomic relations. Such tasks benefit from
text annotation tools that integrate a search
which covers the text, the annotations, as well
as the knowledge resource. However, to the
best of our knowledge, no current tools integrate knowledge-supported search as well as
entity linking support. We address this gap by
introducing knowledge-supported search functionality into the INCEpTION text annotation
platform. In our approach, cross-document references are created by linking entity mentions
to a knowledge base in the form of a structured
hierarchical vocabulary. The resulting annotations are then indexed to enable fast and yet
complex queries taking into account the text,
the annotations, and the vocabulary structure.

1 Introduction

In many domains, annotating documents is a key requirement to solve complex problems like identifying sentiment targets in customer reviews, or identifying disease symptoms in medical texts. Traditionally, annotation tasks involved creating dense layers
of annotation, e.g. part-of-speech or dependency
annotations made on every single word, single or
multi-token named entity mentions. Nowadays, the
information to be annotated is often sparsely distributed, e.g. the mentions of particular types of
entities. Finding spans of text which are candidates
for a particular annotation type has thus become an
important and challenging aspect of the annotation
process. Therefore, it is essential that annotators
can search the corpus, making queries over the full
text as well as over the annotations. Linking entity mentions to a structured knowledge resource
(e.g. a taxonomy) allows them to be disambiguated,

which facilitates interpreting, processing, and navigating the annotated texts by effectively creating
cross-document coreferences.

Consider a wine market specialist analysing a
corpus of wine reviews. She wants to annotate mentions of different types of wines and link them to
a knowledge resource, more specifically to a wine
taxonomy. However, since annotating the entire
corpus would take too much time, she wants to
focus on statements made about certain properties
of specific wines. Thus, she needs to search for
keywords (*"price"*, *"quality"*, etc.), mentions of
wines of certain types (*"Bordeaux"*, *"Burgundy"*),
or already annotated statements (e.g. to find com-
parative reviews). Thus, the specialist might pose
queries such as *"sentences containing statements
about the price of all kinds of Bordeaux wines"*
in order to completely perform her corpus analysis. Note that the analyst cannot prepare a task-
specific corpus in advance, because she only discovers which properties of the wines are addressed
by the reviews as she goes along with the analysis.

We are not aware of any web-based text annotation tool that supports this kind of explorative
annotation tasks requiring full-text search, cross-
document entity linking, and annotation search,
and, at the same time, takes into account the hierarchical relations of a taxonomy in a tightly integrated way. To address this gap, we integrate
knowledge-supported search capabilities into the
INCEpTION annotation platform (Klie et al., 2018)
to provide a flexible way of searching the corpus
during the annotation process. The corpus and
annotations are indexed at token level. Primitive
attributes (string, numeric, boolean) and attributes
linking annotations to a knowledge base are indexed and can be queried. For linked annotations,
it also considers the super-type/hypernym relations
in the respective knowledge resource.

Section 2 highlights use cases in which those

Proceedings of the 2018 Conference on Empirical Methods in Natural Language Processing (System Demonstrations), pages 127–132
Brussels, Belgium, October 31–November 4, 2018. ©2018 Association for Computational Linguistics

functionalities are beneficial. Section 3 briefly introduces the INCEpTION annotation platform. Section 4 describes the knowledge-supported search functionality. Section 5 describes which types of knowledge resources the platform supports. Finally, Section 6 describes the related work.

2 Use cases

This section examines three exemplary scenarios of increasing complexity that highlight the benefits of knowledge-supported search in an annotation tool. We consider a wine market specialist who is investigating a corpus of wine reviews to identify the qualities most valued by the consumers and for which they may be willing to pay more. Her goal is to gain insights on consumer preferences, and the annotations she performs are a means to achieve this goal. The examples use the wine ontology from the W3C's *OWL Web Ontology Language Guide*,[1] a popular example of an OWL-based ontology.

Scenario I: Mention identification. The user wants to annotate mentions of a certain concept, e.g. types of wines. She starts with an initial list of wine types and uses the full text search to locate potential mentions, e.g. Bordeaux. Since the query is ambiguous (e.g. it could refer to the city or to the region instead of the wine type), she reviews each match and annotates it only when appropriate. If she discovers a wine type during this process that is not yet on her list, she adds it and again uses the full text search to locate and annotate its mentions.

Scenario II: Concept linking. The user now links the previously identified mentions to a taxonomy where the types of wines are organized into a tree or directed acyclic graph. For example, the vocabulary encodes that *Château d'Yquem* is a wine belonging to the *Sauternes* type, which in turn is a subtype of *Bordeaux*. These links effectively introduce cross-document coreferences within the corpus. Using the annotation search capabilities, the user wants to locate mentions of a wine type. This should consider the vocabulary structure, such that a search for a general wine type (e.g. Bordeaux) also finds mentions of all its subtypes.

Scenario III: Concepts in context. In addition to the linked concept mentions from the previous scenario, we assume that the corpus also carries other types of annotation, e.g. a custom claim annotation which identifies text spans containing statements made about properties of the wine. The user

now wants to query the linked concept mentions in conjunction with these claims, e.g. to locate claims about particular types of wines. She may search for *"claims about wines either from the* Bordeaux *or from the* Burgundy *types, containing words matching the pattern* 'expensive.*'" (Figure 1).

These scenarios underline the benefit of integrating full text and knowledge-supported annotation search into an annotation tool. The next sections shows how INCEpTION addresses these needs.

3 The INCEpTION platform

INCEpTION[2] is a generic multi-user annotation platform aiming to cover three essential aspects of text annotation in a single tool: 1) corpus building, 2) knowledge modelling, and 3) annotation, and to combine them with machine-learning-based assistive mechanisms (so-called *recommenders*) to improve the annotation efficiency and quality.

INCEpTION is implemented as a Java-based web application using Tomcat, Spring Boot and Wicket. It is partially based on WebAnno (Eckart de Castilho et al., 2016), which we have modularized step-by-step to accommodate the needs of INCEpTION. This has allowed us to exclude certain WebAnno modules, e.g. the original automation module, which we replace with our own *recommender* framework, as well as to add new modules such as the search capabilities and knowledge base integration discussed here. We retain the WebAnno modules for project management, inter-annotator agreement calculation, adjudication, etc. as they are compatible with our new modules. The platform is open source software licensed under the Apache License 2.0.

This paper focusses on the annotation search capabilities of INCEpTION together with its knowledge base support. For the *recommender* mechanism, please refer to Klie et al. (2018).

4 Search

The search functionality of INCEpTION is accessible through a sidebar ① in the annotation editor (Figure 1). It allows searching within the documents of the project the user is currently working on. After executing a query, the corresponding results are displayed grouped by document ②. Clicking on a result causes the annotation area to switch to the corresponding document/text span ③. Attributes that link an annotation to a knowledge

<hr>

[1]https://www.w3.org/TR/owl-guide/wine.rdf

[2]https://inception-project.github.io

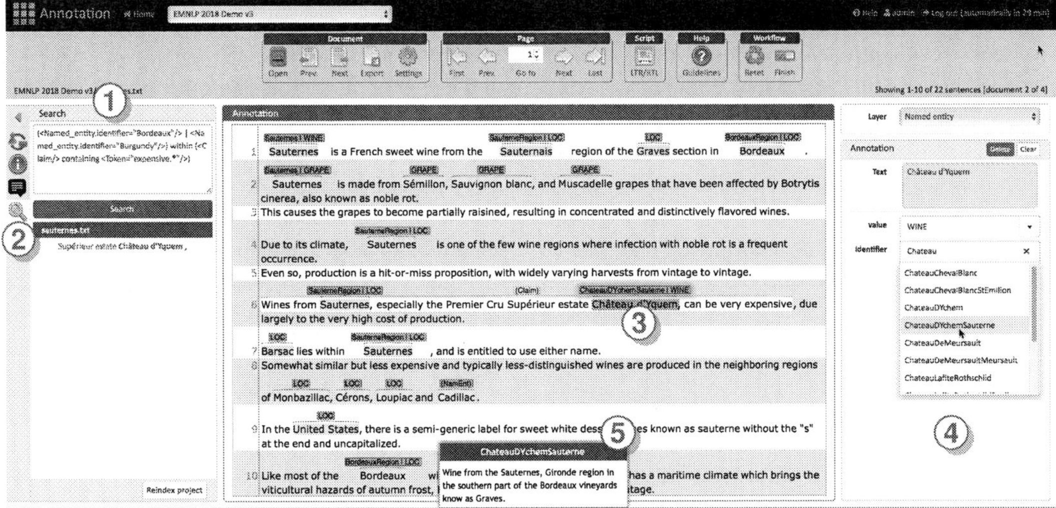

Figure 1: (1) Search sidebar with the query *"all mentions of wines belonging either to the Bordeaux or to the Burgundy type, located inside a claim which contains the pattern expensive.* "*; (2) search results grouped by document; (3) annotation area with a highlighted result; (4) auto-complete field allowing to select an entity from the knowledge base; (5) description of the entity the mouse cursor hovers over.

base item are conveniently editable through an auto-complete field (4).

4.1 Choosing a search framework

The knowledge-supported search functionality called for a search framework that met three requirements: 1) supporting text and annotation search; 2) supporting frequent updates, since the index needs to be updated whenever the user creates, changes or deletes an annotation; 3) it can be embedded directly in the annotation tool (i.e. no separate installation required). We considered three frameworks: the IMS Open Corpus Workbench, Mímir and MTAS.

The IMS Open Corpus Workbench (Christ, 1994) (IMS CWB) is an old but powerful tool to index and search annotated corpora. It introduced the popular Corpus Query Language (CQL).

Using Mímir (Tablan et al., 2015), queries over the annotated text can be combined with information from an knowledge base through SPARQL. This permits queries such as *find all mentions X of persons that were born in London*, where *X* is annotated as a person in the text, and *X was born in London* is contained in the knowledge base.

MTAS (Brouwer et al., 2017) is a recent framework which implements a large part of CQL on top of Apache Lucene.[3]

All frameworks support searching the full text as well as span annotations and their attributes.

Mímir and IMS CWB both assume that corpora are indexed once and queried often. Indexed documents can neither be updated nor easily be deleted and replaced. MTAS does not support updates to documents, but it allows deleting and then re-indexing individual documents.

IMS CWB is implemented in C and can be run either as a server or in an interactive mode. It cannot be easily embedded into a Java application such as INCEpTION. Mímir is implemented in Java, but its architectural design assumes that it is being used as a server. MTAS can be run as a server, but it can also be embedded into a Java-based application.

In conclusion, this made MTAS the best choice to be integrated with INCEpTION.

4.2 Integrating the search framework

To manage the annotations, INCEpTION uses UIMA (Ferrucci and Lally, 2004). For the knowledge base (KB), it uses RDF4J[4]. Thus, it was necessary to first implement a bridge from the UIMA data model to the MTAS data model while supporting the customizable layer configuration provided by INCEpTION. The ability to index annotation

---

[3]http://lucene.apache.org/

[4]http://rdf4j.org

attributes that link to KB items, i.e. classes and instances, was then added as a plugin to this bridge.

The bridge equally supports the built-in annotation layers (e.g. NAMED ENTITY) as well as user-defined layers (e.g. CLAIM). It indexes all the spans associated with all types of annotation layers (spans, relations, and chains). However, queries over relations and chains are limited since MTAS does not offer specific query operators for them. Indexed annotations must start and end at a token boundary. Subtoken annotations are not supported.

Each layer defines a set of attributes. E.g. the NAMED ENTITY layer defines a string attribute VALUE, which usually takes values such as LOC, PER, ORG and OTH for standard named entity annotation tasks. For our examples, we have also added WINE and GRAPE to that list. It also provides the attribute IDENTIFIER which can be used to link an annotation to a KB item (class or instance).

4.3 Full-text, annotation and attribute search

The token layer is built into INCEpTION and can be used to perform full-text queries. E.g., this query locates all occurrences of the token Bordeaux:

```
"Bordeaux"
```

Layers are referenced by their name. Attributes can be addressed using the syntax [layer].[attribute]. Assuming that wine mentions are annotated as named entities of type WINE, the following query finds all mentions of wines. This addresses the needs of Scenario I (Section 2).

```
<Named_entity.value="WINE"/>
```

4.4 Knowledge-supported search

Consider that the named entity annotation layer carries an IDENTIFIER attribute that holds the IRI (Internationalized Resource Identifier) of a KB item (Figure 2). These IRIs are included in the index, together with the IRIs of any items located higher in the ontology hierarchy. As IRIs are hard to read, the index also includes the human-readable labels associated with the entries, so that the user can query using these labels instead.

A KB item can either be a class in the ontology hierarchy (e.g. a wine type or subtype) or an instance (e.g. a specific wine). The following types of queries can be performed to search for annotations linked to the KB: 1) mentions of a specific

KB item; 2) mentions of a KB item, including the mentions of its descendants.

The syntax for addressing the attributes linked to the knowledge base is the same as for normal attributes. The user can either match against the IRI of the linked KB item or against its label. This will retrieve all mentions of the given item, plus all mentions of its descendants in the ontology. Thus, the query effectively traverses the ontology hierarchy, starting in the given item and going down its corresponding subtree. This addresses queries like the one highlighted in Scenario II (Section 2).

```
<[layer].[attribute]="[label | IRI]" />
```

The following example matches all mentions of wines under the *Bordeaux* branch of the ontology:

```
<Named_entity.identifier="Bordeaux"/>
```

By appending -exact to the attribute name, it is possible to limit the query to mentions of exactly one particular item:

```
<[layer].[attribute]-exact="[label | IRI]" />
```

Note that multiple KB items may in principle carry the same label. To avoid this ambiguity, it may be necessary to query using the IRI.

Considering again that annotations are linked to the wine ontology, the following query locates all exact mentions of the *Clos de Vougeot* wine:

```
<Named_entity.identifier-exact =
    "http://www.w3.org/TR/2003/PR-owl-guide-
    20031209/wine#ClosDeVougeotCotesDOr"/>
```

The rich query language provided by MTAS allows to combine different query types like the ones previously introduced, using operators such as within or containing. Considering that our example dataset includes the custom CLAIM annotation type, we can address Scenario III (Section 2) by writing the following query, which retrieves all mentions of wines belonging to the Burgundy or Bordeaux types (and their subtypes), located inside a claim that matches the regular expression pattern expensive.* (Figure 1).

```
(<Named_entity.identifier="Burgundy"/> |
 <Named_entity.identifier="Bordeaux"/>)
within (<Claim/> containing "expensive.*")
```

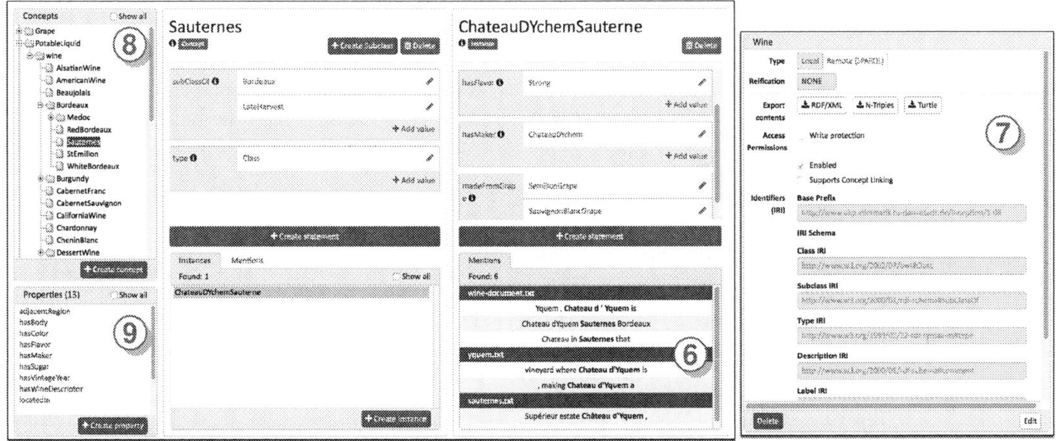

Figure 2: Knowledge base page (left): (8) concept explorer; (9) property explorer; (6) annotated mentions of the seleted KB item. Right: (7) mapping configuration editor.

5 Knowledge-base integration

The knowledge-oriented search capabilities of INCEpTION are enabled by its KB module. This module allows the user to create a KB from scratch or to import one from an RDF file. Remote KBs can be accessed in a read-only mode via the SPARQL.

The KB management page (Figure 2) allows editing classes, properties, instances and the corresponding statements they are defined by. Using the search module, it also displays any annotated mentions (6) of the currently selected KB item.

As the KB module is RDF-based, every piece of information is stored as a triple <subj, pred, obj>. Since this model is very abstract, there are a number of different schemas defining common identifiers (IRIs) that provide additional semantics, e.g. RDF Schema[5] uses the IRI rdfs:subClassOf to encode a subclass relation between the items identified by the subject and the object of a triple.

To support a broad range of different knowledge resources, INCEpTION offers a configurable mapping (7) (Figure 2). The user can choose from several predefined mappings (e.g. RDF, OWL, or SKOS) or define a custom mapping. The mapping mechanism relies on a minimal set of IRIs that must be defined for any KB used with the platform: the INSTANCE-OF relation is required to be able to identify instances, classes and properties within the ontology (<X, instance-of, Y>). Commonly rdf:type is used here, but e.g. the RDF version of Wikidata uses a different IRI. Addition-

ally IRIs identifying CLASS and PROPERTY definitions are required in order to populate the concept explorer (8) and the property explorer (9) (Figure 2) - e.g. <X, instance-of, class>. The class hierarchy is defined via the SUBCLASS-OF IRI. Thus, hierarchies defined e.g. via rdfs:subClassOf or skos:broader are supported, but not hierarchies defined via skos:narrower.[6] While INCEpTION tries to detect root classes automatically, the corresponding query is resource intensive and may eventually time out on some large knowledge resources. Thus, it is also possible to bypass the automatic detection by manually specifying the IRIs of root classes. Finally, IRIs for LABELs and DESCRIPTIONs can be defined. If present, labels are used instead of the IRI when referring to a class, property or instance. Descriptions are shown as a tooltip (Figure 1) when linking an annotation to a KB item.

6 Related work

Several annotation tools support structured vocabularies or KBs and some can be used for cross-document annotation tasks. As INCEpTION is a generic annotation tool, we compare our work to the other generic tools.

WebAnno (Eckart de Castilho et al., 2016), while not offering explicit support for structured vocabularies, can approximate them by combining two of its features: tagsets and constraints. Constraints allow to show a certain attribute of an annotation only when another attribute has a specific value, e.g. to show a COUNTRY attribute only if the TYPE

---

[5]https://www.w3.org/TR/rdf-schema/

[6]https://www.w3.org/2004/02/skos/

property of the entity has the value location. Tagsets can then be used to control which values are acceptable for the entity type or country properties. However, WebAnno has no support for search.

AlvisAE (Papazian et al., 2012) supports linguistic and semantic annotations and can connect them to a structured vocabulary. However, it does not offer the ability to search over annotations and consequently also has no ability to make use of the vocabulary structure in such queries.

CROMER (Girardi et al., 2014) is a tool for entity and event coreference annotation. It allows to annotate and link entity mentions to entities defined in a knowledge base and in this way to create implicit cross-document coreference links. It also offers a simple string-based search to locate potential entity mentions. However, it does not allow to perform further searches involving the created annotations or the structure of the vocabulary.

NeuroCurator (O'Reilly et al., 2017) is a collaborative framework for annotating experiment parameters in scientific papers using an ontology-driven approach. It is rather an interactive knowledge base population tool than a tool for cross-document coreference. Queries over the texts that make use of the information of the KB are not possible.

7   Conclusion and Future Work

We have introduced a knowledge-supported search mechanism into a generic text annotation tool, INCEpTION, to support entity linking and cross-document coreference annotation tasks. The need for such a functionality was motivated using three scenarios, all of which are facilitated using the knowledge-supported search mechanism. In future work, we plan to further extend the search mechanism, e.g. allowing to search over annotation suggestions provided by the *recommender* framework of INCEpTION and by further enhancing the ability to match against information contained in the knowledge bases.

Acknowledgments

We thank Wei Ding, Peter Jiang, Marcel de Boer and Michael Bugert for their valuable contributions. This work was supported by the German Research Foundation under grant No. EC 503/1-1 and GU 798/21-1 (INCEpTION).

References

Matthijs Brouwer, Hennie Brugman, and Marc Kemps-Snijders. 2017. MTAS: A Solr/Lucene based Multi Tier Annotation Search solution. In *Selected papers from the CLARIN Annual Conference 2016, Aix-en-Provence, 26–28 October 2016*, 136, pages 19–37. Linköping University Electronic Press, Linköpings Universitet.

Richard Eckart de Castilho, Éva Mújdricza-Maydt, Seid Muhie Yimam, Silvana Hartmann, Iryna Gurevych, Anette Frank, and Chris Biemann. 2016. A Web-based Tool for the Integrated Annotation of Semantic and Syntactic Structures. In *Proceedings of the workshop on Language Technology Resources and Tools for Digital Humanities (LT4DH) at COLING 2016*, pages 76–84, Osaka, Japan.

Oli Christ. 1994. A modular and flexible architecture for an integrated corpus query system. In *Proceedings of COMPLEX'94 3rd Conference on Computational Lexicography and Text Research*, pages 23–32, Budapest, Hungary.

David Ferrucci and Adam Lally. 2004. UIMA: An Architectural Approach to Unstructured Information Processing in the Corporate Research Environment. *Natural Language Engineering*, 10(3-4):327–348.

Christian Girardi, Manuela Speranza, Rachele Sprugnoli, and Sara Tonelli. 2014. CROMER: a Tool for Cross-Document Event and Entity Coreference . In *Proceedings of the Ninth International Conference on Language Resources and Evaluation (LREC-2014)*, pages 3204–3208, Reykjavik, Iceland. ELRA.

Jan-Christoph Klie, Michael Bugert, Beto Boullosa, Richard Eckart de Castilho, and Iryna Gurevych. 2018. The INCEpTION Platform: Machine-Assisted and Knowledge-Oriented Interactive Annotation. In *Proceedings of the 27th International Conference on Computational Linguistics - COLING 2018*, pages 5–9, Santa Fe, New-Mexico, USA.

Christian O'Reilly, Elisabetta Iavarone, and Sean L. Hill. 2017. A Framework for Collaborative Curation of Neuroscientific Literature. *Frontiers in Neuroinformatics*, 11(27):1–16.

Frèdèric Papazian, Robert Bossy, and Claire Nèdellec. 2012. AlvisAE: a collaborative Web text annotation editor for knowledge acquisition. In *Proceedings of the Sixth Linguistic Annotation Workshop*, pages 149–152, Jeju, Republic of Korea. Association for Computational Linguistics.

Valentin Tablan, Kalina Bontcheva, Ian Roberts, and Hamish Cunningham. 2015. Mímir: An open-source semantic search framework for interactive information seeking and discovery. *Web Semantics: Science, Services and Agents on the World Wide Web*, 30(0):52–68.

CytonMT: an Efficient Neural Machine Translation Open-source Toolkit Implemented in C++

Xiaolin Wang   Masao Utiyama   Eiichiro Sumita
Advanced Translation Research and Development Promotion Center
National Institute of Information and Communications Technology, Japan
{xiaolin.wang,mutiyama,eiichiro.sumita}@nict.go.jp

Abstract

This paper presents an open-source neural machine translation toolkit named CytonMT[1]. The toolkit is built from scratch only using C++ and NVIDIA's GPU-accelerated libraries. The toolkit features training efficiency, code simplicity and translation quality. Benchmarks show that CytonMT accelerates the training speed by 64.5% to 110.8% on neural networks of various sizes, and achieves competitive translation quality.

1 Introduction

Neural Machine Translation (NMT) has made remarkable progress over the past few years (Sutskever et al., 2014; Bahdanau et al., 2014; Wu et al., 2016). Just like Moses (Koehn et al., 2007) does for statistic machine translation (SMT), open-source NMT toolkits contribute greatly to this progress, including but not limited to,

- RNNsearch-LV (Jean et al., 2015)[2]

- Luong-NMT (Luong et al., 2015a)[3]

- DL4MT by Kyunghyun Cho et al.[4]

- BPE-char (Chung et al., 2016)[5]

- Nematus (Sennrich et al., 2017)[6]

- OpenNMT (Klein et al., 2017)[7]

- Seq2seq (Britz et al., 2017)[8]

- ByteNet (Kalchbrenner et al., 2016)[9]

- ConvS2S (Gehring et al., 2017)[10]

- Tensor2Tensor (Vaswani et al., 2017)[11]

- Marian (Junczys-Dowmunt et al., 2018)[12]

These open-source NMT toolkits are undoubtedly excellent software. However, there is a common issue – they are all written in script languages with dependencies on third-party GPU platforms (see Table 1) except Marian, which is developed simultaneously with our toolkit.

Using script languages and third-party GPU platforms is a two-edged sword. On one hand, it greatly reduces the workload of coding neural networks. On the other hand, it also causes two problems as follows,

- The running efficiency drops, and profiling and optimization also become difficult, as the direct access to GPUs is blocked by the language interpreters or the platforms. NMT systems typically require days or weeks to train, so training efficiency is a paramount concern. Slightly faster training can make the difference between plausible and impossible experiments (Klein et al., 2017).

- The researchers using these toolkits may be constrained by the platforms. Unexplored computations or operations may become disallowed or unnecessarily inefficient on a third-party platform, which lowers the chances of developing novel neural network techniques.

---

[1] https://github.com/arthurxlw/cytonMt
[2] https://github.com/sebastien-j/LV_groundhog
[3] https://github.com/lmthang/nmt.hybrid
[4] https://github.com/nyu-dl/dl4mt-tutorial
[5] https://github.com/nyu-dl/dl4mt-cdec
[6] https://github.com/EdinburghNLP/nematus
[7] https://github.com/OpenNMT/OpenNMT-py
[8] https://github.com/google/seq2seq

[9] https://github.com/paarthneekhara/byteNet-tensorflow (unofficial) and others.
[10] https://github.com/facebookresearch/fairseq
[11] https://github.com/tensorflow/tensor2tensor
[12] https://github.com/marian-nmt/marian

Proceedings of the 2018 Conference on Empirical Methods in Natural Language Processing (System Demonstrations), pages 133–138
Brussels, Belgium, October 31–November 4, 2018. ©2018 Association for Computational Linguistics

Toolkit	Language	Platform
RNNsearch-LV	Python	Theano,GroundHog
Luong-NMT	Matlab	Matlab
DL4MT	Python	Theano
BPE-char	Python	Theano
Nematus	Python	Theano
OpenNMT	Lua	Torch
Seq2seq	Python	Tensorflow
ByteNet	Python	Tensorflow
ConvS2S	Lua	Torch
Tensor2Tensor	Python	Tensorflow
Marian	C++	–
CytonMT	C++	–

Table 1: Languages and Platforms of Open-source NMT toolkits.

CytonMT is developed to address this issue, in hopes of providing the community an attractive alternative. The toolkit is written in C++ which is the genuine official language of NVIDIA – the manufacturer of the most widely-used GPU hardware. This gives the toolkit an advantage on efficiency when compared with other toolkits.

Implementing in C++ also gives CytonMT great flexibility and freedom on coding. The researchers who are interested in the real calculations inside neural networks can trace source codes down to kernel functions, matrix operations or NVIDIA's APIs, and then modify them freely to test their novel ideas.

The code simplicity of CytonMT is comparable to those NMT toolkits implemented in script languages. This owes to an open-source general-purpose neural network library in C++, named CytonLib, which is shipped as part of the source code. The library defines a simple and friendly pattern for users to build arbitrary network architectures in the cost of two lines of genuine C++ code per layer.

CytonMT achieves competitive translation quality, which is the main purpose of NMT toolkits. It implements the popular framework of attention-based RNN encoder-decoder. Among the reported systems of the same architecture, it ranks at top positions on the benchmarks of both WMT14 and WMT17 English-to-German tasks.

The following of this paper presented the details of CytonMT from the aspects of method, implementation, benchmark, and future works.

2 Method

The toolkit approaches to the problem of machine translation using the attention-based RNN encoder-decoder proposed by Bahdanau et al. (2014) and Luong et al. (2015a). Figure 1 illus-

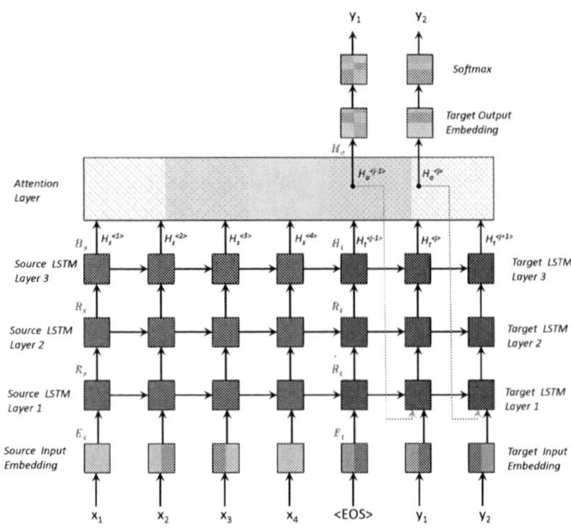

Figure 1: Architecture of CytonMT.

trates the architecture. The conditional probability of a translation given a source sentence is formulated as,

$$log\,p(\mathbf{y}|\mathbf{x}) = \sum_{j=1}^{m} log(p(y_j|H_o^{\langle j \rangle}))$$

$$= \sum_{j=1}^{m} \log(\text{softmax}_{y_j}(\tanh(W_o H_o^{\langle j \rangle} + B_o))) \quad (1)$$

$$H_o^{\langle j \rangle} = \mathcal{F}_{\text{att}}(H_s, H_t^{\langle j \rangle}), \quad (2)$$

where $\mathbf{x}$ is a source sentence; $\mathbf{y}=(y_1, \ldots, y_m)$ is a translation; H_s is a source-side top-layer hidden state; $H_t^{\langle j \rangle}$ is a target-side top-layer hidden state; $H_o^{\langle j \rangle}$ is a state generated by an attention model $\mathcal{F}_{\text{att}}$; W_o and B_o are the weight and bias of an output embedding.

The toolkit adopts the multiplicative attention model proposed by Luong et al. (2015a), because it is slightly more efficient than the additive variant proposed by Bahdanau et al. (2014). This issue is addressed in Britz et al. (2017) and Vaswani et al. (2017). Figure 2 illustrates the model, formulated as ,

$$a_{st}^{\langle ij \rangle} = \text{softmax}(\mathcal{F}_{\text{a}}(H_s^{\langle i \rangle}, H_t^{\langle j \rangle}))$$

$$= \frac{e^{\mathcal{F}_{\text{a}}(H_s^{\langle i \rangle}, H_t^{\langle j \rangle})}}{\sum_{i=1}^{n} e^{\mathcal{F}_{\text{a}}(H_s^{\langle i \rangle}, H_t^{\langle j \rangle})}}, \quad (3)$$

$$\mathcal{F}_{\text{a}}(H_s^{\langle i \rangle}, H_t^{\langle j \rangle}) = H_s^{\langle i \rangle \top} W_{\text{a}} H_t^{\langle j \rangle}, \quad (4)$$

$$C_s^{\langle j \rangle} = \sum_{i=1}^{n} a_{st}^{\langle ij \rangle} H_s^{\langle i \rangle}, \quad (5)$$

$$C_{st}^{\langle j \rangle} = [C_s; H_t^{\langle j \rangle}], \quad (6)$$

$$H_o^{\langle j \rangle} = \tanh(W_c C_{st}^{\langle j \rangle}), \quad (7)$$

where $\mathcal{F}_{\text{a}}$ is a scoring function for alignment; W_{a} is a matrix for linearly mapping target-side hidden

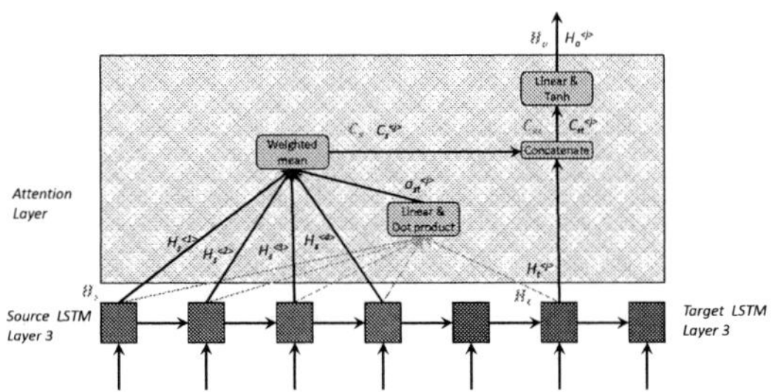

Figure 2: Architecure of Attention Model.

states into a space comparable to the source-side; $a_{st}^{\langle ij \rangle}$ is an alignment coefficient; $C_s^{\langle j \rangle}$ is a source-side context; $C_{st}^{\langle j \rangle}$ is a context derived from both sides.

3 Implementation

The toolkit consists of a general purpose neural network library, and a neural machine translation system built upon the library. The neural network library defines a class named *Network* to facilitate the construction of arbitrary neural networks. Users only need to inherit the class, declare components as data members, and write down two lines of codes per component in an initialization function. For example, the complete code of the attention network formulated by the equations 3 to 7 is presented in Figure 3. This piece of code fulfills the task of building a neural network as follows,

- The class of *Variable* stores numeric values and gradients. Through passing the pointers of *Variable* around, component are connected together.

- The data member of *layers* collects all the components. The base class of *Network* will call the functions *forward*, *backward* and *calculateGradient* of each component to perform the actual computation.

The codes of actual computation are organized in the functions *forward*, *backward* and *calculateGradient* for each type of component. Figure 4 presents some examples. Note that these codes have been slightly simplified for illustration.

```
class Attention: public Network
{
 DuplicateLayer dupHt;          // declare components
 LinearLayer linearHt;
 MultiplyHsHt multiplyHsHt;
 SoftmaxLayer softmax;
 WeightedHs weightedHs;
 Concatenate concateCsHt;
 LinearLayer linearCst;
 ActivationLayer actCst;

 Variable* init(LinearLayer* linHt,
     LinearLayer* linCst, Variable* hs,
     Variable* ht)
 {
  Variable* tx;
  tx=dupHt.init(ht);             // make two copies
  layers.push_back(&dupHt);

  tx=linearHt.init(linHt, tx);             // WaHt
  layers.push_back(&linearHt);

  tx=multiplyHsHt.init(hs, tx);            // Fa
  layers.push_back(&multiplyHsHt);

  tx=softmax.init(tx);                     // ast
  layers.push_back(&softmax);

  tx=weightedHs.init(hs, tx);              // Cs
  layers.push_back(&weightedHs);

  tx=concateCsHt.init(tx, &dupHt.y1);      // Cst
  layers.push_back(&concateCsHt);

  tx=linearCst.init(linCst, tx);           // WcCst
  layers.push_back(&linearCst);

  tx=actCst.init(tx, CUDNN_ACTIVATION_TANH);// Ho
  layers.push_back(&actCst);

  return tx; //pointer to result
 }
};
```

Figure 3: Complete Code of Attention Model Formulated by Equations 3 to 7

```
void LinearLayer::forward()
{
 cublasXgemm(cublasH, CUBLAS_OP_T, CUBLAS_OP_N,
  dimOutput, num, dimInput,
  &one, w.data, w.ni, x.data, dimInput,
  &zero, y.data, dimOutput)
}

void LinearLayer::backward()
{
 cublasXgemm(cublasH, CUBLAS_OP_N, CUBLAS_OP_N,
  dimInput, num, dimOutput,
  &one, w.data, w.ni, y.grad.data, dimOutput,
  &beta, x.grad.data, dimInput));
}

void LinearLayer::calculateGradient()
{
 cublasXgemm(cublasH, CUBLAS_OP_N, CUBLAS_OP_T,
  dimInput, dimOutput, num,
  &one, x.data, dimInput, y.grad.data, dimOutput,
  &one, w.grad.data, w.grad.ni));
}

void EmbeddingLayer::forward()
{
 ...
 embedding_kernel<<<grid, blockSize>>>(words,
  firstOccurs, len, dim, stride,
  wholeData, y.data, true);
}
```

Figure 4: Codes of Performing Actual Computation.

4 Benchmarks

4.1 Settings

CytonMT is tested on the widely-used benchmarks of the WMT14 and WMT17 English-to-German tasks (Bojar et al., 2017) (Table 2). Both datasets are processed and converted using byte-pair encoding(Gage, 1994; Schuster and Nakajima, 2012) with a shared source-target vocabulary of about 37000 tokens. The WMT14 corpora are processed by the scripts from Vaswani et al. (2017)[13]. The WMT17 corpora are processed by the scripts from Junczys-Dowmunt et al. (2018)[14], which includes 10 million back-translated sentence pairs for training.

The benchmarks were run on an Intel Xeon CPU E5-2630 @ 2.4Ghz and a GPU Quadro M4000 (Maxwell) that had 1664 CUDA cores @ 773 MHz, 2,573 GFLOPS . The software is CentOS 6.8, CUDA 9.1 (driver 387.26), CUDNN 7.0.5, Theano 1.0.1, Tensorflow 1.5.0. Netmaus, Torch and OpenNMT are the latest version in December 2017. Marian is the last version in May 2018.

CytonMT is run with the hyperparameters settings presented by Table 3 unless stated otherwise. The settings provide both fast training and competitive translate quality according to our experiments on a variety of translation tasks. Dropout is applied to the hidden states between non-top recurrent layers R_s, R_t and output H_o according to (Wang et al., 2017). Label smoothing estimates the marginalized effect of label-dropout during training, which makes models learn to be more unsure (Szegedy et al., 2016). This improved BLEU scores (Vaswani et al., 2017). Length penalty is applied using the formula in (Wu et al., 2016).

4.2 Comparison on Training Speed

Four baseline toolkits and CytonMT train models using the settings of hyperparameters in Table 3. The number of layers and the size of embeddings and hidden states varies, as large networks are often used in real-world applications to achieve higher accuracy at the cost of more running time.

Table 4 presents the training speed of different toolkits measured in source tokens per second. The results show that the training speed of CytonMT is much higher than the baselines.

[13]https://github.com/tensorflow/tensor2tensor

[14]https://github.com/marian-nmt/marian-examples/tree/master/wmt2017-uedin

Data Set	# Sent.	# Words	
		Source	Target
WMT14			
Train.(standard)	4,500,966	113,548,249	107,259,529
Dev. (tst2013)	3,000	64,807	63,412
Test (tst2014)	3,003	67,617	63,078
WMT17			
Train.(standard)	4,590,101	118,768,285	112,009,072
Train.(back trans.)	10,000,000	190,611,668	149,198,444
Dev. (tst2016)	2,999	64,513	62,362
Test (tst2017)	3,004	64,776	60,963

Table 2: WMT English-to-German corpora.

Hyperparameter	Value
Embedding Size	512
Hidden State Size	512
Encoder/Decoder Depth	2
Encoder	Bidirectional
RNN Type	LSTM
Dropout	0.2
Label Smooth.	0.1
Optimizer	SGD
Learning Rate	1.0
Learning Rate Decay	0.7
Beam Search Size	10
Length Penalty	0.6

Table 3: Hyperparameter Settings.

OpenNMT is the fastest baseline, while CytonMT achieves a speed up versus it by 64.5% to 110.8%. Moreover, CytonMT shows a consistent tendency to speed up more on larger networks.

4.3 Comparison on Translation Quality

Table 5 compares the BLEU of CytonMT with the reported results from the systems of the same architecture (attention-based RNN encoder-decoder). BLEU is calculated on cased, tokenized text to be comparable to previous work (Sutskever et al., 2014; Luong et al., 2015b; Wu et al., 2016; Zhou et al., 2016).

The settings of CytonMT on WMT14 follows Table 3, while the settings on WMT17 adopt a depth of 3 and a hidden state size of 1024 as the training set is three times larger. The cross

Embed./State Size	512	512	1024	1024
Enc./ Dec. Layers	2	4	2	4
Nematus	1875	1190	952	604
OpenNMT	2872	2038	1356	904
Seq2Seq	1618	1227	854	599
Marian	2630	1832	1120	688
CytonMT	**4725**	**3751**	**2571**	**1906**
speedup $\geqslant$	64.5%	84.1%	89.6%	110.8%

Table 4: Training Speed Measured in Source Tokens per Second.

System	Open Src.	BLEU
WMT14		
Nematus(Klein,2017)	√	18.25
OpenNMT(Klein,2017)	√	19.34
RNNsearch-LV(Jean,2015)	√	19.4
Deep-Att(Zhou,2016)		20.6
Luong-NMT(Luong,2015)	√	20.9
BPE-Char(Chung,2016)	√	21.5
Seq2seq(Britz, 2017)	√	22.19
CytonMT	√	**22.67**
GNMT (Wu, 2015)		24.61
WMT17		
Nematus(Sennrich,2017)	√	27.5
CytonMT	√	**27.63**
Marian(Junczys,2018)	√	27.7

Table 5: Comparing BLEU with Public Records.

entropy of the development set is monitored every $\frac{1}{12}$ epoch on WMT14 and every $\frac{1}{36}$ epoch on WMT17, approximately 400K sentence pairs. If the entropy has not decreased by $max(0.01 \times learning\_rate, 0.001)$ in 12 times, learning rate decays by 0.7 and the training restarts from the previous best model. The whole training procedure terminates when no improvement is made during two neighboring decays of learning rate. The actual training took 28 epochs on WMT14 and 12 epochs on WMT17.

Table 5 shows that CytonMT achieves the competitive BLEU points on both benchmarks. On WMT14, it is only outperformed by Google's production system (Wu et al., 2016), which is very much larger in scale and much more demanding on hardware. On WMT17, it achieves the same level of performance with Marian, which is high among the entries of WMT17 for a single system. Note that the start-of-the-art scores on these benchmarks have been recently pushed forward by novel network architectures such as Gehring et al. (2017), Vaswani et al. (2017) and Shazeer et al. (2017)

5   Conclusion

This paper introduces CytonMT – an open-source NMT toolkit – built from scratch only using C++ and NVIDIA's GPU-accelerated libraries. CytonMT speeds up training by more than 64.5%, and achieves competitive BLEU points on WMT14 and WMT17 corpora. The source code of CytonMT is simple because of CytonLib – an open-source general purpose neural network library – contained in the toolkit. Therefore, CytonMT is an attractive alternative for the research community. We open-source this toolkit in hopes of benefiting the community and promoting the field. We look forward to hearing feedback from the community.

The future work of CytonMT will be continued in two directions. One direction is to further optimize the code for GPUs, such supporting multi-GPU. The problem we used to have is that GPUs proceed very fast in the last few years. For example, the microarchitectures of NVIDIA GPUs evolve twice during the development of CytonMT, from Maxwell to Pascale, and then to Volta. Therefore, we have not explored cutting-edge GPU techniques as the coding effort may be outdated quickly. Multi-GPU machines are common now, so we plan to support them.

The other direction is to support latest NMT architectures such ConvS2S (Gehring et al., 2017) and Transformer (Vaswani et al., 2017). In these architectures, recurrent structures are replaced by convolution or attention structures. Their high performance indicates that the new structures suit the translation task better, so we also plan to support them in the future.

References

Dzmitry Bahdanau, Kyunghyun Cho, and Yoshua Bengio. 2014. Neural machine translation by jointly learning to align and translate. *Proceedings of the 3rd International Conference on Learning Representations.*, pages 1–15.

Ondřej Bojar, Rajen Chatterjee, Christian Federmann, Yvette Graham, Barry Haddow, Shujian Huang, Matthias Huck, Philipp Koehn, Qun Liu, Varvara Logacheva, Christof Monz, Matteo Negri, Matt Post, Raphael Rubino, Lucia Specia, and Marco Turchi. 2017. Findings of the 2017 conference on machine translation (wmt17). In *Proceedings of the Second Conference on Machine Translation, Volume 2: Shared Task Papers*, pages 169–214, Copenhagen, Denmark. Association for Computational Linguistics.

Denny Britz, Anna Goldie, Minh-Thang Luong, and Quoc Le. 2017. Massive exploration of neural machine translation architectures. In *Proceedings of the 2017 Conference on Empirical Methods in Natural Language Processing*, pages 1442–1451, Copenhagen, Denmark. Association for Computational Linguistics.

Junyoung Chung, Kyunghyun Cho, and Yoshua Bengio. 2016. A character-level decoder without explicit segmentation for neural machine translation. In *Proceedings of the 54th Annual Meeting of the Association for Computational Linguistics (Volume 1: Long Papers)*, pages 1693–1703, Berlin, Germany. Association for Computational Linguistics.

Philip Gage. 1994. A new algorithm for data compression. *The C Users Journal*, 12(2):23–38.

Jonas Gehring, Michael Auli, David Grangier, Denis Yarats, and Yann N Dauphin. 2017. Convolutional Sequence to Sequence Learning. *ArXiv e-prints*.

Sébastien Jean, Kyunghyun Cho, Roland Memisevic, and Yoshua Bengio. 2015. On using very large target vocabulary for neural machine translation. In *Proceedings of the 53rd Annual Meeting of the Association for Computational Linguistics and the 7th International Joint Conference on Natural Language Processing (Volume 1: Long Papers)*, pages 1–10, Beijing, China. Association for Computational Linguistics.

Marcin Junczys-Dowmunt, Roman Grundkiewicz, Tomasz Dwojak, Hieu Hoang, Kenneth Heafield, Tom Neckermann, Frank Seide, Ulrich Germann, Alham Fikri Aji, Nikolay Bogoychev, Andr F. T. Martins, and Alexandra Birch. 2018. Marian: Fast neural machine translation in c++. *arXiv preprint arXiv:1804.00344*.

Nal Kalchbrenner, Lasse Espeholt, Karen Simonyan, Aäron van den Oord, Alex Graves, and Koray Kavukcuoglu. 2016. Neural machine translation in linear time. *CoRR*, abs/1610.10099.

Guillaume Klein, Yoon Kim, Yuntian Deng, Jean Senellart, and Alexander Rush. 2017. Opennmt: Open-source toolkit for neural machine translation. In *Proceedings of ACL, System Demonstrations*, pages 67–72, Vancouver, Canada. Association for Computational Linguistics.

Philipp Koehn, Hieu Hoang, Alexandra Birch, Chris Callison-Burch, Marcello Federico, Nicola Bertoldi, Brooke Cowan, Wade Shen, Christine Moran, Richard Zens, et al. 2007. Moses: Open source toolkit for statistical machine translation. In *Proceedings of ACL, Interactive Poster and Demonstration Sessions*, pages 177–180. Association for Computational Linguistics.

Thang Luong, Hieu Pham, and Christopher D. Manning. 2015a. Effective approaches to attention-based neural machine translation. In *Proceedings of the 2015 Conference on Empirical Methods in Natural Language Processing*, pages 1412–1421, Lisbon, Portugal. Association for Computational Linguistics.

Thang Luong, Ilya Sutskever, Quoc Le, Oriol Vinyals, and Wojciech Zaremba. 2015b. Addressing the rare word problem in neural machine translation. In *Proceedings of the 53rd Annual Meeting of the Association for Computational Linguistics and the 7th International Joint Conference on Natural Language Processing (Volume 1: Long Papers)*, pages 11–19, Beijing, China. Association for Computational Linguistics.

Mike Schuster and Kaisuke Nakajima. 2012. Japanese and korean voice search. In *Acoustics, Speech and Signal Processing (ICASSP), 2012 IEEE International Conference on*, pages 5149–5152. IEEE.

Rico Sennrich, Orhan Firat, Kyunghyun Cho, Alexandra Birch, Barry Haddow, Julian Hitschler, Marcin Junczys-Dowmunt, Samuel L"aubli, Antonio Valerio Miceli Barone, Jozef Mokry, and Maria Nadejde. 2017. Nematus: a toolkit for neural machine translation. In *Proceedings of the Software Demonstrations of the 15th Conference of the European Chapter of the Association for Computational Linguistics*, pages 65–68, Valencia, Spain. Association for Computational Linguistics.

Noam Shazeer, Azalia Mirhoseini, Krzysztof Maziarz, Andy Davis, Quoc V. Le, Geoffrey E. Hinton, and Jeff Dean. 2017. Outrageously large neural networks: The sparsely-gated mixture-of-experts layer. *CoRR*, abs/1701.06538.

Ilya Sutskever, Oriol Vinyals, and Quoc V Le. 2014. Sequence to sequence learning with neural networks. In *Advances in neural information processing systems*, pages 3104–3112.

Christian Szegedy, Vincent Vanhoucke, Sergey Ioffe, Jonathon Shlens, and Zbigniew Wojna. 2016. Rethinking the inception architecture for computer vision. *Proceedings of the Conference on Computer Vision and Pattern Recognition*, pages 2818–2826.

Ashish Vaswani, Noam Shazeer, Niki Parmar, Jakob Uszkoreit, Llion Jones, Aidan N Gomez, Ł ukasz Kaiser, and Illia Polosukhin. 2017. Attention is all you need. In I. Guyon, U. V. Luxburg, S. Bengio, H. Wallach, R. Fergus, S. Vishwanathan, and R. Garnett, editors, *Advances in Neural Information Processing Systems 30*, pages 6000–6010. Curran Associates, Inc.

Xiaolin Wang, Masao Utiyama, and Eiichiro Sumita. 2017. Empirical study of dropout scheme for neural machine translation. In *Proceedings of the 16th Machine Translation Summit*, pages 1–15.

Yonghui Wu, Mike Schuster, Zhifeng Chen, Quoc V Le, Mohammad Norouzi, Wolfgang Macherey, Maxim Krikun, Yuan Cao, Qin Gao, Klaus Macherey, et al. 2016. Google's neural machine translation system: Bridging the gap between human and machine translation. *arXiv preprint arXiv:1609.08144*.

Jie Zhou, Ying Cao, Xuguang Wang, Peng Li, and Wei Xu. 2016. Deep recurrent models with fast-forward connections for neural machine translation. *Transactions of the Association for Computational Linguistics*, 4:371–383.

OpenKE: An Open Toolkit for Knowledge Embedding

Xu Han[1,2,3*]   **Shulin Cao**[2,3,4,5*]   **Xin Lv**[1,4]   **Yankai Lin**[1,2,3]
Zhiyuan Liu[1,2,3†]   **Maosong Sun**[1,2,3]   **Juanzi Li**[1,4]

[1]Department of Computer Science and Technology, Tsinghua University, Beijing, China
[2]Institute for Artificial Intelligence, Tsinghua University, Beijing, China
[3]State Key Lab on Intelligent Technology and Systems, Tsinghua University, Beijing, China
[4]Knowledge Engineering Laboratory, Tsinghua University, Beijing, China
[5]College of Information Science and Technology, Beijing Normal University, Beijing, China

Abstract

We release an open toolkit for knowledge embedding (OpenKE), which provides a unified framework and various fundamental models to embed knowledge graphs into a continuous low-dimensional space. OpenKE prioritizes operational efficiency to support quick model validation and large-scale knowledge representation learning. Meanwhile, OpenKE maintains sufficient modularity and extensibility to easily incorporate new models into the framework. Besides the toolkit, the embeddings of some existing large-scale knowledge graphs pre-trained by OpenKE are also available, which can be directly applied for many applications including information retrieval, personalized recommendation and question answering. The toolkit, documentation, and pre-trained embeddings are all released on `http://openke.thunlp.org/`.

1 Introduction

People construct various large-scale knowledge graphs (KGs) to organize structured knowledge about the world, such as WordNet (Miller, 1995), Freebase (Bollacker et al., 2008) and Wikidata (Vrandečić and Krötzsch, 2014). Most KGs are typically organized in the form of triples (h, r, t), with h and t indicating *head* and *tail* entities, and r indicating the relation between h and t, e.g., (*Mark Twain*, `PlaceOfBirth`, *Florida*). Abundant structured information in KGs is widely used to enhance various knowledge-driven NLP applications (e.g., information retrieval, question answering and dialogue system) with the ongoing effective construction of KGs.

Limited by the scale and sparsity of KGs, we have to represent KGs with corresponding distributed representations. Therefore, a variety of knowledge embedding (KE) approaches have been proposed to embed both entities and relations in KGs into a continuous low-dimensional space, such as linear models (Bordes et al., 2011, 2012, 2014), latent factor models (Sutskever et al., 2009; Jenatton et al., 2012; Yang et al., 2015; Liu et al., 2017), neural models (Socher et al., 2013; Dong et al., 2014), matrix factorization models (Nickel et al., 2011, 2012, 2016; Trouillon et al., 2016), and translation models (Bordes et al., 2013; Wang et al., 2014; Lin et al., 2015; Ji et al., 2015).

These models have achieved great performance on benchmark datasets. However, there exist two main issues which may lead to difficulty in full utilization and further development. On the one hand, the existing implementations are scattered and unsystematic to some extent. For example, the interfaces of these model implementations are inconsistent with each other. On the other hand, these model implementations mainly focus on model validation and are often time-consuming, which makes it difficult to apply them for real-world applications. Hence, it becomes urgent to develop an efficient and effective open toolkit for KE, which will definitely benefit both the communities in academia and industry. For this purpose, we develop an open KE toolkit named "OpenKE". The toolkit provides a flexible framework and unified interfaces for developing KE models. While taking in some training and computing optimization methods, OpenKE makes KE models efficient and capable of embedding large-scale KGs. The features of OpenKE are threefold:

(1) At the data and memory level, the unified framework of OpenKE manages data and memory for KE models. Model developments based on OpenKE no longer require complicated data processing and memory allocation.

(2) At the algorithm level, OpenKE unifies the mathematical forms of various specific models to

---

* indicates equal contribution
† Corresponding author: Z.Liu(liuzy@tsinghua.edu.cn)

139

Proceedings of the 2018 Conference on Empirical Methods in Natural Language Processing (System Demonstrations), pages 139–144
Brussels, Belgium, October 31–November 4, 2018. ©2018 Association for Computational Linguistics

Model	Scoring Function	Parameters	Loss Function
RESCAL (Nickel et al., 2011)	$\mathbf{h}^{\top}\mathbf{M}_r\mathbf{t}$	$\mathbf{M}_r \in \mathbb{R}^{k \times k}, \mathbf{h} \in \mathbb{R}^k, \mathbf{t} \in \mathbb{R}^k$	margin-based loss
TransE (Bordes et al., 2013)	$-\|\mathbf{h} + \mathbf{r} - \mathbf{t}\|_{L_1/L_2}$	$\mathbf{r} \in \mathbb{R}^k, \mathbf{h} \in \mathbb{R}^k, \mathbf{t} \in \mathbb{R}^k$	margin-based loss
TransH (Wang et al., 2014)	$-\|(\mathbf{h} - \mathbf{w}_r^{\top}\mathbf{h}\mathbf{w}_r) + \mathbf{r} - (\mathbf{t} - \mathbf{w}_r^{\top}\mathbf{t}\mathbf{w}_r)\|_{L1/L2}$	$\mathbf{w}_r \in \mathbb{R}^k, \mathbf{r} \in \mathbb{R}^k, \mathbf{h} \in \mathbb{R}^k, \mathbf{t} \in \mathbb{R}^k$	margin-based loss
TransR (Lin et al., 2015)	$-\|\mathbf{M}_r\mathbf{h} + \mathbf{r} - \mathbf{M}_r\mathbf{t}\|_{L_1/L_2}$	$\mathbf{M}_r \in \mathbb{R}^{k_r \times k_e}, \mathbf{r} \in \mathbb{R}^{k_r}, \mathbf{h} \in \mathbb{R}^{k_e}, \mathbf{t} \in \mathbb{R}^{k_e}$	margin-based loss
TransD (Ji et al., 2015)	$-\|(\mathbf{r}_p\mathbf{h}_p^{\top} + \mathbf{I})\mathbf{h} + \mathbf{r} - (\mathbf{r}_p\mathbf{t}_p^{\top} + \mathbf{I})\mathbf{t}\|_{L1/L2}$	$\mathbf{r}_p \in \mathbb{R}^{k_r}, \mathbf{h}_p \in \mathbb{R}^{k_e}, \mathbf{t}_p \in \mathbb{R}^{k_e}, \mathbf{I} \in \mathbb{R}^{k_r \times k_e},$ $\mathbf{r} \in \mathbb{R}^{k_r}, \mathbf{h} \in \mathbb{R}^{k_e}, \mathbf{t} \in \mathbb{R}^{k_e}$	margin-based loss
DistMult (Yang et al., 2015)	$< \mathbf{h}, \mathbf{r}, \mathbf{t} >$	$\mathbf{r} \in \mathbb{R}^k, \mathbf{h} \in \mathbb{R}^k, \mathbf{t} \in \mathbb{R}^k$	logistic loss
HolE (Nickel et al., 2016)	$\mathbf{r}^{\top}\left(\mathcal{F}^{-1}\left(\overline{\mathcal{F}(\mathbf{h})} \odot \mathcal{F}(\mathbf{t})\right)\right)$	$\mathbf{r} \in \mathbb{R}^k, \mathbf{h} \in \mathbb{R}^k, \mathbf{t} \in \mathbb{R}^k$	logistic loss
ComplEx (Trouillon et al., 2016)	$\Re(< \mathbf{h}, \mathbf{r}, \overline{\mathbf{t}} >)$	$\mathbf{r} \in \mathbb{C}^k, \mathbf{h} \in \mathbb{C}^k, \mathbf{t} \in \mathbb{C}^k$	logistic loss

Table 1: The brief introduction of some typical KE models. For most models, k is the dimension of both entities and relations. For some other models, K_e is the dimension of entities and k_r is the dimension of relations. $\mathcal{F}$ denotes the Fourier transform. $\odot$ denotes the element-wise product. $< a, b, c >$ denotes the element-wise multi-linear dot product.

implement them under the unified framework. We also propose a novel negative sampling strategy for further acceleration.

(3) At the computation level, OpenKE can separate a large-scale KG into several parts and adapt KE models for parallel training. Based on the underlying management of data and memory, we also adopt TensorFlow (Abadi et al., 2016) and Py-Torch (Paszke et al., 2017) to build a convenient platform to run models on GPUs.

Besides the toolkit, we also provide the pre-trained embeddings of several well-known large-scale KGs, which can be used directly for other relevant works without repeatedly spending much time for embedding KGs. In this paper, we mainly present the architecture design and implementation of OpenKE, as well as the benchmark evaluation results of some typical KE models implemented with OpenKE. Other related resources and details can be found on `http://openke.thunlp.org/`.

2 Background

For a typical KG $\mathcal{G}$, it expresses data as a directed graph $\mathcal{G} = \{\mathcal{E}, \mathcal{R}, \mathcal{T}\}$, where $\mathcal{E}$, $\mathcal{R}$ and $\mathcal{T}$ indicate the sets of entities, relations and facts respectively. Each triple $(h, r, t) \in \mathcal{T}$ indicates there is a relation $r \in \mathcal{R}$ between $h \in \mathcal{E}$ and $t \in \mathcal{E}$. For the entities $h, t \in \mathcal{E}$ and the relation $r \in \mathcal{R}$, we use the bold face $\mathbf{h}, \mathbf{t}, \mathbf{r}$ to indicate their low-dimensional vectors respectively.

For any entity pair $(h, t) \in E \times E$ and any relation $r \in \mathcal{R}$, we can determine whether there is a fact $(h, r, t) \in \mathcal{T}$ via their low-dimensional embeddings learned by KE models. These embeddings learned by KE models. These embeddings greatly facilitate understanding and mining knowledge in KGs. In practice, the KE models

define a scoring function $S(h, r, t)$ for each triple (h, r, t). In most cases, there are only true triples in KGs and non-existing triples can be either false or missing. Local closed world assumption (Dong et al., 2014) has been proposed to solve this problem, which requires existing triples to have higher scores than those non-existing ones. Hence, the scoring function $S(h, r, t)$ returns a higher score if (h, r, t) is true, vice versa.

Based on the above-mentioned scoring functions, some KE models formalize a margin-based loss as the training objective to learn embeddings of the entities and relations:

$$\mathcal{L} = \sum_{t \in \mathcal{T}} \sum_{t' \in \mathcal{T}'} \left[\gamma + S(t') - S(t)\right]_+. \tag{1}$$

Here $[x]_+$ indicates keeping the positive part of x and $\gamma > 0$ is a margin. $\mathcal{T}'$ denotes the set of non-existing triples, which is constructed by corrupting entities and relations in existing triples,

$$\mathcal{T}' = \mathcal{E} \times \mathcal{R} \times \mathcal{E} - \mathcal{T}. \tag{2}$$

Some other KE models cast the training objective as a classification task. The embeddings of the entities and relations can be learned by minimizing the regularized logistic loss,

$$\mathcal{L} = \sum_{t \in \mathcal{T}} \log(1 + \exp(-S(t))) + \sum_{t' \in \mathcal{T}'} \log(1 + \exp(S(t'))). \tag{3}$$

The main difference among various KE models is scoring functions. Hence, we briefly introduce several typical models and their scoring functions in Table 1. These models are state-of-the-art and widely introduced in many works. We systematically incorporate all of them into our OpenKE.

3 Design Goals

Before introducing the concrete toolkit implementations, we report the design goals and features of OpenKE, including system encapsulation, operational efficiency, and model extensibility.

3.1 Encapsulation

Developers tend to maximize the reuse of code to avoid unnecessary redundant development in practice. For KE, its task is fixed, and its experimental settings and model parameters are also similar. However, previous model implementations are scattered and lack of necessary interface encapsulation. Thus, developers have to spend extra time reading obscure open-source code and writing glue code for data processing when they construct models. In view of this issue, we build a unified underlying platform in OpenKE and encapsulate various data and memory processing which is independent of model implementations. As is shown in Figure 1, the system encapsulation makes it easy to train and test KE models. Thus, we just need to set hyperparameters via interfaces of the platform to construct KE models.

3.2 Efficiency

Previous model implementations focus on model validation and enhancing experimental results rather than improving time and space efficiency. In fact, as real-world KGs can be very large, training efficiency is an important concern. Hence, OpenKE integrates efficient computing power, training methods, and various acceleration strategies to support KE models. We adopt TensorFlow and PyTorch to implement the model training and test modules based on the interfaces of underlying platform. These machine learning frameworks enable models to be run on GPU, with just few minutes needed for training and testing models on benchmark datasets. In order to train existing large-scale KGs, we also implement lightweight C/C++ versions for quick deployment and multi-threading acceleration of KE models, in which some models (e.g. TransE) can embed more than $100M$ triples in a few hours on ordinary devices.

3.3 Extensibility

Since different KE models have different design solutions, we make OpenKE fully extensible to future variants. For the underlying platform, we encapsulate data processing and memory manage-

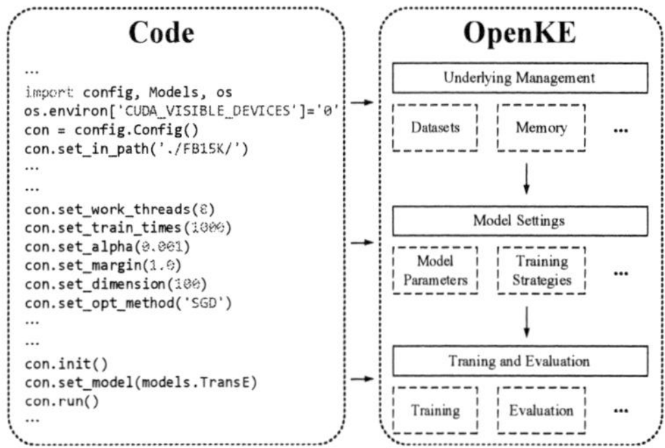

Figure 1: An example for training a KE model (TransE) via OpenKE.

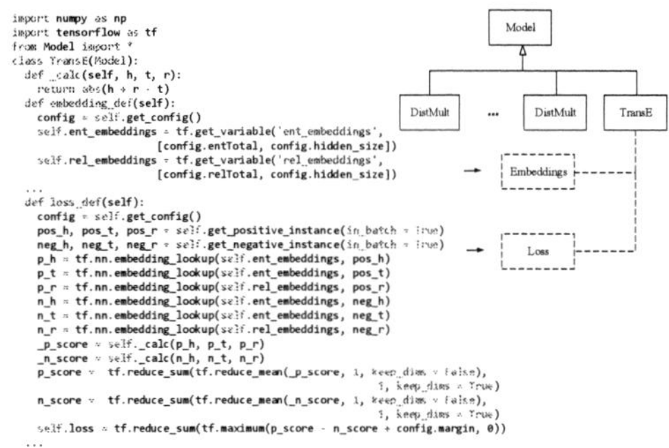

Figure 2: An example for implementing a KE model (TransE) via OpenKE.

ment, and then provide various data sampling interfaces. For the training modules, we provide enough interfaces for possible training methods. For the construction of KE models, we unify their mathematical forms and encapsulate them into a base class. These framework designs can greatly meet the needs of current and future models, and customized interfaces to meet individual requirements are also available in OpenKE. As shown in Figure 2, all specific models are implemented by inheriting the base class with designing their own scoring functions and loss functions. In addition, models in OpenKE can be placed into the framework of TensorFlow and PyTorch to interact with other machine learning models.

4 Implementations

In this section, we mainly present the implementations of acceleration modules and special sampling algorithm in OpenKE. OpenKE has been available to the public on GitHub [1] and is open-source under the MIT license.

---

[1] http://github.com/thunlp/OpenKE

Algorithm 1 Parallel Learning

Require: Entity and relation sets $\mathcal{E}$ and $\mathcal{R}$, training triples $\mathcal{T} = \{(h, r, t)\}$.

1: **Initialize** all model embeddings and parameters.
2: **for** $i \leftarrow 1$ to *epoches* **do**
3:     In each thread:
4:     **for** $j \leftarrow 1$ to *batches/threads* **do**
5:         **Sample** a positive triple (h, r, t)
6:         **Sample** a corrupted triple (h', r', t')
7:         **Compute** the loss function $\mathcal{L}$
8:         **Update** the gradient $\nabla \mathcal{L}$
9:     **end for**
10: **end for**
11: **Return** all embeddings and parameters

4.1 GPU Learning

GPUs are widely used in machine learning tasks to speed up model training in recent years. In order to accelerate KE models, we integrate GPU learning mechanisms into OpenKE. We build the GPU learning platform based on TensorFlow (branch master) and PyTorch (branch OpenKE-PyTorch). Both TensorFlow and PyTorch are machine learning libraries, providing effective hardware optimizations and abundant arithmetic operators for convenient model constructions, especially the stable environments for GPU learning. The autograd packages also bring additional convenience. TensorFlow and PyTorch enable us to coustruct models without manual back propagation implementations, further reducing the programming complexity for GPU Learning. We develop necessary encapsulation modules aligning to TensorFlow and PyTorch so that the development and deployment of KE models can be faster and further convenient. Models can be deployed easily on a variety of devices without implementing complicated device setting code, even for multiple GPUs.

4.2 Parallel Learning

Abundant computing resources (e.g Servers with multiple GPUs) do not exist all the time. In fact, we often rely on simple personal computers for model validation. Hence, we enable OpenKE to adapt models for parallel learning on CPU [2] besides employing GPU learning, which allow users to make full use of all available computing resources. The parallel learning method is shown in Algorithm 1. The main idea of parallel learning method is based on data parallelism mechanism, which divides training triples into several parts and trains each part of triples with a corresponding

---

² `https://github.com/thunlp/Fast-TransX`

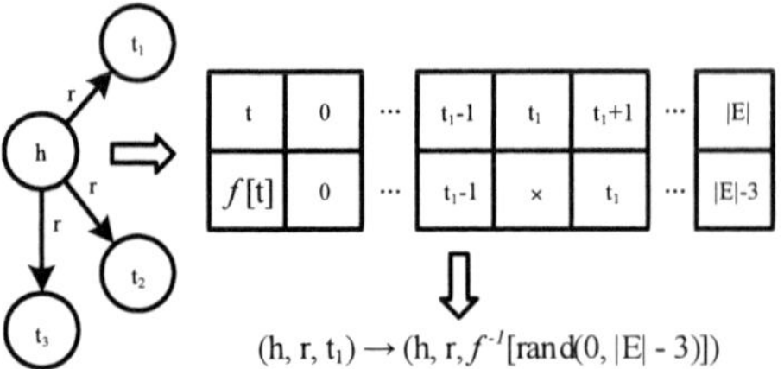

Figure 3: An example for the offset-based negative sampling algorithm.

thread. In parallel learning, there are two strategies implemented to update gradients. One of the methods is the lock-free strategy, which means all threads share the unified embedding space and update embeddings directly without synchronized operations. We also implement a central synchronized method, where each thread calculates its own gradient and results will be updated after summing up the gradients from all threads.

4.3 Offset-based Negative Sampling

All KE models learn their parameters by minimizing the margin-based loss function Eq. (1) or the regularized logistic loss Eq. (3). Both of these loss functions need to construct non-existing triples as negative samples. We have empirically found that the corrupted triples have great influence on final performance. Randomly replacing entities or relations with any other ones may make the negative triple set $\mathcal{T}'$ contain some positive triples in $\mathcal{T}$, which would weaken the performance of KE models. The original sampling algorithm will spend much time checking whether generated triples are in T and filtering them out. In OpenKE, we propose an offset-based negative sampling algorithm to generate negative triples. As shown in Figure 3, we renumber all entities with new serial numbers. Each entity's new number is obtained by adding an offset to its original ID, and the offset is the total number of positive entities which have lower IDs. Our algorithm first randomly sample a new number and then map the new number back to its corresponding entity. This algorithm can directly generate negative triples without any checking. Since the relation set is very small, we still directly replace positive relations for relation corruption.

5 Evaluations

Link prediction has been widely used for evaluating KE models, which needs to predict the tail entity when given a triple $(h, r, ?)$ or predict the

Dataset	Rel	Ent	Train	Valid	Test
FB15K	1,345	14,951	483,142	50,000	59,071
WN18	18	40,943	141,442	5,000	5,000

Table 2: Statistics of FB15K and WN18.

Datasets Models	FB15K		
	TF	PT	MT
TransE	75.6(+28.5)	75.4(+28.3)	74.3(+27.2)
TransH	72.8(+14.3)	72.7(+14.2)	74.8(+16.3)
TransR	74.9(+6.2)	75.7(+7.0)	75.6(+6.9)
TransD	74.3(+0.1)	74.2(+0.0)	75.2(+1.0)
RESCAL	49.1(+5.0)	57.2(+13.1)	-
DistMult	73.4(+15.7)	75.4(+17.4)	-
HolE	70.4(−3.5)	-	-
ComplEx	72.3(−11.7)	80.5(−3.5)	-

Table 3: Experimental results of link prediction on FB15K (%).

Datasets Models	WN18		
	TF	PT	MT
TransE	90.5(+1.3)	90.0(+0.8)	83.3(−5.9)
TransH	94.6(+7.9)	94.4(+7.7)	92.5(+5.8)
TransR	93.8(+1.8)	94.4(+2.4)	94.6(+2.9)
TransD	94.2(+1.7)	94.3(+1.8)	91.9(−0.3)
RESCAL	80.2(+27.4)	80.2(+27.4)	-
DistMult	93.6(−0.6)	93.6(−0.6)	-
HolE	94.4(−0.5)	-	-
ComplEx	94.0(−0.7)	94.0(−0.7)	-

Table 4: Experimental results of link prediction on WN18 (%).

Models	Time (s)
TransE (KB2E, CPU)	7124
TransE (OpenKE, CPU, 1-Thread)	386
TransE (OpenKE, CPU, 2-Thread)	206
TransE (OpenKE, CPU, 4-Thread)	118
TransE (OpenKE, CPU, 8-Thread)	76
TransE (OpenKE, GPU, TensorFlow)	178
TransE (OpenKE, GPU, PyTorch)	266

Table 5: Training time of different implementations of TransE on FB15K.

head entity when given a triple $(?, r, t)$. In order to evaluate OpenKE, we implement various KE models with OpenKE, and compare their performance with previous works on link prediction task.

Some datasets are usually used as benchmarks for link prediction, such as FB15K and WN18. FB15K is the relatively dense subgraph of Freebase; WN18 is the subset of WordNet. These public datasets are available online [3]. Following previous works, We adopt them in our experiments. The statistics of FB15K and WN18 are listed in Table 2, including the number of entities, relations, and facts.

As mentioned above, OpenKE supports models with efficient learning on both CPU and GPU. For CPU, the benchmarks are run on an Intel(R) Core(TM) i7-6700K @ 3.70GHz, with 4 cores and 8 threads. For GPU, the models in both TensorFlow and PyTorch versions are trained by GeForce GTX 1070 (Pascal), with CUDA v.8.0 (driver 384.111) and cuDNN v.6.5. To compare with the previous works, we simply follow the parameter settings used before and traverse all training triples for 1000 rounds. Other detailed parameters and training strategies are shown in our source code. We show these results in Table 3 and Table 4. In these tables, the difference between our implementations and the paper reported results are listed in the parentheses. To demonstrate the efficiency of OpenKE, we select TransE as a representative and implement it with both OpenKE and KB2E [4], and then compare their training time. KB2E is a widely-used toolkit for KE models on GitHub. These results can be found in Table 5.

From the results in Table 3, Table 4 and Table 5, we observe that: (1) Models implemented with OpenKE have the comparable accuracies compared to the values reported in the original papers. These results are compatible with our expectations. For some models, their accuracies are slightly higher due to OpenKE. These results indicate our toolkit is effecive. (2) OpenKE significantly accelerates the training process of the models trained both on CPU and GPU. As compared to the model implemented with KB2E, all models in OpenKE achieve more than $10\times$ speedup. These results show that our toolkit is efficient.

The evaluation results indicate that our toolkit significantly handles the time-consuming problem and can support existing models to learn large-scale KGs. In fact, TransE based on OpenKE only spends about 18 hours training the whole Wikidata for 10000 rounds and gets stable embeddings. There are more than $40M$ entities and $100M$ facts in Wikidata. We also evaluate the embeddings learned on the whole Wikidata on the link prediction task. Because the whole Wikidata is quite huge, we emphasize link prediction of Wikidata more on ranking a set of candidate entities rather than requiring one best answer. Hence, we report the proportion of correct entities in top-N ranked entities (Hits@10, Hits@20, Hits@50 and Hits@100) in Table 6. To our best knowledge, this is the first time that adopting KE models to embed an existing large-scale KG. The results shown in Table 6 indicate that OpenKE enables models to effectively and efficiently embed large-scale KGs.

---

[3] https://everest.hds.utc.fr/doku.php?id=en:transe

[4] https://github.com/thunlp/KB2E

Metric	Hits@10	Hits@20	Hits@50	Hits@100
Head	29.6	36.2	46.7	56.3
Tail	66.8	75.2	84.9	90.6

Table 6: Experimental results of link prediction on the whole Wikidata.

6 Conclusion

We propose an efficient open toolkit OpenKE for knowledge embedding. OpenKE builds a unified underlying platform to organize data and memory. It also applies GPU learning and parallel learning to speed up training. We also unify mathematical forms for specific models and encapsulate them to maintain enough modularity and extensibility. Experimental results demonstrate that the models implemented by OpenKE are efficient and effective. In the future, we will incorporate more knowledge embedding models and maintain the stable embeddings of some large-scale knowledge graphs.

Acknowledgments

This work is supported by the 973 Program (No. 2014CB340501) and the National Natural Science Foundation of China (NSFC No. 61572273, 61661146007) and Tsinghua University Initiative Scientific Research Program (20151080406). This research is part of the NExT++ project, supported by the National Research Foundation, Prime Ministers Office, Singapore under its IRC@Singapore Funding Initiative.

References

Martín Abadi, Paul Barham, Jianmin Chen, Zhifeng Chen, Andy Davis, Jeffrey Dean, Matthieu Devin, Sanjay Ghemawat, Geoffrey Irving, Michael Isard, et al. 2016. Tensorflow: A system for large-scale machine learning. In *Proceedings of OSDI*.

Kurt Bollacker, Colin Evans, Praveen Paritosh, Tim Sturge, and Jamie Taylor. 2008. Freebase: a collaboratively created graph database for structuring human knowledge. In *Proceedings of KDD*.

Antoine Bordes, Xavier Glorot, Jason Weston, and Yoshua Bengio. 2012. Joint learning of words and meaning representations for open-text semantic parsing. In *Proceedings of AISTATS*.

Antoine Bordes, Xavier Glorot, Jason Weston, and Yoshua Bengio. 2014. A semantic matching energy function for learning with multi-relational data. *Proceedings of ML*.

Antoine Bordes, Nicolas Usunier, Alberto Garcia-Duran, Jason Weston, and Oksana Yakhnenko. 2013. Translating embeddings for modeling multi-relational data. In *Proceedings of NIPS*.

Antoine Bordes, Jason Weston, Ronan Collobert, Yoshua Bengio, et al. 2011. Learning structured embeddings of knowledge bases. In *Proceedings of AAAI*.

Xin Dong, Evgeniy Gabrilovich, Geremy Heitz, Wilko Horn, Ni Lao, Kevin Murphy, Thomas Strohmann, Shaohua Sun, and Wei Zhang. 2014. Knowledge vault: A web-scale approach to probabilistic knowledge fusion. In *Proceedings of KDD*.

Rodolphe Jenatton, Nicolas L Roux, Antoine Bordes, and Guillaume R Obozinski. 2012. A latent factor model for highly multi-relational data. In *Proceedings of NIPS*.

Guoliang Ji, Shizhu He, Liheng Xu, Kang Liu, and Jun Zhao. 2015. Knowledge graph embedding via dynamic mapping matrix. In *Proceedings of ACL*.

Yankai Lin, Zhiyuan Liu, Maosong Sun, Yang Liu, and Xuan Zhu. 2015. Learning entity and relation embeddings for knowledge graph completion. In *Proceedings of AAAI*.

Hanxiao Liu, Yuexin Wu, and Yiming Yang. 2017. Analogical inference for multi-relational embeddings. In *Proceedings of ICML*.

George A Miller. 1995. Wordnet: a lexical database for english. *Communications of the ACM*.

Maximilian Nickel, Lorenzo Rosasco, and Tomaso Poggio. 2016. Holographic embeddings of knowledge graphs. In *Proceedings of AAAI*.

Maximilian Nickel, Volker Tresp, and Hans-Peter Kriegel. 2011. A three-way model for collective learning on multi-relational data. In *Proceedings of ICML*.

Maximilian Nickel, Volker Tresp, and Hans-Peter Kriegel. 2012. Factorizing yago: scalable machine learning for linked data. In *Proceedings of WWW*.

Adam Paszke, Soumith Chintala, Ronan Collobert, Koray Kavukcuoglu, Clement Farabet, Samy Bengio, Iain Melvin, Jason Weston, and Johnny Mariethoz. 2017. Pytorch: Tensors and dynamic neural networks in python with strong gpu acceleration.

Richard Socher, Danqi Chen, Christopher D Manning, and Andrew Ng. 2013. Reasoning with neural tensor networks for knowledge base completion. In *Proceedings of NIPS*.

Ilya Sutskever, Joshua B Tenenbaum, and Ruslan Salakhutdinov. 2009. Modelling relational data using bayesian clustered tensor factorization. In *Proceedings of NIPS*.

Théo Trouillon, Johannes Welbl, Sebastian Riedel, Éric Gaussier, and Guillaume Bouchard. 2016. Complex embeddings for simple link prediction. In *Proceedings of ICML*.

Denny Vrandečić and Markus Krötzsch. 2014. Wikidata: a free collaborative knowledgebase. *Communications of the ACM*.

Zhen Wang, Jianwen Zhang, Jianlin Feng, and Zheng Chen. 2014. Knowledge graph embedding by translating on hyperplanes. In *Proceedings of AAAI*.

Bishan Yang, Wen-tau Yih, Xiaodong He, Jianfeng Gao, and Li Deng. 2015. Embedding entities and relations for learning and inference in knowledge bases. In *Proceedings of ICLR*.

LIA: A Natural Language Programmable Personal Assistant

Igor Labutov   **Shashank Srivastava**   **Tom Mitchell**

School of Computer Science
Carnegie Mellon University
Pittsburgh, PA 15217, USA

ilabutov@cs.cmu.edu ssrivastava@cmu.edu tom.mitchell@cmu.edu

Abstract

We present LIA, an intelligent personal assistant that can be programmed using natural language. Our system demonstrates multiple competencies towards learning from human-like interactions. These include (i) the ability to be taught reusable conditional procedures, (ii) ability to be taught new knowledge about the world (concepts in an ontology) and (iii) the ability to be taught how to ground that knowledge in a set of sensors and effectors. Building such a system highlights design questions regarding the overall architecture that such an agent should have, as well as questions about parsing and grounding language in situational contexts. We outline key properties of this architecture, and demonstrate a prototype that embodies them in the form of a personal assistant on an Android device.

1   Introduction

Today's conversational assistants such as Alexa have the capacity to act on a small number of pre-programmed natural language commands (e.g., "What is the weather going to be like today?"). However, advances in semantic parsing and broader language technologies present the possibility of designing conversational interfaces that enable users to instruct (i.e., program) their assistants using language, similar to how humans teach new tasks to one another. For example, if a user wants Alexa to have a new functionality such as *"whenever there is an important email I haven't seen within an hour, read it out to me"*, she should be able to instruct it verbally. This instruction may include explaining what constitutes an *"important email"*. This, in turn, may involve a description such as *"important emails are from colleagues"*, which may require further background knowledge defining *"colleagues"*, *"friends"*, etc. When humans teach other humans, such knowledge is often imparted naturally through explanations, e.g.,

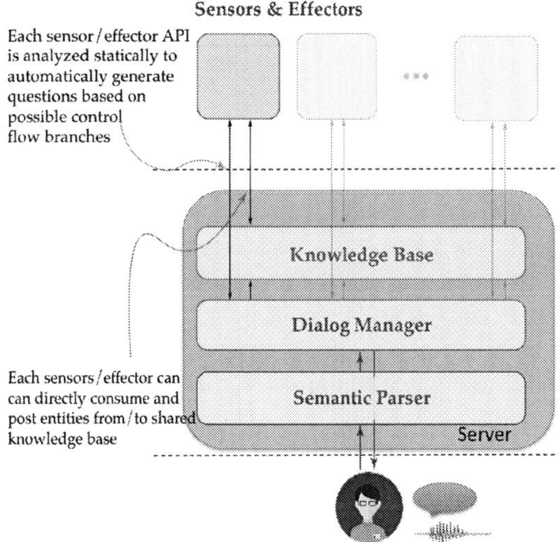

Figure 1: Architecture overview: LIA interacts with the environment through a set of *sensors* and *effectors*, which are mapped to API's of other Android applications. End-users interact with the agent through a text (or voice) interface. User utterances are mapped through a Semantic Parser to logical forms. A Dialog Manager module guides user interactions by grounding logical forms to actions, or asking questions based on possible control flow branches

"my colleagues would have a CMU affiliation" or *"Tom is a colleague"*. If AI assistants could be taught in a similar fashion, this could effectively make every computer user a programmer.

Towards this end, we present a prototype for a personal assistant, **LIA** (for **Learning from Instruction Agent**), which demonstrates some of these capabilities. LIA resides on a typical mobile Android device. It can perceive the external environment through a set of *sensors* (e.g., sensors for detecting new emails, reading the calendar, reading current time, etc.) and perform actions to change the environment through its *effectors* (e.g., send a message, set an alarm, change the calendar, etc.). The set of sensors and effectors are mapped to functions calls of API's for corresponding Android applications (see Figure 1).

145

Proceedings of the 2018 Conference on Empirical Methods in Natural Language Processing (System Demonstrations), pages 145–150
Brussels, Belgium, October 31–November 4, 2018. ©2018 Association for Computational Linguistics

2 Core competencies

LIA demonstrates three core competencies that we consider key for learning from instruction:

2.1 Learning Procedures

Among the main use-cases of being able to teach an agent is being able to define condition-action rules and procedures, such as the following:

```
> If there is an  important email  then  forward
  to my project team
> Whenever it  snows at the night ,  set my alarm
  to 30 minutes earlier
>  Update my calendar  when there is an  important
  meeting request
```

Here, the condition and the effect (action) are highlighted in green and red respectively. The condition in each example requires a check that has to be grounded in the perception sensors. If the condition is satisfied, the required processing consists of calling the execution of actions grounded in the effectors. Giving a conversational assistant the capacity to learn rules verbally opens the possibility of teaching more complex and personalized rules, especially compared to visual programming tools such as IFTTT and Zapier[1]. LIA can ask questions if it cannot parse specifics parts of a user-statement (e.g., if it cannot understand the if-condition, see Figure 2 for an example). Another advantage of a conversational setting is that LIA can take initiative when certain things are left ambiguous by the user (e.g., ask the user what to do if there is a conflict on the calendar for the last rule in the list above) — an issue that cannot be coped with in traditional programming environments.

2.2 Learning World Knowledge

LIA can be taught knowledge about the world by the user (e.g., concepts and ontologies) that can be used as building blocks in teaching new programs.

A key advantage of a conversational interface for teaching new programs is that it allows the user to be naturally expressive about data (i.e., variables/constants) by modelling them after real-world concepts. For example, instead of saying:

```
> If there is an email from Tom, Justine, Oscar
  or Igor, forward it to Mary
```

LIA allows a user to say:

```
> If there is an email from my project team forward
  it to my assistant
```

---

[1] https://ifttt.com/, https://zapier.com/

By relying on the concept of *"my project team"* (instead of listing its members), the second expression is more efficient and natural. It is also better from a programming perspective: if team members change later, the rule will not have to be redefined. LIA enables users to refer to arbitrary concepts such as a *project team* or *colleague*, by declaratively teaching it about them. For example:

```
> Oscar is on my project team
> Everyone on my project team is a colleague
```

The above examples are akin to defining formal data-structures, containing class and field definitions, instance creation and definitions of the natural concept hierarchy (class inheritance). Because the object-oriented programming (OOP) paradigm is designed to model the real world, LIA uses it as the underlying knowledge model that the user can build and modify naturally using language.

2.3 Grounding Knowledge to Perception

Not all knowledge can be easily conveyed through crisp extensional definitions such as in the example of *project team* above. Common concepts such as *important email* or *meeting request* are difficult to declaratively define. In a conventional programming paradigm, the developer may opt to create special functions for grounding such "fuzzy" concepts using machine learning models (i.e., classifiers) that are grounded in attributes of examples (e.g., emails) observed through perceptual sensors.

A conversational programming paradigm offers a natural interface for teaching "fuzzy" and "crisp" concepts alike. Instead of defining hard rules for detecting *important emails* for example, the user may instead opt to provide descriptions that characterize the concept statistically:

```
> An important email will usually be from a
  colleague's email address
> its subject may contain words like urgent or
  important
```

By grounding such natural language descriptions to observable attributes of emails, such descriptions can be used to build classification models for concepts such as 'important emails'.

Example Interaction: Figure 2 shows an example interaction exemplifying these abilities in LIA, and also outlining its working. A video demonstration of the system can be seen at http://y2u. be/YfKqpT0apQw. Next, we describe how these abilities are implemented in LIA, and highlight salient features of its architecture.

Figure 2: Example interaction sequence with LIA. Annotations on the right summarize different parts of the conversation and outline LIA's working

3 Architecture and System Overview

An instructable conversational assistant can be thought of as a new type of programming interface that allows end-users to compose core functionalities (over domains such as email, calendar, etc.) into programs through natural language dialog. Just like conventional programming languages, this needs answers to design questions such as: "how are new components (functions) imported into the instructable agent", and "how do these components communicate (e.g., what are the data types, how do variables get created and passed between functions)". As examples in this paper illustrate, allowing end-users teach an assistant through conversation brings new challenges to the design of a software architecture that facilitates programming via dialog. We outline five features that we see as fundamental to any system which can be "programmed" through conversation, and describe how LIA implements them:

3.1 Verbally Referencing and Passing Data between Sensors and Effectors

In a conventional programming language, formally declared variables allow one to explicitly store and reference information later in the program. A conversational programming interface needs to allow for a similar mechanism by allowing users to refer and reuse data during instruction through verbal references. For example, consider the following instructions that the user can give while teaching a new procedure *"If there is a meeting request, put it on my calendar"*:

```
> Check if there is a time or date mentioned in
  the message
```

```
> Then set the time of the new event to that time
```

This example illustrates the requirement for passing data between two components (*email* and *calendar* APIs), which requires reference resolution on the part of LIA's semantic parser (e.g., which *"event"* did the user refer to in this context?).

LIA solves the problem of interpreting users' utterances and that of resolving references to variables (e.g., *"subject of the received email"* or *"assistant's email address"*) jointly. Reference resolution is context-dependent, and is difficult to solve using rule-based heuristics. The problem of semantic parsing and variable resolution is addressed by LIA using a machine learning based approach. For example, if the user mentions *"Tom's email"*, and there are multiple contacts named Tom, the agent can use its conversational context (e.g., most recently mentioned entities) and world knowledge to help and resolve the reference – both are naturally incorporated as features; weights for these are learned continuously through interactions with the user.

LIA uses a synchronous CFG-based parser implemented using SEMPRE (Berant et al., 2013), and an underlying frame-based meaning representation (i.e., a frame consists of an intent such as *CREATE_NEW_CONCEPT* and any arguments such as the name of the concept), allowing nested frames for certain intents (currently the *IF_THEN* intent). The parser has an underlying log-linear parameterization of the frame/utterance pairs, with weights that can be learned offline and updated online during interactions with the user. LIA uses the following two classes of features to represent utterance/frame pairs:

- **Lexical/logical form features**: these include indicator features for derivation rules used in the parse, as well as the conjunction of nonterminals in the derivation with the part-of-speech tags spanned by the derivation.
- **Variable resolution features**: these include indicator features that fire if the resolved reference matches only partially to the variable name (e.g., if the user mentions *"affiliation"* rather than *"university affiliation"*), and a feature that indicates whether the variable was mentioned recently in the conversational context.

The *variable resolution* features are very powerful in that they allow the incorporation of external context to help the agent resolve references by relying on the aggregate information from all sensor and effectors of the physical device. For example, a reference to a particular person may be ambiguous when interpreted in isolation, but may naturally resolve to the person who recently sent a text-message or an email. External information such as this, can be incorporated into the *variable resolution* features in a scalable way.

3.2 Generalizing Programs from a Single Example

In conventional programming, explicit functions serve as reusable building blocks and must be expressed via specialized syntax to declare what parts of the procedure can be generalized to differ-

ent arguments. In a conversational setting, the user is not likely to be explicit about what parts of what they teach should generalize – this knowledge is often implicit based on the context of the taught program. Thus, programs taught via conversation need to be intelligent in automatically generalizing to future invocations with different arguments where appropriate (e.g., if the user taught the agent how to *"tell colleagues to..."*, the same procedure should correctly generalize to *"tell friends to..."*.

When a user teaches a new procedure to LIA, the interaction is always grounded in the specific context within which the user was teaching it. To explain, when teaching how to *"tell my boss that I will be late"*, the user will narrate the sequence of instructions to the agent that repeat arguments from the original command, e.g.,

```
> Set the recipient to my  boss 's email address
> Then set its subject to  I will be late
```

Here, *"boss"* and *"I will be late"* are arguments repeated from the original utterance that is being taught. In a conventional programming language, the programmer would write a function that would explicitly indicate which parts of the procedure are placeholders and would be replaced with arguments in any future invocations of the program. In a conversational setting, the agent must have the capacity to automatically identify what parts of the taught program are placeholders and should be substituted with different arguments in the future. LIA's algorithm is based on Azaria et al. (2016) – it identifies matches between the command being taught and the references to entities made in the program; it then uses this information to store a templated version of the taught program that can be re-used for future invocations with different arguments, e.g.,: *"tell my friends I am on my way"*.

3.3 Define New Knowledge

In a conventional programming language, data structures and their relationships (e.g., inheritance) must be declared formally. On the other hand, LIA infers the data types and relationships declared by the user from natural language statements (e.g., *"most colleagues have a university affiliation"* declares a new field '*university affiliation*', and *"everyone on the cmu team is a colleague"* creates an class-inheritance relation between a member of a cmu team and a colleague). These are identified through a set of manually defined syntactic patterns in the semantic parser.

LIA represents an agent's knowledge in a traditional object-oriented paradigm: the agent's world consists of classes (referred to as *concepts*), and instances (referred to as *objects*). Classes can extend (i.e., be inherited by) at most one other class, while instances can instantiate multiple classes. Further, if a concept (or instance) in LIA extends other concepts, it also inherits all of its fields.

3.4 Grounding New Knowledge in Sensors and Effectors

An important component of an intelligent assistant is the ability to ground language and abstract concepts in observable perception, through sensors and effectors. We envision enabling the agent to learn concepts (such as important emails) from a combination of explanations, and examples of the concept. This is motivated by our recent research on using natural language to define feature functions for learning tasks (Srivastava et al., 2017), and also work on using declarative knowledge in natural language explanations to supervise training of classifiers (Srivastava et al., 2018). Using semantic parsing, we can map natural language statements to predicates in a logical language, which are grounded in sensor-effector capabilities of the personal agent. These may enable the user to:

1. Mention specific attributes that characterize a concept (e.g., define a boolean feature that checks whether an email comes from a colleague)
2. Assert fuzzy statistical constraints specifying relationships between such feature and labels (e.g., 'emails from my colleagues are usually important')

In combination, these capabilities can potentially allow the agent to be taught classifiers for fuzzy concepts from a blend of natural language explanations of these concepts, and labeled or unlabeled data.

Using these explanations and unlabeled data, an automated learner can output a classifier that can predict the class for a new instance. The system can currently be used to train classifiers for a small number of restricted domains. The classifier learning component is currently a standalone module (separate from rest of LIA). We plan to make this publicly accessible in the future.

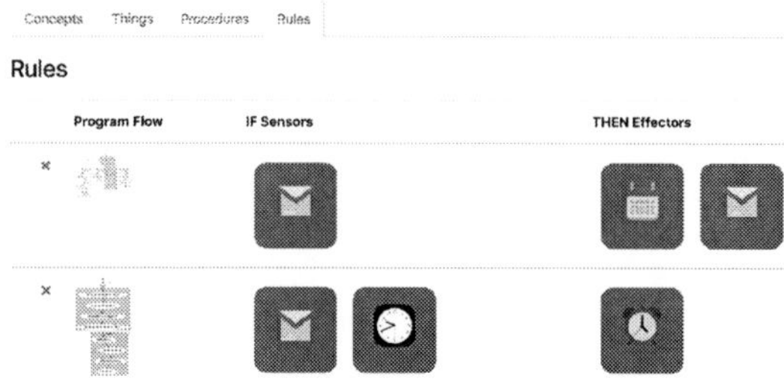

Figure 3: Knowledge View in user interface, which displays procedures taught by a user, along with utilized sensors and effectors

3.5 Mixed-Initiative Interactions

In a conventional programming language, the programmer anticipates all possible outcomes of various API calls made in a program, wrapping these calls with control-flow statements (if/then/else blocks) to account for different return flows. Conversely, end-user programmers must not be required to be explicit about all possible program flows, but rather must inherently be in the form of a mixed-initiative dialog. LIA does this by being pro-active in identifying possible control flow branches based on the instructions the user has provided while teaching. Consider an example:

```
> Check that I am available tomorrow at 2pm

  ...

> What should I do if you are not available?
```

Here, the question creates a control flow branch, from which point on the user instructs a sequence of actions that would be triggered only if the condition that the agent asked about was true. One of the key challenges in providing this mixed-initiative strategy is scaling it to multiple sensors and effectors, where the API for each sensor/effector could trigger a set of potential control flow branches based on the internal execution paths of the individual sensor/effector methods.

LIA's architecture facilitates a generic way of integrating new sensor/effector classes by automatically discovering possible outputs of the API method calls through a static analysis of the API source code. This static code analysis registers this information as possible control flow branches and uses it during the dialog with the user to ask what to do when these control flow branches are reached during execution. Of course, not every possible output of a particular API call (e.g., checking the user's availability) requires asking the user what to

Figure 4: Program flow with conditional branches for an example program visualized in terms of the API method calls. Dashed lines show data (variables) passed between different method calls. White boxes denote branches that were explicitly prompted by the agent by asking a question on what to do in a given situation (see Fig 2)

do. It is up to the API developer to decide what execution paths inside the API call warrant generating a question to the user. To communicate this information explicitly and in a standard way, we require that the API methods always return an object of a special output return type that both (i) contains the message to the user and (ii) encodes the information about whether the execution path resulting in this return value was successful or resulted in an error, and whether the agent should probe the user on what to do when this branch point is reached.

Figure 4 illustrates a full program taught by the user (*"if there is an important meeting request then put it on my calendar"*) with two conditional branches; both branches were prompted by the agent explicitly asking the user for what to do in two scenarios: the user is not available at a particular time, and the original email does not contain a time/date. See Figure 4 for more details.

4 Conclusion and Outlook

We have presented LIA, a natural language programmable assistant that allows users to teach it new procedures, define new concepts and concept hierarchies, and ground these to observable attributes and actions in the agent's repertoire of sensors and effectors. Currently, LIA is limited in some ways. For example, newly taught com-

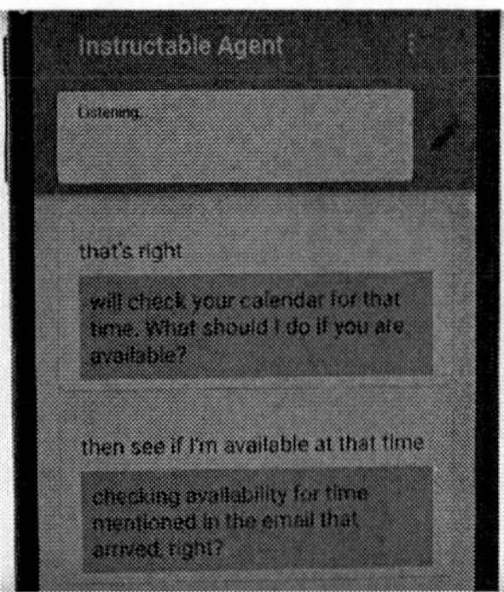

Figure 5: Screenshot of LIA being taught a new procedure on an Android mobile device

mands are incorporated as new grammar rules in the semantic parser. As a result, future invocations of the command that exhibit lexical and syntactic variations may not correctly parse. Also, currently LIA only uses conversational and lexical features to resolve ambiguities in grounding frames to the entities in the knowledge base. The mechanism of incorporating features, however, is general and future efforts can also incorporate external features from multiple sensors (e.g., your location, person you talked to most recently, etc.).

We believe that computers that can be interactively instructed from natural language present an exciting new area, which can have significant implications for both learning and language research, as well as engender a range of creative applications. We hope that through our demonstration, we can engage the community in this direction.

References

Amos Azaria, Jayant Krishnamurthy, and Tom M Mitchell. 2016. Instructable intelligent personal agent. In *AAAI*, pages 2681–2689.

Jonathan Berant, Andrew Chou, Roy Frostig, and Percy Liang. 2013. Semantic parsing on freebase from question-answer pairs. In *Proceedings of the 2013 Conference on Empirical Methods in Natural Language Processing*, pages 1533–1544.

Shashank Srivastava, Igor Labutov, and Tom Mitchell. 2017. Joint concept learning and semantic parsing from natural language explanations. In *Proceedings of the 2017 Conference on Empirical Methods in Natural Language Processing*, pages 1527–1536.

Shashank Srivastava, Igor Labutov, and Tom Mitchell. 2018. Zero-shot learning of classifiers from natural language quantification. In *Proceedings of the 56th Annual Meeting of the Association for Computational Linguistics*.

PizzaPal: Conversational Pizza Ordering using a High-Density Conversational AI Platform

Antoine Raux, Yi Ma, Paul Yang, and Felicia Wong

b4.ai / botbotbotbot, Inc.

3225 Ash Street

Palo Alto, CA, USA

{antoine,yi,paul,felicia}@b4.ai

Abstract

This paper describes PizzaPal, a voice-only agent for ordering pizza, as well as the Conversational AI architecture built at b4.ai. Based on the principles of high-density conversational AI, it supports natural and flexible interactions through neural conversational language understanding, robust dialog state tracking, and hierarchical task decomposition.

1 High-Density Conversational AI

Following the recent rise to prominence of smart speakers, as well as the continuous improvement of core technologies for speech recognition and natural language understanding, voice-only interactive applications, whether in the home or in car, have attracted increasing attention and investment from the industry. Such applications generally fall under two broad categories: assistants and bots. Voice assistants, pioneered by Siri in 2010, aim at providing a broad range of information and services across many domains, primarily by leveraging natural language's evocative power, i.e. its ability to summon any intent, concept or entity at any point in a conversation. On the other hand, bots (also known as skills on Alexa and action on Google Assistant) are much narrower in scope, often providing a voice interface to a single brand, service, or API.

While technological progresses are undeniable, these applications have only met limited success[1], and largely fail to sustain even simple task-oriented conversations with humans. We believe this relatively poor user experience stems from the fact that neither assistants nor bots are able to cover the space of possible (or even reasonable) conversations with enough density. In other words, while a given set of user intents are recognized and supported, even small variations over those are not properly handled. There are several root causes to these limitations. While platforms such as Google's DialogFlow or Facebook's wit.ai provide a simple way of building a relatively small set of distinct intents to a large developer community, these alone cannot support truly natural, sustained, interaction. Therefore, companies (typically startups) that develop bots might not have the necessary resources or knowledge to build truly compelling conversational experiences. On the other hand, some of the largest tech companies are behind most voice assistants (Apple, Google, Amazon) have plenty of resources, financial, human, and intellectual, but they are typically focused on expanding the *breadth* of their applications, to the expense of its *density*. Figure 1 gives an example of the contrast between breadth and density.

At b4.ai, we believe that only *high-density conversational AI* can deliver the seamless, natural experience that matches users' expectations of Artificial Intelligence and leads to truly successful conversational consumer products. The following sections describe how we are tackling this challenge by first focusing on domain-specific applications in the form of Alexa skills and Google Actions.

2 The PizzaPal Conversational Ordering System

The PizzaPal system is a voice-only conversational agent that supports ordering pizza, drinks and side dishes for delivery or pickup. It runs either as an Alexa skill or a Google Assistant action and is connected to the Domino's Pizza API. While there exist other conversational agents (assistants, skills or actions) that support pizza or-

---

[1] According to Smith (2017), the retention rate after two weeks for Alexa skills was only 6% in September 2017.

151

Proceedings of the 2018 Conference on Empirical Methods in Natural Language Processing (System Demonstrations), pages 151–156

Brussels, Belgium, October 31–November 4, 2018. ©2018 Association for Computational Linguistics

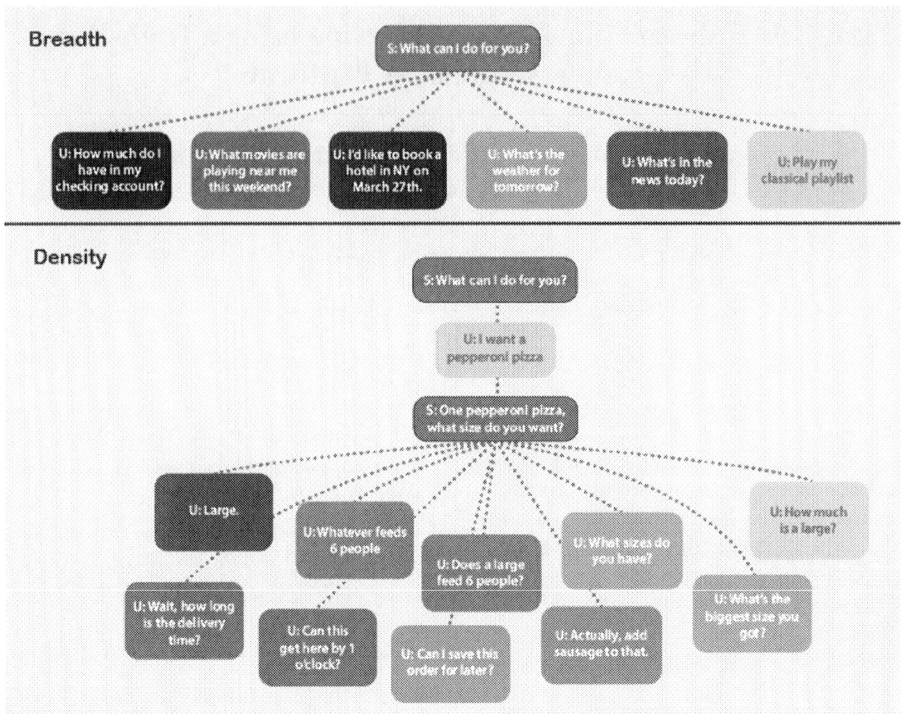

Figure 1: Leveraging Natural Conversation for Breadth vs Density

dering or similar e-commerce tasks, PizzaPal is unique in the naturalness and flexibility of its interactions, as shown in the example of Figure 2.

P: (...) What will you be having?
U: Can I get a large spinach pizza?
P: One large spinach pizza. Can I get you anything else?
U: I'll also take a pepperoni pizza.
P: One pepperoni pizza. *Do you want that in large as well?*[*]
U: How much was the spinach pizza?
P: A large spinach pizza is $18.49. *Let's continue with the pepperoni pizza.*[**] Should I make that a large as well?
U: *Do you have anything smaller?*[***]
P: Medium is smaller. It is 12 inches. Shall I order it for you?
U: Sure.
P: Sure. Can I get you anything else?

Figure 2: Example dialogue with PizzaPal.[2]

The italicized sentences show instances of natu-

ral conversational behavior exhibited by PizzaPal:

* PizzaPal proactively suggests sizes and items based on the dialog history when possible.

** While the system can drive the conversation to completion by asking the user direct questions, it also allows the user to take the initiative at any time.

*** The user can express constraints and intents freely, including using contextual expressions.

These are a few examples of features characteristic of high-density AI, which are implemented in PizzaPal. In the remainder of the paper, we will describe the b4.ai framework architecture and components that support the PizzaPal system.

3 Architecture

3.1 Overview

At a high level, the b4.ai framework is composed of three main services that run on top of a front end platform such as Amazon Alexa or Google Assistant. As illustrated in Figure 3, the front end controls application launch, voice recognition

---

[2]The video of this dialog is available at https://youtu.be/BQrzgJk4-yI

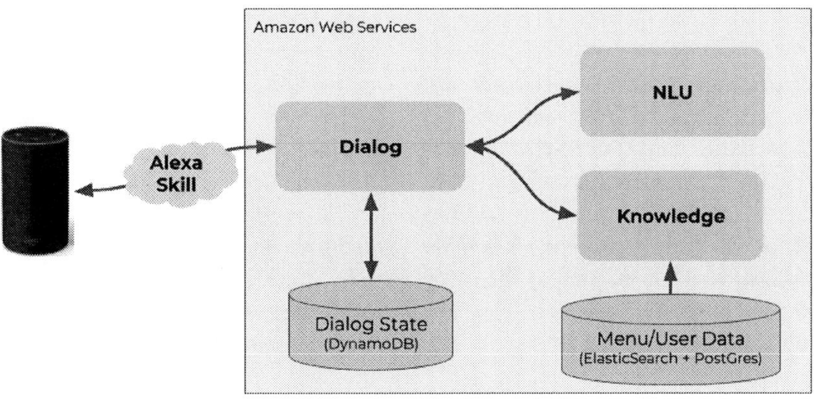

Figure 3: Overview of the b4.ai dialog framework.

and voice synthesis. The front end sends the transcription of each user input to the core dialog service, which first calls the NLU service to extract non-contextual semantic information, and interacts with the knowledge backend, before returning the bot response to the front end as a string to be spoken back to the user. All three services are implemented as REST APIs hosted on AWS EC2 instances.

3.2 Knowledge Service

The role of the Knowledge Service is to retrieve domain knowledge (e.g. menus, restaurant addresses, as well as user prefererences), help resolve references (e.g. when the user says "add chicken to my pizza", "chicken" might match to different possible toppings like "BBQ Chicken", "Garlic Chicken" or "Teriyaki Chicken"), and execute transactions with 3rd party services (e.g. placing the order for delivery). Even for a single domain application such as pizza ordering, this requires access to a variety of databases, APIs and services. The Knowledge Service abstracts away these different source schemas and allows unified access from the dialog service. In general, the Knowledge Service supports a variety of queries, both structured (e.g. getting the menu of a given store given its store ID) and unstructured (e.g. finding menu items matching certain keywords and key phrases), which are performed via an API defined in terms of questions about entities and properties (e.g. "get the available toppings for menu item X", "resolve ingredient named N for dish type T"). The initial implementation of the Knowledge Service relies on 3rd party REST

APIs, and our own PostGres and ElasticSearch databases to access restaurant and menu information.

3.3 Natural Language Generation

The NLG service takes the semantic output generated by the Dialog service and converts it to natural language. We have implemented a simple, scalable template based approach to NLG, that allows to control the language used by the system with some amount of variation. The templates incorporate some conditionals so that entities such as menu items or ingredients can be rendered differently based on entity properties and context.

4 Natural Language Understanding

The Natural Language Understanding (NLU) service of PizzaPal converts the surface text of a user's request (taken from Alexa or Google Assistant's APIs) into a structured semantic representation that serves as the input for the Dialog Manager. The output of the NLU follows a food ordering schema that defines what a `MenuItem` consists of.

Conventional task-oriented dialog systems use intent detection and slot filling to identify user's intention and extract semantic constituents from the natural language query. This intent-slot configuration might suffice when the backend task is outlined as a database lookup operation where the extracted slots are used as constraints and the retrieved information is presented to the user by populating fixed language templates. However, it is not sufficient for building a genuinely natural conversational system that requires frequent elaborate high-density actions. Consider the following user input:

*"I want **three large pizzas**, the **Honolulu Hawaiian**, and **two with cheese and chicken**."*

The NLU should identify three separate entities (in bold) in order to resolve the ambiguity that the user requested two kinds of pizzas with different quantities instead of three *Honolulu Hawaiian* with extra *chicken*, which is inferred by the entity model. The Subsection 4.1.1 and 4.1.2 describe the intent and slot model; with Subsection 4.1.3 explains the entity model.

4.1 Model Description

All the neural networks for our NLU service are trained and run using the Python deep learning library Keras (Chollet et al., 2015), with a TensorFlow backend (Abadi et al., 2015).

4.1.1 Intent Model

The intent model learns a Convolutional Neural Networks (CNN) with multiple filters and fixed kernel size from an $n \times k$ representation of sentence using GloVe word embeddings (Pennington et al., 2014). Random word vectors were generated for Out-of-vocabulary (OOV) words before training. In addition to the word embedding features, we are adding a few more dimensions to the word representation with additional one-hot encoding categorical features based on whether the word appears in different sets of collections of phrases that specify *ingredients*, *dish names*, or *portion sizes* etc. At the time of writing, there are 26 intents in the current model. A few example intents include `RequestItem`, `GivePortionSize`, and `AddToppings` etc.

4.1.2 Slot Model

Slot model is independent of the intent model, which allows different intents to share the same set of slots. The input for learning the slot model is identical to that for learning the intent model. The slot model learns a Bidirectional Long Short-Term Memory (LSTM) Networks with dropout and emits a slot label for each token in the word sequence. Currently, the slot model predicts a label from a total of 21 slots. Example slots include `dish_name`, `portion_size`, and `ingredient` etc.

4.1.3 Entity Model

Similar to the slot model, the entity model learns a Bidirectional LSTM Networks with dropout that emits one of the B, I, O labels for each token in the word sequence to indicate the boundaries of separate entities. Usually an entity corresponds to a `MenuItem` in the schema. As shown in the example user request below, each underlined chunk of text represents an entity.

*"I'd like **two large hand tossed Hawaiian** and a **medium cheese pizza with double pepperoni**."*

In addition to the word embedding and categorical features as used for learning the intent and slot model, the input for learning the entity model additionally contains the one-hot encoding of the slot label information. The ground truth slot labels are used for training the entity model, while during prediction the output of the slot model is used as features.

4.2 Data Collection

In order to bootstrap our NLU models before we obtain real user data from the released product, we have been leveraging crowdsourcing to generate reasonable sentences for the various intents, slots and entities. We have collected both freeform sentences by giving crowdworkers a general scenario and asking them what they would say to PizzaPal, as well as paraphrases, for which we provide a target sentence with known annotation and ask workers to provide variations with the same meaning. The first approach has proven useful to uncover intents, slots and ways to formulate queries, while the paraphrase approach allows us to rapidly collect data for specific intents and scenarios.

5 Dialog Management

5.1 Overview

Once the NLU service has extracted intents, slots and entities from a user utterance, the Dialog service first updates the persistent state of the dialog based on the new input, and second decides what response to give to the user. Recent work on dialog management has focused on Deep Learning based approaches (Liu et al., 2018), showing great promise when large amounts of training dialog data are available. We also believe that such data-driven approaches are part of the solution to scale high-density AI. However, in order to bootstrap an initial system that displays our target flexibility and naturalness, we opted for an engineered solution based on data structures and algorithms inspired by computational linguistics research. Specifically, the two core components of

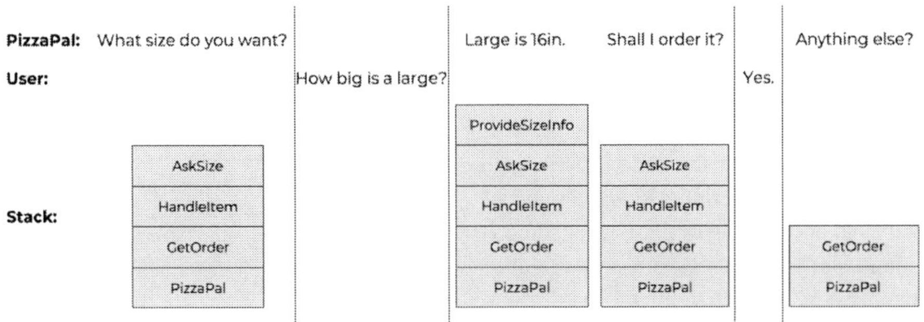

Figure 4: Example of Dialog Flow

our dialog state are:

- A *topic stack* which tracks the hierarchical topic structure of the conversation and allows switching to new topics and coming back to previous topics. This is inspired by the RavenClaw architecture (Bohus and Rudnicky, 2009). Practically speaking, the stack contains modules, each in charge of a particular subdialog.

- An *entity reference set* that can be retrieved by content as well as recency to match referring expressions provided by the user such as "my pizza", "the large one", "the pepperoni", etc.

In the current implementation, the domain logic within each module is implemented in Python code. We are also exploring ways of implementing modules as Deep Networks trained on example dialogs for both state tracking and decision making.

5.2 Example Runtime Flow

Initially, the stack contains the root module. After each user input, the stack is traversed from top to bottom and each module attempts to interpret the NLU according to its own context to update the dialog state. As soon as a module does so, the iteration stops and the decision making phase starts, where the module at the top of the stack can either output a prompt to the user, push another module, or pop itself from the stack, indicating that it has completed its intended subtask. For example, one module might be in charge of handling the specification of one item from the menu (`HandleItem`). When executing this module, it might decide (e.g. based on information from the backend about the given item) that it needs to enquire about the size of the item, and

push another module specialized in this subtask `AskSize`. If, instead of answering the question by providing a size, the user asks a question (e.g. "How big is a large?"), the corresponding module is pushed on top of the stack and handles the question (`ProvideSizeInfo`). Once it is done (presumably by providing the answer), `ProvideSizeInfo` pops itself from the stack and `AskSize` is back on top and tries again to obtain a size from the user. Figure 4 shows a simplified example of a dialog flow and the evolution of the stack.

Modules operate as asynchronous functions that perform a task. Once a module is completed (which could involve several turns of interactions with the user), it returns the information that it was able to obtain from the user to its calling module via callback function. This asynchronous mechanism allows the system to both lead the conversation to complete the task, while also leaving the option of the user to switch topics and ask questions, without losing track of the main task.

6 Challenges

The ambitious goals of high-density AI outlined in section 1 raise significant challenges on all components of the system. First, of course, are speech recognition errors, which, even given the high quality of ASR provided by today's voice platforms, are still prominent for certain idiosyncratic words or phrases. Since we do not control the ASR module, there is little we can do here, though we have observed that training the NLU on properly annotated ASR output help resolves the most common issues (e.g. "I want two pizzas" misrecognized as "I want to pizzas").

Even when ASR faithfully transcribes the utterances, some nuances that are essential to understanding the user intent are sometimes minute such as the difference between "I want a pepperoni pizza" and "I just want a pepperoni pizza" which, in some contexts, means that the user wants to remove all other items from the order. This type of small but crucial distinctions, characteristic of high-density AI, point to the limitations of the traditional intent/slot approach where every nuance must be captured by a different intent. In addition, while it is more practical to implement NLU as independent of context (and leave the contextual interpretation to the Dialog service), the strong influence of context on interpretation makes NLU labeling (both by human annotators, particularly when crowdsourcing the task, and by the trained DNNs) a challenging task. For these reasons, we are exploring new approaches to conversational NLU that avoid these pitfalls by integrating Dialog and NLU more tightly.

Finally, we found that project and product management tasks for high-density AI, while critical to the development of a robust and useful product, present some significant challenges too. Because dialog flows are never rigidly defined and the user can always say anything at any point of the conversation, representing different features of the agent (e.g. "supporting crust customization") for purposes of communication between product, engineering and QA teams is a non trivial problem. Similarly, traditional metrics used for tracking progress toward milestones and product releases often fail to capture the seemingly infinite number of ways users can interact with each feature. We believe that new metrics, tools and processes appropriate to high-density AI systems are a critical requirement toward the development of large scale successful conversational products and we are actively working on building them.

7 Conclusion

In this paper, we present PizzaPal, a pizza ordering bot that customers can interact with through Amazon Alexa and Google Assistant using multi-turn dialogs with natural language. It is based on a proprietary dialog framework developed by b4.ai and is the first implementation of High-Density Conversational AI (#highdensityai) as a commercially viable product.

References

Martín Abadi, Ashish Agarwal, Paul Barham, Eugene Brevdo, Zhifeng Chen, Craig Citro, Greg S. Corrado, Andy Davis, Jeffrey Dean, Matthieu Devin, Sanjay Ghemawat, Ian Goodfellow, Andrew Harp, Geoffrey Irving, Michael Isard, Yangqing Jia, Rafal Jozefowicz, Lukasz Kaiser, Manjunath Kudlur, Josh Levenberg, Dandelion Mané, Rajat Monga, Sherry Moore, Derek Murray, Chris Olah, Mike Schuster, Jonathon Shlens, Benoit Steiner, Ilya Sutskever, Kunal Talwar, Paul Tucker, Vincent Vanhoucke, Vijay Vasudevan, Fernanda Viégas, Oriol Vinyals, Pete Warden, Martin Wattenberg, Martin Wicke, Yuan Yu, and Xiaoqiang Zheng. 2015. TensorFlow: Large-scale machine learning on heterogeneous systems.

Dan Bohus and Alexander I. Rudnicky. 2009. The ravenclaw dialog management framework: Architecture and systems. *Comput. Speech Lang.*, 23(3):332–361.

François Chollet et al. 2015. Keras. `https://keras.io`.

Bing Liu, Gokhan Tur, Dilek Hakkani-Tur, Pararth Shah, and Larry Heck. 2018. Dialogue learning with human teaching and feedback in end-to-end trainable task-oriented dialogue systems. In *NAACL*.

Jeffrey Pennington, Richard Socher, and Christopher D. Manning. 2014. Glove: Global vectors for word representation. In *Empirical Methods in Natural Language Processing (EMNLP)*, pages 1532–1543.

Jessica Smith. 2017. The Voice Apps Report. Technical report, BI Intelligence.

Developing Production-Level Conversational Interfaces with Shallow Semantic Parsing

Arushi Raghuvanshi
Cisco Systems
arushi@cisco.com

Lucien Carroll
Cisco Systems
lucienc@cisco.com

Karthik Raghunathan
Cisco Systems
ktick@cisco.com

Abstract

We demonstrate an end-to-end approach for building conversational interfaces from prototype to production that has proven to work well for a number of applications across diverse verticals. Our architecture improves on the standard domain-intent-entity classification hierarchy and dialogue management architecture by leveraging shallow semantic parsing. We observe that NLU systems for industry applications often require more structured representations of entity relations than provided by the standard hierarchy, yet without requiring full semantic parses which are often inaccurate on real-world conversational data. We distinguish two kinds of semantic properties that can be provided through shallow semantic parsing: entity groups and entity roles. We also provide live demos of conversational apps built for two different use cases: food ordering and meeting control.

1 Introduction

Conversational interfaces are a prominent feature of many consumer technology products today. Popular voice assistants, such as Alexa, Siri, Google Assistant, and Cortana, have been built using a methodical approach of domain-intent-entity classification and dialogue management that is becoming an industry standard (Dialogflow, 2018; Wit.ai, 2018; Amazon, 2018; Microsoft, 2018).

In this demo, we share best practices on developing production conversational interfaces. We provide attendees with an interactive demo which illustrates the live classification of each model in the end-to-end pipeline for different queries and use cases. The demo systems focus on two use cases in English—food ordering and meeting control—though the architecture is broadly applicable to other languages and use cases.

Furthermore, we introduce two components of the pipeline that are improvements over the indus-

try standard—entity grouping and entity roles—which are forms of shallow semantic parsing. We demonstrate the value of these shallow semantic parses, going beyond named entity recognition without exhaustive semantic or syntactic parsing, or even full relation extraction. We first give an overview of the system architecture, then describe the shallow semantic parsing problems in more detail and compare our approach to related systems.

2 Architecture

The NLP pipeline is broken down into a series of components as illustrated in Figure 1: Intent Classifier, Entity Recognizer, Entity Resolver, Semantic Parser, Dialogue Manager, Question Answerer and Application Manager. For each component, the model type, features, and hyperparameters are tuned for the use case.

This architecture allows us to bootstrap applications with few queries per intent—tens or hundreds of queries for narrow vocabulary intents and thousands of queries for open vocabulary intents—and smoothly transition as data sets increase. Getting a deployable version of a conversational assistant on small data set sizes is key, since generating conversational data is expensive, and early in development, product decisions can often change, requiring relabeling the data. Once a model is in production, dataset sizes can grow by labeling queries from user logs. This architecture scales well and continues to give robust performance as query sizes increase by orders of magnitude. As the dataset sizes grow, the most optimal model type, features, and hyperparameters will change.

2.1 Intent Classification

A **Domain Classifier** assigns an incoming query into one of a set of pre-defined topical buckets or domains. This is a classification model that uses

157

Proceedings of the 2018 Conference on Empirical Methods in Natural Language Processing (System Demonstrations), pages 157–162
Brussels, Belgium, October 31–November 4, 2018. ©2018 Association for Computational Linguistics

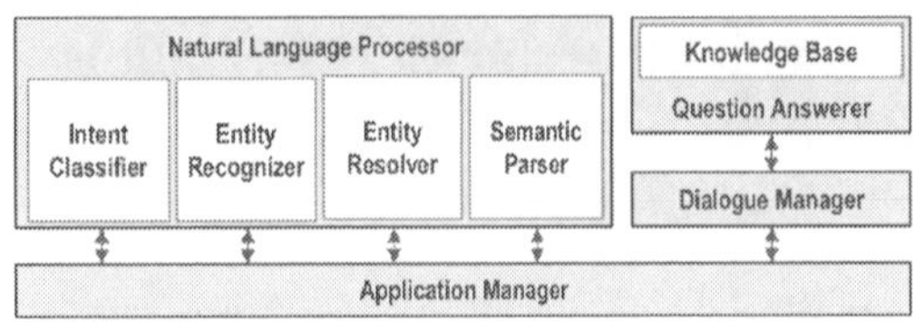

Figure 1: Natural language processing pipeline

text features like n-grams and gazetteer matches to determine which domain the vocabulary of the query is most likely in. In addition to these features that capture language and sentence structure, this component has access to the user context and the history of previous queries in the conversation. Different models such as logistic regression (LR), support vector machine (SVM), decision tree, or random forest can be selected for different use cases based on the data set size and distribution.

Intent Classifiers predict which of the domain's intents is expressed in the request. It is a text classification model like the domain classifier, but trained on data to distinguish among the types of intended dialogue acts within a domain.

Figure 2 illustrates the domain and intent classifications for the input query "I'd like a plain bagel that's warmed up and with cream cheese" for a food ordering app. In the demo, users can try tweaking the language of the query and see how it affects the model prediction. For example, when keeping the phrase "I'd like a", but changing the rest of the query to an unrelated item (e.g. "I'd like a link to a funny video"), the domain classification changes to UNRELATED. When tweaking the language from "I'd like a bagel" to a more explicit "I want to order a bagel" increases the confidence of the ORDER intent classification.

2.2 Entity Recognition

Entity Recognizers identify and label entities— the words and phrases that must be represented and interpreted to fulfill requests. It is a sequence tagging model such as a Maximum Entropy Markov Model (MEMM), Long Short-Term Memory recurrent neural network (LSTM), or a Conditional Random Field (CRF). The features depend on the model type used but can include word embeddings or gazetteer matches. The optimal model is dependent on dataset size. A MEMM model with gazetteer and n-gram features may be most robust when trained on a few hundred queries, but the LSTM model with character and

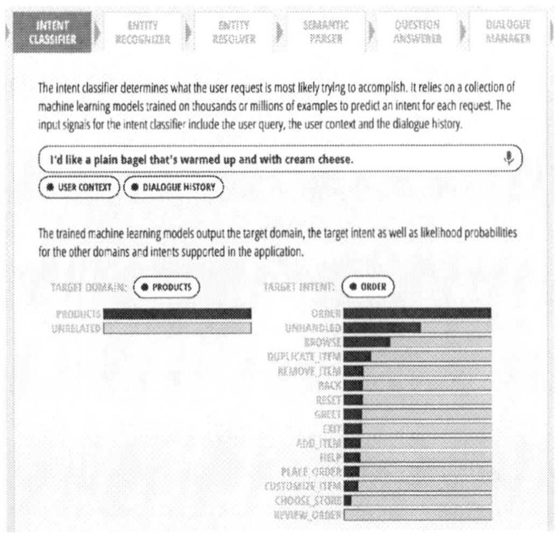

Figure 2: Domain and intent classifier demo view

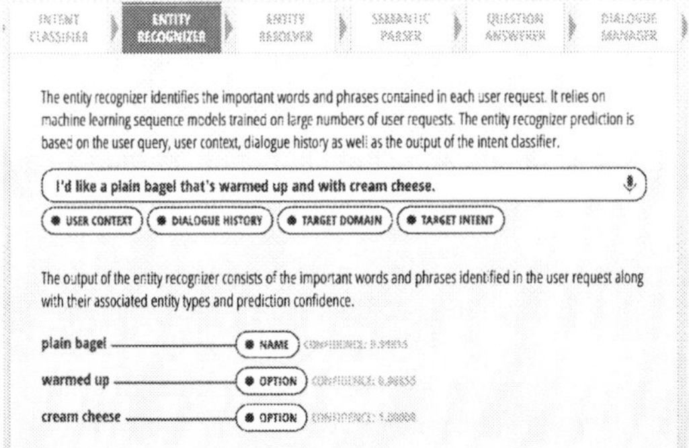

Figure 3: Entity recognizer demo view

word embeddings can have better accuracy when trained on a few hundred thousand queries.

In Figure 3 we illustrate the extracted entities from an example query and the confidence of those predictions.

2.3 Entity Resolution

An **Entity Resolver** maps each identified entity to a canonical value. For example, in the food ordering use case, the text "plain bagel" needs to be mapped to a canonical id that can be use to make an API call to place the order.

The entity resolver uses an information retrieval (IR) approach to resolve to the correct canonical form by doing text matching against an index of canonical entities. This matching uses common IR techniques of character n-gram, token n-gram, and fuzzy matching as well as tf-idf scoring. The index also contains information like synonyms for entities, so the model can correctly resolve items

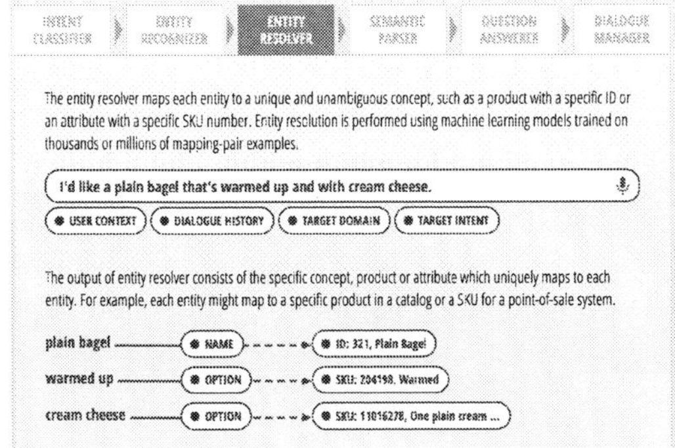

Figure 4: Entity resolver demo view

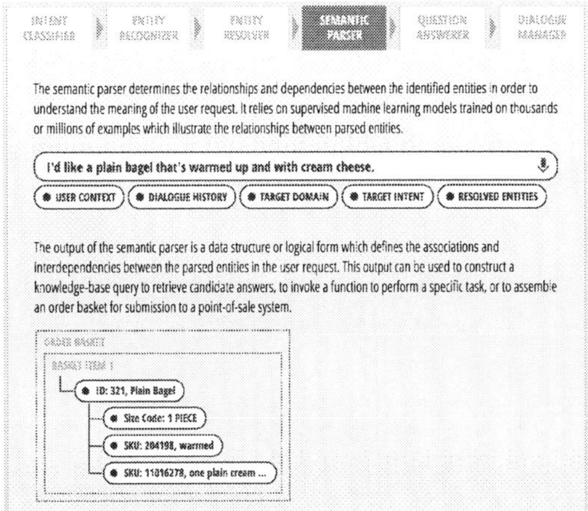

Figure 5: Semantic parser demo view

that are semantically similar but syntactically different. For example, "pasta with tomato sauce" can be resolved to "spaghetti marinara". In Figure 4, the entity text "warmed up" is resolved to the "Warmed" (SKU: 204198) as an example.

2.4 Semantic Parser

The interpretation of some queries requires a more structured representation than domains, intents and entities provide. We decompose entity relation extraction into two degenerate cases: assignment of entity relation type or **role** and association of dependent 'child' entities to a head 'parent' entity in an entity **group**. Though some use cases require both kinds of information, many use cases only require one of these, and it is productive to treat them as separable problems.

Entity Role Classifiers add another level of labeling when knowing an entity's type is not enough to interpret the entity correctly. E.g., a role label can be used to classify a numerical entity as a SIZE versus a QUANTITY. In the case "I'll have the 12 oz soda", the role of the entity "12" should be SIZE, but in the case "I'll have 3 sodas", the role of the entity "3" should be a QUANTITY.

The addition of the role classification is novel to our architecture. It is an intermediate between using only NER and doing a full semantic or syntactic parse. The benefit of doing role classification is that you can get important semantic and syntactic information in a targeted way for entities that are predefined to take multiple roles, rather than having to generate a full parse for each query. Without this learned role classification, systems often have to rely on heuristics in the dialogue manager to determine the roles of the entities. Unlike our approach, the alternative of using ruled-based heuristics does not scale to unseen language patterns.

Our role classifier can be a logistic regression, SVM, decision tree, or random forest model. The best model is selected based on the data distribution and use case. Features include n-grams, bag of words, and other entities present in the query.

A **Entity Group Parser** finds relationships between the extracted entities and groups them into a meaningful hierarchy as illustrated in Figure 5.

The language parser for entity grouping is another novel component of our architecture. A small number of configuration parameters generates a weighted context-free grammar (WCFG) over entities and the words not in entities. The developer can specify whether to allow parent-child attachment to the left or right, what the minimum or maximum number of dependent entities should be, and the preferred direction of attachment. The developer can also specify certain 'linking' words, whose occurrence between two entities increases the chance of the entities being in the specified head-dependent relationship. More details on the semantic parser are given in section 3.

2.5 Question Answerer

A **Question Answerer** queries a Knowledge Base, which encompasses all of the important world knowledge for a given application use case, to find answers to user queries. The example in Figure 6 demonstrates the ranked list of relevant results for the request "what pastries are available?".

2.6 Dialogue Manager

A **Dialogue Manager** analyzes each processed query, executes the required logic, and returns an appropriate natural language response. The lan-

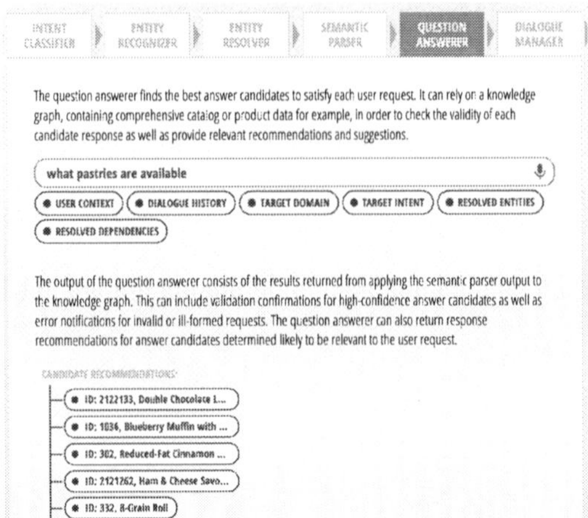

Figure 6: Question answerer demo view

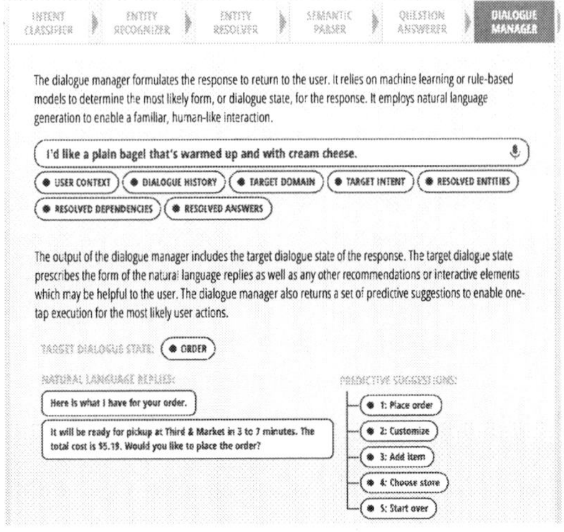

Figure 7: Dialogue manager demo view

guage of the response itself is often templated, but the appropriate template is selected based on the context of the target domain, intent, entities, and results from the question answerer. In the example in Figure 7, the user's query was classified as the order intent with the correct entity and options filled in, so the dialogue manager prompts the user to confirm their order and informs them of the pickup time.

2.7 Application Manager

An **Application Manager** orchestrates the query workflow. It receives requests from the client including both text queries and context information, processes the requests by passing them through each of the other components, and then returns the final response to the client endpoint.

3 Shallow Semantic Parsing

In conventional semantic parsing, a single tree of dependency relations is constructed to cover approximately a whole sentence, enabling a translation from natural language to logical form for each sentence. In the example below, the dependencies OWNER, POSSESSION and QUANTITY can be assigned within a sentence in which a NUMBER entity and DRINK entity are already recognized.

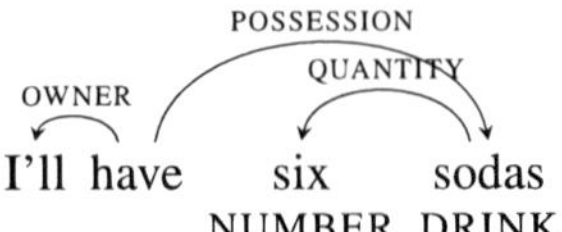

For many information retrieval tasks, including this task-oriented dialogue system, it is sufficient to just extract the relations among entities, in this case QUANTITY.

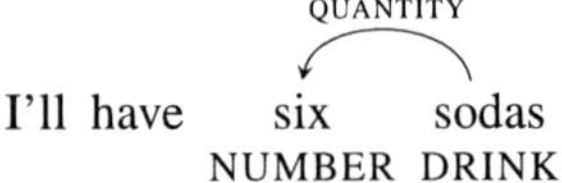

The QUANTITY relation enables the system to distinguish the sentence above from the sentence below, for example, where the same NUMBER entity has a SIZE relation.

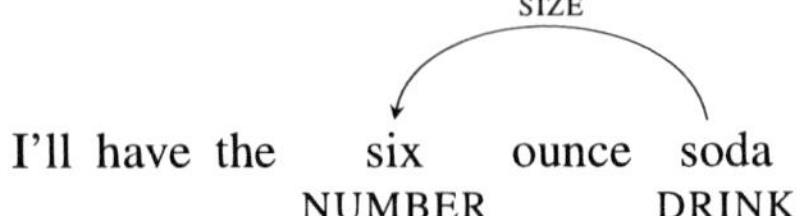

But beyond that, it is often sufficient for the trained model to recognize the relation type, without specifying the parent. When this is the case, we can treat the relation type as a role label on the entity.

I'll have the   six   ounce   soda
NUMBER   DRINK
SIZE

I'll have   six   sodas
NUMBER DRINK
QUANTITY

This unifies the classification problem with cases where the same disambiguation is required even though there is no explicit head, as in the query below.

I'll have   six
NUMBER
QUANTITY

In contrast, entity grouping associates child entities to a parent entity without specifying a relation type, such as the OPTION entities to the corresponding DISH entities below.

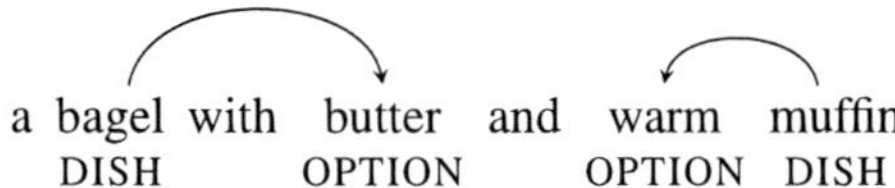

Entity grouping is sufficient in cases where there is only one relation type relevant to a particular intent, or in cases where the relation type is fully determined by the associated entity types. But even when both relation type and parent-child links are required, as below, we benefit from decomposing the problem.

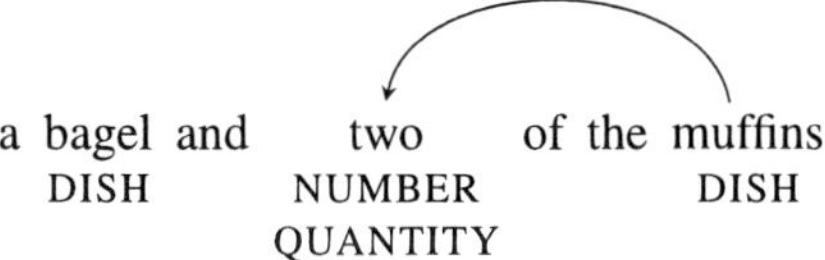

In the initial stages of development, when training data is limited, this allows the system to use a probabilistic model for role labeling which generalizes across cases with and without explicit heads, while using a simple deterministic parser for entity grouping. Once training data is sufficient, these can be smoothly transitioned to a fully probabilistic dependency parser, performing joint learning of entity roles and entity groups.

4 Evaluation of the Semantic Parser

To illustrate the trade-off in model approaches within this architecture as development matures, we provide an evaluation of different entity grouping systems in Table 1. The test data in this evaluation is 200 food ordering queries with more than one DISH entity, and we focus on query-level accuracy—the percentage of queries with correct labels. The baseline system Nearest Head simply assigns any dependent entity to the nearest available head entity. The Default WCFG system uses NLTK (Bird et al., 2009) to construct a CFG over entities and assigns domain-general costs to select a parse, while the Tuned WCFG uses preferences specified by the developer for this use case (e.g. particular entities tend to associate left vs. right) to adapt the cost calculation to the use case. Tuning the WCFG on 1225 queries with multiple dish entities provides an acceptable 97% accuracy. The DepP system trains the transition-based

System	Train #	Test %
Nearest Head	N/A	86.0
Default WCFG	N/A	91.5
Tuned WCFG	1225	97.0
DepP	1225	86.0
DepP + Fixups	1225	95.5
DepP	5106	92.0
DepP + Fixups	5106	98.5

Table 1: Evaluation of approaches to entity grouping for a food ordering use case.

dependency parser from Spacy v. 1.9 (Honnibal and Johnson, 2015) on the entity grouping problem. With only 1225 training queries, the parser is not able to learn the structure of the problem well, sometimes leaving dependent entity types unassociated or producing impossible tag sequences. Fixup rules that force dependent entities to associate to a head entity improve the accuracy, and adding nearly 4000 training queries that only have one DISH name allows the parser to learn the basic structure better. The combination of these allows the DepP system to reach 98.5% accuracy. With smaller training data set sizes the DepP system is not viable, but once training data increases, we can expect more robust performance from the more powerful model.

5 Related Work

Our approach extends a long history of work in shallow semantics for NLU. Conceptually the most similar is work on relation extraction, as established by the Automatic Content Extraction (ACE) program (Doddington et al., 2004). For example, Culotta and Sorensen (2004) and Bunescu and Mooney (2005) use full syntactic dependency parses as features in tree-kernel SVMs to recognize relations among entities. Similarly, semantic role labeling (Màrquez et al., 2008; Palmer et al., 2010) constructs event representations by identifying arguments of predicate heads, typically treating it as a sequence labeling task. More recently, neural network models that combine sequential representations with dependency structures have obtained improvements on both relation extraction (Miwa and Bansal, 2016) and semantic role labeling (Roth and Lapata, 2016), and similar models have the power to jointly learn role labels and entity groups. However, these methods only perform well with abundant training data, so while product decisions are in flux, working with simpler models facilitates the quick development of a production app on smaller data sets.

Some researchers have attempted full semantic parsing for task-oriented systems similar to ours. Berant et al. (2013) induce a semantic parser from question–answer pairs, and then these parses can be used to find answers for unseen questions. Chen et al. (2014) combine a semantic parser with word embeddings to induce mappings from the semantic parser's relations to the slots of a task-oriented dialogue system. In customer-facing products, systems trained by unsupervised learning have too high risk of misbehavior. Moreover, in our applied domains, either the relation head or the relation type is often predetermined or irrelevant, so that information can remain undefined or implicit, leaving a simpler problem.

6 Conclusion

We have described a dialogue system interface for an architecture which extends the traditional NLU pipeline with entity role labeling and entity grouping, forms of shallow semantic parsing. The described methodology has allowed us to consistently build production-level conversational assistants. In this demo, we hope to share these insights in an interactive way.

7 Acknowledgements

The software presented in this paper has greatly benefited from the comments and code contributions of Tim Tuttle, J.J. Jackson, Vijay Ramakrishnan, Marvin Huang, Jui-Pin Wang, Minh Tue Vo Thanh, Amrut Nagasunder, and Varsha Embar.

References

Amazon. 2018. Create the interaction model for your skill. https://developer.amazon.com/docs/custom-skills/create-the-interaction-model-for-your-skill.html.

Jonathan Berant, Andrew Chou, Roy Frostig, and Percy Liang. 2013. Semantic parsing on freebase from question-answer pairs. In *Proceedings of the 2013 Conference on Empirical Methods in Natural Language Processing*, pages 1533–1544. Association for Computational Linguistics.

Steven Bird, Edward Loper, and Ewan Klein. 2009. *Natural Language Processing with Python*. O'Reilly Media Inc.

Razvan C. Bunescu and Raymond J. Mooney. 2005. A shortest path dependency kernel for relation extraction. In *Proceedings of the conference on Human Language Technology and Empirical Methods in Natural Language Processing - HLT '05*, pages 724–731, Morristown, NJ, USA. Association for Computational Linguistics.

Yun-Nung Chen, William Yang Wang, and Alexander I. Rudnicky. 2014. Leveraging frame semantics and distributional semantics for unsupervised semantic slot induction in spoken dialogue systems. In *2014 IEEE Spoken Language Technology Workshop (SLT)*, pages 584–589. IEEE.

Aron Culotta and Jeffrey Sorensen. 2004. Dependency tree kernels for relation extraction. In *Proceedings of the 42nd Annual Meeting on Association for Computational Linguistics - ACL '04*, pages 423–es, Morristown, NJ, USA. Association for Computational Linguistics.

Dialogflow. 2018. Create and query your first agent. https://dialogflow.com/docs/getting-started/first-agent.

George Doddington, Alexis Mitchell, Mark Przybocki, Lance Ramshaw, Stephanie Strassel, and Ralph Weischedel. 2004. The Automatic Content Extraction (ACE) Program Tasks, Data, and Evaluation. *Proceedings of LREC 2004*, pages 837–840.

Matthew Honnibal and Mark Johnson. 2015. An Improved Non-monotonic Transition System for Dependency Parsing. *Proceedings of the 2015 Conference on Empirical Methods in Natural Language Processing*, pages 1373–1378.

Lluís Màrquez, Xavier Carreras, Kenneth C. Litkowski, and Suzanne Stevenson. 2008. Semantic Role Labeling: An Introduction to the Special Issue. *Computational Linguistics*, 34(2):145–159.

Microsoft. 2018. Building conversations. https://docs.microsoft.com/en-us/cortana/skills/mva32-building-conversations.

Makoto Miwa and Mohit Bansal. 2016. End-to-End Relation Extraction using LSTMs on Sequences and Tree Structures. *Proceedings of the 54th Annual Meeting of the Association for Computational Linguistics*, pages 1105—-1116.

Martha Palmer, Daniel Gildea, and Nianwen Xue. 2010. Semantic Role Labeling. *Synthesis Lectures on Human Language Technologies*, 3(1):1–103.

Michael Roth and Mirella Lapata. 2016. Neural Semantic Role Labeling with Dependency Path Embeddings. *Proceedings of the 54th Annual Meeting of the Association for Computational Linguistics*, pages 1192–1202.

Wit.ai. 2018. Build your first app. https://wit.ai/docs/quickstart.

When science journalism meets artificial intelligence : An interactive demonstration

Raghuram Vadapalli[1]*, **Bakhtiyar Syed**[1]*, **Nishant Prabhu**[1]*, **Balaji Vasan Srinivasan**[2], **Vasudeva Varma**[3]

[1,3] IIIT Hyderabad, [2] Adobe Research

{raghuram.vadapalli, syed.b, nishant.prabhu}@research.iiit.ac.in

balsrini@adoWhen be.com, vv@iiit.ac.in

Abstract

We present an online interactive tool[1] that generates titles of blog titles and thus take the first step toward automating science journalism. Science journalism aims to transform jargon-laden scientific articles into a form that the common reader can comprehend while ensuring that the underlying meaning of the article is retained. In this work, we present a tool, which, given the title and abstract of a research paper will generate a blog title by mimicking a human science journalist. The tool makes use of a model trained on a corpus of $87,328$ pairs of research papers and their corresponding blogs, built from two science news aggregators. The architecture of the model is a two-stage mechanism which generates blog titles. Evaluation using standard metrics indicate the viability of the proposed system.

1 Introduction

With approximately 2.5 million new scientific papers being published every year (Jinha, 2010), there is an ever growing need to make this vast trove of scientific knowledge accessible to the common man. This accessibility of scientific knowledge plays an important role in key political, economic, cultural and social policy discussions and also in public dialogue. Websites like *sciencedaily.com*, *phys.org*, *eurekalert.org* aim to address this problem by aggregating and showcasing the top science news stories from the worlds leading universities and research organizations.

News-writing bots have captured the headlines in the recent past, leading to the growing popularity of "Robo Reporting"[2,3]. However, extending this framework to be used for science journalism is a non-trivial task as that would entail understanding scientific content and translating it to simpler language without distorting its underlying semantics. To our knowledge, there have been no prior attempts within the scientific community to extend "Robo Reporting" to science journalism, and this dearth of research in this area can be partially attributed to the lack of suitable data for AI algorithms to be trained. To address this lack of an appropriate training corpus, we have created a parallel corpus of scientific paper titles and abstracts, and their corresponding blog titles with the aim of initiating this foray into automated science journalism and engendering further research.

This initiative is an initial step towards the larger goal of understanding the entire research paper and generating a complete blog. The system makes use of a pipeline-based architecture that uses a combination of the title of the research paper and its abstract to generate the title of the blog. Sample of an abstract, paper title and its corresponding blog title is given in Table 1.

Table 1: Sample - Blog Title, Paper Title and Abstract from our corpus

Blog title: Applying machine learning to the universe's mysteries
Paper title: An equation-of-state-meter of quantum chromodynamics transition from deep learning
Abstract: A primordial state of matter consisting of free quarks and gluons... Here we use supervised learning with a deep convolutional neural network to identify the EoS employed...

Our system models the blog title generation task via a two-stage process: first, it uses a heuristic function mechanism to extract relevant information from the title and abstract of the research

---

* The authors contributed equally.

[1] https://irel.iiit.ac.in/science-ai/

[2] Washington Post's robot reporter has published 850 articles.

[3] New York Times is using bots to create more one-to-one experiences.

Proceedings of the 2018 Conference on Empirical Methods in Natural Language Processing (System Demonstrations), pages 163–168
Brussels, Belgium, October 31–November 4, 2018. ©2018 Association for Computational Linguistics

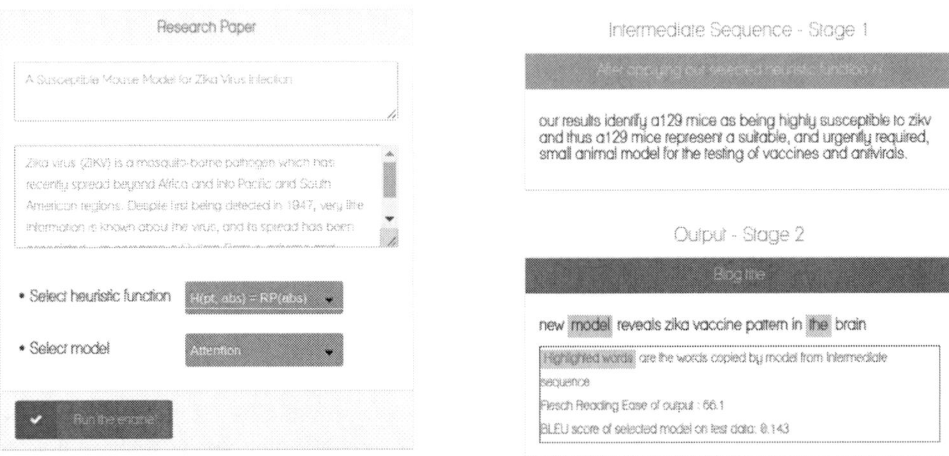

Figure 1: Layout of the web application for our prototype, demonstrating blog title generation

paper and then it it uses the extracted information to generate the blog title. The state-of-the-art sequence-to-sequence neural networks for natural language generation like the Pointer Generator Network (See et al., 2017) are used in the second stage of the pipeline. The generated blog titles are evaluated using all standard metrics for natural language generation tasks and the results indicate the viability of the proposed model to produce semantically sound blog titles. Our contributions can be summed up as follows:

1. A new parallel corpus of $87,328$ pairs of research paper titles and abstracts and their corresponding blog titles.

2. Demonstrating the web application, which uses a pipeline-based architecture that can generate blog titles in a step-by-step fashion, while enabling the user to choose between various heuristic functions as well as the neural model to be used for generating the blog title.

3. Analyzing the outcomes of the experiments conducted to find the best heuristic function as well as network architecture.

We have thus taken the first steps towards building an automated science journalism system by generating blog titles with a long-term vision of generating an entire blog from a given research paper - thereby paving the way for future research in the area.

2 Related Work

Recently, a lot of activity in the space of advances in natural language generation has resulted from pioneering works in building sequence-to-sequence neural networks. Among these advances, two particular areas relevant to the problem we have formulated are *neural headline generation* and *style transfer*.

In the space of **Neural Headline Generation**, *Long Short Term Memory* (LSTM) based sequence-to-sequence architectures for headline generation using the attention mechanism have been explored (Ayana et al., 2017). However, the authors generate headlines for the same domain which effectively means we cannot apply the architectures directly to our problem where the domains and vocabulary are very different. While directly using seq2seq architectures was somewhat helpful in our case - as we will show later; cross domain headline generation requires the consideration of aspects such as style, readability, etc in the two different domains of study.

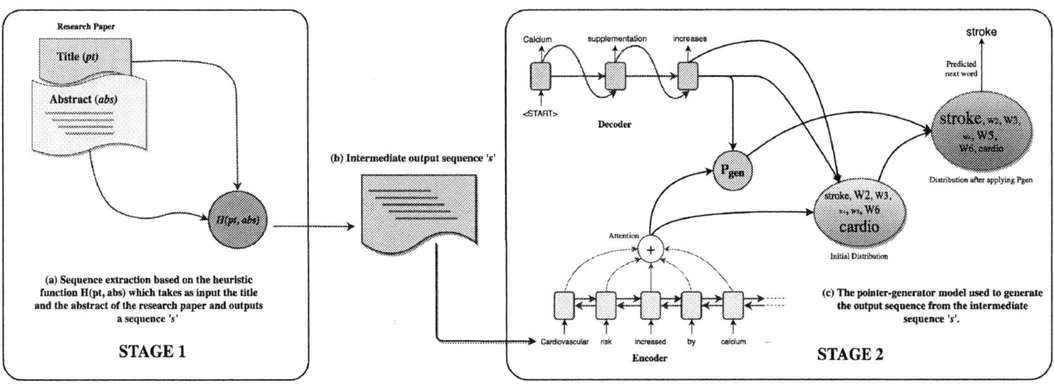

Figure 2: Model of pipeline architecture, describing the two stages in which we model blog title generation

Existing literature in **non-parallel style transfer** assumes the unavailability of sufficient parallel data (Shen et al., 2017; Fu et al., 2018; Kabbara and Cheung, 2016). In first trying to address the problem of style transfer on non-parallel data, Shen et al. (2017) tried to separate the content from the style of the article. It was assumed that a shared latent content distribution exists across different text corpora, and proposed a method that leveraged refined alignment of latent representations to perform style transfer. While Shen et al. (2017) demonstrated their results on sentiment transfer, this cannot be accepted as style transfer from a linguistic point of view.

In other recent works, Fu et al. (2018) address the style-transfer problem by learning separate content and style representations using adversarial networks. Their reported results are on their custom Paper-News Title dataset and the samples reported by the authors either copy the entire source text or replace a few words. Their evaluation criteria leaves a lot to be desired as they evaluate transfer strength using a classifier and content preservation using word embeddings. A lack of parallel data again presents a drawback. While Kabbara and Cheung (2016) presented a variant of an autoencoder where the latent representation had two separate components: one for style and one for content, the authors do not report results on any dataset and hence is not useful in our context.

One key assumption across all the non-parallel style transfer works is a significant overlap between the vocabulary of the source and target style. On the other hand, in the context of science journalism - the overlap in vocabulary between the source and the target is not significant which is one of the prime reasons why the non-parallel style transfer methods cannot be directly extended to our problem. This puts our problem in the bracket of content re-purposing, for which we give a demonstrable prototype.

3 Parallel Corpus for Science Journalism

In the process of building a solution to address the problem of automated science journalism, we built a corpus of parallel data consisting of scientific papers and their corresponding blog articles from two science news aggregation websites: *sciencedaily.com* and *phys.org*. Both these websites publish articles explaining the latest scientific advancements and are rich sources of parallel data. Though we were able to obtain over $300,000$ blog titles, only around $100,000$ of those articles had links to original research papers. These $100,000$ or so research papers were published on over 1000 different research publication websites and we used manual rules to extract abstracts and titles from the research papers that were published on the more frequent research publication websites like *nature.com, pnas.org*. Our final dataset comprises of $87,328$ (blog title, paper title, abstract) triples.

Out of $87,328$ triples, $77,604$ are obtained from *sciencedaily.com*, 9724 tuples are obtained from *phys.org*. The statistical analysis of the dataset is as presented below:

1. Average length of blog titles: 9.55 words
2. Average length of research paper titles: 12.07 words
3. Average length of research paper abstracts:

179.54 words

4. Average word overlap between blog titles and paper titles: 1.93 words

5. Average word overlap between the paper abstracts and blog titles: 3.64 words.

The models must therefore learn which words in the target vocabulary correspond to which words in the source, so that the generated output adheres to the target style.

4 Blog Title Generation

Figure 2 illustrates the proposed architecture. Our demonstrable prototype consists of a two-stage pipeline, which is described in detail as follows:

1. A heuristic function takes the title and abstract of the research paper and extracts relevant information which is then used for further processing.

2. The output of the previous step is fed into a sequence-to-sequence neural generation model in order to generate the title of the blog post.

The dataset is of the format $\mathcal{T} = \{ (bt, pt, abs) \}$, where, bt is the blog title, pt is the paper title and abs is the abstract. We define a **heuristic function** $\mathcal{H}(pt, abs)$ which takes a paper title and abstract as parameters and outputs a sequence s. The various heuristic functions $\mathcal{H}$ we explored are outlined below:

$\mathcal{H}(pt, abs) = pt$: In this heuristic, we assume that the paper title will encapsulate sufficient information to generate the blog title.

$\mathcal{H}(pt, abs) = \mathcal{RP}(abs)$: TF-IDF based measure that selects the sentence that best represents the abstract. (Allahyari et al., 2017)

$\mathcal{H}(pt, abs) = \mathcal{RD}(abs)$: Flesch Reading Ease based measure that selects the most readable sentence in the abstract.

$\mathcal{H}(pt, abs) = \mathcal{RPD}(abs)$: Selects the sentence that maximizes the product of normalized $\mathcal{RD}(abs)$ and $\mathcal{RP}(abs)$ scores, where normalization is performed across all sentences.

We also experimented with different combinations of the above heuristics: $\mathcal{H}(pt, abs) = pt \mid \mathcal{RD}(abs)$, $\mathcal{H}(pt, abs) = pt \mid \mathcal{RP}(abs)$, $\mathcal{H}(pt, abs) = pt \mid \mathcal{RPD}(abs)$ and $\mathcal{H}(pt, abs) = pt \mid abs$; where $\mid$ implies concatenation of the associated heuristics.

In **stage 2**, neural natural language generation models are used to generate the blog title. The system provides a baseline **attention network** which defines 'attention' over the input sequence to allow the network to focus on specific parts of the input text and the **pointer-generator** (See et al., 2017) network which extends the attention-network to compute a probability P_{gen} that decides whether the next word in sequence should be copied from the source or generated from the rest of the vocabulary. The pointer-generator aids in copying factual information from the source, and we hypothesize that this will be useful when generating blog titles. Formally, the sequence s obtained from the first stage is the input to the neural natural language generation model which generates bt' as output with a loss function $\mathcal{L}(bt, bt')$, given by sum of cross entropy loss at all time-steps:

$$\mathcal{L}(bt, bt') = -\sum_{t=0}^{t=T} P(bt'_t)$$

5 Demonstration

Figure 1 illustrates the layout of our demonstrable web application. It can be accessed publicly at the following URL: `https://irel.iiit.ac.in/science-ai`. The layout of the web application is broadly divided into two parts. the left half of the page has the necessary text fields and drop down menus to accept inputs from the user and the right half of the page displays the outputs- both the intermediate sequence, which is the output of the first stage of the pipeline, and the blog title, which is the output of the second stage of the pipeline. The application accepts two text inputs from the user: the **title** of the research paper and the **abstract** of the research paper. The application also allows the user to select the heuristic function to be used in the first stage of the pipeline as well as the neural generation model to be used in the second stage of the pipeline. Running the engine will parse the inputs and pass them on to the appropriate heuristic function, which will produce an intermediate sequence viewable on the right side of the page. This intermediate sequence is then passed on to the neural generation model that is selected by the user which then generates the final output, which can be viewed below the intermediate sequence.

$\mathcal{H}(pt, abs)$	BLEU		ROUGE_L		CIDEr		SkipThought Sim.		Flesch Reading Ease	
	$\mathcal{PG}$	*Attn*	$\mathcal{PG}$	*Attn*	$\mathcal{PG}$	*Attn*	$\mathcal{PG}$	*Attn*	$\mathcal{PG}$	*Attn*
pt	0.157	0.149	0.157	0.138	0.453	0.433	0.430	0.432	46.481	43.069
abs	0.135	0.095	0.136	0.089	0.359	0.123	0.444	0.119	45.484	39.021
$\mathcal{RD}(abs)$	0.091	0.142	0.09	0.137	0.161	0.450	0.403	0.431	**57.468**	**47.521**
$\mathcal{RP}(abs)$	0.101	0.143	0.105	0.134	0.183	0.571	0.414	0.429	46.338	41.179
$\mathcal{RPD}(abs)$	0.096	0.134	0.097	0.126	0.179	0.543	0.415	0.428	43.89	40.761
$pt \mid \mathcal{RD}(abs)$	0.139	0.152	0.129	**0.145**	0.351	0.754	0.435	0.444	49.504	42.964
$pt \mid \mathcal{RP}(abs)$	0.142	**0.153**	0.137	0.144	0.372	0.745	0.431	**0.448**	40.856	35.311
$pt \mid \mathcal{RPD}(abs)$	0.151	0.152	0.158	0.140	0.399	**0.759**	0.435	0.433	40.193	44.339
$pt \mid abs$	**0.171**	0.096	**0.172**	0.091	**0.523**	0.123	**0.446**	0.219	41.307	45.641

Table 2: Performance of the various heuristic functions contrasted with the proposed sequence-to-sequence generation framework

Figure 3: Results in the application

It is important to note that our research prototype is still in a nascent stage and the problem of automated science journalism is far from being solved. The same heuristic function or neural generation model might not exhibit the best results for all possible inputs. Thus, it is of exceptional importance to provide the users fine grained control over the individual components of the model. The system does this by allowing the user the freedom to select a heuristic function and neural generation model of their choice. This allows for more flexibility for the users to experiment with various heuristic functions and neural generation models and ensures better results than forcing the user to use one particular configuration for all inputs.

If not selected by the user, the heuristic function $\mathcal{H}(pt, abs) = pt$ and the **attention network** neural generation model are used as defaults as this configuration has consistently exhibited good results.

In order to further facilitate experimentation by the user, the web application shows the performance of the user-selected configuration on our test dataset, it displays the readability scores of the generated output, and also highlights the words in the output that were copied from the source. All these features give anyone using this system a detailed view of how various configurations work and provide the flexibility to select the one that works best of their use-case. Figure 3 showcases the above mentioned features.

6 Evaluation and Analysis

We evaluate the generated titles using various metrics surveyed by Sharma et al. (2017) for task-oriented language generation.

1. **BLEU** (Papineni et al., 2002): It uses a modified precision to compare generated text against multiple reference texts
2. **ROUGE_L** (Lin, 2004): It is an F-measure that is based on the Longest Common Subsequence (LCS) between the candidate and reference utterances
3. **CIDEr** (Vedantam et al., 2015): It is based on n-gram overlap
4. **Skip Thought Cosine Similarity** (Kiros et al., 2015): It is based on a continuous representation of sentences known as skip-thought vectors

5. **Flesch Reading Ease** (Flesch, 1948): It measures the readability of the sentence based on the number of syllables and words

Table 2 shows the performance of our proposed input functions of the architecture contrasted with the proposed neural generation models pointer-generator (*abbr.* $\mathcal{PG}$) and the attention-network (*abbr. Attn*).

The blogs had a *Flesch Reading Ease* of around 30-35, while the research paper's reading ease was between 15-20. Our generated samples have a reading ease *(>30)* highlighting the transfer in style from research paper to the blog. The higher *FRE* indicates that the generated titles are easier to understand than the paper titles.

To further shed some light on the quality of the generated blog titles, Table 3 shows a few sampled sentences generated by the best performing models in our architecture. Based on our experiments, we conclude that our system learns to generate titles similar to a human expert for scientific blogs.

Table 3: Samples generated by our prototype

Blog title: Safer alternatives to nonsteroidal antinflamatory pain killers **Model-generated title:** New hope for treating inflammatory cardiovascular disease
Blog title: The effects of soy and whey protein supplementation on acute hormonal responses to resistance exercise in men **Model-generated title:** Soy protein supplementation linked to resistance exercise in men
Blog title: Scientists reconcile three unrelated theories of schizophrenia **Model-generated title:** A new way to fight psychiatric disorders

7 Conclusion and Future Work

This work serves as a baseline first attempt toward automating science journalism. We proposed an architecture with a two stage pipeline and have developed a demonstrable web application that accepts the title and abstract of a research paper and outputs a blog title, while also giving the user the flexibility to tinker with the individual components of the system. Future work would include using more advanced architectures to generate the body of the blog.

References

Mehdi Allahyari, Seyed Amin Pouriyeh, Mehdi Assefi, Saeid Safaei, Elizabeth D. Trippe, Juan B. Gutierrez, and Krys Kochut. 2017. Text summarization techniques: A brief survey. *International Journal of Advanced Computer Science and Applications*.

Ayana, Shi-Qi Shen, Yan-Kai Lin, Cun-Chao Tu, Yu Zhao, Zhi-Yuan Liu, and Mao-Song Sun. 2017. Recent advances on neural headline generation. *Journal of Computer Science and Technology*.

Rudolph Flesch. 1948. A new readability yardstick. *Journal of Applied Psychology*.

Zhenxin Fu, Xiaoye Tan, Nanyun Peng, Dongyan Zhao, and Rui Yan. 2018. Style transfer in text: Exploration and evaluation. *AAAI*.

Arif E. Jinha. 2010. Article 50 million: an estimate of the number of scholarly articles in existence. *Learned Publishing*.

Jad Kabbara and Jackie Chi Kit Cheung. 2016. Stylistic transfer in natural language generation systems using recurrent neural networks. In *Proceedings of the Workshop on Uphill Battles in Language Processing: Scaling Early Achievements to Robust Methods*.

Ryan Kiros, Yukun Zhu, Ruslan R Salakhutdinov, Richard Zemel, Raquel Urtasun, Antonio Torralba, and Sanja Fidler. 2015. Skip-thought vectors. In *Advances in Neural Information Processing Systems 28*.

Chin-Yew Lin. 2004. Rouge: A package for automatic evaluation of summaries. In *Proc. ACL workshop on Text Summarization Branches Out*.

Kishore Papineni, Salim Roukos, Todd Ward, and Wei-Jing Zhu. 2002. Bleu: A method for automatic evaluation of machine translation. In *40th Annual Meeting on Association for Computational Linguistics*.

Abigail See, Peter J. Liu, and Christopher D. Manning. 2017. Get to the point: Summarization with pointer-generator networks. In *55th Annual Meeting of the Association for Computational Linguistics*.

Shikhar Sharma, Layla El Asri, Hannes Schulz, and Jeremie Zumer. 2017. Relevance of unsupervised metrics in task-oriented dialogue for evaluating natural language generation. *CoRR*.

Tianxiao Shen, Tao Lei, Regina Barzilay, and Tommi S. Jaakkola. 2017. Style transfer from non-parallel text by cross-alignment. *Advances in Neural Information Processing Systems*.

Ramakrishna Vedantam, C. Lawrence Zitnick, and Devi Parikh. 2015. Cider: Consensus-based image description evaluation. In *IEEE Conference on Computer Vision and Pattern Recognition*.

Universal Sentence Encoder for English

Daniel Cer[a†], **Yinfei Yang**[a†], **Sheng-yi Kong**[a], **Nan Hua**[a], **Nicole Limtiaco**[b],
Rhomni St. John[a], **Noah Constant**[a], **Mario Guajardo-Céspedes**[a], **Steve Yuan**[c],
Chris Tar[a], **Yun-Hsuan Sung**[a], **Brian Strope**[a], **Ray Kurzweil**[a]

[a]Google AI
Mountain View, CA

[b]Google AI
New York, NY

[c]Google
Cambridge, MA

Abstract

We present easy-to-use TensorFlow Hub sentence embedding models having good task transfer performance. Model variants allow for trade-offs between accuracy and compute resources. We report the relationship between model complexity, resources, and transfer performance. Comparisons are made with baselines without transfer learning and to baselines that incorporate word-level transfer. Transfer learning using sentence-level embeddings is shown to outperform models without transfer learning and often those that use only word-level transfer. We show good transfer task performance with minimal training data and obtain encouraging results on word embedding association tests (WEAT) of model bias.

1 Introduction

We present easy-to-use sentence-level embedding models with good transfer task performance even when using remarkably little training data.[1] Model engineering characteristics allow for trade-offs between accuracy versus memory and compute resource consumption.

2 Model Toolkit

Models are implemented in TensorFlow (Abadi et al., 2016) and are made publicly available on TensorFlow Hub.[2] Listing 1 provides an example

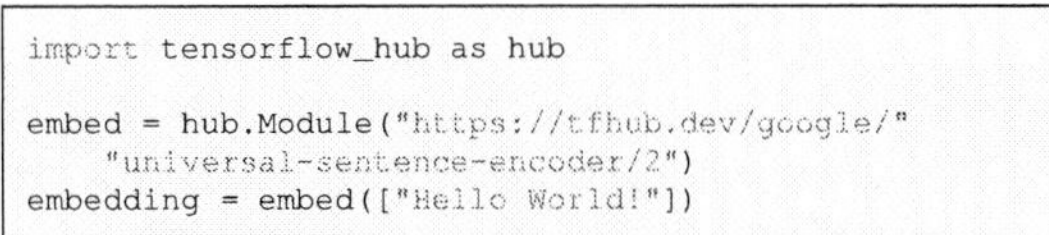

```python
import tensorflow_hub as hub

embed = hub.Module("https://tfhub.dev/google/"
    "universal-sentence-encoder/2")
embedding = embed(["Hello World!"])
```

Listing 1: Python sentence embedding code.

code snippet to compute a sentence-level embedding from a raw untokenized input string.[3] The resulting embedding can be used directly or incorporated into a downstream model for a specific task.[4]

3 Encoders

Two sentence encoding models are provided: (i) transformer (Vaswani et al., 2017), which achieves high accuracy at the cost of greater resource consumption; (ii) deep averaging network (DAN) (Iyyer et al., 2015), which performs efficient inference but with reduced accuracy.

3.1 Transformer

The transformer sentence encoding model constructs sentence embeddings using the encoding sub-graph of the transformer architecture (Vaswani et al., 2017). The encoder uses attention to compute context aware representations of words in a sentence that take into account both the ordering and identity of other words. The context aware word representations are averaged together to obtain a sentence-level embedding.

We train for broad coverage using multi-task learning, with the same encoding model supporting multiple downstream tasks. The task types include: a Skip-Thought like task (Kiros et al.,

---

† Corresponding authors:
{cer, yinfeiy}@google.com

[1]We describe our publicly released models. See Yang et al. (2018) and Henderson et al. (2017) for additional architectural details of models similar to those presented here.

[2] https://www.tensorflow.org/hub/, Apache 2.0 license, with models available as saved TF graphs.

[3]Basic text preprocessing and white-space tokenization is performed internally. Preprocessing lowercases the text and removes punctuation. OOV items are handled using string hashing to index into 400,000 OOV embeddings.

[4]Visit https://colab.research.google.com/ to try the code snippet in Listing 1. Example code and documentation is available on the TF Hub website.

Proceedings of the 2018 Conference on Empirical Methods in Natural Language Processing (System Demonstrations), pages 169–174
Brussels, Belgium, October 31–November 4, 2018. ©2018 Association for Computational Linguistics

2015);[5] conversational response prediction (Henderson et al., 2017); and a select supervised classification task that improves sentence embeddings.[6] The transformer encoder achieves the best transfer performance. However, this comes at the cost of compute time and memory usage scaling dramatically with sentence length.

3.2 Deep Averaging Network (DAN)

The DAN sentence encoding model begins by averaging together word and bi-gram level embeddings. Sentence embeddings are then obtain by passing the averaged representation through a feedforward deep neural network (DNN). The DAN encoder is trained similar to the transformer encoder. Multitask learning trains a single DAN encoder to support multiple downstream tasks. An advantage of the DAN encoder is that compute time is linear in the length of the input sequence. Similar to Iyyer et al. (2015), our results demonstrate that DANs achieve strong baseline performance on text classification tasks.

3.3 Encoder Training Data

Unsupervised training data are drawn from a variety of web sources. The sources are Wikipedia, web news, web question-answer pages and discussion forums. We augment unsupervised learning with training on supervised data from the Stanford Natural Language Inference (SNLI) corpus (Bowman et al., 2015) in order to further improve our representations (Conneau et al., 2017). Since the only supervised training data is SNLI, the models can be used for a wide range of downstream supervised tasks that do not overlap with this dataset.[7]

4 Transfer Tasks

This section presents the data used for the transfer learning experiments and word embedding association tests (WEAT): (**MR**) Movie review sentiment on a five star scale (Pang and Lee, 2005); (**CR**) Sentiment of customer reviews (Hu and Liu, 2004); (**SUBJ**) Subjectivity of movie reviews and plot summaries (Pang and Lee, 2004);

DATASET	TRAIN	DEV	TEST
SST	67,349	872	1,821
STS Bench	5,749	1,500	1,379
TREC	5,452	-	500
MR	-	-	10,662
CR	-	-	3,775
SUBJ	-	-	10,000
MPQA	-	-	10,606

Table 1: Transfer task evaluation sets.

(**MPQA**) Phrase opinion polarity from news data (Wiebe et al., 2005); (**TREC**) Fine grained question classification sourced from TREC (Li and Roth, 2002); (**SST**) Binary phrase sentiment classification (Socher et al., 2013); (**STS Benchmark**) Semantic textual similarity (STS) between sentence pairs scored by Pearson r with human judgments (Cer et al., 2017); (**WEAT**) Word pairs from the psychology literature on implicit association tests (IAT) that are used to characterize model bias (Caliskan et al., 2017).[8] Table 1 gives the number of samples for each transfer task.

5 Transfer Learning Models

For sentence classification transfer tasks, the output of the sentence encoders are provided to a task specific DNN. For the pairwise semantic similarity task, the similarity of sentence embeddings u and v is assessed using $- \arccos \left(\frac{uv}{||u|| \, ||v||} \right)$.[9]

5.1 Baselines

For each transfer task, we include baselines that only make use of word-level transfer and baselines that make use of no transfer learning at all. For word-level transfer, we incorporate word embeddings from a word2vec skip-gram model trained on a corpus of news data (Mikolov et al., 2013). The pretrained word embeddings are included as input to two model types: a convolutional neural network model (CNN) (Kim, 2014); a DAN. The baselines that use pretrained word embeddings allow us to contrast word- vs. sentence-level transfer. Additional baseline CNN and DAN models are trained without using any pretrained word or sentence embeddings. For reference, we compare with InferSent (Conneau et al., 2017) and

---

[5] The Skip-Thought like task replaces the LSTM (Hochreiter and Schmidhuber, 1997) in the original formulation with a transformer model.

[6] SNLI (Bowman et al., 2015; Conneau et al., 2017)

[7] For questions on downstream evaluations possibly overlapping with the encoder training data, visit the TF Hub discussion board, `https://groups.google.com/a/tensorflow.org/d/forum/hub`, or e-mail the corresponding authors.

[8] For MR, CR, SUBJ, SST, and TREC we use the preparation of the data provided by Conneau et al. (2017).

[9] arccos converts cosine similarity into an angular distance that obeys the triangle inequality. We find that angular distance performs better on STS than cosine similarity.

Skip-Thought with layer normalization (Ba et al., 2016) on sentence-classification tasks. On the STS Benchmark, we compare with InferSent and the state-of-the-art neural STS systems CNN (HCTI) (Shao, 2017) and gConv (Yang et al., 2018).

5.2 Combined Transfer Models

We explore combining the sentence and word-level transfer models by concatenating their representations prior to the classification layers. For completeness, we report results providing the classification layers with the concatenating of the sentence-level embeddings and the representations produced by baseline models that do not make use of word-level transfer learning.

6 Experiments

Experiments use our most recent transformer and DAN encoding models.[10] Transfer task model hyperparamaters are tuned using a combination of Vizier (Golovin et al., 2017) and light manual tuning. When available, model hyperparameters are tuned using task dev sets. Otherwise, hyperparameters are tuned by cross-validation on task training data or the evaluation test data when neither training nor dev data are provided. Training repeats ten times for each task with randomly initialized weights and we report results by averaging across runs. Transfer learning is important when training data is limited. We explore using varying amounts of training data for SST. Contrasting the transformer and DAN encoders demonstrates trade-offs in model complexity and the training data required to reach a desired level of task accuracy. Finally, to assess bias in our encoders, we evaluate the strength of biased model associations on WEAT. We compare to Caliskan et al. (2017) who discovered that word embeddings reproduce human-like biases on implicit association tasks.

7 Results

Table 2 presents results on classification tasks. Using transformer sentence-level embeddings alone outperforms InferSent on MR, SUBJ, and TREC. The transformer sentence encoder also strictly outperforms the DAN encoder. Models that make use of just the transformer sentence-level embeddings tend to outperform all models that only use word-level transfer, with the exception of TREC and

---

10universal-sentence-encoder/2 (DAN); universal-sentence-encoder-large/3 (Transformer).

MODEL	MR	CR	SUBJ	MPQA	TREC	SST
Sentence Embedding Transfer Learning						
U_T	**82.2**	**84.2**	**95.5**	**88.1**	**93.2**	**83.7**
U_D	72.2	78.5	92.1	86.9	88.1	77.5
Word Embedding Transfer Learning						
CNN_{w2v}	**75.1**	**80.5**	**91.1**	80.3	**96.6**	**84.1**
DAN_{w2v}	74.7	75.3	90.2	**82.1**	83.5	80.6
*Sentence Embedding Transfer Learning + DNN/CNN **with** word-level transfer*						
U_T+CNN_{w2v}	80.1	85.2	<u>**95.8**</u>	88.4	<u>**98.7**</u>	85.3
U_T+DAN_{w2v}	**81.4**	**86.4**	93.7	87.5	97.0	**86.0**
U_D+CNN_{w2v}	76.7	82.0	91.2	85.2	97.1	85.1
U_D+DAN_{w2v}	76.4	81.0	94.0	88.0	92.6	82.2
*Sentence Embedding Transfer Learning + DNN/CNN **without** word-level transfer*						
U_T+CNN_{rnd}	<u>**82.7**</u>	**88.6**	93.6	**87.8**	98.5	<u>**88.9**</u>
U_T+DAN_{rnd}	80.6	84.8	**94.3**	86.0	**98.6**	86.2
U_D+CNN_{rnd}	78.0	82.9	90.2	**87.8**	96.2	83.2
U_D+DAN_{rnd}	76.4	84.9	94.0	85.3	98.1	86.2
Baselines with No Transfer Learning						
CNN_{rnd}	**76.5**	81.0	89.6	**82.2**	97.9	**85.0**
DAN_{rnd}	74.6	**81.2**	**91.8**	79.9	93.9	82.0
Prior Work						
InferSent	**81.1**	**86.3**	92.4	<u>**90.2**</u>	88.2	84.6
Skip Thght	79.4	83.1	**93.7**	89.3	-	-

Table 2: Classification tasks. U_T uses the transformer encoder for transfer learning, while U_D uses the DAN encoder. DAN/CNN$_{w2v}$ use pre-trained w2v emb. DAN/CNN$_{rnd}$ train rand. init. word emb. on the final classification task.

SST, on which CNN$_{w2v}$ performs better. Transfer learning with DAN sentence embeddings tends to outperform a DAN with word-level transfer, except on MR and SST. Models with sentence- and word-level transfer often outperform similar models with sentence-level transfer alone.

MODEL	DEV	TEST
Transformer Encoder	**0.802**	**0.766**
DAN Encoder	0.760	0.717
Prior Work		
gConv (Yang et al., 2018)	<u>**0.835**</u>	<u>**0.808**</u>
CNN (HCTI) (Shao, 2017)	0.834	0.784
InferSent (Conneau et al., 2017)	0.801	0.758

Table 3: STS Benchmark Pearson's r. Our prior gConv model (Yang et al., 2018) is a variant of our TF Hub transformer model tuned to STS.

Table 3 compares our models to strong baselines on the STS Benchmark. Our transformer embeddings outperform the sentence representations produced by InferSent. Moreover, computing similarity scores by directly comparing the representations produced by our encoders approaches the performance of state-of-the-art neural models whose representations are fit to the STS task.

Table 4 illustrates transfer task performance for varying amounts of training data. With small quantities of training data, sentence-level transfer achieves surprisingly good performance. Using only 1k labeled examples and the transformer embeddings for sentence-level transfer *surpasses* the performance of transfer learning using InferSent on the full training set of 67.3k examples. Training with 1k labeled examples and the transformer sentence embeddings surpasses word-level transfer using the full training set, CNN_{w2v}, and approaches the performance of the best model without transfer learning trained on the complete dataset, CNN_{rnd}@67.3k. Transfer learning is not always helpful when there is enough task training data. However, we observe that our best performing model still makes use of transformer sentence-level transfer but combined with a CNN with no word-level transfer, U_T+CNN_{rnd}.

Table 5 contrasts Caliskan et al. (2017)'s findings on bias within GloVe embeddings with results from the transformer and DAN encoders. Similar to GloVe, our models reproduce human associations between flowers vs. insects and pleasantness vs. unpleasantness. However, our models demonstrate weaker associations than GloVe for probes targeted at revealing ageism, racism and sexism.[11] Differences in word association patterns can be attributed to training data composition and the mixture of tasks used to train the representations.

8   Resource Usage

This section describes memory and compute resource usage for the transformer and DAN sentence encoding models over different batch sizes and sentence lengths. Figure 1 plots model resource consumption against sentence length.[12]

Compute Usage   The transformer model time complexity is $O(n^2)$ in sentence length, while the

---

[11] The development of our models did not target reducing bias. Researchers and developers are strongly encouraged to independently verify whether biases in their overall model or model components impacts their use case. For resources on ML fairness visit https://developers.google.com/machine-learning/fairness-overview/.

[12] All benchmark values are averaged over 25 runs that follow 5 priming runs. CPU and mem. benchmarks are performed on a machine with an Intel(R) Xeon(R) Platinum P-8136 CPU @ 2.00GHz CPU. GPU benchmarks use an Intel(R) Xeon(R) CPU E5-2696 v4 @ 2.20GHz CPU and NVIDIA Tesla P100 GPU.

MODEL	SST 1K	SST 4K	SST 16K	SST 67.3K
Sentence Embedding Transfer Learning				
U_T	**84.8**	**84.8**	**84.8**	**83.7**
U_D	78.7	78.6	76.9	77.5
Word Embedding Transfer Learning				
CNN_{w2v}	**70.7**	73.8	**81.5**	**84.1**
DAN_{w2v}	67.5	**75.1**	78.4	80.6
Sentence Embedding Transfer Learning				
*+ DNN/CNN **with** word-level transfer*				
U_T+CNN_{w2v}	84.9	84.9	**85.4**	85.3
U_T+DAN_{w2v}	<u>**85.1**</u>	<u>**85.4**</u>	85.0	**86.0**
U_D+CNN_{w2v}	78.6	79.7	80.9	85.1
U_D+DAN_{w2v}	78.7	79.1	81.6	82.2
Sentence Embedding Transfer Learning				
*+ DNN/CNN **without** word-level transfer*				
U_T+CNN_{rnd}	83.1	**83.3**	84.9	<u>**88.9**</u>
U_T+DAN_{rnd}	**84.9**	84.2	<u>**86.0**</u>	86.2
U_D+CNN_{rnd}	77.5	77.9	81.3	83.2
U_D+DAN_{rnd}	78.5	78.8	82.5	86.2
Baselines with No Transfer Learning				
CNN_{rnd}	**68.9**	**74.6**	**81.5**	**85.0**
DAN_{rnd}	68.4	73.1	78.0	82.0
Prior Work				
InferSent	-	-	-	84.6

Table 4: SST performance varying the amount of training data. Model types are the same as Table 2. Using 1k examples, U_T transfer learning rivals models trained on the full training set, 67.3k.

DAN model is $O(n)$. As seen in Figure 1 (a-b), for short sentences, the transformer encoding model is only moderately slower than the much simpler DAN model. However, compute time for transformer increases noticeably with sentence length. In contrast, the compute time for the DAN model stays nearly constant across different lengths. When running on GPU, even for large batches and longer sentence lengths, the transformer model still achieves performance that can be used within an interactive systems.

Memory Usage   The transformer model space complexity also scales quadratically, $O(n^2)$, in sentence length, while the DAN is linear, $O(n)$. Similar to compute usage, memory for the transformer model increases quickly with sentence length, while the memory for the DAN model remains nearly constant. For the DAN model, memory is dominated by the parameters used to store the model unigram and bigram embeddings. Since the transformer model only stores unigrams, for

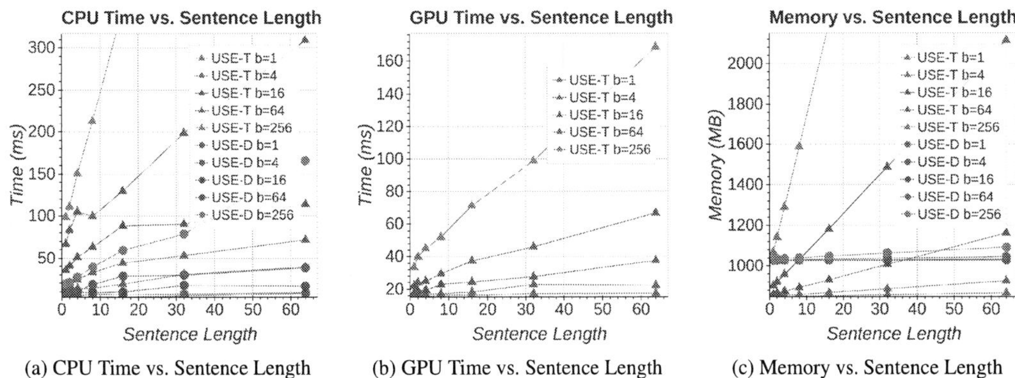

(a) CPU Time vs. Sentence Length   (b) GPU Time vs. Sentence Length   (c) Memory vs. Sentence Length

Figure 1: Resource usage for the Universal Sentence Encoder DAN (USE-D) and Transformer (USE-T) models for different batch sizes and sentence lengths.

Target words	Attrib. words	Ref	GloVe		U. Enc. DAN		U. Enc. Trans.	
			d	p	d	p	d	p
Eur.- vs. Afr.-American names	Pleasant vs. Unpleasant	a	1.41	10^{-8}	0.36	0.04	0.22	0.14
Eur.- vs. Afr.-American names	Pleasant vs.Unpleasant from (a)	b	1.50	10^{-4}	-0.37	0.87	0.21	0.27
Eur.- vs. Afr.-American names	Pleasant vs. Unpleasant from (c)	b	1.28	10^{-3}	0.72	0.02	0.93	10^{-2}
Male vs. female names	Career vs. family	c	1.81	10^{-3}	0.02	0.48	0.95	0.03
Math vs. arts	Male vs. female terms	c	1.06	0.02	0.59	0.12	0.12	0.41
Science vs. arts	Male vs. female terms	d	1.24	10^{-2}	0.24	0.32	-0.21	0.67
Mental vs. physical disease	Temporary vs. permanent	e	1.38	10^{-2}	1.60	10^{-2}	0.42	0.23
Young vs old peoples names	Pleasant vs unpleasant	c	1.21	10^{-2}	1.01	0.02	0.06	0.46
Flowers vs. Insects	Pleasant vs. Unpleasant	a	1.50	10^{-7}	1.38	10^{-6}	1.47	10^{-7}
Instruments vs. Weapons	Pleasant vs Unpleasant	a	1.53	10^{-7}	1.44	10^{-7}	1.65	10^{-7}

Table 5: WEAT for GloVe vs. our DAN and transformer encoding models. Effect size is reported as Cohen's d over the mean cosine similarity scores across grouped attribute words. Statistical significance uses one-tailed p-scores. The *Ref* column indicates the source of the IAT word lists: (a) Greenwald et al. (1998) (b) Bertrand and Mullainathan (2004) (c) Nosek et al. (2002a) (d) Nosek et al. (2002b) (e) Monteith and Pettit (2011).

very short sequences transformer requires almost half as much memory as the DAN model.

9 Conclusion

Our encoding models provide sentence-level embeddings that demonstrate strong transfer performance on a number of NLP tasks. The encoding models make different trade-offs regarding accuracy and model complexity that should be considered when choosing the best one for a particular application. Overall, our sentence-level embeddings tend to surpass the performance of transfer using word-level embeddings alone. Models that make use of sentence- and word-level transfer often achieve the best performance. Sentence-level transfer using our models can be exceptionally helpful when limited training data is available. The pre-trained encoding models are publicly available for research and use in industry applications that can benefit from a better understanding of natural language.

Acknowledgments

We thank our teammates from Descartes, Ai.h and other Google groups for their feedback and suggestions. Special thanks goes to Ben Packer and Yoni Halpern for implementing the WEAT assessments and discussions on model bias.

References

Martín Abadi, Paul Barham, Jianmin Chen, Zhifeng Chen, Andy Davis, Jeffrey Dean, Matthieu Devin, Sanjay Ghemawat, Geoffrey Irving, Michael Isard, Manjunath Kudlur, Josh Levenberg, Rajat Monga, Sherry Moore, Derek G. Murray, Benoit Steiner, Paul Tucker, Vijay Vasudevan, Pete Warden, Martin Wicke, Yuan Yu, and Xiaoqiang Zheng. 2016. Tensorflow: A system for large-scale machine learning. In *Proceedings of USENIX OSDI'16*.

Lei Jimmy Ba, Ryan Kiros, and Geoffrey E. Hinton. 2016. Layer normalization. *CoRR*, abs/1607.06450.

Marianne Bertrand and Sendhil Mullainathan. 2004. Are emily and greg more employable than lakisha and jamal? a field experiment on labor market discrimination. *The American Economic Review*, 94(4).

Samuel R. Bowman, Gabor Angeli, Christopher Potts, and Christopher D. Manning. 2015. A large annotated corpus for learning natural language inference. In *Proceedings of EMNLP*.

Aylin Caliskan, Joanna J. Bryson, and Arvind Narayanan. 2017. Semantics derived automatically from language corpora contain human-like biases. *Science*, 356(6334):183–186.

Daniel Cer, Mona Diab, Eneko Agirre, Inigo Lopez-Gazpio, and Lucia Specia. 2017. Semeval-2017 task 1: Semantic textual similarity multilingual and crosslingual focused evaluation. In *Proceedings of SemEval-2017*.

Alexis Conneau, Douwe Kiela, Holger Schwenk, Loic Barrault, and Antoine Bordes. 2017. Supervised learning of universal sentence representations from natural language inference data. *arXiv preprint arXiv:1705.02364*.

Daniel Golovin, Benjamin Solnik, Subhodeep Moitra, Greg Kochanski, John Karro, and D. Sculley. 2017. Google vizier: A service for black-box optimization. In *Proceedings of KDD '17*.

Anthony G. Greenwald, Debbie E. McGhee, and Jordan L. K. Schwartz. 1998. Measuring individual differences in implicit cognition: the implicit association test. *Journal of personality and social psychology*, 74(6).

Matthew Henderson, Rami Al-Rfou, Brian Strope, Yun-Hsuan Sung, László Lukács, Ruiqi Guo, Sanjiv Kumar, Balint Miklos, and Ray Kurzweil. 2017. Efficient natural language response suggestion for smart reply. *CoRR*, abs/1705.00652.

Sepp Hochreiter and Jürgen Schmidhuber. 1997. Long short-term memory. *Neural Comput.*, 9(8):1735–1780.

Minqing Hu and Bing Liu. 2004. Mining and summarizing customer reviews. In *Proceedings of KDD '04*.

Mohit Iyyer, Varun Manjunatha, Jordan Boyd-Graber, and Hal Daumé III. 2015. Deep unordered composition rivals syntactic methods for text classification. In *Proceedings of ACL/IJCNLP*.

Yoon Kim. 2014. Convolutional neural networks for sentence classification. In *Proceedings of EMNLP*.

Ryan Kiros, Yukun Zhu, Ruslan R Salakhutdinov, Richard Zemel, Raquel Urtasun, Antonio Torralba, and Sanja Fidler. 2015. Skip-thought vectors. In *In Proceedings of NIPS*.

Xin Li and Dan Roth. 2002. Learning question classifiers. In *Proceedings of COLING '02*.

Tomas Mikolov, Ilya Sutskever, Kai Chen, Greg Corrado, and Jeffrey Dean. 2013. Distributed representations of words and phrases and their compositionality. In *Proceedings of NIPS'13*.

Lindsey L. Monteith and Jeremy W. Pettit. 2011. Implicit and explicit stigmatizing attitudes and stereotypes about depression. *Journal of Social and Clinical Psychology*, 30(5).

Brian A. Nosek, Mahzarin R. Banaji, and Anthony G. Greenwald. 2002a. Harvesting implicit group attitudes and beliefs from a demonstration web site. *Group Dynamics*, 6(1).

Brian A. Nosek, Mahzarin R. Banaji, and Anthony G Greenwald. 2002b. Math = male, me = female, therefore math me. *Journal of Personality and Social Psychology,*, 83(1).

Bo Pang and Lillian Lee. 2004. A sentimental education: Sentiment analysis using subjectivity summarization based on minimum cuts. In *Proceedings of the 42nd Meeting of the Association for Computational Linguistics (ACL'04), Main Volume*.

Bo Pang and Lillian Lee. 2005. Seeing stars: Exploiting class relationships for sentiment categorization with respect to rating scales. In *Proceedings of ACL'05*.

Yang Shao. 2017. Hcti at semeval-2017 task 1: Use convolutional neural network to evaluate semantic textual similarity. In *Proceedings of the 11th International Workshop on Semantic Evaluation (SemEval-2017)*, pages 130–133.

Richard Socher, Alex Perelygin, Jean Wu, Jason Chuang, Christopher D. Manning, Andrew Ng, and Christopher Potts. 2013. Recursive deep models for semantic compositionality over a sentiment treebank. In *Proceedings of EMNLP*.

Ashish Vaswani, Noam Shazeer, Niki Parmar, Jakob Uszkoreit, Llion Jones, Aidan N Gomez, Ł ukasz Kaiser, and Illia Polosukhin. 2017. Attention is all you need. In *Proceedings of NIPS*.

Janyce Wiebe, Theresa Wilson, and Claire Cardie. 2005. Annotating expressions of opinions and emotions in language. *Language Resources and Evaluation*, 39(2):165–210.

Yinfei Yang, Steve Yuan, Daniel Cer, Sheng yi Kong, Noah Constant, Petr Pilar, Heming Ge, Yun-Hsuan Sung, Brian Strope, and Ray Kurzweil. 2018. Learning semantic textual similarity from conversations. *Proceedings of RepL4NLP workshop at ACL*.

Author Index

Özenç, Berke, 25

Adejoh, Rosemary, 60
Adel, Heike, 42
Ajjour, Yamen, 60
Ananiadou, Sophia, 108
Apidianaki, Marianna, 120

Beck, Eugen, 84
Bhattacharya, Indrani, 96
Biemann, Chris, 48, 78
Boratko, Michael, 102
Bostan, Laura Ana Maria, 42
Boullosa, Beto, 127
Bremer, Peer-Timo, 36

Callison-Burch, Chris, 120
Cao, Shulin, 139
Carroll, Lucien, 157
Castiglia, Giuliano, 60
Cer, Daniel, 169
Chang, Maria, 102
Constant, Noah, 169

Das, Rajarshi, 102
Dou, Longxu, 13

Eckart de Castilho, Richard, 127
Ehsani, Razieh, 25
Eirew, Alon, 19

Fan, Fan, 60
Feng, Zhili, 72
Fokoue, Achille, 102
Fröhlich, Bernd, 60

Green, Yael, 19
Guajardo-Cespedes, Mario, 169
Gurevych, Iryna, 114, 127
Guskin, Shira, 19

Han, Xu, 139
Hua, Nan, 169

Izsak, Peter, 19

Ji, Heng, 96

Kapanipathi, Pavan, 102
Kawahara, Daisuke, 54
Kiesel, Dora, 60
Klie, Jan-Christoph, 127
Klinger, Roman, 42
Kong, Sheng-yi, 169
Korat, Daniel, 19
Kudo, Taku, 66
Kumar, Naveen, 127
Kurohashi, Sadao, 54
Kurzweil, Ray, 169

Labutov, Igor, 145
Lakomkin, Egor, 90
Li, Juanzi, 139
Li, Tao, 36
Li, Zhimin, 36
Limtiaco, Nicole, 169
Lin, Chin-Yew, 13
Lin, Yankai, 139
Liu, Shusen, 36
Liu, Zhiyuan, 139
Loginova, Ekaterina, 30
Lv, Xin, 139

Ma, Yi, 151
Magg, Sven, 90
Mamou, Jonathan, 19
Mattei, Nicholas, 102
McCallum, Andrew, 102
Mikkilineni, Divyendra, 102
Mitchell, Tom, 145
Musa, Ryan, 102

Neubig, Graham, 7
Neumann, Günter, 30
Ney, Hermann, 84
Nghiem, Minh-Quoc, 108
Ning, Qiang, 72

Padó, Sebastian, 42
Padigela, Harshit, 102
Papay, Sean, 42
Pascucci, Valerio, 36
Patel, Ajay, 120

Peng, Haoruo, 72
Pereg, Oren, 19
Peter, Jan-Thorsten, 84
Prabhu, Nishant, 163

Qin, Guanghui, 13

Radke, Rich, 96
Raghunathan, Karthik, 157
Raghuvanshi, Arushi, 157
Raux, Antoine, 151
Richardson, John, 66
Riehmann, Patrick, 60
Roth, Dan, 72

Sands, Alexander, 120
Solak, Ercan, 25
Sorokin, Daniil, 114
Srikumar, Vivek, 36
Srinivasan, Balaji Vasan, 163
Srivastava, Shashank, 145
St. John, Rhomni, 169
Stein, Benno, 60
Strope, Brian, 169
Sumita, Eiichiro, 133
Sun, Maosong, 139
Syed, Bakhtiyar, 163

Talamadupula, Kartik, 102
Tanveer, Md Iftekhar, 1
Tar, Chris, 169
Tolmachev, Arseny, 54
Ture, Ferhan, 1

Utiyama, Masao, 133

Vadapalli, Raghuram, 163
Varma, Vasudeva, 163

Wachsmuth, Henning, 60
Wang, Jinpeng, 13
Wang, Xiaolin, 133
Wasserblat, Moshe, 19
Weber, Cornelius, 90
Wermter, Stefan, 90
Wiedemann, Gregor, 78
Witbrock, Michael, 102
Wong, Felicia, 151

Yang, Paul, 151
Yang, Yinfei, 169
Yao, Jin-Ge, 13
Yimam, Seid Muhie, 48, 78
Yin, Pengcheng, 7

Yuan, Steve, 169
Yuvraj, Pritish, 102

Zhang, Ni, 96
Zhang, Tongtao, 96
Zhou, Ben, 72